Items
below
teler
Fing
ticket
are c.
in rer
bor
—

2

11/4/1

# Irish Protestant identities

MANCHESTER
1824
Manchester University Press

# Irish Protestant identities

Edited by
MERVYN BUSTEED, FRANK NEAL AND
JONATHAN TONGE

Manchester
University Press

Manchester and New York

distributed exclusively in the USA by Palgrave Macmillan

*Published by* Manchester University Press
Oxford Road, Manchester M13 9NR, UK
*and* Room 400, 175 Fifth Avenue, New York, NY 10010, USA
www.manchesteruniversitypress.co.uk

*Distributed exclusively in the USA by*
Palgrave Macmillan, 175 Fifth Avenue, New York,
NY 10010, USA

*Distributed exclusively in Canada by*
UBC Press, University of British Columbia, 2029 West Mall,
Vancouver, BC, Canada V6T 1Z2

*British Library Cataloguing-in-Publication Data*
A catalogue record for this book is available from the British Library

*Library of Congress Cataloging-in-Publication Data applied for*

ISBN    978 07190 7745 6  *hardback*

First published 2008

17  16  15  14  13  12  11  10  09  08          10  9  8  7  6  5  4  3  2  1

Typeset in Sabon
by Servis Filmsetting Ltd, Stockport, Cheshire
Printed in Great Britain
by Biddles Ltd, King's Lynn

# Contents

# List of tables

# List of figures

# List of contributors

**Dr David J. Butler** teaches Human Geography at University College Cork (UCC) and Irish studies at the University of Limerick. He is author of *South Tipperary 1570–1841: Religion, Land and Rivalry* (Four Courts Press, 2007) as well as numerous papers on the reformed churches and inter-church relations in Ireland.

**Mervyn Busteed** lectured in Geography at the University of Manchester and was a previous chair of the British Association of Irish Studies. He is an Honorary Research Fellow of Manchester and Liverpool universities. Recent publications include *Castle Caldwell, Co. Fermanagh: Life on a West Ulster Estate 1750–1800* (Four Courts Press, 2006) and "Fostered to trouble the next generation: contesting the ownership of the martyrs commemoration ritual in Manchester 1888–1921", in Y. Whelan and N. Moore (eds) *Heritage, Memory and the Politics of Identity* (Ashgate, 2007).

**Peter Day** is a postgraduate research student at the Institute of Irish Studies, University of Liverpool, extending his researches into the Orange Order in Liverpool as the subject of his PhD thesis. He is author of "The Orange Order in Liverpool", *Anglofiles*, 141 (September 2006).

**Dr Naomi Doak** completed her PhD in the Faculty of Languages and Literature at the University of Ulster in 2006 on the topic: "Assessing an absence: Ulster Protestant women writers, 1900–1965". Recent publications include "Ulster Protestant women authors, Olga Fielden's *Island Story*", *Irish Studies Review*, 15.1 (2007); "Lost voices: Ulster Protestant women writers", in Eadaoin Agnew, Eamonn Hughes, Caroline Magennis and Christina Morin (eds) *A Further Shore: Essays in Irish and Scottish Studies* (Aberdeen University Press, 2007) and "A case study of Mrs F. E. Crichton and *The Precepts of Andy Saul* (1877–1918) (*The Irish Feminist Review*, January 2008).

**James E. Doan** is Professor of Humanities at Nova Southeastern University, Fort Lauderdale, USA and founding President of the South Florida Irish Studies Consortium Inc. His publications include *Encyclopedia of Irish History and Culture* (2004) co-edited with James Donnelly et al. and *On the Side of Light: Critical Essays on the Poetry of Cathal O'Searcaigh* (2002) co-edited with Frank Sewell.

**Hastings Donnan** is Professor of Social Anthropology at Queen's University Belfast. He is the author, editor or co-editor of more than fifteen books including, most recently, *The Anthropology of Ireland* (Berg, 2006), *Culture and Power at the Edges of the State* (Lit Verlag, 2005), *Interpreting Islam* (Sage, 2002), *Borders: Frontiers of Identity, Nation and State* (Berg, 2001) and *Border Identities: Nation and State at International Frontiers* (Cambridge University Press, 1998).

**Mark Doyle** completed his PhD at Boston College, USA in 2006, and is now a Mellon Postdoctoral Fellow at the University of Pennsylvania Humanities Forum. His research is focused on communal and religious violence, imperialism, comparative urban history and migration.

**Dr Aaron Edwards** completed his PhD in the School of Politics, International Studies and Philosophy at Queen's University Belfast in 2006. He has published several articles in the journals *Politics*, *Journal of Contemporary History*, *Irish Political Studies* and *Peace Review*. His recent books include *Transforming the Peace Process in Northern Ireland: From Terrorism to Democratic Politics* (Irish Academic Press, 2008, co-edited with Stephen Bloomer) and *Democratic Socialism and Sectarianism: A History of the Northern Ireland Labour Party* (Manchester University Press, forthcoming).

**Tony Fahey** is Senior Research Officer in the Economic and Social Research Institute, Dublin. He has published extensively on various political and social aspects of life in the Republic of Ireland.

**Dr John Gibney** is a Government of Ireland Postdoctoral Fellow at the Moore Institute, NUI Galway. He was previously National Endowment for the Humanities Faculty Fellow in Irish Studies at the University of Notre Dame in Indiana. He is currently completing a book entitled *Ireland and the Popish Plot* (Palgrave, forthcoming).

**Brian Graham** is Professor of Human Geography at the University of Ulster. He has extensive research interests in the broad field of cultural geography with a particular focus on the island of Ireland. His most recent book is *Pluralising Pasts: Heritage, Identity and Place in Multicultural Societies* (Pluto Press, 2007) (with G. J. Ashworth and J. E. Tunbridge). He is also co-editor (with P. Howard) of the *The Ashgate Research Companion to Heritage and Identity* (Ashgate, 2008).

**Lyndsey Harris** is an Associate Lecturer at the School of Economics and Politics at the University of Ulster at Jordanstown, and visiting lecturer at the Department of Social and Communications Studies at the University of Chester. Lyndsey is Chair of the Political Studies Association's Post Graduate Network (PGN); a Student Associate of INCORE; a Council member of the Conflict Research Society; and an IUS Armed Forces and Society Fellow. Her recent publications include "Introducing the strategic approach: an examination of loyalist paramilitaries in Northern Ireland", *British Journal of Politics and International Relations*, 8.4: 539–49.

**Bernadette C. Hayes** is Professor of Sociology at the University of Aberdeen. She has published extensively in the areas of gender, religion and politics. Her most recent book, *Conflict and Consensus: A Study of Values and Attitudes in the Republic of Ireland* (Brill, 2006) co-authored with Tony Fahey and Richard Sinnott, provides a detailed and comparative account of the complex value patterns in Ireland, North and South.

**Dr Thomas Hennessey** is Reader in History at Canterbury Christ Church University and a Fellow of the Royal Historical Society. Among his publications are: *The Evolution of the Troubles 1970–72* (Irish Academic Press, 2007); *Northern Ireland: The Origins of the Troubles* (Gill & Macmillan, 2005); *The Northern Ireland Peace Process: Ending the Troubles?* (Palgrave Macmillan, 2000); *Dividing Ireland. World War One and Partition* (Routledge, 1998); and *A History of Northern Ireland* (Palgrave Macmillan, 1997).

**Dr Myrtle Hill** is Director of the Centre for Women's Studies at Queen's University Belfast. A senior lecturer in social, religious and women's history, she has published many articles and chapters in these areas. Her books include *Women in Ireland: A Century of Change* (Blackstaff, 2003), *The Time of the End: Millenarian Beliefs in Ulster* (Ulster Historical Foundation, 2000) *and Women of Ireland: Image and Experience c.1880–1920* (Blackstaff, 1999, second edition) co-authored with Vivian Pollock.

**Dr Stephen Hopkins** is Lecturer in Politics in the Department of Politics and International Relations at the University of Leicester. His latest work on the politics of auto/biography in Northern Ireland is "Fighting without guns? Political autobiography in contemporary Northern Ireland", in Liam Harte (ed.) *Modern Irish Autobiography: Self, Nation and Society* (Palgrave, 2007).

**William Jenkins** is an Associate Professor in the Department of Geography at York University, Toronto. His research interests centre on the comparative study of Irish immigrants and their descendants in urban North America in the nineteenth and twentieth centuries. His most recent publications have appeared in journals such as *Immigrants and Minorities* and *Society and Space* and he is presently completing a volume on the Irish in Buffalo and Toronto between 1867 and 1916.

**James W. McAuley** is Professor of Political Sociology and Irish Studies at the University of Huddersfield. He has written extensively on political sociology, social movements and the politics of Northern Ireland. His most recent book is *Politics, State and Society* (Sage Press, 2004). He recently completed ESRC and Leverhulme Trust funded research in Northern Ireland.

**Dr Ian McKeane** lectures in the Institute of Irish Studies at the University of Liverpool and develops the work of the Institute within the wider community. His research interests include famine migration to Liverpool, aspects of the Irish independence struggle and French perceptions of Ireland.

**Dr Patrick Mitchel** is Director of Studies and Lecturer in Theology at the Irish Bible Institute in Dublin. His research interests include evangelical theology and history. His recent publications include *Evangelicalism and National Identity in Ulster 1921–1998* (Oxford University Press, 2003), "Evangelical Diversity", in R. Dunlop (ed.) *Evangelicals in Ireland: An Introduction* (Columba, 2004). He is editor of *Together We Believe: A Common Faith, a Common Purpose* (IBI, 2005).

**Sarah Morgan** is a civil servant based in London who retains an interest in Irish diaspora studies and particularly the Irish in Britain. Prior to becoming a civil servant, she was based at the Irish Studies Centre, University of North London (now London Metropolitan University). Sarah has worked on a number of research projects, dealing with the Irish in Britain, most recently the Irish2Project.

**Deidre O'Byrne** lectures in Irish and other literatures at Loughborough University. She is an active member of Nottingham Irish Studies Group and enjoys promoting Irish culture in the academic and wider community. Her main area of research is Irish women's rural writings.

**Dr Catherine O'Connor** teaches in the Department of History at the University of Limerick. Her research interests include Irish women's history, oral history and the Irish rebellion of 1798. Her most recent publication is "Women and the rebellion, Wexford 1798, in *History Studies*, 4, 2003.

**Dr Daithí Ó Corráin** is a research fellow in the Centre for Contemporary Irish History, Trinity College Dublin. He is author of *Rendering to God and Caesar: The Irish Churches and the Two States in Ireland 1949–73* (Manchester University Press, 2006) and has published a number of articles and chapters on aspects of church history and partition. He is currently completing *The Dead of the Irish Revolution 1916–21* (Yale University Press, forthcoming).

**Dr Neil Southern** is a lecturer in the Department of Education and Social Science at the University of Central Lancashire, where he teaches modules on Ethnicity and Human Rights, and Politics. Recent articles include items in *Nationalism and Ethnic Politics, Irish Political Studies* and the *Journal of Contemporary Religion*.

**Jonathan Tonge** is Professor of Politics at the University of Liverpool His recent books include *Northern Ireland* (Polity, 2006) *The New Northern Irish Politics* (Palgrave, 2005) *Sinn Fein and the SDLP: From Alienation to Participation* (Hurst 2005, with Gerard Murray) and *Northern Ireland: Conflict and Change* (Pearson, 2002). He has also published a wide range of journal articles and book chapters on Northern Ireland, based mainly on ESRC and Leverhulme Trust research awards.

**Fintan Vallely** is a musician and writer on traditional music who lectures at Dundalk Institute of Technology. His research is focused on music and identity. He edited *The Companion to Irish Traditional Music* (Cork University Press, 1999) and is the author of *Tuned Out: Protestant Perceptions of Traditional Music* (Cork University Press, 2008).

**Graham Walker** is Professor of Political History at Queen's University of Belfast. His most recent book is *A History of the Ulster Unionist Party: Protest, Pragmatism and Pessimism* (Manchester University Press,

2004). He is currently working on a study of devolution in relation to Scotland and Northern Ireland since 1945.

**Bronwen Walter** is Professor of Irish Diaspora Studies at Anglia Ruskin University, Cambridge. Her research interests include Irish settlement in Britain, with particular reference to women's experiences and multigenerational identities in England, New Zealand and Newfoundland. She has written *Outsiders Inside: Whiteness, Place and Irish Women* (Routledge, 2001) and co-authored *Discrimination and the Irish Community in Britain* (Commission for Racial Equality, 1997).

# Acknowledgements

The editors acknowledge with grateful thanks the help of a number of people and organisations in the construction of this volume. Debbie Hughes and the European Studies Research Institute at the University of Salford offered enormous help in facilitating the "Irish Protestant identities" international conference in September 2005. Except for the final chapter, the contributions in this volume were first aired at that well-attended event, which was generously sponsored by the British Academy. The British Association of Irish Studies also provided generous support and publicity. The conference was marked by high quality plenary sessions and papers, leading to enthusiastic participation from delegates drawn from thirteen different disciplines and seven countries. Since the conference, Tony Mason at Manchester University Press has been a helpful and supportive publisher. Other acknowledgements are contained within individual chapters.

# List of abbreviations

| | |
|---|---|
| DUP | Democratic Unionist Party |
| FAIR | Families Acting for Innocent Relatives |
| IOO | Independent Orange Order |
| IPBS | Irish Protestant Benevolent Society |
| IRA | Irish Republican Army |
| LAW | Loyalist Association of Workers |
| NAVER | North Armagh Victims Encouraging Recognition |
| NILP | Northern Ireland Labour Party |
| OYB | Orange Young Britons |
| PIRA | Provisional Irish Republican Army |
| PUP | Progressive Unionist Party |
| RHC | Red Hand Commando |
| RUC | Royal Ulster Constabulary |
| SAVER | South Armagh Victims Encouraging Recognition |
| SF | Sinn Fein |
| UDA | Ulster Defence Association |
| UDR | Ulster Defence Regiment |
| UPRG | Ulster Political Research Group |
| UULA | Ulster Unionist Labourist Association |
| UUP | Ulster Unionist Party |
| UVF | Ulster Volunteer Force |
| UWC | Ulster Workers Council |

# Introduction

*Mervyn Busteed, Frank Neal and Jonathan Tonge*

Protestantism in Ireland is almost entirely an innovation imposed by the British administration or introduced by successive waves of migrants from Britain from the sixteenth century onwards. Such immigration was encouraged and in many cases organised by British governments for whom the transformation of Ireland into a Protestant country was a significant aspiration. Though such a large-scale shift of ecclesiastical allegiance never took place and was never likely, nevertheless, the religious geography of the island was transformed. Protestant majorities emerged in some parts of the north-east, with much smaller communities scattered throughout the rest of the island. This Protestant population of approximately 25 per cent was itself internally divided. Just over half belonged to the Church of Ireland, the Irish branch of the Anglican communion, and for almost two hundred years after the close of the Williamite wars in 1692 provided the ruling elite in Ireland. Slightly less numerous were the Presbyterians who were mostly descended from Scottish settlers, and subject to much of the penal legislation which also applied to Catholics for most of the eighteenth century. Small groups of dissenters made up the balance and experienced the same discriminatory laws until the early nineteenth century.

The rise of a more assertive Irish nationalism, with a strong Catholic and later Gaelic revivalist emphasis demanding various forms of self-government, provoked a variety of responses from the Protestant population. Some shared nationalist aspirations and became prominent in the leadership cadre, but the great majority responded by becoming more strongly, and in some cases stridently, pro-union in outlook and unionist in politics. This culminated in the partition of the island in 1920. Northern Ireland politics and society were dominated by a unionist majority with a large Catholic and nationalist minority, whilst the new Irish Free State/Republic was characterised by an overwhelming Catholic majority embarking upon the creation of the new Irish state and a small Protestant minority cut off from both Britain and Northern Ireland. In each of these situations, Irish Protestants were repeatedly challenged about their basic identity and loyalties in relation to both Britain and Ireland. Moreover, it was also a question for those who left Ireland, since, like all migrants they faced an identity crisis, caught between the land of their birth and their new homeland.

Developments from the late 1960s onwards sharpened the challenge. The collapse of the political system in Northern Ireland, the abolition of devolved government, the Troubles, political divisions in the previously monolithic unionists, the emergence of paramilitary loyalism, a lack of empathy with the unionist outlook by British governments, Conservative and Labour, and the search for a political solution, which would involve both Irish nationalists and unionists in joint government, challenged many of the basic assumptions which had long underlain the northern Protestant world view.

The very different situation of the small Protestant minority in the Irish Republic had seen them experience numerical decline and a process of adjustment to their radically reduced circumstances as a community marginalised by the triumph of Irish nationalism. They too had to decide where their loyalties lay, in a lingering nostalgia for ascendancy now long past or with the newly emerging Irish nation state. In so doing they had to face the danger of being overwhelmed by the strongly Catholic ethos of Irish society and latterly by the frenetic materialism which came with the prosperity of the 1990s, both of which could so easily smother their distinctive traditions.

Twenty-five of the chapters which follow are a selection of the papers which were presented at a conference on "Irish Protestant Identities" organised by the British Association for Irish Studies (BAIS) and the European Studies Research Institute of the University of Salford on 15–17 September 2005, an event which marked the twentieth anniversary of BAIS. The final chapter was added after the 2007 Northern Ireland Assembly elections. All are based on original research. The collection does not try to cover every aspect of a topic, which is affected by ongoing change. However, they do attempt to investigate a theme, which we believe is central to an understanding not merely of Irish Protestantism but Ireland in general.

## An overview of the contents of the book

The position of the Anglican ascendancy is discussed in three chapters, which examine its situation at formative periods and in each case emphasise the response to a basic insecurity. John Gibney (Chapter 1) discusses how, regardless of what actually happened, Anglican Protestants in Restoration and Jacobean Ireland crafted a group memory of events in the Irish rising of 1641, which they used to justify legislative measures to secure their elite status. He notes the recurring emphasis on Catholic Irish barbarity, disloyalty and untrustworthiness and the need to guard against a further outbreak – themes that were to recur down the centuries. Mervyn Busteed (Chapter 2) analyses the outlook of a leading member of one Fermanagh ascendancy family in the period 1740–84. With the passage of time many members of the ascendancy class had become deeply rooted in Ireland. He shows how one of the more conscientious landowners, aware of wider European cultural and economic trends, was subject to a conflicting pull on his loyalty and sense of identity, caught between Ireland and Britain, the ideas of the Enlightenment and the demographic and political realities of Ireland. Deirdre O'Byrne (Chapter 3) discusses how this same group is represented in the fiction and autobiography of the twentieth century, by which time they were well aware that they were no longer the ruling landowning elite. She notes the sense of a quietly desperate and declining minority living amongst the decaying grandeur of neglected gardens and houses, and their ghosts, seeking comfort in a myth of wartime sacrifice and conscious of their drift to gentle extinction, eroded by emigration, intermarriage with Catholics and the lack of male heirs.

Three studies demonstrate more active Protestant coping strategies in the face of radical change. David Butler (Chapter 4) examines the fate of the smaller Protestant dissenting groups (Congregationalist, Baptist and Quaker) in Munster in the years 1660–1810. He notes how some congregations died out while others survived and some flourished. In some cases immigration helped, but he emphasises the key role of wealthy, committed families, energetic, gifted leaders and shrewd forward-thinking financial management as keys to survival in a hostile cultural environment. Hayes and Fahey (Chapter 5) examine the political attitudes of Protestants in the Republic in the final two years of the twentieth century. Noting a sense of disengagement in the early years of the newly independent Irish state, they analyse data sets which suggest that, while Protestants have slightly less interest in politics than others, they share the same levels of confidence and participation in Irish political institutions and have an equal or even slightly higher level of civic awareness, suggesting they are now full citizens in every sense. Daithí Ó Corráin notes, in Chapter 6, how the Church of Ireland had always been very aware of the all-Ireland dimension, while simultaneously recognising that the great majority of its members lived in Northern Ireland. He analyses how between 1949 and 1973 it strove to accommodate the political partition of the island and the development of two contrasting regimes and differing sets of loyalties by adjustments to the order of worship and administrative structures, and how it had to cope with the sometimes fierce anti-Catholicism of some northern members.

Irish Protestantism – like Irish Catholicism – has, on the whole, generated rather conservative social attitudes on the role of women, especially in religious life. However, Myrtle Hill (Chapter 7) in a study largely concentrating on the missionary societies of the Presbyterian Church, shows how women were able to carve out a distinctive role for themselves. While some took on traditional roles as home makers for their missionary husbands and domestic role models for indigenous women, in the novel circumstances of overseas service many, especially single women, took on active leadership roles organising and administering clinics, schools and classes, and building up support groups at home, sometimes to the dismay of male colleagues. In Chapter 8, Catherine O'Connor analyses the role of Church of Ireland women in the life of the Ferns diocese in south-east Ireland in the 20 years after 1945. She shows how much of their quietly devout lives was focused around community preservation and welfare, providing music at church services, putting great effort into organising and catering for events designed not only to raise funds for church work at home and abroad but to provide social occasions when suitable Anglican marriage partners might be encountered.

In Chapter 9, Naomi Doak switches the focus to the north and draws attention to the fact that relatively little has been written about the work of Ulster Protestant women authors. She suggests that the intellectual orthodoxy of the post-colonial paradigm in Irish studies may be partly responsible, since it seems to imply that the north is still a colony and Protestants the colonists. She also argues that much of the discussion of the north has focused on the Protestant/Catholic conflict to the detriment of other cleavages and that the overt masculinity of unionist culture and the assignment of women to domestic roles have both discouraged female literary effort and downgraded what has been produced.

Religious belief is clearly central to the Irish Protestant sense of identity, but chapters by Doyle, Mitchel, and Morgan and Walter emphasise how its significance varies with time and place. Both Doyle and Mitchel focus on the evangelical tradition, so strong in both historic and contemporary Irish Protestantism. Doyle (Chapter 10) discusses the remarkable 1859 revival in Ulster and its impact in sharpening the sense of communal identity among the Belfast Protestant working class. In particular, he argues that the highly visible manifestations of the movement – open air meetings and preaching, worshippers crying out, swooning, claiming visions – proclaimed and heightened group awareness and underlined contrasts with Catholic belief and practice. Mitchel, in Chapter 11, examines the changing outlook of evangelical Protestants in independent Ireland. He notes the significance of evangelicalism in nineteenth-century Protestantism, especially among those elements of the governing ascendancy who saw the converting of Catholics as a means of strengthening the Union as well as weaning them from the errors of Rome. After partition he relates how their persistently anti-Catholic outlook and evangelistic efforts led to a mixture of hostility in some areas, condemnation by Catholic bishops and general incomprehension. However, by the early twenty-first century, he notes how generational change, the absence of any political agenda, an influx of migrants from evangelical backgrounds and efforts to engage in meaningful fashion with contemporary Irish society have transformed evangelicalism in the Republic.

It has proved extremely difficult to isolate the Protestant element in Irish migration to Britain. However, in Chapter 12, and Morgan and Walter have succeeded where few others have managed, in that they have been able to pick out a small group of second generation Irish Protestant migrants willing to talk about their attitudes to things Irish. They find these individuals have an awareness of difference from British fellow citizens but also that they very consciously stand aside from Irish migrant social and sporting club networks in Britain. Among the second generation they find an awareness of Irish sectarian divisions and parental anti-Catholicism, but little desire to claim an Irish Protestant identity.

By contrast, the Irish Protestant element in emigration to North America has received rather more attention, much of it focused on the "Ulster Scots", descendants of planters who moved on across the North Atlantic. James Doan (Chapter 13) focuses on the notably self-aware and well-organised Presbyterians in the 100 years from the late seventeenth century. He notes the economic and religious reasons for their departure and the somewhat disgruntled reactions of the Anglican authorities and other Protestant groups in their new homeland. He traces their movement into the western and south-western fringes of the colonies and notes how their role as defenders of the frontier against the natives echoed their relationship with Ulster Catholics. He also remarks how their critical attitude towards any authority but their own helped fuel critical colonial attitudes towards British government. William Jenkins moves the emphasis on to later Protestant settlement further north, especially in the Toronto area. In Chapter 14, he outlines the key role of a network of Orange Order lodges, evangelical churches and charities in supporting, socialising and affirming the migrants. He notes how they carried much of their ultra-Protestant, anti-Catholic and unionist outlook into Canadian politics, but underlines the fact that the small liberal Protestant home rule element was also represented.

The Irish War of Independence and partition took place against the background of the redrawing of the map of Europe after the First World War. Ian McKeane (Chapter 15) provides a useful reminder that the Protestant situation attracted European attention by examining their treatment in the French press during the period 1919–22, and demonstrates the great value of contemporary newspapers as a resource for historians. He finds a strong element of travelogue in the reportage, a frequent reliance on imagination rather than fact, and only a hazy awareness of the basis of the conflict between nationalists and unionists. Some reporters did attempt interviews, but he notes how Unionist spokesmen (*sic*) were wary, maladroit and sometimes downright uncommunicative – an experience which was to recur in future crises.

Strained relationships also occur *within* the unionist population. In Chapter 16, Hastings Donnan discusses how the Protestant population of South Armagh has coped with the losses and the sense of victimhood resulting from an IRA campaign that lasted almost a quarter of a century. He examines the contrasting narratives put out by two victim support groups. One of these publicises graphic accounts of violent incidents and makes explicit political points by stressing republican paramilitary responsibility. The other presents victim suffering in restrained fashion, focuses on support services for survivors and relatives and eschews political commentary. Fintan Vallely focuses on a cultural aspect of the chronically strained relationships between unionist and nationalist in Chapter 17. He stresses how, while Irish traditional music came to be regarded as part of the cultural package that went with Irish nationalism, there were always Protestants who participated as consumers and performers. But the Unionist loss of control over Northern Ireland's political structures with the abolition of the Stormont parliament and imposition of direct rule in 1972, and the realisation that there is little understanding or empathy for them in Britain, has led some elements to embark on the construction of a sense of identity less tied to the British connection. In casting around for cultural resources he shows how some have fastened upon the traditions of the Scottish element in the seventeenth century Ulster plantation, particularly the music of their descendants, and how they have tried to present it as their exclusive property in isolation from the general corpus of Ulster traditional music.

Discussion of the unionist political outlook has tended to characterise it as unyielding and unchanging. However, Tom Hennessey (Chapter 18) points out how the unionist definition of their national identity has undergone some notable shifts during the twentieth century and has always been multi-layered. He points out how in the early twentieth century, before partition, unionist leaders held to a dual identity, frequently stressing how they held to both Irishness and Britishness within the United Kingdom. But he traces the process by which partition and two world wars led them to downplay the Irish dimension. He notes how the process has continued. At the outset of the Troubles in the late 1960s, surveys revealed that Protestants in Northern Ireland were labelling themselves as "British", some as "Irish" and some as belonging to "Ulster", but by the early 1990s a process of polarisation had obviously taken place, with many more opting for "British", very few for "Irish" and while some chose "Ulster" it had declined notably in favour of "Northern Irish". He stresses that while the Ulster Protestant sense of identity was still multi-faceted, and some were quite ready to acknowledge an Irish dimension, for most this was within a distinctive Northern Irish and British context.

The impact of Protestant Orange identities beyond Ireland is considered in Chapter 19, in Peter Day's study of the Orange Order on Merseyside. Sectarian tensions within Liverpool developed amid Protestant and Catholic Irish immigration to the city during the 1800s. The alignment of the Protestant working class to the Conservative party, or to candidates standing as "Protestants", prevented the Labour party from gaining a majority on the city council until the 1950s. Candidates with religious labels continued to be elected until the 1970s, but a combination of slum clearance and secularism diminished the importance of Orangeism within Liverpool. Day charts the decline in relevance and numbers suffered by the Order, exemplified by diminishing attendance at its flagship 12 July parades in Liverpool and Southport. The Order continues to offer a group identity for a small number of working-class Protestants on Merseyside, but its political and religious impacts have vanished.

Tonge and McAuley (Chapter 20) explore the much larger Orange Order in Northern Ireland. Here too, the Order has suffered substantial decline in terms of membership and has been removed from political influence. Such influence was considerable during the days of Ulster Unionist Party (UUP) hegemony from 1921 until 1972, when the Order's important position within the unionist movement provided voice and made Orange Order membership essential for most unionist politicians. The Order's retreat since 1972 has been considerable, as it has become bereft of political clout and has suffered large reductions in the number of urban and middle-class members.

As the fortunes of the UUP declined after the Good Friday Agreement, the Order severed its historical link to the party, opposing what it perceived as moral equivocations or immoral features within the Agreement, such as prisoner releases. As Tonge and McAuley detail, a significant number of security force victims during the conflict had been members of the Orange Order, heightening Orange perceptions that a process of ethnic cleansing was taking place. The compromises of the Good Friday Agreement were thus strongly opposed by many within the Order. Within three years of the deal, it was evident that a majority of Orangemen were now voting for the (then) anti-Good Friday Agreement Democratic Unionist Party (DUP), even though that party, with the Free Presbyterian connections of its leader, had no connection with the Order.

The final section of the book considers issues of representation and transformation in Northern Ireland since the 1960s, with particular focus on the Protestant working class. The "ultra" wing of the assertion of Protestant identity, loyalist paramilitarism, is explored in Chapters 21 and 22 by Lyndsey Harris and Stephen Hopkins, while Brian Graham (Chapter 23) examines the role of loyalist former prisoners in effecting conflict transformation.

In examining the strategic role of loyalist paramilitaries, Harris draws a distinction between the community defence orientation of the Ulster Defence Association (UDA), which developed as a local response to republican activity and the broader historical fidelity to the principles of defence of the Union, based on the 1912 Solemn Covenant of resistance, articulated by the Ulster Volunteer Force (UVF). Both these positions, argues Harris, are grounded in the rationality of community or constitutional defence. As such, loyalist paramilitarism cannot simply be dismissed as unthinking gangsterism, even though its image may be more negative than that associated with republican "armed struggle".

Stephen Hopkins discusses loyalist paramilitarism from the perspective of loyalist biography and autobiography. Loyalist writings have been underdeveloped compared to the plethora of material emanating from republicans, reinforcing perceptions of loyalist inarticulacy. Hopkins offers several possible explanations for the relative dearth; educational groundings in mathematics and science, rather than literature; the defeatism of the loyalist community; the dominance of state institutions until the 1970s, diminishing the need for narratives of justification and the lack of marketability of such material, compared to the global interest in the IRA. The works that have emerged have tended to be hagiographies of loyalist leaders, or self-justifying autobiographies, with a leaning towards the duplicitous. Nonetheless, Hopkins indicates their value, in that loyalist leaders highlight the structural and political condition which influenced their chosen path of paramilitarism; the importance of the prison experience in shaping ideas and the motivations behind compromise – or, in a few cases, such as that of Johnny Adair, the lack of concession. Like the other contributors in this volume, Hopkins draws distinctions between the UDA and UVF, the latter being more favourably disposed to political discussion and reconciliation.

Graham notes the asymmetry of roles in conflict transformation in the early years of the loyalist ceasefire. While the UVF and its political associates in the Progressive Unionist Party (PUP) were generally committed to developing the peace, sections of the UDA converted into criminal gangs dedicated more to the promotion of drug-dealing than peace. The author notes the particular difficulties for loyalist ex-prisoners in reintegrating into their community, having fewer opportunities for political work than their republican counterparts. Moreover, the experience of having been imprisoned by a state they purported to defend was disorienting for many former prisoners. The insecurities of politically motivated loyalist ex-prisoners are thus acute. Nonetheless, Graham does note two positive contributions from this group. The first is an emphasis by some on the need to protect loyalist communities not from the IRA but from those elements engaged in drug-dealing. Second, amid continuing local territorial squabbles, ex-prisoners have sometimes combined with their republican counterparts to defuse tensions at sectarian interfaces.

Part of the problem for loyalists has rested in their inability to form a mass-support, populist party, in contrast to developments within republicanism. The story since the onset of conflict in the late 1960s has been one of intra-bloc division within unionism. A historical overview of the Protestant working class in Northern Ireland and its modern political fragmentation is offered by Graham Walker in Chapter 25, where he examines the crisis in the relationship between the Protestant working class and its leaders, which developed amid challenges to the state during the 1960s. This breach in relations impacts upon the present, as the UUP failed to retain its utterly dominant position; was rendered largely powerless by direct rule from Westminster from 1972 onwards and eventually, in the post-Good Friday Agreement era, lost the support of the Unionist electorate.

Whilst conceding that it held some advantages over its Catholic counterpart, Walker rejects the notion of a privileged Protestant working class as historical myth. He argues that labourist battles for a better deal for the working class (generally) have tended to be ignored in accounts of Northern Ireland. Protestant trade unionism was important, while the adoption of the British welfare state by Northern Ireland's political leaders contributed to Protestant pride in their British identification. Given this contribution "from below", Walker argues for a historical narrative, which does not merely concentrate upon clichéd, top-down accounts of unionist hegemony.

Some of these themes are developed by Aaron Edwards in Chapter 24. He argues that the possibility of progress for a labourist unionist party, shorn of the sectarian or triumphalist trappings of unionism, disappeared with the arrival of the Troubles. The particular sufferer amid the onset of conflict was the Northern Ireland Labour Party (NILP). Although the NILP was predominantly Protestant, its emphasis was more labourist than unionist. It offered a challenge to the UUP which peaked in the mid-1960s, before the alternative challenges posed by the civil rights movement and the republican armed struggle were accompanied by communal polarisation. After this, the Protestant working class tended to gravitate towards support for the overt communalism of Ian Paisley's DUP or even flirted with loyalist paramilitarism.

Finally, the rise of the DUP in its intra-communal battle with the UUP is explored by Neil Southern in Chapter 26. Southern highlights how the ambiguities within the 1998 Good Friday Agreement, particularly on the issue of the decommissioning of paramilitary weapons, allowed the DUP to prosper, amid fears among unionists that the deal was one based primarily upon concessions to nationalists. The chapter charts how the DUP later managed to enter into government with Sinn Fein within the framework of the Agreement with only minimal internal strife. According to Southern, the UUP could be seen as "unfair losers", given their willingness to negotiate the template for political settlement. However, the party's lack of internal unity over the deal and the failure to close down elements of the agreement amid procrastination by republicans, led to an electoral switch by many insecure unionists to the DUP.

Despite the voluminous literature on Irish conflict, politics, religion and culture, the Protestant tradition on the island remains under-researched in comparison with its Catholic and nationalist counterpart. The purpose of this volume is to partially redress the imbalance by analysing diverse aspects of the minority grouping in a polity and society where the importance of religious and denominational affiliation remains high.

# Part I

# Aspects of ascendancy

# 1

# The memory of 1641 and Protestant identity in Restoration and Jacobite Ireland

*John Gibney*

## Introduction

In October 1641 Catholics in Ulster embarked upon a rebellion against Protestant colonists in the province, which rapidly escalated across the island. The subsequent wars of the 1640s became a parallel theatre to the British civil wars as well as an internecine conflict, and would only be ended by the parliamentarian reconquest of Ireland in 1649–53. However, the initial months of the rebellion could be (and were) seen as markedly distinct from the remainder of the conflict and fears of a repeat of this rebellion would prey on the minds of Irish Protestants in the late seventeenth century. The reason was simple: it was perceived as having been a concerted attempt to wipe out the Protestant presence in Ireland. Given the levels of violence in early modern Ireland, it was probably inevitable that it could be seen to retain the potential for more.

After the restoration of the monarchy in 1660, 1641 came to be seen as ultimate proof of the barbarity of the Catholic Irish, and the reiteration of these perceived proofs of their irredeemable brutality found a role within political discourse in both islands. The spectre of 1641 would be employed for specific political purposes: to justify the continued dispossession of the Catholic Irish under the land settlement of the early 1660s; to justify the attempts to exclude the Catholic James, Duke of York, from the succession to the crown in 1680; and to procure military assistance for Irish Protestants during the Williamite War of 1689–91. What follows is an attempt to examine how such perceptions acquired their polemical purpose in relation to these three examples.

## 1641: a defining moment?

The political utility of 1641 depended on a specific perception of the rebellion that was obvious to many in the Stuart kingdoms, and which was continually reiterated in print. For example, an anonymous pamphlet reprinted in London during the Popish Plot in late 1678 took 1641 as its subject or, more particularly, the atrocities against Protestant settlers allegedly carried out during the rebellion by the native Irish: burial alive, burning, exposure to the elements, hanging, mutilation, starvation and inventive torture, among other things. Children were fed to dogs, boiled alive and had their skulls smashed in, families were forced to kill one another, and "such was their malice against the English, that they forced their children to kill English children". Wives and daughters were raped in front of their husbands and fathers "with the basest villains they could pick out", and usually murdered afterwards. Neither the persons nor the religious symbols of Protestants were respected. In Sligo the bodies of men and women would be stripped and rearranged into what was delicately termed "a most immodest posture". Graves were desecrated and Bibles set alight, for "it was hell-fire they burnt". In Kilkenny the head of a minister was attached to a cross in the market place, the mouth was cut open to the ears, and the rebels "laid a leaf of a Bible upon it, and bid him preach, for his mouth was wide enough". In an ignominious if no less cruel demise, a fat man was supposedly melted down to make candles for a mass. This account was reproduced from Sir John Temple's influential *Irish Rebellion*, as was an obvious question to be considered.

> All this wickedness they exercised upon the English, without any provocation given them. Alas! Who can comprehend the fears, terrors, anguish, bitterness and perplexity that seized upon the poor Protestants, finding themselves so suddenly surprised without remedy, and rapt up in all kinds of outward miseries which could possibly by man be inflicted upon human kind?[1]

The question remained relevant. 1641 resonated in the Protestant imaginations of both Ireland and England. It was an obvious benchmark for what Irish Catholics might potentially do again should they ever have the chance.

Such an exaggerated perception of the rebellion was by no means untypical: it was commonly held throughout the late seventeenth century and beyond (Love, 1966; Barnard, 1991; Donovan, 1995; Shagan, 1997). It undoubtedly resembled, and was influenced by, the stock imagery and rhetoric of anti-Popery in early modern Britain and Europe, but this perception contributed to the development of a specifically Irish tradition of sectarian anti-Popery that derived its potency from the reality that Protestants in Ireland were vastly outnumbered by Catholics (Clarke, 1997). Confessional allegiance had become increasingly important in

Irish society from the mid-to-late sixteenth century onwards, with the introduction of the Reformation, the parallel activities of an increasingly militant British Protestant state, and the responses of Irish Catholic communities that increasingly adhered to the Counter-Reformation in the face of these twin challenges. The Anglo-Scottish Ulster plantation of the early seventeenth century was one result of the eventual military defeat of Catholic Ireland in the Nine Years War (1596–1603). The Protestant nature of the British colonial presence in Ireland prior to 1641 guaranteed a sectarian dimension in Irish society, and Anglican hostility to Catholicism had long been enshrined in the theology of the Church of Ireland (Ford, 1987). However, popular Protestant attitudes to Catholicism may well have been influenced less by doctrinal consider-ations than by a visceral distinction between the generally Catholic native and generally Protestant—both Anglican and Presbyterian—newcomer, especially after the brutal events of the 1640s (Ford, 2005). The blunt reality was that in 1641 the Catholic Irish embarked upon what eventu-ally became a nationwide rebellion "wherein the force of religion was so much greater than that of birth" (Gibney, 2005: 458), and which was directed at the Protestant colonists who had benefited from their dispos-session. The consequence in subsequent decades was that, despite the diversity of Irish Protestant communities, 1641 became a touchstone for that aspect of their developing identity that perceived their position in Ireland as besieged and under threat.

Virtually since its outbreak, the 1641 rebellion was rightly assumed to be a defining moment in Irish history. But what actually happened to Protestants in the rebellion? They perceived that they had been subjected to a brutally sectarian onslaught, and had narrowly escaped extermina-tion. The most recent and substantive study readily identifies the basis for such Protestant fears, outlining the extent of violence against the set-tlers, and its politicised and ritualistic nature (Canny, 2001). But the sheer extent of the assault across the country was undoubtedly exagger-ated; the polemical estimation of Protestant casualties afterwards ranged from 10,000 to 1,000,000, though Catholic casualties were passed over in silence (Donovan, 1995). The atrocity stories published in the after-math, and decades later, emphasised the supposed lack of provocation, or of a rationale, for the attacks upon Protestants, thereby highlighting their sectarian aspects. The published accounts of the rebellion that emerged in the seventeenth century (such as the pamphlet cited above) often borrowed their details wholesale from a handful of works, such as Henry Jones's *Remonstrance*[2] and Temple's *Irish Rebellion* (Cope, 2001; Gillespie, 2005a). Both of these works were written at specific junctures, and for specific political purposes, and both reproduced many of the

extensive (and visceral) witness depositions collected after 1641 that
have preoccupied historians ever since (Clarke, 1986).

When stripped of the complexity of its background, the technical
reality of a rebellion against a colony was that the battle lines
inevitably adopted a religious tinge. In time, 1641 could be depicted as
a purely religious war, and its events would retain a resonance for generations. Protestant political argument in the decades after the event
became predicated on the fact that they remained an embattled minority, endangered in Ireland and aware that they had come under attack
in the past. The atrocities directed at Protestants during the rebellion,
both real and exaggerated, loomed large in the memory and imagination of the Irish Protestant community. Given the fact that the most
significant consequence of the wars in mid-century had been the crys-
tallisation of a nascent Protestant "ascendancy", in an Irish context, the
utility of anti-Catholicism in political and social life would inevitably
(and by definition) be at the expense of those Catholics whom they had
supplanted. The view of 1641 as having been an attempt at sectarian
genocide was thus intended to justify the new Protestant dispensation,
by highlighting the danger that the Protestant interest was assumed to
be in.

This was not an abstraction: there were very real issues at stake.
Naturally, there was a vigorous tradition of Catholic refutation of such
assertions. Predicated ultimately on the basis of Catholic loyalty to a
Protestant state, the Catholic position could be defended in numerous
ways. One anonymous tract, published in 1662, was prompted by the
publication in London of Protestant atrocity stories of 1641 that were
intended "to render all the Catholics there (in all good men's opinions)
blasted and unfit to partake of his Majesties grace and favour".[3] It sought
to refute such claims, balancing them against atrocities committed by
English forces.

This was one means of defence from vilification, but there were others.
John Lynch wrote an elaborate history to counter English views of the
barbarity of the Irish, Peter Walsh emphasised Catholic loyalty to the
crown, and Nicholas French, in numerous works, bluntly rebutted
the allegations made against Catholics since the 1640s.[4] Yet the bulk of
such pro-Catholic publications were large, sophisticated works written
by the Catholic elite, particularly the clergy (Lynch, Walsh and French
were all Catholic clerics), usually printed on the continent, and effectively
accessible only to the wealthy and the learned: printing restrictions kept
them out of Ireland, and they were difficult to get into the country
(Barnard, 2001; Pollard, 1989). There were links that could overcome
these difficulties, but British print culture naturally made greater inroads

into Ireland as commercial and ecclesiastical networks facilitated the spread of books, and increases in literacy, and thus demand for reading material, inevitably extended the reach of the printed word (Barnard, 1998; Gillespie, 2005b).

Alongside this was the intangible reality that oral culture, of communal reading, rumour, gossip and hearsay, and reading aloud would also bring the contents of books (and other printed media) to a greater audience. For example, numerous proclamations issued in Ireland during the Popish Plot in 1678–79 dealt with issues such as the presence of Catholic clergy, Catholics within towns, and Catholic ownership of weapons.[5] Inevitably reminders of the potential danger posed by Catholics, such proclamations were seen, read and heard in public. Oral communication and rumour filled the gaps between the literate and non-literate. Beyond this was the parallel oral and scribal culture of Gaelic Ireland, but within Anglophone print culture, authors and publications propagating a Protestant view of 1641 as unmitigated sectarian massacre vastly outnumbered pro-Catholic writers. This was an aspect of explicitly Irish Protestant memory, but that perception of 1641 and their relation to it was also shaped by the reality of the Irish Protestant experience for, at least until the 1680s, the rebellion was within living memory.

Revived fears of another rebellion recurred throughout the second half of the seventeenth century within specific and explicit contexts, and became more pertinent at moments of real and perceived crisis. Between their exposure to danger in 1641 and their seeming salvation after 1691, Irish Protestants found the memory of what had allegedly happened in 1641 particularly (and inevitably) relevant. But equally, it was useful, being revived at moments of crisis to bolster their position in the face of real or perceived danger. The issue is not 1641 in itself, but what it was believed to be. Writings that touched upon 1641 were polemical by definition, intending to provoke a reaction and hopefully garner influence at some level, whether published in Ireland or Britain. Public and private references to 1641 did not necessarily require detailed explication; intimation often seemed to be enough, which suggests a set of automatic assumptions about what had actually happened, and thereby what it meant.

## 1641 after 1660

The restoration of the monarchy across the three kingdoms in 1660 was to be the restoration of the old order in a manner that would render irrelevant and consign to history the extraordinary events of the 1640s

and 1650s. The logic of eradicating the commonwealth was the eradica-
tion of all it had done, which in Ireland meant reversing the massive
confiscation and redistribution of Catholic-owned lands in the 1650s; and
those Protestant inhabitants who had benefited from this would strongly
oppose its reversal (Clarke, 1999). The maintenance of a particular view
of 1641 became a part of this opposition. The Protestant experience of
1641, as interpreted by figures such as Temple, could suggest that their
survival was due to divine providence. Indeed, in the early 1660s the commemoration of its outbreak on 23 October received legislative and liturgical sanction, even though the divisive nature of such commemorations
was not lost on figures such as the viceroy James Butler, Duke of Ormond
(Barnard, 1991). And the 1662 Act of Settlement that confirmed most of
the Cromwellian confiscations proceeded from the assumption that the
"unnatural insurrection" of 1641 had become "a formed and almost
national rebellion of the Irish Papists . . . to the destruction of the English
and Protestants inhabitants in Ireland". Alongside such a damning indict-
ment were concomitant assurances of Protestant loyalty, but the basis for
the content of the act remained a constant, "forasmuch as the rapines,
depredations and massacres committed by the said Irish and Popish rebels
and enemies are not only well known to this present parliament, but are
notorious to the whole world".[6] Therein lay the justification for the for-
feiture of the properties of Irish Catholics, as converted into law.

Given the changes that the Protestant community underwent between
1641 and 1660, it was understandable that they would exert themselves
to defend their new interests, but it was inevitable that such sweeping
assumptions were contested. The Franciscan Peter Walsh, in *A letter
desiring a just and merciful regard of the Roman Catholicks of Ireland*,
petitioned Ormond for Catholic redress, made no denial of Catholic
involvement in warfare in Ireland. "But you know, my Lord, there are
many thousands of Protestants in the three kingdoms, who have been far
more heinously criminal, both against his Majesty and against his
father."[7] Given the protean career of a figure such as Roger Boyle, Lord
Broghill (rewarded at the Restoration as Earl of Orrery despite a successful Cromwellian interlude), one could see his point. Yet the coun-
terblast to Walsh, *The Irish colours displayed*, was credited to Orrery,
and argued to extremity, deeming the inherent savagery of the Irish
Catholic to be an evident reality. The "bloody animosities were constant
and hereditary to them, so long before any division between them in
matters of religion, and withal how much they have been sharpened by
that accident", an idea neatly extended to the Catholic Old English,
thereby exonerating all but the newer, Protestant colonists from complicity in conflict.

Religion here exposed another facet of political loyalty, with the misguided inclination of the Irish to follow their clergy making them little more than "Spanish Papists"; the well-worn theme of foreign (Catholic) intervention in Ireland remained a constant. The limited restoration of some previous Catholic occupants to their lands in the early 1660s had gone too far as it was, and the implicit invocation of violence came with a polemical purpose, as "the only good effect of such infinite slaughters and murders as have hitherto infamed [*sic*] that kingdom . . . has been the producing of this conjuncture wherein his Majesty hath gained an occasion of setting it upon lasting foundations." Walsh's statement, as cited above, received a direct rebuttal, for "the cold and treacherous murders . . . of above two hundred thousand in the first two years, makes the massacres unparalleled, and excuses all cruelties [that] may have been returned by the English in the heat of war."[8] The Irish Catholic was the bedrock of this argument: 1641 (and a massively exaggerated casualty figure) the evidence and rationale. The double standard is evident; British Protestant forces could readily engage in massacres such as that at Dungans Hill in 1647 that readily obviated moral equivalency or superiority (Lenihan, 2001). Yet in the eyes of the author of this tract, such actions were defensible. Cannily, Orrery (if he was indeed the author) refused to enter into debate over a key issue raised by Walsh: the terms of the 1649 peace treaty negotiated between the Confederate Catholics and Charles I, which became the bedrock of Catholic claims on the crown throughout the Restoration period.

With regards to the specific nature of the claims on which Catholic spokesmen stood, the question of whether the treaty remained binding was bound to be anathema to the Protestant interest in Ireland after 1660. In 1649 it had prompted a furious denunciation by officers in Munster who declared their allegiance to Parliament; the treaty was depicted as wholesale surrender, with a proposed act of oblivion "but a fair inducement to allure the Irish to attempt once more to take away the lives of the rest which remained, and then our lands were their own also".[9] Symbolically, this tract was dated 23 October 1649, eight years to the day of the outbreak of the rebellion. In 1678 the issue recurred again, as it was reported to Ormond (who was serving as viceroy for a third time), that "the French ambassador has given out that his master would see the benefit of the peace the Catholics made with you".[10] A more tangible concern for Irish Protestants was felt over time.

*The Irish colours displayed* also argued from implication: 1641 proved the untrustworthy and dangerous nature of Catholics. The massive exaggeration of Protestant casualties vindicated this militant stance. Given the events of the 1640s and 1650s, the restitution of the Catholic community could only come at the expense of Protestants, theoretically exposing both themselves and England to danger once again.[11] But the utility of scaremongering was not lost on those in the 1660s (such as Orrery) who sought to block the implications of the Restoration land settlement (Creighton, 2000). Certainly, John Lynch took the view that the maintenance of the confiscations of the 1650s was the principal motivation for inciting hatred against Catholics, and that rumours of their treasonable activities inevitably followed rumours of concessions to them, thus providing a pretext for further repression.[12]

The perception of 1641 as unnatural rebellion was essential to this Irish Protestant perspective: the threat of a repeat of 1641 was vital to its maintenance. This is not to ascribe purely material notions to Irish Protestants; fears of 1641 recurring again may have served a purpose, but they were also quite genuine, and in this sense seemed to become an integral element of their mental world. "Less will not content the Irish than the rooting out all English interest here" was one observation, and there is no reason to doubt the sincerity of the belief, even if the reality could differ.[13] Such fears never quite went away. In 1676 Henry Jones, as bishop of Meath, returned to the theme, preaching a sermon at Christ Church in Dublin warning Ireland's Protestants of the dangers they faced. He proceeded from the assumption that "Ireland . . . is above all other nations in Europe, influenced by the power of Rome." In the form of the Papacy, Antichrist had sought to destroy Christ's Protestant witnesses across Europe.

> And can the bloody butcheries of poor Protestants by the cruel Irish in Ireland be in this forgotten, when about one hundred thousand perished anno 1641? Yet to that impudence is that now risen, as to disavow any such rebellion of the Irish, or such their murders of the innocent Protestants in Ireland; but daring to aver on the contrary, that they themselves were the sufferers, and that by the English and Protestants.[14]

Scepticism about the nature of a Catholic plot, not to mention the events of 1641, would be notably absent in August 1678, when the first allegations about a Popish Plot were presented to the English government. One part of the plot was to be the securing of Ireland "to the tyranny of the Pope . . . by a general rebellion and massacre as formerly".[15] The assumption was deemed to reflect the danger, and the Catholic was the enemy. For Irish Protestants, the most immediate danger, as illustrated by their own historical experience, would again be from the Irish Catholics amongst whom they lived.

## The Popish Plot and the Williamite war

The Popish Plot was the outburst of anti-Catholic fear in England prompted by Titus Oates' allegations in August 1678 that there was a Catholic conspiracy in Britain and Ireland to wipe out Protestantism. No hard evidence about any conspiracy came to light, but despite the absence of evidence, fear of Catholicism remained widespread in Ireland. In late 1678 two Catholics, Walter and Thomas Eustace, advised a Protestant, Walter Harris of Dublin, who owned lands in Wicklow, against further purchases in the county. They had previously urged it on him as a good deal, but now changed their minds because of "some fears . . . of the French King". Reminding Harris of the hardships suffered in the "late rebellion", they assured him that "there were much sadder times at hand than ever". Harris did not buy the land, but concluded "that there may be some evil design of the Papists in hand".[16] The assumption was automatic, and was by no means unique. Vague and sinister reports sent to Dublin told of suspicious contacts between members of the Connaught gentry and the unspecified figures on the continent, of the presence of a Jesuit in Sligo attempting to recruit to the French and Papal cause, along with questionable rumours that unusually large numbers of Catholics were suddenly attending mass in Athy.[17] And the gentry of Queens County suspected that the captain of their county militia was a Catholic.[18] Ormond's reluctance to sanction repressive measures against Catholics during the Popish Plot made him the subject of a whispering campaign in Ireland and England claiming him to be a covert Catholic, intimately involved in plans to orchestrate a rising.[19]

The fear of Catholic subversion in the highest echelons of the Irish administration would be confirmed in Protestant eyes by the activities of Richard Talbot, Earl of Tyrconnell a decade later. Reference to 1641 was never far away: the pedigree of Ormond's brother-in-law Colonel John Fitzpatrick was that "his father was a heinous rebel, and his mother hanged for making candles of Englishmen's grease in the time of the late rebellion".[20] Such assertions raised the spectre of another assault upon Protestants in Ireland, and by extension upon Protestants in Britain. This would be especially evident when such fears of an Irish plot were seized upon by the nascent Whig opposition in England to strengthen their campaign to exclude the Catholic James, Duke of York, from the succession, which in itself reached a high point with the execution of Oliver Plunkett, the Catholic primate and archbishop of Armagh. The smallest of rumours offered the basis for implicit assumptions of Catholic intentions, and Whig propaganda emphasised the supposed reality of this "Irish plot", with 1641 alleged to have caused the deaths of 250,000 "without any provocation save they were Protestants".[21] The assumptions upon which such claims depended had not abated. The fear of another Irish rebellion remained and was real, corresponding as it did to the pattern of previous decades; the possibility of another attempted massacre could stand alone without a definite purpose.

But such fears could also be harnessed in the service of specific causes. The 1680s retained an undercurrent of unease facilitated by uncertainty about the present and certainty about the past. After all, the exclusion campaign had failed, as in 1685 York succeeded to the thrones of the three kingdoms as James II. Yet "the Irish talk of nothing now but recovering their lands and bringing the English under their subjection, which they who have been the masters for above 400 years know not how well to bear".[22] Unsurprisingly, given the Catholic revival of the late 1680s (especially the danger to the land settlement posed by the 1689 Jacobite Parliament), and the stark fact that (Catholic) French forces were in Ireland supporting a Catholic monarch, the Williamite war triggered an outburst of printed material similar in tone to that employed in previous generations. As in the 1640s, much, if not all, of this, was intended for an English audience, in order to procure English—or as it turned out, Dutch—military assistance for an increasingly beleaguered Protestant community in Ireland. Naturally, James was vilified. For one observer, Ireland had long overcome "that great devastation caused by that tedious and bloody rebellion begun in the year '41'" to attain a level of prosperity and happiness, "for all affairs were managed with the same equality and indifference towards all manner of persons; so that the very Papists could not complain of an unequal distribution of justice". The depoliticised nature of such an idyllic scene ensured that when "malicious and prying Popish neighbours" began "without doubt, to think of some such bloody practices as were put in execution in the year forty-one", they may have been inclined to emulate them.[23]

But "'tis certain, that the Irish never had power to hurt the English and Protestants of that kingdom, but for the advantage they had of a Popish king who divested the Protestants of all power, civil and military" and placing it instead "into the hands of Irish papists".[24] Another account of James's alleged conduct assured readers that the author would not "enter into a tedious discourse of all the measures taken since 1660 to subvert the Protestant religion"; to the appropriate audience it would be unnecessary.[25] The involvement of Catholic clergy and the French, as had been alleged in 1680, was discerned once more.[26] Again, the spectre of 1641 remained near to hand; "a day never to be forgot, notwithstanding the late pretended Irish parliament, made an act for abolishing the remembrance of that day".[27] The current assault upon Protestants by James's viceroy, the Old English Catholic Richard Talbot, Earl of Tyrconnell, and his forces "so nearly resemble their beginnings in their last so horrid rebellion in forty one".[28] Some attempted to draw a distinction between the two, "as the late King coming for Ireland. . .gave us some hopes, it would abate the cruelty of the enraged Tyr——l".[29] But in rhetorical terms the distinction was irrelevant. The more imaginative pamphleteers put words into Tyrconnell's mouth to emphasis the point, and in doing so collapsed any distinctions between himself and his royal superiors, especially his Catholic queen: "It was but in the year 1641 200,000 heretics fell victims to the holy cause, in this island; and were I master of as many islands, they should all be offered up a tribute to your majesties shrine."[30] It was from such perennial fears, now transformed into reality, which Irish Protestants sought to secure themselves. The soliciting of English support, as in the 1640s, was an obvious way out of a dilemma that seemed to present them with the prospect of their destruction for, arguably, the events of 1689–91 suggested confirmation of what had been feared since 1641. As the Jacobite cause was defeated in Ireland, the Protestant community transferred allegiance to a new king, and thereby sought to preserve themselves. The legislative victory extracted by that community in the 1690s proved a durable one. But the memory from which it drew purpose never passed out of history.

### Conclusion

The rebellion that broke out in October 1641 was the single most notorious sequence of violence in a remarkably violent era, ushering in two decades of war and upheaval in Ireland. As for the eventual losers, it also opened up the question of what place Catholics were to occupy within Irish society under a British system, and that question would only be conclusively answered with the victory of an Irish Protestant state in the 1690s. As the perceived victims and ultimate victors of the 1640s, Irish Protestants had a powerful weapon in the shape of the memory of 1641. The prominence accorded to the perception of its events stemmed from their relevance to the contemporary status of the Protestant interest, and their utility in attempting to change or maintain this. Yet it seemed to have a deeper, more visceral resonance at other moments of crisis. Some Protestants perceived the 1798 rebellion as a potential rerun of what their ancestors had faced (Kelly, 2003). Equally, a video produced by the Orange Order in Portadown in 1991, during the Troubles, reiterated the exaggerated casualty figures for 1641, comparing the sectarian dimension of the rebellion with the Nazi Holocaust, and explicitly stating that 1641 is crucial to understanding the "siege mentality of the Ulster

Protestant".[31] And the siege mentality is surely an element of an identity that has perceived itself (rightly or wrongly) as being *under* siege.

The impact of 1641 upon the identity of the Irish Protestant community was of fundamental importance. But that identity played a part in the shaping of Ireland's history in the decades and centuries after the event. Between their exposure to danger in 1641 and their seeming salvation after 1691, Irish Protestants found the memory of what had allegedly happened in 1641 particularly relevant. From the end of the seventeenth century it was superseded by the victory of William of Orange, and the salvation this was taken to entail. But from the seventeenth century onwards, 1641 had become part of the recurring process that sought to make sense of Ireland's past to shed light upon its present (Kelly, 1994; Moody, 1994; Walker, 1996). What was seen as the salvation of Ireland's Protestants in July 1690 was salvation from the recurrence of what was potentially a catastrophe for them, and them alone. And with the constant reiteration each summer of the events of 1690, it should perhaps be borne in mind that behind them lies the enduring shadow of 1641.

## Notes

1 *An account of the bloody massacre in Ireland: acted by the instigation of the Jesuits, Priests, and Friars* (London, 1679), pp. 4, 8, 6, 5. This latter passage is taken from Sir John Temple, *The Irish rebellion* (London, 1646), p. 104. I would like to thank Aidan Clarke, Dave Edwards, Kevin Forkan, Éamonn Ó Ciardha and Jane Ohlmeyer for their assistance with earlier drafts of this essay. Where possible, spelling in quotations from primary sources has been modernised. Interpolations have been indicated in square brackets.

2 Henry Jones, *A remonstrance of divers remarkable passages concerning the Church and Kingdom of Ireland* (London, 1642).

3 "R. S.", *A collection of some of the murthers and massacres committd on the Irish in Ireland since the 23rd of October 1641* (London, 1662), p. 6.

4 John Lynch, Cambrensis Eversus, Matthew Kelly (ed.) (2 vols, Dublin, 1848); Peter Walsh, *The history and vindication of the loyal formulary, or Irish remonstrance* (London, 1674); Nicholas French, *The historical works of the right Rev. Nicholas French* (2 vols, Dublin, 1846).

5 Richard Steele (ed.), *A Bibliography of Royal Proclamations of the Tudor and Stuart Sovereigns, 1485–1714* (2 vols, Oxford, 1910), ii, pp. 114–16.

6 "An act for the better execution of his Majesties gracious declaration for the settlement of the Kingdom of Ireland" (14 and 15 Cha. II) in *The Irish Statutes (rev. edn): 3 Edward II to the Union, AD 1310–1800* (Dublin, 1995 edn), pp. 85, 86–7.

7 Peter Walsh, *A letter desiring a just and merciful regard of the Roman Catholicks of Ireland* (Dublin, 1662), n.p.

8  The Irish colours displayed, in a reply of an English Protestant to a late letter of an Irish Roman Catholique, both address'd to his grace the Duke of Ormond (London, 1662), pp. 4, 5, 8, 12.

9  The remonstrance and resolutions of the Protestant army of Munster (Cork, 1649).

10  Ossory to Ormond, 16 Nov. 1678 (Historical Manuscript Commission, *Calendar of the manuscripts of the marquess of Ormonde, new series* (8 vols, London, 1902–20), iv, p. 235).

11  Calendar of the state papers relating to Ireland [in the reign of Charles II] . . . 1660–70 (4 vols, London, 1905–10), 1660–62, pp. 167–8, 173–6.

12  Lynch, *Cambrensis Eversus*, i, pp. 35, 59.

13  John Dillingham to Lord Montagu, 26 May 1664 (Historical Manuscripts Commission, *Report on the manuscripts of Lord Montagu* (London, 1900), p. 166.

14  [Henry Jones], *A sermon of Antichrist, preached at Christ-Church*, Dublin, Novemb. 12, 1676 (2nd edn, London, 1679), A2, p. 23.

15  Coventry to Ormond, 13 Aug. 1678 (*HMC Ormonde*, new ser., iv, p. 183).

16  "Examination of Walter Harris", 17 Oct. 1678 (Bodleian Library, Oxford, Carte Mss 38, fo. 703).

17  Anonymous deposition, 23 Oct. 1678 (Bodleian Library, Oxford, Carte Mss. 38, fo. 715); Jeremiah Jones to Ormond, 12 Nov. 1678 (Bodleian Library, Oxford, Carte Mss. 38, fo. 709); William Addis to Henry Benn, Lt. Richard Locke to Henry Benn, 30 Nov. 1678 (*HMC Ormonde*, new ser, iv, p. 256).

18  Captain Robert Fitzgerald to Ormond, 7 Nov. 1678 (Bodleian Library, Oxford, Carte Mss. 214, fo. 328).

19  "A coppy of som discovery of ye plott", 5 Feb. 1679 (National Library of Ireland, Mss 13,014).

20  *Ireland's sad lamentation* (London, 1681), n.p.

21  *The Third part of No Protestant plot* (London, 1682), p. 3.

22  Patrick Melvin (ed.), "Sir Paul Rycaut's memoranda and letters from Ireland, 1686–1687", *Analecta Hibernica* 27 (1972), pp. 156–8.

23  *A short view of the methods made use of in Ireland for the subversion and destruction of the Protestant religion and interest in that kingdom* (London, 1689), pp. 2, 11.

24  *Reasons for his Majesties issuing a general pardon to the rebels of Ireland* (London, 1689), n.p.

25  *A true representation to the king and people of England; how matters were carried on all along in Ireland by the late King James* (London, 1689), A2.

26  *A confession of faith of the Roman Catholics of Ireland* (London, 1689); *Tyrconnel's letter to the French king from Ireland* (London, 1690).

27  *Dublin Intelligence*, 5 (21–28 October 1690).

28  *An account of the late barbarous proceedings of the Earl of Tyrconnel* (London, 1689); *A brief and modest representation of the present state & condition of Ireland* (London, 1689).

29  *An account of the present, miserable state of affairs in Ireland* (1689).

30  *A letter from MonsieurTyrconnel . . . to the late queen* (London, 1690), p. 4.
31  "Mini-twelfth and re-enactment, 15 June 1991", New Way Video, Portadown. I would like to thank Elizabethanne Boran for providing me with a copy of this.


# References

Barnard, T. C. (1991) "The uses of 23 October 1641 and Irish Protestant celebrations", *English Historical Review*, 106: 889–920.

Barnard, T. C. (1998) "Learning, the learned and literacy in Ireland, *c*.1660–1760", in T. Barnard, D. Ó Cróinín and K. Simms (eds) *A Miracle of Learning: Studies in Manuscripts and Irish Learning* (Aldershot: Ashgate), pp. 209–35.

Barnard, T. C. (2001) "'Parlour entertainment in an evening?' Histories of the 1640s", in M. Ó Siochrú (ed.) *Kingdoms in Crisis: Ireland in the 1640s* (Dublin: Four Courts Press, 2001), pp. 20–43.

Canny, N. (2001) *Making Ireland British, 1580–1650* (Oxford: Oxford University Press).

Clarke, A. (1986) "The 1641 depositions", in Peter Fox (ed.) *Treasures of the Library, Trinity College Dublin* (Dublin: Royal Irish Academy), pp. 111–22.

Clarke, A. (1997) "The 1641 rebellion and anti-popery in Ireland", in Brian MacCuarta (ed.) *Ulster 1641: Aspects of the Rising* (Belfast: Institute of Irish Studies, 2nd edn), pp. 139–57.

Clarke, A. (1999) Prelude to Restoration in Ireland: The End of the Commonwealth, 1659–1660 (Cambridge: Cambridge University Press).

Cope, J. (2001) "Fashioning victims: Dr Henry Jones and the plight of Irish Protestants, 1642", *Historical Research*, 74: 370–91.

Creighton, A. (2000) "The Catholic interest in Irish politics in the reign of Charles II, 1660–85" (unpublished PhD thesis, Queen's University, Belfast).

Donovan, L. (1995) "'Bloody news from Ireland': the pamphlet literature of the Irish massacres of the 1640s" (unpublished MLitt thesis, Trinity College, Dublin).

Ford, A. (1987) *The Protestant Reformation in Ireland, 1590–1641* (Frankfurt am Main: Verlag Peter Lang).

Ford, A. (2005) "Living together and living apart: sectarianism in early modern Ireland", in A. Ford and J. McCafferty (eds) *The Origins of Sectarianism in Early Modern Ireland* (Cambridge: Cambridge University Press), pp. 1–23.

Gibney, J. (2005) "Select document: A discourse of Ireland, 1695", *Irish Historical Studies*, 34: 449–61.

Gillespie, R. (2005a) "Temple's fate: reading *The Irish Rebellion* in late seventeenth-century Ireland", in C. Brady and J. Ohlmeyer (eds) *British Interventions in Early Modern Ireland* (Cambridge: Cambridge University Press), pp. 315–33.

Gillespie, R. (2005b) *Reading Ireland: Print, Reading and Social Change in Early Modern Ireland* (Manchester: Manchester University Press).

Kelly, J. (1994) "'The Glorious and Immortal memory': commemoration and Protestant identity in Ireland, 1660–1800", *Proceedings of the Royal Irish Academy*, 94/c/2, pp. 25–52.

Kelly, J. (2003) "'We were all to have been massacred': Irish Protestants and the experience of rebellion", in T. Bartlett, D. Dickson, D. Keogh and K. Whelan (eds) *1798: A Bicentenary Perspective* (Dublin: Four Courts Press), pp. 312–30.

Lenihan, P. (2001) *Confederate Catholics at War, 1641–49* (Cork: Cork University Press).

Love, W. (1996) "Civil War in Ireland: appearances in three centuries of historical writing", *Emory University Quarterly*, 22: 57–72.

Moody, T. W. (1994) "Irish history and Irish mythology", in C. Brady (ed.) *Interpreting Irish History: The Debate on Historical Revisionism, 1938–1994* (Dublin: Irish Academic Press), pp. 71–86.

Pollard, M. (1989) *Dublin's Trade in Books, 1550–1800* (Oxford: Oxford University Press).

Shagan, E. H. (1997) "Constructing discord: ideology, propaganda, and English responses to the Irish rebellion of 1641", *Journal of British Studies*, 36: 4–34.

Walker, B. (1996) "1641, 1689, 1690 and all that: the unionist sense of history", in B. Walker (eds) *Dancing to History's Tune: History, Myth and Politics in Ireland* (Belfast: Institute of Irish Studies), pp. 1–14.

# 2

# Ascendancy insecurities: cross pressures on an eighteenth-century improving landlord

*Mervyn Busteed*

## Introduction

For almost two centuries after the conclusion of the Williamite Wars Ireland was governed by an exclusively Anglican elite, which never numbered more than 12 per cent of the population, or about 300,000 in the 1760s (Connolly, 1995). Their hyphenated designation "Anglo-Irish" indicates that the great majority were the descendants of migrants from Britain who had settled in Ireland during the sixteenth and seventeenth centuries. By the eighteenth century they were overwhelmingly dominant in the ownership of land, the key to political and social as well as economic dominance. In the 1780s approximately 5,000 Anglo-Irish families owned 95 per cent of the productive land of Ireland (Proudfoot, 1998). Their position was buttressed by legislation barring Catholics and, to a lesser extent, non-conformists from local and national public life and severely restricting access to education and the professions.

There has been a marked duality in discussion of the Anglo-Irish. Their literary and architectural achievements and their assertion of Irish parliamentary rights against the London parliament have long been acclaimed, but there has also been a long-lived stereotype amounting to caricature, which has presented them as raffish, eccentric, irresponsible and hard drinking absentees living off rents extracted from their oppressed peasantry. (Somerville-Large, 2003). However, recent work has revealed that some elements were well educated, widely travelled in Ireland, Britain and Europe, fully aware of contemporary cultural trends and quite sophisticated in their tastes and interests (Barnard 2004, Clarke 2003, Cronin 1995, Friel 2000).

This chapter discusses the outlook and activities of the head of the Caldwell family of county Fermanagh in the mid-eighteenth century and the combination of, sometimes, conflicting influences which bore down on him, thereby illustrating some of the cross pressures inherent in Anglo-Irish society.

## Sir James Caldwell and family

Originally from Prestwick in Ayrshire, the Caldwells arrived in Ulster during the early seventeenth-century plantation of British Protestant colonists in Ulster and settled in Enniskillen, where John Caldwell became active in the commercial life of the region. Clearly ambitious and upwardly mobile, by the 1660s they were renting part of the estate of the Blennerhassetts, another planter family. In 1671 they purchased the estate and in June 1683 the head of the family was granted a hereditary baronetcy (Bagshawe 1886, Cunningham 1980). The estate comprised 2,370 acres, of which 2,100 were on the western and northern shores of Lower Lough Erne and 270 acres around Belturbet in County Cavan.

The fourth and by far the most active baronet was Sir James Caldwell. He was born about 1720 and educated privately and at Trinity College, Dublin, graduating in 1740. Following the conventional pattern, he set out to travel in Europe, but early in 1744 he learned that his father had died and, not for the last time in his life, seems to have been disoriented by grief. He remained on the continent for another five years serving in military and diplomatic posts with Empress Maria Theresa of Austria and the King of Sardinia during the War of Austrian Succession (1743–48). The formidable empress was so impressed that she offered him the post of Chamberlain in the imperial household, but he found that as a Protestant he could not take the necessary oath. Nevertheless, on 15 March 1749 he recorded that she gave him one of her diamond rings and

> bestowed upon me and my male heirs for ever the first honours of the country, such as never before were conferred upon a Protestant and alien, except the Duke of Marlborough, creating me a Count of Milan of the Holy Roman Empire and granting me the imperial eagle crowned as an addition to my arms.[1]

Sir James returned to the family home of Castle Caldwell on a scenic wooded peninsula at the western end of the lough. On 18 December 1753 he made what contemporaries would have described as a "good" marriage to Elizabeth, third daughter of Archbishop Hort of Tuam, niece of Lord Shelburne, later Prime Minister 1783–84. As he described it to his sister Catherine, it was clearly a glittering affair, and as with most marriages within a landed elite, material concerns had not been neglected

> Our wedding was at my Lord Shelburne's. My Lord Primate married us,
> and my Lord Chancellor gave her away, Lord George [Sackville] with many
> other people of great distinction were at the wedding, the fortune is above
> 10,000 pounds and everything has been settled by my Lord Chancellor in
> as generous and honourable a way for me as is possible.[2].

Sir James quickly took his place in Fermanagh's local affairs, but there
was also wider recognition. In February 1753 he was unanimously
elected a Fellow of the Royal Society, in 1762 he became a Gentleman of
the King's Privy Chamber and, in recognition of having raised a body of
volunteers from his tenantry, in 1764 a Freeman of the city of Dublin. He
had three sons and four daughters and clearly enjoyed family life.
However, in September 1778, Lady Caldwell, his "dear Lizzie" as he
called her in his letters, died. Sir James, distraught with grief, left Castle
Caldwell and for three years lived in England with his daughters. He
returned to Castle Caldwell in 1781, but his earlier energy and ebullience
had deserted him. He died in February 1784.

Sir James confessed that "the principal and great pursuit of my life"[3]
was a peerage, which would have completed the upward trajectory of a
family with its origins in trade. He was never granted this step and suffered an overwhelming sense of disappointment. But it is to this unful-
filled ambition that we owe much of our insight into Anglo-Irish life. In
his pursuit of the peerage he carefully preserved all documentation which
he believed would support his case. When the estate was bankrupt and
auctioned in 1877, a relative, Mr W. H. G. Bagshawe, bid successfully
for these archives. A keen amateur historian, he incorporated them into
the Bagshawe family documents and in 1950 Major F. E. G. Bagshawe
donated the collection to the John Rylands University Library,
Manchester (Taylor, 1955). The 3,500 documents relating to the
Caldwells cover the period 1637–1830, but unsurprisingly they are most
numerous for 1750–84, when Sir James was head of the family. They
closely reflect his interests and outlook and provide a window into the
sometimes conflicting forces which bore down on this ruling elite.

## Enlightenment and tradition

In many ways Sir James was a product of the eighteenth-century
Enlightenment, with its emphasis on rationality, modernity and the possibility of improvement (Porter, 2000). Yet, in many ways, he occupied a
deeply traditional role in the society of north-west Ulster and demonstrates how enlightenment was applied in Ireland (Denby, 2005). His
private schooling, university education, travels and army service on
the continent had widened his horizons, but these experiences were

enhanced by time spent in Europe with the essayist and letter writer Lady Mary Wortley Montagu and the French philosopher Baron Montesquieu. Service with the Austrian army had brought him into contact with Irish exiles in Austrian service and this may have encouraged the tolerance he displayed towards Catholicism as a religion without, however, tempering his political outlook.

He had the broad interests of the enlightened gentleman, as reflected in the extensive nature of his correspondence. It ranges over political, economic and ecclesiastical affairs in Ireland, Britain, Europe and North America. Among his correspondents were peers, bishops, politicians, including the Prime Minister William Pitt the Elder, economists and literary figures, including Dr Samuel Johnson and David Garrick. He wrote 23 pamphlets on aspects of Irish economic and political life and British military affairs and in 1764 produced his *Debates*, a widely acclaimed verbatim report on the proceedings of the Irish Parliament in 1763.

But perhaps the most notable outworking of Sir James's approach was his dedication to the characteristic enlightenment philosophy of "improvement", with its belief in the possibility of moral, spiritual and material uplift of individuals and society by the application of rational effort and experiment under the guidance of the enlightened leaders of society. Such like-minded people shared ideas and experiences through reading, visiting and gathering in clubs and organisations (Barnard, 2003). Sir James was a frequent visitor to other estates and a notably hospitable host. Late in November 1771 he issued an invitation to an acquaintance: "I hope with all my heart you are not engaged this Christmas, the beauties of ye lake are well worth seeing, even at that season. You shall have excellent shooting, pleasant outlets for riding or walking, a full family in which ceremony is not known and a very hearty welcome."[4]

In Ireland the most notable grouping of those dedicated to improvement was the Dublin Society, founded in 1731 "for the improvement of husbandry and other useful arts"( Maxwell, 1936: 8). Sir James was an energetic member of what he described as "that benevolent and useful institution". He participated fully in almost every aspect of its activities, planting and conserving woodland, exchanging cuttings, encouraging the linen industry, selectively breeding livestock, experimenting with new implements and crops and reporting the results to the Society (Busteed, 2000). He was an energetic advocate of the society's schemes granting premiums for land reclamation and early in 1774 he explained

> the efforts which I have made with much trouble and some expense to forward and make known the benevolent intentions of the Society . . . The counties of Fermanagh and Donegal . . . abound . . . with vast tracts of

uncultivated land . . . The rise of lands had caused a great spirit of reclaiming . . . but . . . so far from knowing how to put in their claims, I found none
that knew that premiums were offered . . . I send printed advertisements to
all the neighbouring towns and villages setting forth the encouragement the
Dublin Society gave to poor renters for reclaiming of land, and that on Lady
Day in March 1772 . . . I would pay my tenants the premiums they had got
publicly and . . . a present of a cockade . . . this brought a vast concourse
of people to my house it cost me ten pounds in ribbons and I entertained
them with music and dancing and sent them away very happy.[5]

While he was an enlightened, modern-minded improving landlord, Sir
James was also very much a landed proprietor of the *ancien régime*. He
was very aware not only of his responsibilities towards his tenants but of
his role and status in society, and he defended them with vigour. On at
least three occasions he was ready to call someone out when he believed
family honour impugned, and following an insult at a dance in Bath in
early 1752 he fought a duel (Busteed, 2006). In a society where land was
central to power and status, he took a keen interest in all matters relating to property. Though the marriage was very successful, it was preceded by careful negotiations, Sir James noting that in the nuptial
negotiations "there was a necessity for having 6000 pounds of her
fortune placed in trustee hands for the discharge of the debts that affected
my estate".[6]

As the local proprietor he was viewed as the natural source of influence to be used to protect and further the interests of all who came under
his protection. He was frequently asked to provide references and use his
leverage to obtain posts on other estates or in the church, army, navy or
local administration. Looking back on this period in 1827, Sir Jonah
Barrington wrote that from the local landlord's house "all disputes
amongst the tenants were then settled—quarrels reconciled—all debts
arbitrated" (Barrington 1977: 3). There is no doubt that many landlords
were readily deferred to as natural sources of order and justice. Sir James
certainly acted as local arbiter. In 1763 there was widespread agitation
in parts of Ulster by the "Oakboys", drawn from all religious denominations protesting against tithes and the county cess or tax. In September,
Revd Henry Tuthill wrote to Sir James in great distress, explaining how
the local people were "at present unhappily disposed against us poor
parsons. Sorry I am to say the Oaken infatuation is, I fear, abroad . . . I
know not where it will end." He was convinced that "your presence
would, in an instant, set all things right but sir, if I am not to have that
happiness I am certain a letter from you . . . will soften the minds of the
people."[7]. Just over a week later he wrote, "Your letters carried with
them the force of an act of parliament, everything is now quiet . . . and

if gentlemen of fortune and resolution will show themselves forward on this occasion, I shall speedily hope to see our present confusion replaced by peace and good order."[8]

The key role of a resident landlord is revealed by the reactions when Sir James was absent. His three years in England following the death of his wife late in 1778 generated considerable correspondence, itself an indication of his centrality. Many of the letters were to and from William Tredenick, who reported on local news, transactions at fairs and markets, progress of crops and negotiations over tenancies. But there is a persistent undercurrent of anxiety at the proprietor's absence: in July 1779 he remarked gloomily, "I suppose we need not expect you home this winter";[9] in February 1780 he was writing, "I hope by the time this comes to hand you will be ready to set out for Ireland",[10] but almost exactly a year later he wrote with some asperity, "I hope in your next letter you will be able to inform me when you will come home."[11] In his letter of 22 July 1781 he undoubtedly wrote from the heart: "It gives me infinite pleasure to find you have arrived safe with your family in Dublin."[12]

In common with many Anglo-Irish landlords, Sir James played a role with even deeper roots. The sixteenth and seventeenth century plantations had seen the native Irish Catholic Gaelic-speaking landed elite replaced by Protestant English-speaking settlers from Britain. However, with his generous hospitality, proprietorial concern for the welfare of his tenants, leadership and arbitration in local affairs and raising soldiers from among his tenants, Sir James was taking on the role of the native leadership he and his caste had replaced, though this was by no means the only paradox in the Anglo-Irish situation.

### Ireland and Britain

Like many of the Anglo-Irish, Sir James felt the pull of loyalties to both Ireland and Britain. As Anglo-Irish families settled into their estates, succeeding generations developed a strong affection for the island. This fed into a sense of "colonial nationalism" (Bartlett, 1990), particularly when the London government embarked on economic policies contrary to Anglo-Irish interests. Resistance was rationalised by the argument that the descendants of British settlers had the same liberties and rights of self-government as their ancestors in Britain and that Ireland was a distinct kingdom in no way subordinate, but linked by common loyalty to the Protestant crown of Great Britain. Sir James displayed his attachment to Ireland in several ways. Like many of the Anglo-Irish, he spent part of each year in Dublin (at 56 Dawson Street) and regularly visited the great social centre of Bath, but he abhorred absenteeism and from the outset he adopted Castle Caldwell as his chief residence, thereby making a very public political statement.

He also demonstrated his loyalties when he defended the rights of the Irish Parliament, especially on economic matters. Past British governments had banned Irish cattle and woollen exports and direct participation in colonial trade. Such restrictions irked Sir James, who argued that they were unconstitutional, "by subjecting Ireland to laws made in another kingdom". But he also argued against such measures in practice on the grounds that "his majesty's dominions, including both England and Ireland, suffer by the distresses of Ireland" since Ireland was "a sister kingdom, subject to the same prince and united by the same interest".[13]

But running parallel to and often cutting across this outlook was Sir James's foundational loyalty to the British crown. The first Sir John had been active in the defence of Enniskillen in 1689 and Sir James repeatedly cited how his ancestors "had signal service in the late happy revolution".[14] He upheld the tradition in 1759 during the Seven Years War when a French invasion seemed likely, and he raised and equipped a light horse troop of 200 from his own pocket. Of his brothers, Henry was wounded serving with Wolfe at Quebec and went on to help defend that city in the American War of Independence, and John was killed in this same conflict. The tradition continued into the next generation with Sir James's son Fitzmaurice serving in that war and his son and heir John acting as liaison officer with Britain's native allies in the north west, Sir James proudly noting that he "was entrusted to give and receive the war hatchet and to distribute the presents to the Indian nations and by many accounts [was] very useful in keeping them to our interest".[15]

Nonetheless, one of Sir James's overriding concerns was always the conduct of government business. In 1755, when there was heated public controversy over the disposal of a revenue surplus resulting in some reallocation of government posts, Sir James was chiefly concerned that the affair "inflamed the country very much . . .What government hopes to gain by these condescensions is hard to say."[16] In 1767 the new Viceroy Lord Townshend broke with precedent in taking the management of government parliamentary business away from the "Undertakers" previously responsible. In the ensuing pamphlet war Sir James supported Townshend (Busteed, 2000) and in recommending him to one of his successors Townshend noted "the particular zeal he expressed during my administration in promoting most essential points of English government".[17] For Sir James, these loyalties were mutually reinforcing: "Though the sea divides England from Ireland, both are subject to the same sovereign, parts of the same dominion, have the same friends and the same enemies, are connected by a common interest."[18]

But the outbreak of the American War of Independence in 1776 led to a crisis when these loyalties clashed and Sir James had to choose. In the early days of the conflict he recognised the problems Britain faced, but was convinced that wider imperial interests were at stake: "It would be difficult to find a method of keeping a country of such extent in subjection and yet Britain must have pusillanimously give up its natural rights if it had suffered its colonies to shake off their dependence without any effort to prevent it let the consequences be what it may".[19]

By late 1778 renewed fears of French invasion ignited a volunteer movement in Ireland, which, by 1780, numbered almost 40,000 and was imbued with a political agenda advocating the exploitation of British weakness to press for Irish legislative independence (Foster, 1988). For Sir James this was going too far. He argued that in return for all the benefits derived from the British connection, Ireland should stand by "the sister kingdom". As for the volunteers, he regarded them as "unprecedented, illegal and dangerous", arguing that the best way to deal with them was to "make it the interest of a part to disunite from the rest".[20] Believing that those in power had shirked their duty "to give such associations a proper turn . . . they were therefore left entirely to themselves and . . . under no restraint" he described how

> Tho' I very much disapprove of independent associations . . . I though it incumbent on me to take some part . . . and to try whether it not be in my power with a small handful of 100 men to set such an example and offer such hints as might be improved by others of superior influence and abilities . . . and appointed officers well attached to government.

He was pleased to report that he found their disposition "highly praiseworthy"—hardly surprising since "they had a confidence in me as being all my tenants or in my manor".[21] However, when he suggested they give up their arms he had to report they refused.

Clearly this crisis had caused Sir James to fall back on his ancestral loyalties, but it had also revealed how his pro-government sympathies allied to his three-year absence after 1778 had rendered him out of touch with the ebb and flow of opinion in Ireland. But alongside this set of conflicting loyalties lay another, related dilemma common to the more perceptive Anglo-Irish.

## The status and role of Catholics in eighteenth-century Ireland

In his attitudes towards Catholics, Sir James displayed a combination of religious toleration and unyielding political suspicion. The estate rent roll for 1770 lists 16 of the 35 tenants with the 31-year lease allowed to

Catholics (Busteed, 2000), and the religious census of 1766 suggests that the area of Fermanagh covered by the estate was about 60 per cent Catholic (Crawford, 1989). Sir James was remarkably solicitous of the Catholics under his care, probably due to a combination of family tradition, noblesse oblige, Christian charity and his encounters with Irish exiles in Austrian service. As for Catholic worship, he believed "toleration . . . should be allowed".[22] Consequently, he ensured the Catholics of Enniskillen paid the relatively small annual rent of 6 pounds when the lease on their church was renewed, permitted and partly financed a chapel on his estate, entertained Catholic clergy at Castle Caldwell and actively supported a local priest in his (successful) bid to become Bishop of Clogher (Busteed, 2000).

His cultural sensitivity also extended to the Irish language, still widely spoken in the area at that time. In late 1765 the Guardian (Principal) of the Irish College in Prague, wrote: "I had forgot, until I was folding my letter, returning you my thanks for your Irish compliment of Kede Mile Failte. This compliment of 100,000 welcomes, which had its origin in the sincere hospitality of our ancestors . . . is excessively kind."[23] His outlook was much appreciated by local Catholics, whose priest assured him: "it is with the liveliest feeling of gratitude that I come on behalf of all those of the Roman Catholic religion in this town and indeed the neighbourhood to render you a thousand thanks", though the same writer was aware that "some in your own communion have maliciously censured you with respect to the protection you constantly extend to the poor Roman Catholics".[24]

Such people need not have worried because in political matters Sir James was a totally unyielding upholder of an exclusively Protestant polity. He argued from both principle and practice. Because of their religion, he asserted that Catholics were "bad subjects, though good men . . . a Papist, consistent with his principles and the duties and discipline of his religion, cannot, in Ireland, be a loyal subject, or take oaths of allegiance to the Protestant Prince under whose government he lives."[25] On a practical level, he was well aware that "the number of Papists in Ireland [is] to the number of Protestants as at least three to one"[26] and was convinced: "Popery, notwithstanding the laws now in being, is still growing".[27] Nor was he satisfied with the stance of the Protestant churches. Presbyterians he noted were characterised by "a general discontent"[28] at having to pay tithes and the county cess. As for the Church of Ireland, he noted that only 800 of the 2,300 parishes had clergy, asserted half of these were non-resident and that many were forced by poverty to take up farming, compromising their standing and leading to neglect of spiritual duties.

It is unsurprising, therefore, that when in 1763 the first effort was made to ease the penal legislation by allowing Catholics to accept land as security for loans, Sir James went into print to oppose the measure. He argued that the proposed bill was "a project to increase the number of Protestant debtors to Popish creditors".[29] Protestants would lose their lands and be "turned adrift, or perhaps profess themselves Papists, or marry Popish wives, and the lower class of Papists will gain settlements, will marry and increase".[30] As for Catholic landholders, "there is scarce a single instance of a Papist, having let a lease to a Protestant, hired a Protestant servant or ever employed a Protestant tradesman, when a Papist could be got".[31]

Regardless of his generous attitudes towards his Catholic tenants, it is clear that Sir James believed the Anglo-Irish position in Ireland was precarious, insecure, easily destabilised and required constant unyielding defence.

## Conclusion

The Anglo-Irish were subject to many cross pressures, but this was perhaps particularly true of those influenced by the mid-eighteenth century Enlightenment with its emphasis on rationalism and improvement. But in the case of Sir James he was also very much a self-aware member of this exclusive, hierarchical, paternalistic ruling elite, exercising and defending all the rights and privileges involved. There are also distinct continuities between the roles he played and those exercised by the native Irish leadership displaced at the plantation.

A second set of cross-pressures was generated by dual loyalties to both Britain, their country of origin, and Ireland, especially in the face of British interference in Irish economic matters. Yet, they were always conscious of their British and Protestant origins and loyalties and in the last analysis their dependence on British military might to uphold their minority position in Ireland. In the case of Sir James, ancestral loyalties proved the stronger. A similarly conflicted situation emerges with attitudes towards Catholics. Sir James was relatively liberal towards Catholicism as a religion but, fully aware of demographic realities, he was an uncompromising opponent of granting Catholics any political role in Ireland.

This chapter has focused on Sir James Caldwell, but notwithstanding the inevitable personal idiosyncrasies, his situation can be seen as personifying some of the pressures bearing down on the Anglo-Irish, especially those who were more aware of contemporary European cultural trends and were consequently caught between modernity and tradition, Britain and Ireland, Enlightenment values and Irish realities.

## Notes

1 Sir James Caldwell to Lord Townshend, 27 November 1772. John Rylands University Library Bagshawe Muniments B 3/19/71.
2 Sir James Caldwell to Catherine Bagshawe (nee Caldwell), 25 December 1753 B 2/3/384.
3 Sir James Caldwell to Lord Townshend, 2 July 1778 B 3/19/95.
4 Sir James Caldwell to John White, 25 November 1771 B 3/16/396.
5 Sir James Caldwell to the Royal Dublin Society, 16 February 1774 B 3/16/415.
6 Sir James Caldwell to Catherine Bagshawe, 25 December 1753 B 2/3/384.
7 Rev Henry Tuthill to Sir James Caldwell, 15 September 1763 B 3/16/366.
8 Rev Henry Tuthill to Sir James Caldwell, dated 26 September 1762, but sequence and context strongly suggest 1763 B 3/16/367.
9 William Tredenick to Sir James Caldwell, 3 July 1779 B 3/16/345.
10 William Tredenick to Sir James Caldwell, 29 February 1780 B 3/16/353.
11 William Tredenick to Sir James Caldwell, 4 February 1781 B 3/16/357.
12 William Tredenick to Sir James Caldwell, 22 July 1781 B 3/16/363.
13 An Enquiry Into How Far the Restrictions Laid Upon the Trade of Ireland by British Acts of Parliament are a Benefit or a Disadvantage to the British Dominions in General and to England in Particular for Whose Advantage they were intended. 1764. p. 768. B 3/21/20.
14 Sir James Caldwell to Lord Grandison, October 1760 B 3/19/10.
15 Sir James Caldwell to Lord Shelburne, 1781 B 3/19/57.
16 Sir James Caldwell to Col. S. Bagshawe, 1 October 1755 B 2/3/389.
17 Lord Townshend to Lord Buckingham, 1778 B 3/19/2.
18 An Enquiry, p. 778.
19 Sir James Caldwell to General Vaughan, 15 August 1775 B 3/16/376.
20 Sir James Caldwell to Lord Townshend, 1781 or 1782 B 3/19/131.
21 Sir James Caldwell to Lord Townshend, June 1780 B 3/19/107.
22 A Brief Examination of the Question Whether it is expedient either in a Religious or Political View, to pass an Act to enable Papists to take Real Securities for Money which they may Lend, 1764, p. 27. 3/21/25.
23 Revd Peter Kelly to Sir James Caldwell, 21 September 1765 B 3/17/40.
24 Revd Denis Maguire to Sir James Caldwell, 20 June 1765. Letter Book vol.3: B 3/10/176.
25 A Brief Examination, p. 10.
26 A Brief Examination, p. 22.
27 A Brief Examination, p. 32.
28 An Address to the House of Commons by a Freeholder, 1771, p. 28. B 3/21/17.
29 A Brief Examination, p. 11.
30 A Brief Examination, p. 15.
31 A Brief Examination, p. 18.

# References

Bagshawe, W. E. G. (1886) *The Bagshawes of Ford: A Biographical Pedigree* (London: Mitchell & Hughes).

Bartlett, T. (1990) " 'A people made for copies rather than originals': the Anglo-Irish, 1760–1800", *International History* Review, 13.1: 11–25.

Barnard, T. (2003) *A New Anatomy of Ireland: The Irish Protestants, 1649–1770* (New Haven: Yale University Press).

Barnard, T. (2004) *Making the Grand Figure: Lives and Possessions in Ireland, 1641–1770* (New Haven: Yale University Press).

Barrington, J. (1997) *Personal Sketches and Recollections of his Own Time* (Dublin: Ashfield Press).

Busteed, M. (2000) "Identity and economy on an Anglo-Irish estate: Castle Caldwell, Co. Fermanagh, *c.*1750–1793", *Journal of Historical Geography*, 26.2: 174–202.

Busteed, M. (2006) *Castle Caldwell, County Fermanagh: Life on a West Ulster Estate, 1750–1800* (Dublin: Four Courts Press).

Clarke, J. (2003) *Christopher Dillon Bellew and his Galway Estates, 1763–1826* (Dublin. Four Courts Press).

Connolly, S. J. (1995) *Religion, Law and Power: The Making of Protestant Ireland 1660–1760* (Oxford: Oxford University Press).

Crawford, W. H. (1989) "The political economy of linen: Ulster in the eighteenth century", in C. Brady, M. O'Dowd and B. Walker (eds) *Ulster: An Illustrated History* (London: Batsford), pp. 135–57.

Cronin, D. (1995) *A Galway Gentleman in the Age of Improvement: Robert Francis French of Monivea, 1716–69* (Blackrock: Irish Academic Press).

Cunningham, J. (1980) *Castle Caldwell and its Families* (Enniskillen: Watergate Press).

Denby, D. (2005) "The Enlightenment in Ireland" *Eighteenth Century Studies*, 38.2: 385–91.

Foster, R. (1988) *Modern Ireland 1600–1972* (London: Allen Lane).

Friel, P. (2000) *Frederick Trench (1746–1836) and Heywood, Queen's County: The Creation of a Romantic Demesne* (Dublin: Irish Academic Press. 2000).

Maxwell, C. (1936) *Dublin Under the Georges 1714–1830* (Dublin: Gill & Macmillan).

Porter, R. (2000) *Enlightenment: Britain and the Creation of the Modern World* (London: Allen Lane).

Proudfoot, L. (1998) "Landlords", in S. J. Connolly (ed.) *The Oxford Companion to Irish History* (Oxford: Oxford University Press).

Somerville-Large, P. (2003) "Anglo-Irish society", in *The Encyclopaedia of Ireland* (Dublin: Gill & Macmillan), p. 57.

Taylor, F. (1955) *Hand-list of the Bagshawe Muniments Deposited in the John Rylands Library* (Manchester: Manchester University Press).

# 3

# Last of their line: the disappearing Anglo-Irish in twentieth-century fictions and autobiographies

## Deirdre O'Byrne

### Introduction

It is a truism that the Anglo-Irish ascendancy class in twentieth-century Ireland declined in numbers, until they could more accurately be described as a descendency. They were unusually fecund in the charting of their own demise, producing an impressive range of fiction and non-fiction. Here, I explore a selection of their writings which are suffused with a gothically atmospheric depiction of decaying buildings and dwindling dynasties, surrounded by paradoxically flourishing horticulture.

### Gardens, plants and reproduction

Elizabeth Bowen was born in 1899, and *Bowen's Court*, a history of her Anglo-Irish family and their home, was published in 1942. A few years after the publication of *Bowen's Court*, Annabel Goff was born. She too wrote a history of her family, *Walled Gardens: Scenes from an Anglo-Irish Childhood*, first published in 1990. Like Elizabeth Bowen, Goff is a writer of fiction. It is interesting that these two Anglo-Irish authors, moved to produce histories of their families, both named their texts after actual built structures, as if to create tangible monuments to a fast disappearing sector of Irish society.

Gearóid Cronin notes that, in Bowen's fiction, "the Big House, like an archetype or an obsession, haunts [her writing] as an icon and a spectre . . . It is represented as a symbol . . . of the Anglo-Irish species" (Cronin, 1991a: 143–4). Annabel Goff does not directly refer to walled gardens as emblematic of her species, but makes the connection with what is grown within those enclosures. She recalls at some length the exotic fruits, including figs, grown in her childhood home, and tells us that "The greenhouses at Glenville were full of . . . delicious things to eat. On the walls, peach trees were espaliered against the peeling white brick . . . Vines grew opposite the peach trees . . . there was a sparse patch of Cape gooseberries." Goff points out that the strange and exotic fruit typically grown by her parents and their peers can be read symbolically: "[a]s the period of affluence ended . . . the imported plants and shrubs were left to become . . . a metaphor for the new, drastically reduced and unprotected state of the Anglo-Irish" (Goff, 1994: 11, 15).

In *The Irish Country House: A Social History*, Peter Somerville-Large reports that "the Ascendancy . . . had always considered gardening to be a particularly Anglo-Irish occupation" (Somerville-Large, 1995: 348), and it is one which surfaces in both fiction and non-fiction. In Molly Keane's novel *Good Behaviour*, for example, the narrator's mother loves to spend time in the greenhouses, "which had once sheltered peaches and nectarines" (Keane, 1982: 10). In Jennifer Johnston's novel, *The Invisible Worm* (1992), Laura spends much of her time in the garden, a place redolent with memories of her Anglo-Irish mother. In Edna O'Brien's short story, "The Connor girls" (1983), Miss Amy, who had scandalised her family and neighbours by a love affair with a Catholic, takes up gardening in her later years. As the story begins with information about her father's horticultural pursuits, the implication is that she has returned to the fold, and become a typical Anglo-Irish spinster, upholding the traditions she once sought to spurn. Major Connor, we are told, plants trees "for the important occasions of his life—the Coronation, the birth of his children, England's victory in the last war". He plants quinces for his daughters, though the Gaelic-Irish narrator tellingly adds: "What were quinces we wondered and never found out" (O'Brien, 1983: 12). The parallel is obvious: the Anglo-Irish, like quinces, are transplanted from another country and culture. They are an incongruous feature of the Irish landscape, not quite fitting in and, as we see in Edna O'Brien's story, regarded with curiosity by the Gaelic-Irish.

According to Annabel Goff, the growing of fruit and vegetables was an economic necessity, as few Anglo-Irish were in paid employment, and were therefore required to be self-sufficient (Goff, 1994). It is ironic, however, that their propensity for growth and cultivation in horticultural terms is paralleled by a lack of propagation of their own human kind. Terence Dooley reports that "Down through the years . . . many landowners and their heirs . . . died unmarried or childless and caused . . . a dislocation of continuity" (Dooley, 2001: 125). Goff recalls that she grew up in "an atmosphere of decay" (Goff, 1994: 39). In Jennifer Johnston's novel *The Invisible Worm*, Laura's Catholic, Gaelic-Irish father voices the death knell of his wife's lineage: "They've lost.

Your swanky lot. Lost. And about time too" (Johnston, 1992: 116), although, according to his daughter, he is attracted to Anglo-Irish women specifically because they possess the perceived "glamour of being an endangered species" (1992: 121).

Endangered they certainly were. In his book *Ascendancy to Oblivion: the Story of The Anglo-Irish* (1986), Michael McConville notes that, due to the exodus of Anglo-Irish after the setting up of the Irish state, membership of the Church of Ireland fell from 146,000 in 1926 to 10,000 in 1985, and most of those lived in Dublin. The sparsity of the population is particularly noticeable on Sundays. In Johnston's *The Invisible Worm*, Protestant Laura only goes to church when her Catholic husband Maurice is away, because, she says, "It irks him to watch me going in there. I can see the irritation in his face. He doesn't have much time for failures and I think he reckons the Church of Ireland to be some sort of pathetic failure" (Johnston, 1992: 64). Maurice's judgement seems to rest on attendance: "He looked at the six cars parked along the road by the gate" (1992: 148). In Edna O'Brien's short story, church attendance is even sparser, her "Connor girls" are two of only "four Protestant souls comprising the congregation in a stone church which was the oldest in our parish" (O'Brien, 1983: 11). Goff's autobiography suggests that the very scarcity of Protestants led to their seeing church attendance as a duty, but it is a social obligation rather than a religious one. "If you were Church of Ireland you went to church. The empty pews reflected lack of population, not lack of enthusiasm—that was taken for granted and not considered an excuse to stay at home", even though the "churches were cold" and, not surprisingly, "the Church of Ireland clergy were a depressed lot, badly paid and expected to have families" (Goff, 1994: 89, 90).

The pressure to reproduce was equally felt by the non-clerical members of the Anglo-Irish population. In *Bowen's Court*, for instance, Elizabeth Bowen, writing of her parents' marriage, tells us: "When they had been married some years, Florence and Henry began to wonder why they did not have an heir." They are not alone in wondering, as according to Bowen: "Bowen's Court asked for an heir, who was to be called Robert" (Bowen, 1998: 403), thus characterising the building itself as a somewhat querulous ancestor vocally reminding the conjugal pair of their duty, and even having a name in mind for the tardy male incumbent-to-be.

This personification of the ancestral residence is not unusual in Anglo-Irish writing. As Jean Lozes points out, "in [Sheridan] Le Fanu's fiction, the Big House is not only a full persona but often the main character" (Lozes, 1991: 104). Despite the requests of the expectant Bowen's Court building, and the hopes of the pregnant Florence who fervently wished to comply with the surrounding architecture, the recalcitrant "Robert" never materialises, but Elizabeth does, to inherit her mother's procreative burden. Bowen describes her situation following her father's death in a short paragraph of clipped phrases: "So, Henry VI died, and I as his only child inherited Bowen's Court . . . I had changed my father's name for my husband's. We had no children" (Bowen, 1998: 448). In *The Invisible Worm*, Jennifer Johnston presents us with a novelistic version of Elizabeth Bowen's dilemma. Laura explains her reasons for marrying a man she did not love in similarly brief sentences: "I wanted a child. I wanted to secure my line. Keep this house in the family" (Johnston, 1992: 59). The very syntax of the writing in both cases suggests the attenuation of the family line.

As the wife of a baronet, Annabel Goff's mother is well aware of her obligations, and her daughter recognises the dilemma: "A male heir was needed. My mother, I know, felt some pressure." With a messianic turn of phrase, Goff reports that her brother, after three daughters, was "born to great rejoicing" (Goff, 1994: 223, 244). The proud parents' marriage breaks down soon afterwards, as if, having fulfilled her propagatory function, the baronet's wife then departs.

Annabel Goff is explicit about both the duties and the difficulties entailed in matching and hatching if you were Anglo-Irish: "We belonged to a stratum of society which was more than waning, it was facing extinction . . . It was necessary to procreate. Some procedure for marriage followed by breeding was necessary for survival." However, the "procedures" were not simple: "It was as though we had a lunatic obstacle course to run if we were to avoid breaking the genetic chain." She describes their youthful gatherings as resembling "a small bunch of lemmings running around in circles pretending not to see the cliff" (Goff, 1994: 195, 196).

### Rationalising decline

Anglo-Irish writer Molly Keane voices a popular theory regarding the failure of her peers to reproduce themselves: "A whole generation of men had been practically wiped out in the [First World] war" (Quinn 1990, 74–5). However, in *The Decline of the Big House in Ireland*, Terence Dooley disputes this version of events. He reports that "almost three quarters of those from the 100 families who served, returned from the war", and that the "idea of the 'lost generation' seems to have grown in mythical proportions, becoming for some the primary catalyst in the decline of the big house" (Dooley, 2001: 125).

However, a crack had appeared in the veneer of the ascendancy class before hostilities broke out. A letter from Charles Monck, heir to Charleville, makes it clear that joining up represented a means of escape from financial worries in Ireland. Monck never returned. He was killed in what could be interpreted as a fulfilment of his death-wish. Writing to his solicitor, he says: "if I die today my difficulties and those of my family would to a great extent disappear" (Dooley, 2001: 124).

The prevailing myth that most of a generation of Anglo-Irish died out in the First World War is a psychologically understandable rewriting of their decline. Rather than presenting an unflattering assessment of themselves as what Jennifer Johnston's Maurice would call "some sort of pathetic failure" (Johnston, 1992: 64), it allows them to envisage themselves as heroic and self-sacrificing in a patriotic cause. This may to some extent be an unconscious effort to counteract or even emulate the dominant myths surrounding Gaelic-Irish republican heroes. In Bowen's 1929 novel *The Last September*, for instance, the trench-coated man who, unawares, passes Lois in the dark, is imbued with an air of mystery and excitement entirely missing from the young men of her own circle. He is described as possessing "a resolute profile, powerful as a thought", and Lois sees him as "inspired" (Bowen, 1942: 34). Tom Garvin attests that during the War of Independence, "The IRA man as a figure of popular glamour was born" (Garvin, 1996: 41). Republican leader Michael Collins was a native of County Cork, the setting of *Bowen's Court*. Photographs of Collins and fellow members of the IRA often show them in a military-style trench coat (see for instance, Coogan, 1995), and folk-stories of Collins wandering the countryside incognito still abound in Ireland. At the time of Bowen's writing of *The Last September*, he had been assassinated (Connolly, 1998), and his "glamorised image" (Lee, 1989: 66) thus acquired overnight an air of romantic martyrdom. It is possible that the Anglo-Irish may have wished to claim a similar glamour for their own dead combatants.

The belief that an entire segment of Anglo-Irish society was killed may also be read as a patriotic wish to project an alliance with England in its time of trouble. Goff's father tells her, somewhat inaccurately, that "The entire English upper class was killed in the First World War" (Goff, 1994: 105). Whatever the actual numbers of Anglo-Irish lost, the effect of that war was traumatic on their caste. Dooley comments: "The First World War proved an important watershed in big house life. The casualty rate amongst the landed class, the loss of sons, relatives or friends, may not have had serious socio-economic consequences but it did have a psychological effect" (Dooley, 2001: 275).

### Self-destruction, rejects, widows and orphans

This may be one reason why death is such a pervasive presence in Anglo-Irish writing. The dominant tone is elegiac (Powell, 2004), and there is a recurring theme of self-destruction. Maud Ellmann notes this feature in the writings of Elizabeth Bowen and opines that it is a matter of caste, referring to "the self-destruction of her class, the Anglo-Irish Protestant Ascendancy" (Ellmann, 2004: 8). Consider the practice which Goff describes, not without humour, in her autobiography: "Traditionally, unsatisfactory males were dumped in outlying areas of the Commonwealth (still thought of by those who consigned them as the Empire or, at least, the Colonies). I can safely say that for a long period of time the sun never set on the rejects of my family" (Goff, 1994: 134, parentheses Goff's).

Goff elaborates on the history of one such "reject" in an account of her paternal grandmother's siblings: "In addition to the five sisters, there had also been a brother, my great-uncle Charles. He was the fourth of the six children . . . and the eagerly awaited son." Despite the eagerness, Charles disappears: "I never heard my grandmother or great-aunts mention his name." Goff subsequently discovers that as a "classic black sheep . . . he'd been sent to Canada . . . Drink, my father hinted, had been the problem". Goff's mother "also had an uncle who proved unsatisfactory", who pre-empted what Goff calls "the classic formula" by taking himself abroad and committing suicide (Goff, 1994: 152, 154–5).

No doubt this export of recalcitrant males was regarded as a protective measure, and may even have been seen as keeping the genetic strain purer by weeding out unwanted stock. Given the dearth of men, however, this culling process seems less like pruning and more like a wanton waste of potential breeding material. It is tempting to conjecture that the high expectations placed on an inheriting son, especially if combined with indulgence, could result in the so-called "unsatisfactory" nature of these young men. In the case of Elizabeth Bowen's father, who wished to make law his career instead of running the family estate at Bowen's Court, paternal disapproval was immense and, in Elizabeth's opinion, the "struggles against his father" contributed to Henry Bowen's subsequent poor mental health (Bowen, 1998: 409; Glendinning, 1977) and early death.

This tendency towards self-destruction seeps into the fiction. In Jennifer Johnston's *The Invisible Worm* (1992), Harriet O'Meara kills herself, but she had at least married and produced a child, albeit a daughter. In Molly Keane's *Good Behaviour*, the only son, Hubert, is killed in a car accident (Keane, 1982), and his sister, hopelessly infatuated with her brother's lover Richard, does not marry. In Edna O'Brien's short story "The Connor girls", the Major's only son is also killed in a motoring incident, though O'Brien imbues this apparent chance occurrence with sinister undertones: "It was said that the accident was due to his father's bullying of him, always urging him to drive faster since he had the most expensive car in the neighbourhood" (O'Brien, 1983: 9). Once again, we see parental pressure to perform as a hindrance, and a factor in subsequent obsolescence. In Jennifer Johnston's *How Many Miles to Babylon?*, the doomed Alec Moore tells us: "They all wanted me to become a man. I found it hard to grasp what this entailed" (Johnston, 1988: 124). Alec's closest relationship is with another man, and he dies childless.

The atmosphere which pervades Anglo-Irish writing, both fiction and non-fiction, is moribund. As David Burleigh comments in an article significantly entitled "Dead and Gone": "In the world Jennifer Johnston sets before us, there are a great many elderly men, whom we usually encounter in the advanced stages of decrepitude" (Burleigh, 1985: 1). Although her fiction, especially in later years, depicts many female characters, they also tend to be of melancholic nature and prone to nostalgia. Jennifer Johnston acknowledges the influence of her Anglo-Irish heritage and of "rather crumbly country houses" on her writing: "Even though my parents were not immediately 'big house' people, that was their sort of background and there were always undertones of that background in my life and in my writing" (Quinn, 1990: 59). If Anglo-Irish characters are in a state of decrepitude, so are the houses. Virginia Woolf describes Bowen's Court as containing "decayed eighteenth-century furniture and carpets all in holes" (Keane, 1982: ix).

Growing up in a succession of similarly crumbling edifices, surrounded by "the weight of Anglo-Irish gloom which hung over the whole household" (Goff, 1994: 52), it is no wonder that Annabel Goff records a childhood beset by anxiety: "I was afraid that my parents would die" (Goff, 1994: 43). She was also worried about ghosts and, to her mind, "Life was clearly full of dangers [and] fears" (44). This anxious morbidity may not be totally unfounded, as early death seems to haunt ascendancy families. Elizabeth Bowen writes that "Like all the Bowens whose dates are known, I had inherited before I was thirty-one" (Bowen, 1998: 446). Thomas McCarthy tells us that, "Misfortune stalked the Bowens. Elizabeth lost her aunt to consumption and her younger uncle went down with the *Titanic*" (Bowen, 1998: xiv). Such tragedies may account in part for the strong Gothic tendency in much Anglo-Irish fiction, from the works of C. R. Maturin and Sheridan Le Fanu to the twentieth-century works of Aidan Higgins and John Banville (Genet, 1991).

Ann Owens Weekes points out that "the orphan is a common symbol for the Anglo-Irish", who felt "abandoned by the natural parent, England" (Weekes, 1990: 196). I would add to this another preponderant stereotype, that of the childless woman, and especially, the childless unmarried woman. Such a figure occurs again and again in the fictions and non-fictions about the Anglo-Irish. For instance, in Aidan Higgins's 1966 novel *Langrishe, Go Down*, four unmarried Langrishe sisters inhabit Springfield House, and, as Imogen reports: "Offers of marriage had not come" (Higgins, 1993: 48). In *The Story of Lucy Gault*, William Trevor creates a character who seems trapped in a tragedy of mythical, fairy-tale dimensions, but without any happy-ever-after ending to reprieve her, or us as readers. Lucy is an only daughter. Her love for Ralph is unconsummated, and she remains unmarried and childless. Her household is seen by the family solicitor as "something petrified . . . Lucy was stilled too, a detail in one of her own embroidered compositions" (Trevor, 2002: 139). The similarity to Tennyson's "Lady of Shalott" (Tennyson, 1971) is inescapable—Lucy is trapped in a world of mirrors and shadows, a world which bears much resemblance to that inhabited by Laura in Johnston's *The Invisible Worm*.

The unmarried daughter also occurs in Molly Keane's work, most memorably in Aroon, the monstrous narrator of *Good Behaviour*. In that novel too we meet the unmarried and childless Crowhurst sisters, known as Nod and Blink (Keane, 1982). Keane is obviously drawing from life in her depiction of unwed females, though her portraits are tinged with comedy. In interview, she is more sympathetic. She recalls that, "When [she] was growing up there was an extraordinarily high proportion of marriageable young women to men. It was a sad time for some of those women; a great deal of them did not have much chance of marrying" (Quinn, 1990: 74–5).

A previously rich source of potential husbands, the English army, disappeared with Independence, taking the officers with it. Growing up a few decades later, Annabel Goff is amusing on the topic of the shortage of young men:

> hostesses were sometimes forced to resort of desperate measures such as including the occasional larger schoolboy who could find a dinner-jacket that fit [*sic*] him. This kind of behaviour was considered unacceptable, but the condemnation always had an implied "there, but for the grace of God, go I" modification. (Goff, 1994: 196)

Goff puts the lack of eligible men in rather more contemporary language than that of Molly Keane. Obviously influenced more by her later years in the United States than by her formative years in Anglo-Irish Waterford society, Goff wryly recalls that, "It was clear to me that no one was going to get laid in the Republic of Ireland; not if she were Anglo-Irish, at least" (Goff,1994: 93).


## Marrying out, fading away, leaving ghosts

Given the dearth of men, it is unsurprising that some Anglo-Irish chose to defy convention and marry outside their religious group. Goff's father, she reports, "took a philosophical view . . . 'I have four children . . . The odds are that at least one of you will marry a Catholic' " (Goff, 1994: 65). His was an unusual attitude, as his daughter is aware. She writes:

> Both Catholics and Protestants were violently opposed to what we called "mixed marriages" . . . It was, regardless of any money or social standing involved, considered a disaster by both sides. For the Catholics, immortal souls were in danger, and for the Protestants there was the crossing of social and cultural barriers and the further erosion of the shaky rock on which they had built. (1994: 65)

The Catholic hierarchy's *Ne Temere* decree that children of "mixed" marriages had to be brought up as Catholics was, according to Phyllis Harrison Browne, "one of the[ir] cleverest ideas [and] was possibly the final reason for the almost complete disappearance of the Church of Ireland congregations". Born in 1920, she comments on the lack of eligible males in her courting years: "the number of suitable young men for young Protestant girls to marry were becoming fewer and fewer" (Murphy and Adair, 2002: 35). Lady Augusta Gregory recalls in her journal that her daughter-in-law worries that "the children will marry peasants" (Pakenham, 2000: 181). Such prejudices are fictionalised in Edna O'Brien's short story, "The Connor girls", as the narrator tells us that her mother is firmly against the romance between Anglo-Irish Miss Amy and her lapsed Catholic boyfriend: "She could not abide it, she said that Catholics and Protestants just could not mix . . . Her mind was firmly made up about the incompatibility of Catholics and Protestants' (O'Brien, 1983: 15). Miss Amy's father, Major Connor, is similarly against the match: "the postman who was a Protestant said that the Major would not travel one inch to see his daughter marry a Papist" (1983: 16). The engagement is subsequently broken off, apparently due to "a clash of family interests" (1983: 17). The Protestant postman, we are told, "was pleased with the outcome" (1983: 17). Phyllis Harrison Browne's recollections of childhood rhymes show that Catholic children noticed the smaller families of their non-Catholic peers: "Proddy, Proddy on the wall, half a loaf would feed you all" (Murphy and Adair, 2002: 34).

Both Edna O'Brien's and Jennifer Johnston's fictions represent inter-marriage as a hoped-for resolution, which actually resolves nothing. In Johnston's *The Invisible Worm*, Protestant Laura sleeps in a separate bedroom from Maurice, her Catholic husband, and they have no children. Laura, who is a keen gardener, tells her friend Dominic of her failure to reproduce her own genes: "All those seeds were rejected" (Johnston, 1992: 4). Laura's grasp on the present is shown to be impaired by her focus on the past and, she says, the "future has no reality for me" (Johnston, 1992: 83). This perceived lack of a future is another constant motif in Anglo-Irish writings. Commenting on the departure of many ascendancy families at the birth of Irish Independence, Goff attests that those who left were "not driven out—but aware that the future held little for them in Ireland" (Goff, 1994: 37). Not all memoirs are as lenient on the sectarianism in Irish society; Robert Ernest Armitage reports that his "family had suffered threats, and the family business was robbed and unjustly boycotted in the early decades of the twenti-eth century" (Murphy and Adair, 2002: 23), which almost led to their emigration.

In both Bowen's and Goff's autobiographical works, the focus is very much on preceding generations, even though Bowen herself had certainly lived a noteworthy and interesting enough life to warrant more attention on herself and her achievements, and has been the subject of several crit-ical and biographical works, for instance those by Patricia Craig (1986), Maud Ellmann (2004) and Victoria Glendinning (1993). Bowen did write accounts of her own life, for instance, *Seven Winters* (1943) and *Collected Impressions* (1950), but they are much shorter texts than *Bowen's Court*.

Jose Lanters writes that, "The past is important in all [of Jennifer] Johnston's novels . . . and many of her characters find themselves dis-turbed by ghosts of the past" (Lanters, 1989: 209). *The Invisible Worm* is certainly haunted. The big house which Laura has inherited is full of an "air of history" evoked by "crests on the spoons, book plates, family portraits, all those museumlike objects collected down through the years . . . We use those artefacts every day, we live . . . with the ghosts of the past" (Johnston, 1992: 121). She tells her friend Dominic: "I guard this house, this mad museum. I am the curator of my ancestor's folly" (1992: 24) and says: "I am tired now of meeting the dead wherever I turn. I am tired of hearing their voices" (1992: 159). Annabel Goff describes one childhood home, Glenville, as composed somewhat paradoxically of "empty rooms, full of ghosts and treasures", and recalls that she and her sister "saw a ghost in the stable attic" (Goff, 1994: 254). Elizabeth Bowen writes of Bowen's Court: "With each death, the air of the place

had thickened: it had been added to. The dead do not need to visit
Bowen's Court rooms . . . we had no ghosts in that house—because they
already permeated them" (Bowen, 1998: 451). This strikes me as an even
more alarming abode than one inhabited by a single ghost. Bowen con-
jures up her home as a sort of spectral soup, "thickened" by the addition
of each dead inhabitant.

This sense of being haunted by one's predecessors is also strong in
Edna O'Brien's short story. The Connor family inherit a Big House on
whose walls hang portraits "glum puffy dark-looking ancestors"
(O'Brien, 1983: 18). The air of decrepitude is pronounced. Their local
church is described as follows: "Moss covered the stones and various
plants grew between the cracks so that in the distance the side wall . . .
was green" (1983: 11–12). The Connor family vault is "smothered in
creeper" (1983: 9). When the Major's death eventually gives the locals a
chance to investigate the Big House on the inside, we discover: "It was
much more simply furnished than [previously] imagined and the loose
linen covers on the armchairs were a bit frayed" (1983: 18). The fraying
covers metaphorically represent the disintegration of the façade of gen-
tility, which characterises the Anglo-Irish as a class.

## Conclusion

As I have pointed out, many writers have used metaphors to convey the
decline of the Anglo-Irish: exotic fruits, walled gardens, frayed covers. I
end on a similarly metaphorical note. If the Anglo-Irish failed to reproduce themselves as a race, they have succeeded in producing a compen-
satory fruitful harvest of artistic endeavours. As Gearóid Cronin notes:
"Paradoxically, the Big House, although having undergone a total demise
in Irish history, has not experienced a parallel demise in Irish literature;
rather, it seems to have been given a new lease of life" (Cronin, 1991b:
215). Valerie Pakenham commends the "indefatigable" habit of the
ascendancy in memoir-keeping (Pakenham, 2000: 6). By taking us inside
the Big Houses and their walled gardens, writers achieve, between the
covers of their books, what the structures themselves could not—they
preserve a fascinating if vanished way of life for posterity.

## References

Bowen, E. (1942) *The Last September* (London: Penguin).
Bowen, E. (1943) *Seven Winters* (London: Longman).
Bowen, E. (1950) *Collected Impressions* (London: Longman).
Bowen, E. (1998) *Bowen's Court* (Cork: Collins).

Burleigh, D. (1985) "Dead and gone: the fiction of Jennifer Johnston and Julia O'Faolain", in M. Sekine (ed.) *Irish Writers and Society at Large* (Gerrards Cross: Colin Smythe), pp. 1–15.

Connolly, S. J. (ed.) (1998) *The Oxford Companion to Irish History* (Oxford: Oxford University Press).

Coogan, T. P. (1995) *De Valera: Long Fellow, Long Shadow* (London: Arrow).

Craig, P. (1986) *Elizabeth Bowen* (London: Penguin).

Cronin, G. (1991a) "The Big House and the Irish landscape in the work of Elizabeth Bowen", in J. Genet (ed.) *The Big House in Ireland: Reality and Representation* (Dingle: Brandon), pp. 143–61.

Cronin, G. (1991b) "John Banville and the subversion of the Big House novel", in J. Genet (ed.) *The Big House in Ireland: Reality and Representation* (Dingle: Brandon), pp. 215–30.

Dooley, T. (2001) *The Decline of the Big House in Ireland: A Study of Irish Landed Families 1860–1960* (Dublin: Wolfhound).

Ellmann, M. (2004) *Elizabeth Bowen: The Shadow Across the Page* (Edinburgh: Edinburgh University Press, 2004).

Garvin, T. (1996) *1922: The Birth of Irish Democracy* (Dublin: Gill & Macmillan).

Genet, J. (1991) *The Big House in Ireland: Reality and Representation* (Dingle: Brandon).

Glendinning, V. (1977) *Elizabeth Bowen: Portrait of a Writer* (London: Phoenix).

Glendinning, V. (1993) *Anthony Trollope* (London: Alfred A. Knopf).

Goff, A. (1994) *Walled Gardens: Scenes from an Anglo-Irish Childhood* (London: Eland).

Higgins, A. (1993) *Langrishe, Go Down* (London: Minerva).

Johnston, J. (1988) *How Many Miles to Babylon?* (London: Penguin).

Johnston, J. (1992) *The Invisible Worm* (London: Penguin).

Keane, M. (1982) *Good Behaviour* (London: Abacus).

Keane, M. and S. Phipps (compilers) (1983) *Molly Keane's Ireland: An Anthology* (London: HarperCollins).

Lanters, J. (1989) "Jennifer Johnston's divided Ireland" in C. C. Barfoot and T. D'haen (eds) *The Clash of Ireland: Literary Contrasts and Connections* Amsterdam: Rodopi), pp. 209–22.

Lee, J. J. (1989) *Ireland 1912–1985: Politics and Society* (Cambridge: Cambridge University Press).

Lozes, J. (1991) "Le Fanu's houses", in J. Genet (ed.) *The Big House in Ireland: Reality and Representation* (Dingle: Brandon), pp. 103–9.

McConville, M. (1986) *Ascendancy to Oblivion: The Story of the Anglo-Irish* (London: Quartet).

Murphy, C. and Adair, L. (2002) *Untold Stories: Protestants in the Republic of Ireland 1922–2002* (Dublin: Liffey).

O'Brien, E. (1983) "The Connor girls", in E. O'Brien, *Returning* (London: Penguin), pp. 9–23.

Pakenham, V. (2000) *The Big House in Ireland* (London: Cassell).

Powell, K. T. (2004) *Irish Fiction: An Introduction* (London: Continuum).

Quinn, J. (ed.) (1990) *A Portrait of the Artist as a Young Girl* (London: Mandarin).

Somerville-Large, P. (1995) *The Irish Country House: A Social History* (London: Sinclair-Stevenson).

Tennyson, A. (1971) "The Lady of Shalott", in *A Choice of Tennyson's Verse*, selected by D. Cecil (London: Faber & Faber), pp. 79–85.

Trevor, W. (2002) *The Story of Lucy Gault* (London: Viking).

Weekes, A. O. (1990) *Irish Women Writers: An Uncharted Tradition* (Lexington: University Press of Kentucky).

# Part II

# Coping strategies in a changing Ireland

# 4

# "Survival of the fittest": Protestant dissenting congregations of south Munster, 1660–1810

*David J. Butler*

## Introduction

This chapter seeks to analyse the spatial distribution and changing circumstances of Protestant dissenting congregations—Presbyterian, Independent/Congregationalist, Society of Friends (Quakers) and Baptist—in the period from the Restoration of the Stuart monarchy in 1660 until 1810, when a new phase of Protestantism evangelism was launched. Protestant dissent arrived on a large scale in southern Ireland with the coming of the Cromwellian armies in 1649–50. During the decade of the Commonwealth (1650–60), the several dissenting denominations enjoyed unprecedented tolerance and practically all dissenting congregations founded in Ireland prior to 1810 resulted from the settlement of Cromwellian families in the mid-seventeenth century.

The restoration of the monarchy in 1660 and the ensuing proclamations against all Christians dissenting from the established church (including Roman Catholics and Quakers) led to a swift fall from grace on the part of these congregations, and to their being forced—like Roman Catholics, a decade earlier—from premier sited meeting-houses to undesirable laneways and obscure rural locations. This chapter describes the formation and progress of the Protestant dissenting community in an important area of Ireland containing the significant walled cities of Cork and Waterford, and important walled towns such as Clonmel, Cashel and Fethard, from the mid-seventeenth century to the early nineteenth century, and its survival through a combination of ingenious schemes devised by leading families, such as careful intermarriage and the financial endowment of congregations.

## Community formation

From the re-establishment of the Church of Ireland in 1660–62, the dissenters were a declining, though still quite powerful group, divided into Presbyterian, Independent/ Congregationalist, Baptist and, subsequently, also Quaker meetings. The survival of dissenting congregations in the period immediately after the Restoration of 1660 depended generally on the numerical, but particularly on the financial, strength of each congregation as, in the absence of any central fund or organisation for any Protestant dissenting denomination, each congregation prevailed or failed on its own resources.

Prior to 1650, there were few dissenting Protestants in southern Ireland beyond the larger port towns and cities and isolated households of the Munster plantation. The decline of the dissenting congregations following the drafting of the Act of Uniformity in 1660–62 was gradual and the distribution of meetings for worship remained largely constant until the late 1680s. The dissenting sects in Ireland had always been heavily dependent on the army, and when many former Cromwellian soldiers left Ireland in the years following the Restoration, selling their estates to those who remained, there were dire consequences for dissenting congregations, particularly those in rural areas. In large part, this dissenter weakness was due to their failure to establish a significant base beyond the military establishment in the 1650s, particularly in the case of the Baptists and Congregationalists. By contrast, the Quakers (see Figure 4.1) continued their expansion through the south, east and north of the province in the later eighteenth century, targeting areas of considerable English settlement and siphoning members from existing congregations, most notably the Baptists. However, as shown in Figure 4.1, Protestantism was an urban phenomenon from the outset, and all of the early congregations founded in the 1660–80 period were urban-based. Towns were to remain the main centres of Protestant dissent in both Britain and Ireland, and as Irish towns were fewer and smaller, offering less diverse employment than those in Britain, most southern dissenting congregations, with the exception of the Quakers, continued to decline throughout this entire period, often until an eleventh-hour revival funded by Irish branches of English missionary organisations in the first decades of the nineteenth century.

Though their distribution was quite dispersed, the membership of dissenting congregations in Munster centred on the urban settlements and their hinterlands, and included a number of wealthy landowners and merchants, the latter occasionally augmented by new arrivals during the eighteenth century. The willingness of the Scottish Presbyterians of Ulster to work with their English brethren in the south of Ireland, and extend

**(a) Denominational distribution**

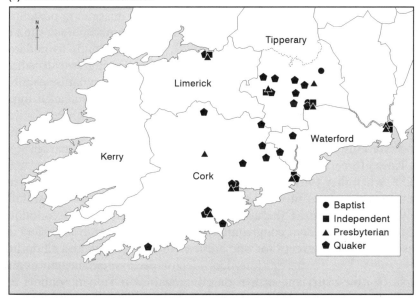

**(b) Foundation date of congregations**

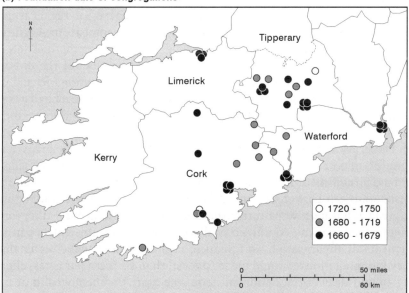

**Figure 4.1** Dissenting congregations of south Munster, 1660–1810

to them the benefit of a ministerial supply, secured the future of these congregations and also the continuance of evangelical missionary preaching in the south of Ireland. In this way, a Presbyterian ministry was begun in the principal Munster towns during 1673, which gradually assimilated the Congregationalists over the course of the following two decades.[1] The Presbyterian Church was the only dissenting denomination capable of providing a resident ministry in this period, a development far more desirable than acquiring a ministerial supply from elsewhere, as was the general lot of the Congregationalists and Baptists. The English Presbyterians and Independents were each represented by congregations at Cork, Limerick, Waterford, Youghal, Clonmel and Tipperary until 1696, when they formalised their cooperation by forming the Presbytery of Munster, where in each area the dominant congregation—usually Presbyterian—became the accepted denomination.[2] Ireland contained just seven Independent congregations in the post-Restoration period, all based in Munster except for one at New Row in Dublin, and all declining causes. These congregations depended on peculiar circumstances and niches for their survival, such as the congregation at Tipperary under the leadership of James Wood, who had been Independent minister at Youghal from 1657 until the Restoration. He did not conform to the established church, and was appointed schoolmaster of the Erasmus Smith School in Tipperary which, crucially, was exempt from Anglican visitation during Smith's lifetime.[3]

As I have argued elsewhere, heritage and origins were of the utmost importance to non-established or proscribed denominations in a state where there was an official religion.[4] However, the maintenance of a separate identity proved virtually impossible as evidenced by the membership of Cloughkeating Baptist Church, near Cloughjordan in the north of Tipperary county, where by the early eighteenth century many had "gon[e] off to a different Profession, and are now so blended, as scarce to be distinguished".[5] Stagnation, followed by gradual decline was the lot of southern Irish dissenting congregations in this period and, of the Baptists, it has been written that the denomination "lingered, rather than lived". Kirtland was an advocate of congregational independence in all elements of organisation and finance, arguing that it was "better that they [congregations] should cease to exist, than be mere parasites, clinging to and drawing nourishment from the State".[6] Their wealth at the Restoration can be seen through the congregation at Clonmel, which had installed Robert Carr as pastor in 1659, while the "hearth money roll" of 1665 lists his successor, a Pastor Hough, living in a substantial eight-hearth house on High Street, which doubtless doubled as manse and discreet meeting place.[7]

## Territorial organisation

Most of the information on the contracting geographical distribution of the Baptist denomination in the south of Ireland is drawn from the Cork [Baptist] church book.[8] The oral testimony deals with Cork congregation and its associated mission stations, and is beneficial in highlighting the intolerance of the Anglican establishment towards the smaller dissenting denominations. At Cork, the Baptists lost their meeting house after the Restoration. But the pastor appointed in 1653 during the Cromwellian Protectorate continued ministering—under the patronage of the Riggs family of Riggsdale—seven miles from Cork city, where meetings were held and the minister was domiciled until his death in 1680. At this point, the Riggs family themselves took on the responsibility for the preaching supply until 1704, when the congregation was rescued from extinction through the provision of a newly trained pastor, a graduate of the "Education Fund for the Baptist Ministry", established in 1700 by a few wealthy Cromwellian families, including Riggs, to provide leadership for their congregations.

> The few members [at Cork] under Mr Coleman were either dead or scattered. Some even of those who continued steadfast in their judgement for believers baptism, for want of a minister, were on the point of joining some other dissenting congregation, but Mr Pettit's coming among them [in 1704] revived a dying cause and united them. Major Riggs [who] was then alive generously promised thirty pounds a year and his [heiress] wife made up considerably more.[9]

The benefit to the Cork church extended far beyond the county boundary, and from the early eighteenth century, the Baptist church in Cork also assumed charge of Clonmel congregation, a mission supply station in South Tipperary, subsequently removed to the home of a member of that congregation at Lismortagh, near Killenaule, some distance to the north-east. The church book records the part played by the ministry of Pettit in extending the life of the remnant congregation there.

> At the same time there was a small people at Clonmel, destitute of a pastor, who though incapable of supporting one, were willing to contribute according to their ability and most anxious for a supply [of preaching]. In line, Mr Pettit was ordained at Clonmel as Pastor of the church of Cork and of that place jointly, and supplied both places during his lifetime.[10]

The reason for selecting Clonmel for the ordination was a practical one, in that it still possessed a house, which had doubled as a chapel and manse since the Protectorate. This is significant, for persecution at Cork had required the congregations to give up their meeting place in the city and retreat to the country estate of the Riggs family.[11]

Surviving documentation relating to the Baptist chapel at Clonmel in this period is limited to entries in the Registry of Deeds, when the manse/chapel, "a stone house slated, with a thatched house backwards in High Street", was put to use generating congregational income, for it was not in use for the great majority of the time, the Cork minister supplying it with preaching a few days in every month.[12] In an instance of inter-church cooperation essential for the survival of outlying congregations relying on preaching supplies, the Presbyterian minister at Cork assisted the Baptist minister by assuming his preaching responsibilities during the one weekend every month when he was away, attending at the supply station.[13]

The Baptist meeting at Clonmel, despite improved finances, dwindled to the point where no members remained in the town and district, other than those living some fifteen miles distant, in the district of the village of Killenaule. In 1723, a lease on the Clonmel premises was agreed and the congregational remnant commenced meeting at Lismortagh, the home of a member.[14] This meeting for worship continued to be important in the linkage with Cork, and in 1729, when Pettit was in his final illness, his successor was ordained at Lismortagh at a general meeting held in the presence of the four Baptist pastors then remaining on the island of Ireland.[15]

The Society of Friends (Quakers) was not, strictly speaking, part of the Cromwellian regime, though they were almost contemporary with it. They made their first appearance in Ireland in 1653, shortly after their foundation, and by 1660 had a reasonably widespread distribution of meetings for worship, held in the homes of member families. The years after 1660, despite widespread anti-Quaker prejudices, saw considerable expansion of the sect through the conversion of some existing Cromwellian families, but predominantly through the arrival of increasing numbers of converts from England who were settling in post-Restoration Ireland. By 1680, Ireland contained 798 Quaker households. Quaker meetings tended, however, to be concentrated in a few areas, rather than being evenly dispersed throughout the island, the primary centres being Cork, Waterford, Limerick and Clonmel.[16] The house-meeting network, as illustrated in Figure 4.2, spread through south Munster, but was largely a short-lived phenomenon, with most meetings lasting no more than three or four decades. While a small community, the Society of Friends—particularly prior to the mid-eighteenth century—was tightly knit, and could not afford many losses if it were to remain viable. This sentiment within the community is illustrated by a

**(a) Meeting facilities**

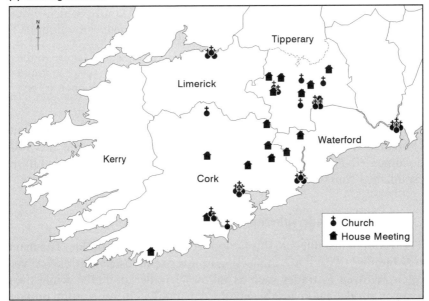

**(b) Congregation status and suvival, circa 1810**

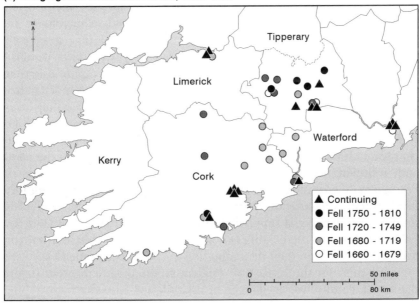

**Figure 4.2** Spatial distribution and status of dissenter meetings for worship, 1660–1810

1714 resolution of the Society of Friends (Tipperary Monthly Meeting), regarding the proposed emigration of a member family, which would constitute a considerable loss to the meeting at Cashel.

> Friends are not willing to part with Thomas Coborne and family to the province of Pennsylvania, America. We dissuade them from such a long and hazardous journey, he being ancient, but they are insisting upon it, and desiring a Certificate [of good standing] from Friends.[17]

A certificate of good standing was essential to any transfer from one Quaker meeting to another, which means that each removal was fully documented. Protestant dissent generally feared community losses to the established church, to Roman Catholicism and to emigration.

### Trade, inheritance, continuity and erosion

The trades of dissenters in this period were often quite humble. The mainstay families of each urban meeting in this pre-industrialisation era were often involved in trades such as tallow chandler, or tailor, while those living in rural areas invariably involved themselves in agricultural pursuits and, subsequently, milling. Some of the dissenters—most notably the Presbyterians—rose quickly to affluence in the aftermath of the Restoration. Many were involved in urban trade and, as merchants and bankers, were enabled, by the turn of the eighteenth century, to invest in the purchase of considerable tracts of urban property and to purchase country estates upon which to retire. Families that exemplify this trend include Vaughan, Riall and Bagwell of Clonmel—a trio of Independent, Unitarian and Presbyterian—who intermarried, founded a banking house and proved the mainstay of the Clonmel dissenting congregation.[18] The Damer family of New Row Independent congregation in Dublin purchased an estate near Tipperary, as part of the Ormond sales of the 1690s and, following the model of the Congregationalist union forming the Presbytery of Munster, they aligned the household to the flagging local Presbyterian congregation, providing meeting facilities and, from 1700, funding and ministerial supply.[19] Among the Baptists, Riggs of Cork and Falkiner of Dublin were bankers who also maintained close marital connections both within their denomination and with each other.[20]

At all times in the history of English colonial settlement in Ireland the settler colony was in danger of assimilation into the Irish population through intermarriage and contact conversion following the Reformation. This phenomenon had occurred within many Old English dynasties by 1650 and numerous acts were consequently passed by the Cromwellians forbidding intermarriage between the New English and the Old English/Gaelic-Irish ethnic groups. The wills and last testaments of this period are particularly illustrative of not only property and kinship networks, but also the religion, English ethnicity and Protestant identity of their testators, particularly those from a dissenting background. One Cromwellian soldier, a collector of the revenue for Clonmel, who died in 1663, bequeathed his estate to his wife "in confidence that she would be a tender mother to his children and improve the estate for her own and their advantage, careful of their breeding".[21] The will of Andrew Roe of Tipperary, a Presbyterian, required that "my daughter Mary shall marry a Protestant who has been educated and bred up on the Protestant religion, either as a Protestant dissenter or according to the established church of this kingdom, for at least twenty years before such marriage".[22] Still more explicit was the last testament of Sir Jerome Alexander of Kilcooley abbey, Co. Tipperary, who left his extensive estates there and at Kilmainham, Dublin, to his only child, Elizabeth, who was to forfeit all if she

> at any time after my decease marry or take [for] a husband any lord of Ireland by what name or title so ever he bears, or the son of any such lord, or nobleman whatsoever, or the son of any archbishop, bishop, or prelate, or any knight, baronet, knight esquire, gentleman or any Irishman, or [anyone] that comes of an Irish extraction and descent, or that hath been borne or bred in the kingdom of Ireland . . . or any papist.[23]

In accordance with her father's wishes, Elizabeth Alexander married in 1676, Sir William Barker of Bocking Hall, Essex, an English baronet.

The consequence of intermarriage with Old English or Gaelic-Irish Roman Catholic dynasties was exclusion from both family and community. In order to limit such occurrences, considerable rigour was attached to inheritance in the dissenter community, as it remained the key to the continuance of small congregations who were dependent on the subscriptions of their membership. Dissenters, in particular, were prominent in the eighteenth century in providing legacies to aid the continuance of the small congregations in which they had been raised, or had spent a considerable portion of their lives. Often in these congregations, leading families were expected to provide premises for worship, and congregations depended solely upon the interest from bequests of money or property to fund a minister's salary. These aspects are well illustrated in the will of Andrew Roe, who besides bequeathing money from his estates to the two local Protestant dissenting ministers—Reverend Nathaniel Card of Clonmel and the Reverend Richard Edge of Tipperary, and their successors—bequeathed in trust for Tipperary dissenting congregation "the house near my dwelling house in the town of Tipperary, commonly called the meeting-house, with the yard or passage leading from the [Main] street of Tipperary thereto, for the remainder of my term of years therein."[24]

## Subscriptions, endowments, offertories and strategies

Irish dissenting churches survived the eighteenth century through a combination of three schemes. The first was by subscription, an arrangement by which as many members as were able and willing undertook to contribute an annual or quarterly fixed sum towards the ministerial stipend. This was the commonest method used and, on the whole, it worked reasonably well. Often in southern Ireland, the resulting stipend was insufficient for a minister with a family, and many supplied more than one congregation with preaching or, where possible, worked as tutors in small private academies. The second tactic was by endowment, where the stipend was derived in part from the interest earned by monies or property left to the church by leading families of the congregation for that specific purpose; the third method involved free-will offerings, pew rents and donations.

The precarious financial position of most dissenting congregations in Ireland during the eighteenth century forced them to rely heavily on the subscriptions of the principal families of their membership. As such families rose in circumstance, they often, through intermarriage or social pressures, converted to the persuasion of their marriage partner, almost always that of the established church. Stipulations designed to ensure that heirs remained within the fold of Protestant dissent occur with remarkable frequency, with the names of executors providing a comprehensive account of kinship networks in the local dissenting communities. The will of John Colsery—after naming as executors two prominent members of the Clonmel dissenting congregation, John Perry and Phineas Riall—demonstrated his wish that his family continue their separate identity outside the established church, in a codicil requiring that each of his sons should obtain

> a certificate of their good behaviour and civil deportment and demeanour from any four or more of the following—John Pyke esq. [of Woodenstown], Mathew Jacob esq. [of Fethard], Mr Andrew Roe of Tipperary, the Revd Mr John Shaw Senior of Clonmell, Charles Alcocke esq., Mr Philip Carleton, Mr John Damer [of Tipperary] and Mr John Bagwell of Ballyboy, or be cut off with five shillings, the rest of the moiety share to go to the others.[25]

These wills and others of the period are valuable for they display a strong desire on the part of the Protestant dissenters, to maintain their own particular religious identity and protect the next generation from conforming with the locals. Such dangers, combined with the increasing difficulty associated with paying a stipend, encouraged individual dissenting congregations to devise financial schemes as a matter of urgency. Members were needed in order to finance a ministerial stipend, and a minister was needed in order to attract and hold a congregation. At Waterford Baptist Church in 1745, the minister—in addition to completing a new meeting-house—was able to build four houses in the city that were let to tenants, the proceeds split between the stipend fund and a fund to aid poor members of the congregation. The Waterford congregation continued investing in property throughout the eighteenth century and was thus enabled to maintain a stable ministerial supply, despite small numbers.[26]

A similar scheme was arranged by the Unitarian Presbyterian congregation at Clonmel, when in 1747, John Perry, a leading member, took a 999-year lease at a peppercorn rent of a piece of ground in the centre of the town. Acting jointly with the senior representatives of the Hutchinson and Bagwell families, this trio of leading families built a number of dwellings upon the site, namely a manse and three houses, with the purpose of generating income for the stipend fund. In addition, Richard Hutchinson of Knocklofty, in covenant with Bagwell and Perry, agreed to contribute £15 annually toward the ministerial stipend, partly composed of a rent charge on his estate.[27] Though the Clonmel congregation went into severe numerical decline during the 1770s—to the extent of losing their descendants to the established church—its finances continued intact, largely due to the efforts of the previous generation in forming trusts and endowments, and the continued association of many of these families with it into the early decades of the nineteenth century.

The second largest dissenting denomination in the first half of the eighteenth century was the Society of Friends. In County Tipperary, the Quaker population prior to 1750 comprised about fifteen families. The earliest settlement at Cashel was failing, as were its outlying house-meetings at Mogorban, near Fethard, and at Tipperary town, while those of Cahir and Clonmel experienced only slight growth, tempered by removals through death and emigration. The static nature of the settlement probably reflected a stagnant economy, with Quakers as the most economically minded of the dissenters, moving "from place to place as the profit dictated".[28] In addition, Quaker austerity resulted in the occasional loss of membership, which combined with the lacklustre economy, kept the Quaker birth rate low. At Cork, the loss of a large estate to the established church was recorded with disdain and a touch of satisfaction at the eventual outcome, when the son and heir "came into his father's inheritance, young and foolish, became a prodigal, purchased at the Heraldry Office the title of knight and baronet, marry'd, and soon after, died".[29]

The upturn in the fortunes of several Quaker meetings in the second half of the eighteenth century centred on the flour milling industry, and led to a vast increase in the Quaker birth rate from 14.2 per decade in 1700–50 to 51 per decade in 1751–1800. During the 1750s, they numerically overtook the Presbyterians as the premier dissenting denomination (numerically) in the province of Munster. These statistics were greatly enhanced by the arrival of Quaker families in the district in the years after 1750 who, attracted by economic opportunity, proceeded to monopolise the corn industry and related trades at the period of their greatest prosperity. In this period, the Quaker population of Munster, with the failing of house meetings and the move from farming to milling, became heavily concentrated in urban areas and their immediate hinterlands. By 1787, though accounting for no more than 3 per cent of the urban population, the Quakers of Clonmel operated some 20 per cent of the business there, with the result it was often referred to as the "Quaker Town".[30] Indeed, at this time, it was remarked that the Quakers of this region "seem to live like princes of the earth more than in any country I have seen [as evidenced by] their gardens, horses, carriages and various conveniences, with the abundance of their tables".[31] Several new meeting-houses were constructed in this period, utilising exclusively the wealth of the members at local and provincial level.

The Baptist church was a far smaller denomination than either the Presbyterians or Quakers, and lacked the landed or mercantile elements present in the other two dissenting groups. It possessed a far greater number of congregational remnants, too small to be representative of social strata. Of the twelve Baptist congregations or remnants then in Ireland, five had a resident pastor, three were supply stations of these congregations and four were destitute of all preaching supplies.[32] It was usually due to at least one family of consequence that some survival strategy was possible. In general, however, the decline of the denomination was widespread and in 1749, the Baptist congregations of all Ireland presented a petition to the Lord Lieutenant, listing the disadvantages experienced through a lack of governmental encouragement and support.

> Arising from want of proper encouragement for the clergy of our persuasion, we ask for a share in His Majesty's Royal Bounty, that we might have in our power, in a more extensive manner, to promote, strengthen and extend the Protestant interest and true zeal, loyalty and love to His Majesties Royal Person and Court, in several places in this kingdom, where popery mostly prevails.[33]

This represented an effort on the part of the denomination to gain access to the *Regium Donum*, the annual Royal Grant to the various Presbyterian congregations, through appealing to the governmental bias in favour of Protestantism. In 1756, the deacon of the Cork church wrote an account of the predicament in which the Baptist denomination of mid-eighteenth century Ireland found itself, which is particularly revealing in its discussion of the manner of collapse of seven congregations through the removal of principal families and a shortage of ministers.

> The meeting at Kilkenny dropped fourteen years ago [1742] at the death of Mr Joseph Geale, who was the principal support of it. That of Clonmel was removed in Mr Pettit's time to Lismortagh [1723] and is now almost extinct; two or three members who remain there are visited twice a year by one of the Cork ministers. In Limerick, there has been no Baptist meeting in our memory, nor in Galway. In the county of Wexford, there were a few members about twenty-five years ago [1731], but are now no more. In the North, there are a few members, but alas, they had no pastor since the death of Mr Giles Mason, who dyed about fifteen years ago [1741]. In Kerry, there has not been one Baptist for some years that we know of.[34]

## Conclusion

Protestant dissenting denominations in Ireland were in gradual decline from 1660 until 1810, during which time many of the larger congregations endured considerable losses to the established church. In this climate of uncertainty, ministerial longevity and strategic financial planning were central to the survival of most congregations during the eighteenth century in particular, with pastorates of 25 to 40 years not uncommon, and various trusts, endowments and interests providing much needed security and continuity. However, as the second map of Figure 4.2 illustrates, this system was only sufficient in holding the position of each denomination. As the eighteenth century progressed, the collapse of the smaller meetings and concentration of Protestant dissent in the major urban centres became more apparent. Of 42 meetings for worship established in counties Cork, Limerick, Waterford and Tipperary in the period from the Restoration to the mid-eighteenth century, only 15 or approximately one-third were still meeting *c.*1810. All of these surviving congregations were urban based. Inheritance stipulation, combined with diverse and innovative territorial strategies, may thus be seen as fundamental in preserving the integrity of the Protestant community in general and Protestant dissent in particular.

## Notes

1  *A History of Congregations in the Presbyterian Church of Ireland, 1610–1982*.
2  Greaves, *God's Other Children*, p. 378.
3  See T. C. Barnard, *Cromwellian Ireland* and P. Kilroy, *Protestant Dissent*.
4  D. J. Butler, *South Tipperary* (Dublin, 2006); "Representing Christianity in Ireland" (2001); "The meeting-house of the Protestant dissenter (1999); "Irish Baptist churches" (1998).
5  Baptist Church, Cork, Cork church book, fo. 17.
6  C. Kirtland, *Baptist* (Belfast, 1868).
7  T. Laffan, *Tipperary's Families*: ville de Clonmel.
8  A bound volume of folio MSS held at Cork Baptist Church, MacCurtain Street, Cork.
9  Cork church book, fo. 19.
10  Cork church book, fos 22–24.
11  Major Riggs lived at Riggsdale, Ballygarvan, some seven miles from Cork City, towards Kinsale.
12  Registry of Deeds, Dublin, R.D. 23/325/13741: registered 6 August 1719, in a bond dated 23 August 1718, between Spencer and Johnson, business partners, Clonmel and Pettit, gent, Cork, the partners to pay Pettit £250 sterling and 8 per cent per annum interest.
13  Pastor Pettit, Cork to Pastor Elisha Callender, America, dated 25 November 1725, cited in K. Herlihy, "The early eighteenth-century Irish Baptists: two letters" (1992).
14  R.D. 42/277/26200: registered 29 April 1724: lease dated 4 March 1723.
15  Cork church book, fo. 25. In 1729, the Cork church had 47 adult members, which probably included those living at Lismortagh.
16  Greaves, *God's Other Children*, p. 308; see also Kilroy, *Protestant Dissent*.
17  Friends Historical Library, Dublin, Grubb Collection S 1856, Ms. Box 56, "Minute of Cashel Monthly Meeting, dated 11 February 1714".
18  W. P. Burke, *Clonmel*, p. 175; T. P. Power, *Land, Politics and Society*, pp. 60–1.
19  See Burke, *Clonmel*; Power, *Land, Politics and Society*.
20  Cork church book.
21  Will of Charles Blount of Clonmel, dated 18 April 1663, cited in Burke, *Clonmel*, pp. 91, 327.
22  Will of Andrew Roe of Tipperary, dated 1713 (transcript), in Grubb (Carrick-on-Suir) collection, National Archives of Ireland, Dublin.
23  Will of Sir Jerome Alexander, proved 1670, cited in W. G. Neely, *Kilcooley*, pp. 33–4; 40.
24  Will of Andrew Roe of Tipperary.
25  Will of John Colsery, dated 7 December 1699 (proved 1709), cited in Burke, *Clonmel*, pp. 329–30.
26  Baptist Union of Ireland, Lisburn Road, Belfast, Old Waterford Deeds Collection.

27 J. Orr, "History of Protestant dissent in Clonmel vicinity, III: old congregational records", *Clonmel Chronicle*, 23 September 1877.
28 C. O'Grada, *Ireland Before and After the Famine*, p. 328.
29 Friends Historical Library, Dublin, Marriage Register, Cork Monthly Meeting, fo. 1.
30 Burke, *Clonmel*, 1907; R. Lucas, "General directory of the Kingdom of Ireland, 1788", *Irish Genealogist* 3.11: 468–76.
31 Friends Historical Library, Dublin, Journal of William Lavery, extract dated 1 January 1792, written while at Clonmel.
32 Cork church book, fo. 88.
33 Kirtland, *Baptist*, pp. 15–16.
34 Cork church book, fo. 308.

## References

Barnard, T. C. (1975) *Cromwellian Ireland: English Government and Reform in Ireland, 1649–60* (Oxford: Oxford University Press).
Burke, W. P. (1907) *History of Clonmel* (Waterford: Harvey).
Butler, D. J. (1998) "An historical geography of the Irish Baptist churches, 1650–1870", *Chimera, UCC Geographical Journal* 13: 56–62.
Butler, D. J. (1999) "The meeting-house of the Protestant dissenter: a study of design, layout and location in southern Ireland", *Chimera: UCC Geographical Journal*, 14: 118–24.
Butler, D. J. (2006) *South Tipperary, 1570–1841: Religion, Land and Rivalry* (Dublin: Four Courts).
Greaves, R. L. (1998) *God's Other Children: Protestant Non-conformists and the Emergence of Denominational Churches in Ireland, 1660–1700* (California: Stanford University Press).
Herlihy, K. (1992) "The early eighteenth-century Irish Baptists—two letters", *Irish Economic and Social History*, 19: 71–3.
Kilroy, P. (1994) *Protestant Dissent and Controversy in Ireland, 1660–1714* (Cork: Cork University Press).
Kingdon, D. P. (1965) *Baptist Evangelism in Nineteenth Century Ireland* (Belfast: Baptist Union of Ireland).
Kirtland, C. (1868) *A History of the Baptist Denomination in Ireland* (Belfast).
Laffan, T. (1911) *Tipperary's Families: The Hearth Money Rolls of 1665-6-7* (Dublin).
Lucas, R. (1966) "General directory of the Kingdom of Ireland, 1788", *Irish Genealogist* 3.11: 468–76.
Neely, W. G. (1983) *Kilcooley: Land and People of Tipperary* (Belfast: Neely).
O'Grada, C. (1988) *Ireland Before and After the Famine: Explorations in Economic History, 1800–1925* (Manchester: Manchester University Press).
Power, T. P. (1993) *Land, Politics and Society in Eighteenth Century Tipperary* (Oxford: Clarendon Press).
Presbyterian Church in Ireland (1982) *A History of Congregations in the Presbyterian Church of Ireland, 1610–1982* (Belfast: Presbyterian Historical Society of Ireland).

# 5

# Protestants and politics in the Republic of Ireland: is integration complete?

*Bernadette C. Hayes and Tony Fahey*

## Introduction

The few available previous accounts of Protestantism in the Republic of Ireland suggest that the Protestant community underwent a period of radical social and political change during the twentieth century. In the early years of national independence, according to these accounts, Protestants felt disengaged from their Catholic neighbours and the newly established Irish state, but in the years following the Second World War they gradually integrated (Acheson, 2002). So great was their believed level of integration that, by the 1980s, some commentators were expressing concerns at the possible demise of the Protestant community as it faced the prospect of being wholly swallowed up and assimilated into Irish society (Bowen, 1983). More recent research, however, has questioned whether integration, much less assimilation, has in fact gone that far. For example, Fahey et al. (2006) found that although both Protestants and Catholics have a clear Irish identity, Protestants were more lukewarm and ambivalent in their attachment to that identity than were Catholics.

The purpose of this chapter is to re-examine the extent of integration among the Protestant community in Irish society by drawing on previously unexamined elements of the data used by Fahey et al. (2006). The key question that is investigated is the degree to which Protestant integration in Irish society can now be said to be complete. Clearly, since integration rather than assimilation is the point at issue here, one would expect the Protestant culture to show some differences from that of the majority Catholic population. The question, though, is whether those differences entail a greater distance from key institutions of Irish society. Are Protestants in any significant ways still disengaged from, rather than integrated into, Irish society? Because of its role as the forum within which diverse cultural sub-groups can be united with a larger whole, this chapter concentrates on the political system (broadly defined) as the most relevant institutional reference point for answering this question.

The next section of the chapter outlines the background that provides the justification for raising this question. Using data from the 1999–2000 European Values Study, the focus turns to the indicators of political engagement, most notably political interest, which provide the main focus for the analysis.

### The post-independence experience of the Protestant community in Ireland, 1922–2000

The initial reaction of the Protestant community to national independence in the new Irish state of the 1920s was to become politically disengaged. As Coakley (1998) notes, independence served a double blow to Protestants: it removed them from the security of membership of the Protestant British state and it deprived them of the strength of numbers provided by their co-religionists in Northern Ireland. The national identity underpinning the independent Irish state linked Irishness with Catholicism and thus had a marginalising effect on the Protestant minority. Many in that minority retained a strong sense of Britishness and a lingering loyalty to the British crown (Acheson, 2002). Aside from religious questions, certain aspects of cultural policy in the new state, particularly the emphasis placed on the restoration of the Irish language, were felt by many Protestants to be an attack on their English cultural heritage (Brown, 1996).

However, despite these inauspicious beginnings, relations between the Protestant minority and the Irish state improved with time. The Free State government scrupulously sought to avoid formal discrimination against Protestants and made significant gestures towards safeguarding their denominational identity as, for example, through the inclusion of Protestant schools within the system of state support for education. As time progressed, these gestures helped take the edge off Protestant attitudes towards the state, and in the years after the Second World War, Protestant detachment gradually evolved towards integration. In his account of this development among members of the Church of Ireland, for example, Acheson (2002: 233) says that in the post-war period "tacit acceptance of the state gave way to positive support, and southern church members, particularly in the cities, became more confident in their citizenship". This "greening" of the Protestant community in the south also led to a growing sense of distance from northern Protestants and a rejection of the characterisation of southern Protestants as an oppressed minority (Brewer and Higgins, 1998). By the 1990s, it was said that Protestants in the Republic had "far more in common with their fellow Catholic citizens than with their Northern co-religionists" (Acheson, 2002: 260).

Looking at these developments in the 1980s, Kurt Bowen, the main sociological analyst of the Protestant community in Ireland, shifted attention away from the former concern with Protestant marginalisation to the new question of whether Protestant integration might go too far and turn into assimilation. Here the issue was whether the Protestant minority would become totally absorbed into Irish society and disappear as a separate identifiable community (Bowen, 1983), a question taken up again by Terence Brown in the mid-1990s (Brown, 1996). Their view was that satisfactory integration rather than overwhelming assimilation was the most likely outcome, largely because Catholicism had lost its former dominant role in shaping identity and social structure and had become more accommodating towards both secularisation and other religions. Paradoxically, therefore, the waning significance of religion in general, and of the Catholic–Protestant divide in particular, could be seen as a source of relief to Protestants and as a boost to the prospect of an integrationist rather than assimilationist future for the Protestant community.

The debate concerning integration versus assimilation undoubtedly captures many of the issues facing the Protestant community in Ireland today—and does so in regard to a dominant culture that is increasingly secular as much as it did in the past when Ireland was overbearingly Catholic. However, there are grounds for continuing to keep in mind older questions about Protestant marginalisation and disengagement in the Irish state. One basis for continuing to ask such questions is the legacy of the long-term *demographic* decline of the Protestant community.

Between the foundation of the state and the early 1990s, the size of the Protestant population was nearly halved, on top of an earlier sharp decline as a consequence of the First World War and the departure of Protestants during the transition to the new state (Sexton and O'Leary, 1996). The pain of this experience was added to the role of intermarriage with Catholics in furthering the Protestant decline. Intermarriage was rare before the 1940s but increased as Protestant-Catholic integration advanced in the post-war period. By the early 1970s, according to Bowen's estimates, one third of Protestants who married had Catholic spouses (Bowen, 1983). Census data from 1981 indicate that 86 per cent of the children of mixed marriages were raised as Catholics, reflecting the long-standing insistence by the Catholic church on a Catholic upbringing for the children of mixed marriages (Sexton and O'Leary, 1996). This "loss" of the children to the Catholic side, combined with a considerable incidence of conversion among the Protestant partners, amounted to a significant demographic drain on the Protestant population. It generated resentment among Protestants as it seemed that the Catholic church was using the numerical superiority of the Catholic population to squeeze the demographic life-blood out of the Protestant population.

Demographic recovery for the Protestant population set in during the 1990s: by 2002, the number of Protestants in the Republic was almost 40 per cent greater than in 1991 (Central Statistics Office, 2004a). However, the social significance of this growth for Protestants was diluted somewhat by the degree to which it was fuelled by inward migration rather than by native demographic vitality: in 2002, about one in four Protestants in the Republic of Ireland was non-national (Central Statistics Office, 2004b). Thus, the long-term demographic experience of the Protestant community reflected its fundamental inability to prosper even up to the recent past, and may have resulted in making it less enthused about its social environment than it might otherwise have been.

There has been little systematic investigation of whether such coolness is in fact present but some recent pointers are available from a study of Catholic and Protestant values and attitudes in both the Republic and Northern Ireland by Fahey et al. (2006). Their analysis suggests that, on the one hand, Protestants in the Republic have adopted a wholly Irish identity: they think of themselves as Irish more or less to the same extent as Catholics do, and the former "west British" associations of Protestantism are largely gone (Fahey et al., 2006).

On the other hand, a closer look reveals some nuances in attitudes among Protestants in the Republic and in the way they relate to their Irish identity that set them somewhat apart from Catholics. For example, they had lower levels of pride in Irish citizenship than Catholics—only 49 per cent of Protestants were "very proud" of their citizenship compared to 75 per cent of Catholics. They were also less "green" on aspects of the "national question". For example, almost one in four Protestants in the Republic were in favour of Northern Ireland remaining in the United Kingdom compared to fewer than one in ten Catholics. Even among Protestants in the Republic, a united Ireland was the option that received the most support: 42 per cent of Protestants in the Republic favoured this outcome, compared to 55 per cent of Catholics in the Republic but only 4 per cent of Protestants in Northern Ireland (Fahey et al., 2006: 90). Therefore, one cannot say that Protestants in the Republic were anti-nationalist or pro-unionist, but simply that there was an element of ambivalence in their attitudes in this area that was absent among Catholics.

These mixed pieces of evidence are inconclusive but they, nevertheless, suggest that it is worth exploring further whether the attitudes of the

Protestant minority in the Republic are not merely somewhat different from those of the majority population but may also be located in a position of greater disengagement from key aspects of the socio-political context—and that some reserve of this kind on the part of the Protestant community would be understandable in the light of the mixed significance of past integration for its demographic survival.

## Data

The data we use for the analysis are drawn from the 1999–2000 European Values Study (EVS) as carried out in the Republic of Ireland. This survey was based on a nationally representative sample of 1,012 adults plus an additional booster sample of 232 Protestants. This booster sample was required to provide a statistically meaningful representation of Protestants, since a strictly representative sample of 1,000 individuals would have included only about 30 Protestants (see Fahey et al., 2006). The sample was drawn at a time when, as already mentioned, the Protestant population was being swelled by inward migration of non-nationals—though the extent to which this was so did not become clear until the population census results for 2002 became available some years later. The sampling method was not designed to capture a representation of this new migrant Protestant population and did not in fact do so—95 per cent of the Protestants sampled in the 1999–2000 EVS identified themselves as Irish citizens. Thus, the Protestant sample examined here could be considered as representative of the settled or native Protestant population rather the larger Protestant population as augmented by in-moving non-nationals. This focus in the sample, while not planned in advance, could be considered an advantage for present purposes, since the concern is to examine the situation of the historic Protestant in Ireland rather than of the newly arrived Protestants in the early twenty-first century.

The main focus in the analysis is on political disengagement. Political disengagement is measured here by reference to a number of different dimensions. Of these, *political interest* is given most attention, as it is often used as key indicator of political alienation or disengagement. Other indicators briefly looked at include *confidence in political institutions, satisfaction with the system of government*, various forms of *political participation*, and *civic morality*.

## Political interest

People's interest in politics, considered as a dimension of political engagement and disengagement, can itself be measured by reference to a range

**Table 5.1 Religious differences in self-reported levels of political interest (%)**

|  | Protestant | Catholic | Total |
|---|---|---|---|
| *Interest in politics:* | | | |
| Very interested | 3.1 | 9.0 | 7.7 |
| Somewhat interested | 30.1 | 35.9 | 34.6 |
| Not very interested | 38.3 | 31.4 | 33.0 |
| Not at all interested | 28.5 | 23.6 | 24.7 |
| (N) | (256) | (884) | (1,140) |
| *Importance of politics:* | | | |
| Very important | 3.5 | 6.1 | 5.5 |
| Quite important | 18.0 | 26.5 | 24.6 |
| Not important | 43.5 | 41.7 | 42.1 |
| Not at all important | 34.9 | 25.7 | 27.8 |
| (N) | (255) | (871) | (1,126) |

*Questions: How interested would you say you are in politics? Please say for each [Politics] how important is it in your life?*
*Source*: Republic of Ireland European Values Study, 1999–2000.

of sub-indicators, of which four are considered here. Two of these relate to self-perceptions of political interest (interest in politics and ratings concerning the importance of politics, as set out in Table 5.1) and two relate more to behavioural manifestations (following politics in the news and frequency of discussion of politics, as set out in Table 5.2). Table 5.1 shows that Protestants in the Republic of Ireland are less interested in politics than Catholics in that they are less likely to think politics is important or to claim an interest in politics. Only around 3 per cent of Protestants claimed to be "very" interested in politics compared to treble this amount—9 per cent—among Catholics. At the other extreme, less than 20 per cent of Catholics claimed to be "not at all" interested in politics compared to 29 per cent of Protestants. Looking at the second indicator, over a third of Protestants reported that political matters were "not at all" important, compared to just over one-fifth of Catholics, while around one third of Catholics saw political matters as either "very or quite" important compared to only 22 per cent of Protestants.

Table 5.2 shows that Protestants also score slightly lower on the two behavioural indicators of political interest: 46 per cent of Protestants said that they never discussed politics, compared to 41 per cent of Catholics. Just under a quarter of Protestants claim to follow politics in the media on a daily basis, compared to almost one third of Catholics.

Factor analysis demonstrates that the four items dealt with in Tables 5.1 and 5.2 can be taken as indicators of a single underlying construct and so can be combined together to form a single index of political interest. The

Table 5.2 **Religious differences in demonstrated levels of political interest (%)**

|  | *Protestant* | *Catholic* | *Total* |
|---|---|---|---|
| *Discuss political matters:* |  |  |  |
| Frequently | 8.9 | 12.3 | 11.5 |
| Occasionally | 45.2 | 46.9 | 46.5 |
| Never | 45.9 | 40.9 | 42.0 |
| (N) | (257) | (881) | (1,138) |
| *Attention to politics in the media:* |  |  |  |
| Every day | 23.8 | 32.2 | 30.4 |
| Several times a week | 15.2 | 16.5 | 16.2 |
| Once or twice a week | 21.9 | 20.2 | 20.6 |
| Less often | 23.0 | 20.4 | 21.0 |
| Never | 16.1 | 10.6 | 11.8 |
| (N) | (256) | (884) | (1,140) |

*Questions: When you get together with your friends, would you say you
discuss political matters frequently, occasionally or never? How often do you
follow politics in the news on television or on the radio or in the papers?*
Source: Republic of Ireland European Values Study, 1999–2000.

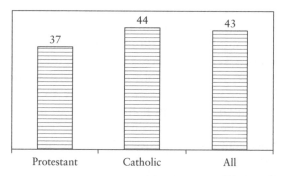

**Figure 5.1** Religious differences in combined index of political interest[1]
*Source*: Republic of Ireland European Values Study, 1999–2000.

comparisons on this index for Protestants and Catholics, as set out Figure
5.1, show an interest score of 37 for Protestants compared to 44 for
Catholics—a modest but nonetheless statistically significant difference.

It is possible that the apparent greater lack of interest in politics
among Protestants compared to Catholics is spurious, in that it is really
accounted for not by their denominational affiliation but by their different social profile. The Protestant population, for example, may have a
distinctive educational or social class composition and so should be
compared with Catholics of a similar composition rather than all

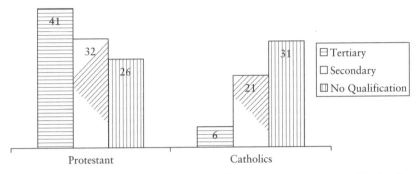

**Figure 5.2** Religious denomination, educational attainment and lack of
political interest[2]
*Source*: Republic of Ireland European Values Study, 1999–2000.

Catholics in order to isolate the denominational effect. To examine this
possibility, a series of multiple regression models were also estimated (not
shown here for space reasons), which measured the denominational
effect on political interest after controlling for the following socio-demo-
graphic characteristics: gender, church attendance, age, education, occupation, employment status and area of residence. The results confirmed
that the denomination effect was real but modest—controlling for the
factors just mentioned, Protestants scored eight points lower on the 100–
point political interest scale than Catholics. Again, this can be considered a modest but, nonetheless, real difference. Further regression
analysis pointed to a striking additional result: while education had an
effect on political interest among both Protestants and Catholics, the
*direction* of the effect among Protestants was the reverse of that among
Catholics. Protestants with third-level education had lower levels of
political interest than Protestants with less education, whereas among
Catholics the opposite pattern holds—political interest is highest among
the best educated.

Figure 5.2 shows these results in bi-variate terms. Among Protestants
with third-level education, just over two-fifths showed little political interest, compared to 6 per cent of corresponding Catholics. The reverse holds
at the other end of the educational spectrum: among those with no educational qualifications, about a quarter of Protestants demonstrated low
political interest compared to just under a third of Catholics. Strikingly,
however, even the least educated Catholics have higher levels of political
interest than the best educated Protestant. The Protestant pattern here is
the unusual one, since the usual situation in developed countries is that
political interest is highest among the best educated (Norris, 2002).

### Confidence, satisfaction and participation

We now consider whether these differing levels of political interest between the two religious communities are reflected in other dimensions of political engagement. Table 5.3 addresses this question by focusing on the relationship between religious denomination and a number of indicators of political engagement. These indicators can be grouped under three headings: *confidence in public institutions, satisfaction with the political system*, and *political participation*.

The results show that, in fact, the relative lack of political interest among Protestants does not consistently carry over into these other aspects of political engagement—there is either no strong difference between Protestants and Catholics on the range of indicators or, where a difference is present, it is as likely to reflect stronger rather then weaker political attachment among Protestants compared to Catholics. This is particularly so in regard to confidence in public institutions: Protestants are more positive than Catholics in regard to seven of the eight institutions listed in the top panel of Table 5.3. In most cases the differences are not statistically significant, yet collectively they clearly enable us to reject the idea that Protestants may have *less* confidence in public institutions than Catholics do. Looking to the two items relating to satisfaction with the political system, we get a less consistent but yet broadly similar finding: Protestants are significantly more satisfied than Catholics with the way democracy is developing in Ireland though they give the present system of government a marginally lower rating. Given that the former result is statistically stronger than the latter, we can take this as a further basis for doubting that Protestants are more alienated from the political system than Catholics.

With the final set of indicators in Table 5.3—those relating to political participation—the general result shows that Protestants and Catholics are more or less similar, or at least are not sufficiently different in a particular direction to support a conclusion that Protestants are less likely to participate in politics. A key item in this list of indicators is the first—likelihood of voting in the next election—since it relates to a core element of citizens' political activity in a democracy. Here, the proportion of Catholics and Protestants who say they would vote is 78 per cent in both cases. This is well above actual turnout in modern elections in Ireland (Lyons and Sinnott, 2003) and so its real meaning is unclear. Yet, for present purposes, it is sufficient to demonstrate that Protestants are no less predisposed to participate in this key aspect of politics than Catholics. Of the remaining indicators, only two—attending lawful demonstrations and occupying buildings or factories—show any notable

Table 5.3 Attitudes towards the political system and political participation (%)

|  | Protestant | Catholic | Total |
|---|---|---|---|
| *Great deal/quite a lot of confidence in public institutions:* | | | |
| Political parties | 17.3 | 19.9 | 19.3 |
| Parliament | 37.6 | 33.1 | 34.1 |
| Armed forces | 62.0 | 61.4 | 61.6 |
| Police | 89.8 | 86.0 | 86.9 |
| Civil service | 65.6 | 62.7 | 63.3 |
| Justice system | 68.2# | 55.4 | 58.2 |
| Health care system | 73.1# | 59.0 | 62.2 |
| Social welfare system | 68.2# | 58.8 | 61.0 |
| *Satisfaction with the political system:* | | | |
| Very/rather satisfied way democracy developing | 72.6# | 65.6 | 67.0 |
| Positive rating of the system of government[a] | 36.7 | 38.6 | 38.1 |
| *Political participation:* | | | |
| Would vote in the next election | 77.3 | 78.0 | 77.8 |
| Have/might help a political party or candidate | 42.5 | 48.2 | 47.0 |
| Have/might sign a petition | 83.8 | 85.3 | 84.9 |
| Have/might attend lawful demonstrations | 55.5# | 64.4 | 62.4 |
| Have/might join in boycotts | 39.0 | 42.4 | 41.7 |
| Have/might occupy buildings or factories | 29.3# | 36.6 | 35.0 |
| Have/might join unofficial strikes | 17.7 | 19.6 | 18.1 |

*Questions*
- Confidence in public institutions: *Please look at this card and tell me, for each item listed, how much confidence you have in them. Is it a great deal, quite a lot, not very much or none at all?*
- Satisfaction with the political system: *On the whole are you very satisfied, rather satisfied, not very satisfied or not at all satisfied with the way democracy is developing in Ireland? People have different views about the system of government in Ireland. Here is a scale for rating the system of government: 1 means very bad; 10 means very good.*
- Political participation: *If there was a general election tomorrow, which political party would you be most likely to vote for? Now I would like you to look at this card. I am going to read out some different forms of political action that people can take, and I'd like you to tell me, for each one, whether you have actually done any of these things, whether you might do it or would never, under any circumstances, do it.*

*Note*: [a], scored 7 or above on a 10–point scale, where 1 represents bad and 10 means very good; #, significant difference between Protestants and Catholics at the 0.05 level or above.
*Source*: Republic of Ireland European Values Study, 1999–2000.

difference between the two religious communities. In both instances, Protestants were less likely to take part than Catholics. Since both of these indicators relate to forms of political protest, the implications of Protestants' lesser willingness to take part are mixed. On the one hand, they could point to a lesser willingness to become politically active and thus reflect disengagement. On the other hand, they could reflect a higher level of satisfaction with the existing political situation and thus point to stronger attachment to the status quo. In any event, it seems unlikely that these two indicators are enough to counter the general pattern of the results in Table 5.3, which is to contradict the idea that Protestants are more disengaged from politics than Catholics.

## Civic morality

The final set of indicators examined here relate to *civic morality*—people's acceptance of the rules of honest and responsible behaviour as laid down in laws and customs, which could be represented as expressing and protecting the common good. The historical stereotypes of Protestant and Catholic attitudes in this area in Ireland were stark, with the contrast typically being drawn between the honest, straightforward and public-spirited Protestant versus the idle, devious Catholic, "happier to 'diddle' the state and whinge than turn an honest penny" (Elliott, 2000: 436; see also Akenson, 1988). In some ways, these stereotypes echoed broader European contrasts between Protestant ethical strictness versus the greater laxity allowed to Catholics by virtue of the forgiveness available in the confessional, but in other ways they reflected the particular historical circumstances associated with British rule and Protestant domination in Ireland. In any event, in the changed circumstances of the Republic of Ireland today, it might be expected that whatever validity the stereotypes had in the past would by now be diluted, if not eliminated. It is even possible that if Protestant disengagement from the civic sphere had proceeded to any great extent, it might be reflected in a reduced sense of civic morality among Protestants, as a form of subtle protest or a sense of detachment from obligations to the wider society.

This question is now examined in relation to seven items dealing with welfare cheating, tax dodging, lying, bribery, public littering and driving under the influence of alcohol (see Table 5.4). The results in Table 5.4 show no indications of a weakened civic sense among Protestants compared to Catholics. If anything, the data lean in the direction of confirming the historical stereotype of the honest Protestant versus the lax Catholic. On five of the seven items, Protestants are more "moral" than Catholics—which is not to say that they are totally on the side of the

Table 5.4 Religious differences in civic morality

| | *(Per cent who say can never be justified)* | | |
| | *Protestant* | *Catholic* | *All* |
| --- | --- | --- | --- |
| Claiming state benefits not entitled to | 82.1# | 68.5 | 71.6 |
| Cheating on tax if have the chance | 65.9# | 58.1 | 59.8 |
| Lying in your own interest | 65.0# | 56.1 | 58.1 |
| Accepting bribe in course of one's duties | 86.7 | 82.5 | 83.4 |
| Throwing away litter in a public place | 75.8# | 69.5 | 70.9 |
| Driving under influence of alcohol | 83.3 | 80.6 | 81.2 |
| Pay cash for services to avoid taxes | 55.8# | 47.2 | 49.1 |

*Question: Please tell me for each of the following statements whether you think it can always be justified, never be justified, or something in between, using this card.*
*Source*: Republic of Ireland European Values Study, 1999–2000.

angels on any issue. Protestants are particularly disapproving of welfare cheating—82 per cent think it never justified to claim state benefits one is not entitled to, compared to 69 per cent of Catholics who take that view. They are not quite so strict on tax dodging but, even so, are still more disapproving than Catholics—for example, 66 per cent of Protestants think it never justified to cheat on tax if they have the chance, which is lower than the 82 per cent who oppose cheating on state benefits but higher than the 58 per cent of Catholics who reject tax cheating. On two items—accepting a bribe and driving under the influence of alcohol—the difference between Protestants and Catholics is not statistically significant, though, even here, the direction of difference is to indicate a marginally more moral position among Protestants.

### Conclusion

Protestant integration into the social and political system in the Republic of Ireland has now proceeded so far that some observers wonder if it is facing an assimilationist fate and heading towards total absorption, with a consequent loss of its identity as a distinct minority. The alternative integrationist outlook is that it has become strongly tied into Irish life while retaining its own cultural distinctiveness. The starting point of the present chapter was that a third possibility should also be considered—that the legacy of the previous history of Protestant disengagement from the Irish state might not yet be fully gone and might have left a residue of coolness towards, and distance from, the mainstream. One ground for raising this possibility was the long-term demographic decline of the Protestant community. This decline persisted up to the 1990s and has only recently been reversed by the in-migration of Protestant non-nationals. This suggests that Irish society has not provided as positive an environment for Protestantism as it might have, with possible consequences for how Protestants might feel about that environment. Another reason was suggested by the previously discussed recent study of values and attitudes in Ireland, which pointed to certain distinctive features of Protestant attitudes in the Republic that might be interpreted as signs of relative disengagement from core institutions in Irish life (see Fahey et al., 2006: 57–86, 195–217).

The chapter examined a range of indicators of political attitudes among Protestants to explore whether this residue of disengagement was in fact present, focusing especially on attitudes towards what could broadly be called the political system. The results point generally towards a rejection of the notion of disengagement. There was one indicator—political interest—where Protestants were significantly less engaged than Catholics, but on all others there was either no significant difference or Protestants were more positive or more attached than Catholics. The overall conclusion, therefore, is to reinforce the thesis of complete Protestant integration into Irish society: Protestants have not become identical to the majority community in the way they relate to the Irish political system, but the ways they differ are within what might be called a normal range of diversity. In fact, in some respects, particularly in the realm of civic morality, they are closer to the ideal of the model citizen than are Catholics.

## Notes

1  These results are mean scores based on a combination of the four items in Tables 5.1 and 5.2. Scores are measured from 0 (no interest) to 100 (complete interest). The difference between Protestants and Catholics is statistically significant at the 0.001 level.
2  Those who scored 20 or less on the scale in Figure 5.1.

## References

Acheson, A. (2002) *A History of the Church of Ireland 1691–2001* (Dublin: Columba Press).
Akenson, D. H. (1988) *Small Differences: Irish Catholics and Irish Protestants 1815–1922* (Montreal and Kingston: McGill-Queen's University Press).

Bowen, K. (1983) *Protestants in a Catholic State* (London: Faber).

Brewer, J. D. and G. I. Higgins (1998) *Anti-Catholicism in Northern Ireland 1600–1998* (London: Gill and Macmillan).

Brown, T. (1996) "Religious minorities in the Irish Free State and the Republic of Ireland (1922–1995)", in *Forum for Peace and Reconciliation, Building Trust in Ireland. Studies Commissioned by the Forum for Peace and Reconciliation* (Belfast: Blackstaff).

Central Statistics Office (2004a) *2002 Census of Population, Volume 12—Religion* (Dublin: Stationery Office).

Central Statistics Office (2004b) *2002 Census of Population, Volume 7—Education and Qualifications* (Dublin: Stationary Office).

Coakley, J. (1998) "Religion, ethnic identity and the Protestant minority in the Republic", in W. Crotty and D. Schmitt (eds) *Ireland and the Politics of Change* (London: Longman).

Coakley, J. (2002) "Religion, national identity and political change in Modern Ireland", *Irish Political Studies*, 17, 4–28.

Elliott, M. (2000) *The Catholics of Ulster* (London: Penguin).

Fahey, T., Hayes, B. C. and Sinnott, R. (2006) *Conflict and Consensus: A Study of Values and Attitudes in the Republic of Ireland and Northern Ireland* (Leiden: Brill).

Lyons, P. and Sinnott, R. (2003) "Voter turnout in 2002 and beyond", in M. Gallagher, M. Marsh and P. Mitchell (eds) *How Ireland Voted 2002* (Basingstoke: Palgrave).

Norris, P. (2002) *Democratic Phoenix: Reinventing Political Activism* (Cambridge: Cambridge University Press).

Sexton, J and O'Leary, R. (1996) "Factors affecting population decline of minority religious communities in the Republic of Ireland", in *Forum for Peace and Reconciliation, Building Trust in Ireland. Studies Commissioned by the Forum for Peace and Reconciliation.* (Belfast: Blackstaff).

# 6

# "If a house be divided against itself that house cannot stand": the Church of Ireland and the political border, 1949–73

*Daithí Ó Corráin*

## Introduction

By dividing Ireland into two states in 1920, political partition separated members of the Church of Ireland across what became a state boundary in 1925. Such division did not lead to ecclesiastical partition; the Church of Ireland remained a unitary all-Ireland organisation. In terms of the church's ecclesiastical geography, the political border, rather like the equator, was an imaginary line. It did not lead to a reconfiguration of diocesan boundaries, which owed their origin to medieval times. In 1949, only two of the church's fourteen dioceses—Down and Dromore and its neighbour Connor—were located entirely within Northern Ireland. Four others—Armagh, Clogher, Kilmore, Elphin and Ardagh and Derry and Raphoe—straddled the political border, and still do. However, despite such continuity, not unexpectedly, political, economic and cultural divergences had by this time distanced church members on either side of the border. Consequently, maintaining its religious unity became a fundamental credo for the Church of Ireland. This was not an easy task for an organisation that operated simultaneously in two political jurisdictions. Unity was something that had to be reinforced and safeguarded. It could not simply be proclaimed. This chapter outlines some of the anxieties and challenges presented by the border in the quarter century between 1949 and the early years of the Northern Ireland Troubles. It also considers how the Church of Ireland surmounted such difficulties.

## The Republic of Ireland Act and state prayers

The impact of partition on the Church of Ireland was cushioned somewhat by the Irish Free State's continued membership of the British Commonwealth. This connection not only served as a bridge between

Ireland and Britain but helped link together northern and southern members of the church. It was an important political, symbolic and even sentimental constant. Despite disestablishment, the liturgy of the Church of Ireland retained prayers for the British monarch and royal family. In 1948 it came as a jolt to the Church of Ireland when the first inter-party government abruptly terminated membership of the Commonwealth and declared the twenty-six counties a republic. John Percy Phair, bishop of Ossory, found it hard "to understand why this measure has been introduced, especially since we were told expressly that no such change was contemplated. It has given a shock to many who like myself supported the ruling party at the election. Who is one to trust these days?"[1] On 23 December 1948, two days after the Republic of Ireland Act was signed into law, the writer St John Ervine wondered if prayers for the king in the Republic would now be "seditious".[2] For the Church of Ireland, the order of public worship would have to reflect the changed constitutional position. But under the shadow of the border this required careful handling. Lack of uniformity in the Book of Common Prayer opened the vista of two prayer books, with one for each state. Such a situation, were it to come to pass, could lead still further to two general synods and, in a worst-case scenario, schism.

At the General Synod in May 1949, John A. F. Gregg, archbishop of Armagh, was adamant that the church's unity would not be sundered. No churchman was better placed to ensure this as Gregg's very career embodied the commitment to bind the church together. He served on both sides of the border, as archbishop of Dublin from 1920 until 1939 and then as archbishop of Armagh and Primate from 1939 until his retirement in February 1959. Gregg was emphatic that "no change of political conditions will ever be allowed to mar the essential oneness of the Church of Ireland . . . 'Hands across the Border' must be the unfailing principle of our common Church life".[3] Though sensitive to those with loyalties to the Crown, he was nonetheless pragmatic:

> Many dwellers in the Republic will regret the loss of the familiar words, but what other way out is there? . . . For in our prayers, above all, there must be reality. And if the Republic of Ireland has left the Commonwealth . . . sad as I am sure the hearts of many will be, we must obey the call of our Christian duty, even if it wounds our sentiment.[4]

Similarly, the *Irish Times* underlined the necessity of recognising the Republic as an accomplished fact: "Henceforward, Irish Protestants in the South . . . can have only one political allegiance; they must be unconditionally loyal to the Republic . . . they must not expose themselves to the taunt that they are in the state while not of it."[5]

However, such "realism" was not universal. Hugh Maude, a prominent Dublin layman and member of the General Synod, instigated an energetic campaign to retain references to the king (Ó Corráin, 2006a). Despite the anxiety in the letter columns of the *Church of Ireland Gazette*, a satisfactory solution did eventually prove possible. As well as safeguarding church unity, Gregg was alert to the danger, should the political loyalty of the church appear ambiguous, of affronting the government in Dublin. He resolutely told Maude that "this matter must, to some extent at any rate, be governed by the wishes of those who live in Éire. Change of some kind, I think, there must be".[6] Gregg described his divided constituency in a letter to Geoffrey Fisher, archbishop of Canterbury:

> It is hard to find anything that suits the conditions in Éire. We have amongst our own people there ardent Republicans who have no wish to hear the King's name—over against them being various of the British regime who will have the King, Republic or no Republic, and, as apart from these extremes, a central body of quiet worshippers who are ready to pray for all, without distinction who are in authority.[7]

Many clergymen occupied the middle ground alluded to by Gregg. For instance, though saddened to see Ireland leave the Commonwealth, Rev. Ernest Bateman was, nonetheless, willing to accept a republic. "As a form of government I dislike it, but I intend to be loyal to it, and I hope that, when the Synod comes to deal with forms of prayer to be used within the new Republic, they will not force upon me a divided loyalty".[8] This captured the potential conflict between obedience to principle and loyalty to the constitution of the state.

A solution had to be found to reflect the political change in the Order of Public Worship in the Republic and, at the same time, ensure that the Book of Common Prayer used in Northern Ireland remained unaltered. To guide the clergy amid the uncertainty, an interim statute was passed at the 1949 General Synod. This granted temporary provision for state prayers in churches outside Northern Ireland until permanent alterations could be made at the 1950 General Synod. In October 1949, the Standing Committee of the General Synod appointed a twelve-member subcommittee chaired by Gregg to report on the matter. Robert McNeill Boyd, Bishop of Derry and Raphoe, neatly defused protest over prayers for the king outside Northern Ireland. He cleverly proposed the addition of the words "in whose dominions we are not counted as aliens", which the bishop regarded as "a reasonable ground why any citizen might pray for the king without imputing disloyalty to his own state".[9] On this basis, a bill was passed at the General Synod in May 1950. The dilemma posed by prayers which contained references to the king, such as Morning Prayer, was solved by the simple expedient of enclosing such references in square brackets prefixed with the letters *N. I.* (Northern Ireland). Conversely, any words prefixed with the letters *R. I.* (Republic of Ireland) were to be used only in the Republic where a prayer for the president and all in authority was also read. Thus only *one* Book of Common Prayer was used. A lingering loyalty to the Crown survived into the 1950s. As Bishop Tyner of Clogher remarked in a diocesan synod address, it would be "manifestly insincere to suggest that a legislative act of either church or state could transform treasured and deep-rooted convictions."[10] This was very much apparent when King George VI died on 6 February 1952. The Standing Committee sent a letter of sympathy signed by Gregg on its behalf. However, such sympathy was not simply confined to members of the Church of Ireland. President Seán T. Ó Ceallaigh felt that the death of the king "caused an extraordinary outburst of feeling everywhere. Even in Ireland, one could sense the depth of the sympathy that arose spontaneously".[11]

## Asymmetrical demographics

The earnestness with which Archbishop Gregg appealed for "hands across the border" was due in part to the Church of Ireland's markedly uneven population distribution. Together, the dioceses of Connor, and Down and Dromore comprised more than 50 per cent of the church's population. By contrast, the diocese of Limerick mustered only 2,000 church members in 1965. The demographic imbalance was succinctly captured in the 1949 report by the diocesan council of Down and Dromore: "Our beloved Church, at the moment, has much cause for anxiety and much occasion for thankfulness. The increase of its numerical strength in the North cheers us; its continuing decrease in the South and West depresses us, but we are one."[12] Concern about the numerical strength of the church was, however, not solely a twentieth-century phenomenon. Between 1861 and 1911 the Church of Ireland's population fell from 693,357 to 576,611. This prompted John Crozier, Archbishop of Armagh, to highlight the church's "diminishing and dwindling population" outside the urban centres of Belfast, Lurgan and Portadown at the General Synod in 1912.[13]

Whereas the church's population subsequently increased in Northern Ireland from 327,076 in 1911 to 344,800 in 1961, the South witnessed a disquieting and steady contraction from 249,535 in 1911 to 104,016 in 1961, or a drop, in proportional terms, from about 8 per cent to about 3.7 per cent (Keane, 1970). Much of the decline was urban, in particular, urban working class. The greatest fall-off occurred between the censuses of 1911 and 1926. These tumultuous years witnessed the First World War and the transition to independence with the consequent withdrawal of public servants, military and their dependants. Kurt Bowen estimated that the departure of the British army accounted for a quarter of the decrease in Irish Anglican numbers (Bowen, 1983). Another important factor was a high emigration rate among the Church of Ireland community of 15 per 1,000, or twice the contemporaneous rate for Catholics (Sexton and O'Leary, 1996).

These combined factors depressed the Church of Ireland birth rate so that by the 1950s and 1960s, the age structure of the Church of Ireland in the South was old with low marriage rates and fertility. Weak natural increase was confirmed by Brendan Walsh in a study on religion and demographic behaviour for the 1946–61 period. The *Ne Temere* decree, by which children of a "mixed marriage" were brought up as Roman Catholics, was highlighted as the primary factor behind low fertility and declining numbers among the Church of Ireland community (Walsh, 1970; Ó Corráin, 2006b). For many the alternative to marriage across denominational boundaries was celibacy. This was singled out by Archbishop Gregg as a significant cause of population decline among his southern flock as early as 1939.[14] The 1961 census reported that over 60 per cent of Protestant males and 40 per cent of Protestant females between the ages of 20 and 40 were unmarried (Whyte, 1975).

The diminished extent of the Church of Ireland population in the Republic forced an inevitable appraisal of the church's infrastructural and clerical resources. The Church of Ireland's *Administration 1967* report instanced one area in the Republic of 50 square miles in which 1,000 people maintained eight churches, six rectories and five halls. Yet, in Northern Ireland, the challenge was that of 'church extension'. The diocesan council reports of the dioceses of Connor, and Down and Dromore catalogued the creation of several new parishes and sustained church building in the 1950s and 1960s. With limited resources, the Church of Ireland had to tighten its organisation in the Republic to provide further finance and manpower for Northern Ireland. Funds for new church buildings, particularly in Belfast, were duly increased during the 1960s.

The situation was exacerbated by falling vocations. Seven of the thirty-four individual dioceses had a ratio of 680:1 laity to clergy in 1965, but in the twenty-seven others, the ratio was 191:1.[15] Although three-quarters of the Church's population lived in the North, there were only three northern divinity students for every five from the Republic. The shortage of vocations and the associated issue of clerical stipends commanded serious and anxious consideration throughout the 1950s because, on average, only fifteen deacons were ordained; this was half the minimum requirement. In a pastoral letter on the subject in March 1952, the bishops of the Church of Ireland warned that the health of the church as a whole was reflected in the extent of its manpower and ability to self-propagate.[16]

In the Republic, the delicate issue of reorganisation was first tackled by the Sparsely Populated Areas Commission (SPAC). It sought to unite small rural parishes. The commission sat between 1956 and 1965 and was responsible for the closure of 144 churches. The City and Town Parishes Commission was the urban equivalent of the SPAC. It faced the phenomenon in Dublin of the church population moving from city centre to the outer suburbs (Milne, 1983). *Administration 67* continued the process of review. This committee was appointed in 1965 to investigate the state of the church at that time, its place in modern society, policy direction and priorities, and reform and reorganisation. Although much fêted, the report was poorly received, partly because many of its proposals were deemed too radical. That plans for rationalisation were treated coolly is hardly surprising given the emotional and sentimental attachments to churches and burial grounds. Nonetheless, financial and infrastructural realities meant that recalibration was inescapable. For example, in 1949 the diocese of Armagh registered 70 parochial units comprising 90 parishes but by 1973 this number had been reduced to 58 units and 80 parishes.

## Administrative structures

It might be supposed that a declining Church of Ireland population with a contracting infrastructural base in the Republic would have attenuated the ties of cross-border unity. Although the church's demographic centre of gravity was firmly in Northern Ireland, this was offset by structural factors, which helped reinforce the all-Ireland nature of the church. Of particular significance was its executive framework.

The administrative structures devised in 1870 to meet the new conditions of disestablishment proved remarkably stable and they survived the upheaval and uncertainty of the Anglo-Irish war, partition and civil war. Dublin, rather than Belfast, remained the church's administrative capital and home to the Representative Church Body. In the absence of state intervention, this entity was established primarily to administer the temporalities of the disestablished church by acting as trustee of money and property at the church's disposal. Its headquarters have always been located in Dublin, first at 52 St Stephen's Green, and from 1968 in

Church of Ireland House, Rathmines. Dublin was the traditional venue for the annual meeting of the church's General Synod. To all intents and purposes, the General Synod is the church's national parliament, which debates and votes on decisions affecting all aspects of church life.

Modelled on Westminster, as it existed in 1870, the General Synod is divided into the House of Bishops and the House of Representatives. The latter is composed of 216 clerical and 432 lay members elected triennially. Each diocese is represented in the ratio of two lay people for every clergyman. However, population changes since 1868 resulted in an over-representation of southern members at the General Synod. For instance, in 1965 the diocese of Armagh had a Church of Ireland population of 41,200 which was a mere 900 fewer than the population of the united diocese of Dublin, Glendalough and Kildare. Yet the latter was represented by 32 clerical and 64 lay synodsmen: more than double the representatives accorded to Armagh (Wilson, 1963). Although three-quarters of the population lived in Northern Ireland, they made up only half the members at the General Synod. While demographically unrepresentative this has ensured that the General Synod has not become intrinsically Northern in character.

Much of the General Synod's work is conducted by committees. This system has quietly been an important means of bolstering church unity. In the view of one church dignitary, the church "holds together and, in my view, the secret to this is that the committees are cross-border and always have been."[17] They have enabled regular interaction between members of the church with potentially different political persuasions. Where political jurisdiction impinged on an issue such as education, with two separate educational systems and government departments, sub-committees have been the norm. The General Synod's Board of Education covers the whole island and is convened annually to approve the recommendations of its Northern Ireland and Republic sub-committees. Both the committee system and the General Synod helped to moderate political diversity and facilitate the appreciation, as one report put it, "that deeply held political views or aspirations are not necessarily incompatible with being a loyal churchman or protestant".[18]

Two other factors merit consideration in the discussion of linkages across the border in this period. First, the vast majority of Church of Ireland ordinands were trained in Trinity College's Divinity School. Ministers were then assigned parishes irrespective of their own origins. Second, the *Church of Ireland Gazette*, the Church's only national weekly publication and the longest running weekly church newspaper in Great Britain and Ireland, had been published in Dublin for 107 years. Though not an official organ, it reported matters of church interest in both jurisdictions. In October 1963 financial difficulty and low reader-ship prompted its relocation to Belfast. With this transfer came a notice-ably more Northern news focus.

### The "Ripon affair"

The sense of unity engendered by the Church of Ireland's diocesan organ-isation came at a price. The IRA's "border campaign" from 1956 until 1962 was largely conducted in the border counties with sporadic guer-rilla-style attacks on military and economic targets. The cross-border dioceses of the Church of Ireland, in common with their Catholic coun-terparts, endured the disruption of spiked roads and suffered the trauma of sectarian murder. Edward Moore, Bishop of Kilmore, Elphin and Ardagh, which included portions of Cavan, Leitrim and Fermanagh, expressed his anxieties to Seán Lemass, the Taoiseach, in September 1961. Moore wrote of "a very real fear that these lawless men will not hold any life sacred. I may also tell you that in the Fermanagh area it has added grave difficulties to my clergy in carrying out their pastoral duties, and damaged bridges and roads have cut off people from the churches."[19] The bishop suggested a review of punishments under the Offences Against the State Act. In his reply, Lemass shared Moore's "concern at the border outrages and their unhappy consequences for all our people", and assured the bishop that all was being done "to bring this futile campaign of violence to an end . . . which the Government have repeatedly condemned as conducive to the perpetuation instead of the abolition of the border".[20] This exchange serves to illustrate the chal-lenges at a diocesan level for a church that operated across political juris-dictions at a time when the legitimacy of Northern Ireland was contested. It was not surprising that the Church of Ireland, just as the other major denominations, welcomed the ground breaking meeting between Lemass and Captain Terence O'Neill, the Northern Ireland prime minister, in January 1965. The General Synod unanimously supported a motion by Canon Henry Lamb, rector of Lisnadill, County Armagh, in favour of cross-border talks and harmony between people of all religious and polit-ical affiliations.[21]

The sense of hopefulness alluded to by Lamb was a part of a zeitgeist. The warmer cross-border political climate was replicated in the inter-church sphere. The papacy of John XXIII, the convocation of the Second Vatican Council, and better relations between Rome and Canterbury generated a palpable sense of anticipation and cautious optimism about ecumenical endeavour. But for a church keen to uphold the principle of all-Ireland unity, therein lurked hidden dangers. Throughout the 1960s the words "ecumenism" and "unity" were invested with political overtones by those who linked together religious and political fears. The "Ripon affair" in 1967 exposed a marked divergence between southern and northern members of the Church of Ireland vis-à-vis ecumenism, in general, and the influence of the Orange Order in particular.

John Moorman, Bishop of Ripon, served as senior Anglican observer at the Second Vatican Council. In February 1967, he was invited to St Anne's Cathedral, Belfast to address the Irish Church Association, which represented a cross-section of clerical and lay opinion, on the conversations between Canterbury and Rome. The threat of an outbreak of violence by the Orange Order and extreme Protestants prompted Dean Cuthbert Peacocke to withdraw the invitation at the behest of the Northern Ireland government, which could not guarantee that the police would be able to maintain the peace. Moorman, himself, received numerous threatening letters.[22] The incident revealed an uncompromising opposition to ecumenism headed by Ian Paisley, who labelled Moorman "the Pope's quisling" (Manktelow, 1999: 72). Moreover, it exposed the inherent contradictions of a dual loyalty to the Church of Ireland and the Orange Order (which denied responsibility for the cancellation) and opened a charged debate on the Orange Order's relationship with the Church of Ireland that persists to this day.

The withdrawal of Moorman's invitation was extremely damaging to the standing of the Church of Ireland. Brian Harvey, canon theologian of St Anne's Cathedral, felt compelled to inform his congregation that the

> Orange Order itself has no constitutional relationship with the Church of Ireland; and no one must ever think that the Orange Order has any constitutional right to dictate or even give the impression of dictating about what the Church of Ireland or any Church of Ireland group does.[23]

The response of the House of Bishops was meek and did not mention the Orange Order by name. A press statement unconvincingly reaffirmed the belief in "freedom of speech throughout the community" and "the right of our Church to order its own affairs without let or hindrance" (Ó Corráin, 2006b: 29). The appearance of such timidity dismayed many southern members and there were several motions at diocesan level calling for stronger church leadership. For instance one diocesan secretary asked:

> Why is there no condemnation of Orangeism? Surely if the Orange Order takes upon itself, as it has done in this instance, to dictate to the Irish Church as to whom it may or may not invite to occupy its pulpits, the time has come for a firm declaration that membership of this organisation is

incompatible with membership of the Church of Ireland. Principle is more important than numbers.[24]

## The role of the Church Committee

The "Ripon affair" was not without beneficial consequence. While the overall number of Church of Ireland members of the Orange Order was small, many northern clergy were affiliates as, indeed, were some bishops. Ironically, John Gregg refused to join either the Masonic or Orange institutions as he believed their members "forfeited independence of judgment" (Seaver, 1963: 334). It was significant, therefore, that on being consecrated bishop of Derry and Raphoe in January 1970, Cuthbert Peacocke resigned from the Orange Order after a membership of more than forty years. That the *Gazette* applauded this decision as "wise, courageous and properly Episcopal" and an example to the clergyman "uncertain about the rightness of his continued membership" of the Orange Order indicates the degree to which the relationship was hitherto unquestioned.[25] Disquiet at the handling of the Moorman debacle also coalesced with a pressing demand for a specialist committee to consider various political, ethical and social issues affecting Church of Ireland members on both sides of the border. The high profile "role of the Church Committee" was established in 1970 and in the years that followed it presented influential annual reports to the General Synod.

The Northern Ireland Troubles forced the Church of Ireland to reconsider the interpenetration of politics and religion. They placed a burden on individual clergy. Victor Griffin recalled, as a southerner in Derry, being subjected to anonymous persecution by letter and telephone from extremist members of the Protestant community whenever he took issue with the Stormont administration or advocated closer links between the churches (Griffin, 1993). Among the laity, some southern members of the church tried to distance themselves from events in the North. In August 1969, a notice in the press by Colonel and Mrs O'Callaghan-Westropp of O'Callaghan's Mills, County Clare declared that they were "so thoroughly ashamed of our co-religionists in the Six Counties of Northern Ireland that we no longer wish to be considered Protestants".[26] There were real fears of church disunity. The Armagh Board of Social Responsibility feared two types of split: first, at parish level, where discontented people might establish a free Church of Ireland, and, second, a rupture between the Church of Ireland in the Republic and that in Northern Ireland. The board emphasised that 'everything possible will have to be done to ensure that the danger is eliminated' and it endorsed especially the need for greater understanding between members of the church, North and South.[27]

This was why the reports of the Role of the Church Committee proved so important. They provided a sort of palliative or safety valve for the Church of Ireland's northern members. Furthermore, they helped deepen the understanding of differing political standpoints across the Church of Ireland and the reasons for them, hitherto often poorly understood. Tellingly, one of the final recommendations of the 1972 report emphasised the importance of developing 'personal contacts and dialogue between members and organisations of the Church of Ireland in parishes and dioceses north and south of the border'.[28] The committee thus ensured that religious unity would not be compromised by competing political aspirations.

### Conclusion

Between 1949 and 1973 the Church of Ireland was mindful of St Mark's warning that a house divided against itself cannot stand. Archbishop Gregg's phrase "hands across the border" summed up the symbolic importance of maintaining religious unity across the political divide, of ensuring that the Church of Ireland's identity and place were firmly on an all-Ireland basis. Achieving this was far from straightforward and, at times, it appeared that the church's unity was in jeopardy. The state prayers issue merely underlined the fact that after thirty years the political border had become entrenched. Public expressions of loyalty to the Crown in the South were adroitly eliminated from the Book of Common Prayer without creating liturgical fissures or damaging ties of creed. By 1973, the volatility of the political crisis in Northern Ireland threatened to hollow out the church's religious union. However, a number of internal factors bound the Church of Ireland together as a unitary all-Ireland entity. Its diocesan organisation long predated political partition. The church's administrative structure reflected a desire to accommodate and moderate political diversity within an all-Ireland framework. Demographics too played their part. Though small in number, southern members of the Church of Ireland were not simply adjuncts to a predominantly Northern church. The significant size of the church's Northern Ireland population was tempered by the nominal nature of some its membership. Despite many challenges, there remained one ministry, one church, one people undivided by political jurisdiction and indivisible in the faith.

## Notes

1 Phair to Lord Templemore, 10 December 1948, Representative Church Body Library (hereafter RCBL), Maude Papers, MS 262/1/1/2/1.
2 *Times*, 23 December 1948.
3 President's address, 10 May 1949, *Journal of the General Synod* (hereafter *JGS*) 1949, p. lxxxiii.
4 Ibid., pp. lxxiii–iv.
5 *Irish Times*, 14 May 1949.
6 Abp. Gregg to H. Maude, 4 February 1949, RCBL, Maude Papers, MS 262/1/1/2/26.
7 Abp. Gregg to Abp. Fisher, 3 January 1950, Lambeth Palace Archives, Fisher Papers, 72, f. 302.
8 *Church of Ireland Gazette* (hereafter *CoIG*), 28 January 1949.
9 Bp Boyd to H. Maude, 3 December 1949, RCBL, Maude Papers, MS 262/1/1/5/178.
10 *Impartial Reporter*, 6 October 1949.
11 S. T. Ó Ceallaigh to S. Leslie, 25 February 1952, NLI, Shane Leslie Papers, MS 22848.
12 Report of the Down and Dromore Diocesan Council to the Diocesan Synod 1949, p. 21.
13 President's address, 17 April 1912, *JGS 1912*, p. lxi.
14 President's address, 9 May 1939, *JGS 1939*, pp. lxxviii–ix
15 Administration 1967, p. 36.
16 *CoIG*, 14 March 1952.
17 Interview with Very Revd Victor Griffin, 15 April 2002.
18 Clerical Society of Ireland, 'Problems and Opportunities for the Church of Ireland,' 17 November 1971, RCBL, MS 142/3.
19 Bp. Moore to S. Lemass, 5 September 1961, National Archives of Ireland, JUS 8/1133.
20 S. Lemass to Bp. Moore, 9 September 1961, ibid.
21 *JGS 1966*, p. lxiii; *Irish Press*, 12 May 1966.
22 Diaries of John Moorman, entries for 17–30 January 1967, MS 3655, Lambeth Palace Archives.
23 *CoIG*, 10 February 1967.
24 *CoIG*, 3 March 1967.
25 *CoIG*, 30 January 1970.
26 *Irish Independent*, 20 August 1969.
27 D. J. Crozier to members of the Board of Social Responsibility, 4 September 1971, RCBL, Simms Papers, MS 238.
28 *JGS 1972*, p. 255.

## References

Bowen, K. (1983) *Protestants in a Catholic State: Ireland's Privileged Minority* (Dublin: Gill & Macmillan, 1983).

Griffin, V. (1993) *Mark of Protest: An Autobiography* (Dublin: Gill and Macmillan).

Keane, T. (1970) 'Demographic trends', in Michael Hurley (ed.) *Irish Anglicanism 1869–1969* (Dublin: Allen Figgis), pp. 168–78.

Manktelow, M. (1999) *John Moorman: Anglican, Franciscan, Independent* (Norwich: Canterbury Press).

Milne, K. (1983) *The Church of Ireland: A History* (Dublin: APCK).

Ó Corráin, D. (2006a) 'We shall find a way through': the Church of Ireland, state prayers and liturgical realities', in T. B. Barnard and W. G. Neely (eds) *The Clergy of the Church of Ireland, 1000–2000: Messengers, Watchmen and Stewards* (Dublin: Four Courts Press), 199–212.

Ó Corráin, D. (2006b) *Rendering to God and Caesar: The Irish Churches and the Two States in Ireland, 1949–73* (Manchester: Manchester University Press).

Seaver, G. (1963) *John Allen Fitzgerald Gregg, Archbishop* (London: Faith Press).

Sexton, J. and O'Leary, R. (1996) 'Factors affecting population decline in minority religious communities in the Republic of Ireland', in *Building Trust in Ireland: Studies Commissioned by the Forum for Peace and Reconciliation* (Belfast: Blackstaff), pp. 255–332.

Walsh, B. (1970) *Religion and Demographic Behaviour in Ireland* (Dublin: ESRI).

Whyte, J. (1975) *Minority Report: The Protestant Community in the Irish Republic* (Dublin: Gill & Macmillan).

Wilson, W. G. (1963) *How the Church of Ireland is Governed* (Dublin: APCK).

# Part III
# The gender dimension

# 7

# Gender, faith and power: negotiating identity in the mission field

*Myrtle Hill*

### Introduction

It is now widely acknowledged that research into women's engagement in the Christian mission to evangelise "heathen" lands—particularly during the period before the Second World War—has made a major contribution to both religious and women's history (e.g. Brouwer, 2002; Bowie et al., 1993; Flemming 1989; Kent, 2004; Rutherdale, 2002). Much of the early interest in female missionaries was generated by feminist historians as part of the wider "second-wave" project of challenging the marginalisation of women in history. In uncovering fresh sources and applying a feminist analysis to more traditional interpretations, they revealed the possibilities of empowerment and independence offered by an area of work which, on the surface, appeared to be one of "service" and support. Later work, drawing on feminist debates on "difference" as well as post-colonial theory, showed greater awareness of the ways in which such women were themselves part of a racially-based power hierarchy while, more recently, the works of postmodernist and poststructuralist theorists have argued against the tendency to see all female missionaries as a hegemonic category.

This brief study of northern Irish female missionary experience, informed by the broader theoretical context, discusses some of the contradictions and ambiguities inherent in their positions. Despite the wealth of literature on American, Canadian and British female missionaries, the role of Irish women in this venture has received relatively little attention, only recently coming under historical investigation (Addeley, 1994; Hill, 2005, 2007). The main focus is on women from Presbyterian backgrounds in the north of Ireland, and within a timeframe *c.*1870–1920, when the female missionary was a relatively new concept.

### Wives and co-workers

The earliest Irish Protestant women to engage in the missionary enterprise did so as wives of male missionaries. Church mission boards considered marriage an important criterion for those representing the
Church in foreign lands for a range of—usually pragmatic—reasons. A
resident wife reduced the risk of clergy forming "unsuitable" relationships and guarded against the taint of scandal, which could so easily mar
the career of unattached men living in an alien culture. The lives of these
men were also, of course, considerably enhanced by the comforts of
western domesticity provided by a dutiful wife. According to the
Reverend William Beatty, senior missionary of the Irish Presbyterian
Church in India,

> A missionary wife, if of the right spirit, must be of immense value, not
> merely as a companion and encourager and a nurse to him, in long and
> dreary isolation from all civilised society and in times of depression and
> sickness, when there might be no European within miles of him, but also
> an actual helper in purely mission work among women and girls of the
> station. (Rea, 1894: 12)

The presence of such Christian women was considered important in
easing social interaction with local communities and in providing the
women of India and China with role models well versed in the "cult of
domesticity" (Robert, 1993). It was hoped they would provide an anti-
dote to the primitive nature of the indigenous family—as seen from the
western perspective. For while recognising, "their considerable power as
mothers in the household", male missionaries claimed that women in
India were "enslaved by fathers, husbands and sons",[1] and "are treated
as chattels, of less importance than animals".[2] However, Beatty's assessment of the role of the missionary wife, which placed her solely in subordinate relation to her husband, greatly underestimates the challenges
posed by her position.

Undoubtedly, replicating family life in a foreign missionary household
was no easy task. In undertaking the expected "wifely duties", women
encountered more than the hardships of travel, language and climate.
Without the comfort and solicitude of family and friends or, more importantly, familiar and regular medical attention, the experiences of preg-
nancy and childbirth were significantly more dangerous, while the health
of those infants who survived childbirth was severely compromised. The
deaths of missionary children were regularly reported in the literature,
while the necessity of sending older children home to be educated
deprived mothers of the normal outlet for exercising their maternal

instincts.[3] Moreover, the additional "mission work" referred to above ranged from teaching and nursing to Bible reading, delivering babies and caring for orphans. Haggis (1998: 52) noted that, "wherever there was a wife a school for girls was established", and education was, of course, regarded as a key means of access and influence. Indeed, both the official records and personal reminiscences leave us in little doubt of the critical importance of wives in establishing a Christian presence in foreign lands. By interacting with local women in the "female" aspects of daily life, they were often able to form bonds at social and emotional levels, and thus act as a bridge to the more formal structures of the mission.

Although their identities were thus mobilised for religious ends, we should not simply assume wives' passive acquiescence. Various accounts testify to the arduous and consistent nature of their involvement in mission work; thus the wife of Rev. Fulton filled her days in India by "dispensing medicine, superintending her girls' boarding school, managing a weekly Inquirers' class for women . . ."[4] It is difficult, however, to capture with greater precision the perceptions and experiences of these women; our analysis is compromised by the power dynamics within marriage which shaped, if not their views, their expression of them. Thus, when Reverend Beatty –having returned home to retire after a full 21 years' service—decided he must depart once more for India, his wife's response was the expected one: "It is my duty to go and help him" (Rea, 1894: 128).

Similarly, in official records, in a direct parallel with the lives of their secular counterparts, the identities of missionary wives are represented as being completely subsumed in those of their husbands. This was reflected in their unpaid status and in the requirement that they leave the mission field on the retirement or death of their husband, whatever their own sense of personal vocation.[5] This lack of recognition must have been particularly galling for those women who, before marriage, had undergone professional training for service in the female missions that were established in the final decades of the nineteenth century. (In the Irish Presbyterian Church alone between 1874 and 1910, more than 25 per cent of trained female missionaries went on to marry serving missionaries). Whereas the career of a male missionary was enhanced by marriage, that of his female counterpart was rendered virtually invisible. Rutherdale (2002: 36) is probably right to conclude that, "women were simultaneously trapped by tradition and liberated by their unique position as missionary wives", but to date, we know rather more of the former than the latter experience.

The introduction of single women missionaries was an acknowledgement that accessing native women—and through them, children—was critical to the success of the entire enterprise. "The women of China cannot be reached in any other way than by women . . . the mothers of China have immense influence in the family, even more so than at home."[6] With eastern cultures denying access to western men, and missionary wives encumbered by family responsibilities, it was considered necessary—"from the point of view of strategy and policy"—to bring on board appropriately trained women who would be able to devote all their energies both to the wives of Christian converts and to the female "heathen" (Boyd, 1908: 79). In typically imperialist mode, the *Presbyterian Missionary Herald* explained to its readers that such female role models were urgently required, since "the women of India are . . . more superstitious, more ignorant, and more attached to their ancestral faiths", while in China, "they are the real conservators of all the old superstitious practices and religious observances, and if China is to be won for Christ, a blow must be struck at the root of the evil".[7]

### A new initiative

By the 1870s the formation of female missionary societies was firmly accepted in mainstream Protestant denominations, with the important caveat that female missionaries confined themselves to "women's work for women". In Ireland, this was reflected in the formation of Hibernian auxiliaries to Anglican and Methodist societies based in Britain, while within Presbyterianism the Female Association for Promoting Christianity among the Women of the East (hereafter, the Female Association), was formed in Belfast in 1873. By 1914, the Female Association had sent a total of 101 Irishwomen to India or China, while a similar number travelled under the auspices of the Church of Ireland.[8]

Because they were a formal part of denominational structures, these new societies amassed extensive organisational, administrative and financial records which, with the addition of literature published for congregational consumption, open up the lives of female missionaries to historical researchers. It is important to note, however, that the interpretation of these records necessitates a careful approach, as the type of discourse generated by missionary activities was overlaid by a combination of traditional masculinist and religious attitudes and assumptions. Intended to inspire new recruits and enlist financial support from the wider Christian community at home, the literature focuses on the most conventionally defining features of femininity. In the first Annual Report of the Female Mission, for example, Reverend Robert H. Boyd declared that the qualities needed for female missionaries were "Christian love and patience and self sacrifice".[9] Biographies and obituaries likewise extolled such virtues: Lucy Jacobs was admired for being "so unobtrusive, yet so thoroughly genuine"; her life "a harmony of saintly service",[10] while Ruth Dickinson had "an amazing humility", and was "always reserved and humble about herself".[11] To uncover the actual experiences of these women is rendered even more difficult by their internalisation of these discourses and their acceptance of the dutiful and secondary role constructed for them in Christian ideology.

### Motivations: service and sacrifice

I have discussed elsewhere, in some detail, the background influences which led young women into a missionary career and several factors emerged as important in predisposing them to take up the mantle of service with such apparent enthusiasm (Hill, 2007). The aspirations of these early female missionaries were shaped by the social, religious and cultural commonalities of middle-class Ulster Protestantism. The majority were from moderately well-off families with strong attachments to their local church or meeting-house, and, through familial and educational influences were well-grounded in the combination of evangelical zeal and piety, which was such a strong feature of northern Protestant identity in late nineteenth and early twentieth-century Ireland. The conversionist zeal associated with evangelicalism had in previous decades been directed towards Ireland's Catholic population, but by this stage it was clear that no "Second Reformation" was likely, rather that their place in the empire, to which Ulster Protestants were so attached, was itself under threat from an increasingly assertive Catholic nationalism. This background gave an added impetus to the desire to win converts for Christ in the India which "God has placed . . . under the control of Britain".[12]

Most missionary candidates were already experienced in "doing God's work" among girls in their local community through the opportunities opened up by the evangelical emphasis on outreach. In temperance and Bible societies, Sunday schools and a range of philanthropic societies, young Christian women received good practical preparation for overseas missionary work, in addition to demonstrating their willingness to serve and their consciousness of their duty towards those less privileged. As one young woman put it, she wished to train as a missionary, not "for love of the Chinese, but because it was her duty to make the best of her talents".[13]

It has been suggested that such church-based work was viewed as a particularly important prerequisite by mission boards, because "there was no desire to send out lay missionaries who would not be prepared to accept male supervision and direction" (Rowbotham, 2002). Certainly, the training provided for potential missionaries was designed to reinforce the Church's gendered hierarchy, to stamp out "the natural individualism of women" and to "relate their personal service . . . to the corporate life of the Training College and the Church".[14]

Given this background, it is not surprising that female missionaries themselves sought to preserve their femininity and were guided by the concept of service and sacrifice. Moreover, though they were not themselves mothers, the "maternal metaphor" was constantly utilised on the mission field with, once again, western standards contrasted with stereotypical assumptions about the local population (Ramusack, 1992). Thus, it was claimed that children "find a wealth of love for them in the hearts of the lady missionaries denied them in their homes. They see in their lives something new—Christian devotion and self-denial—and it is impossible for them to remain uninfluenced."[15] The perceived privilege of white women missionaries was perhaps particularly evident in the common use of the term "Amma" (Indian for mother) given to them by indigenous women as well as children. Amy Carmichael, for example, an independent missionary from county Down, was described as the "powerful matriarch of a large and dependent family" of women and children (Elliot, 1987: 303). This appeal to "woman's sacred role" reflected the power dynamics in cross-cultural relationships where the "benevolent maternal imperialism" of white women both assumed and constructed the passivity and dependency of those they sought to "serve" (Lee, 1996: 624).

### Hierarchies of race and gender

Collins (2005), in his fine study of masculinities, discusses the ways in which the presence of western European colonisers introduced a distinctive set of hierarchical values into colonised nations. In his Indian example, he is concerned with a masculine hierarchy which portrays "civilised" white men at the top, Bengali men as "feminine and inferior" and Sikhs and those from Patan groups as representing a lower form of "fierce" masculinity. The discourse of western Christian communities in Asia reveals how the presence of women missionaries added a further gendered aspect to local power dynamics, with white men at the top and Indian or Chinese women at the bottom. White women were lower than white men and higher than Indian women, but also higher than Indian men. Indeed, indigenous men in missionary literature are often discussed and described in effeminate terms, as weak, emasculated, not "real men" (Lee, 1996: 628). In the hierarchical oppositions created by imperialism in "the Dark Continent", biological explanations of racism were thus underscored by religious values, with gender providing another challenge to cross-cultural dynamics.

Much of the recent historiography on missionary women has focused on their cultural clashes with "local indigenous women [who] were their particular and often deviant and subservient constituency" (Brouwer, 2002: 32). This analysis fits well with Lorde's explanation of how "white women ignore their built-in privilege of whiteness and define woman in terms of their own experience alone, then women of Color become 'other', the outsider whose experience and tradition is too 'alien' to comprehend" (Cranny-Francis et al., 2002: 58). And there is plenty of evidence in the Irish, as in other missionary archives of notions of imperialist superiority and of the tendency to represent "other" identities "one-dimensionally in ways that reinforce and sustain white supremacy" (2002, 34–5). The relationship with "Biblewomen" provides a good example: frequently former inmates of Christian orphanages, who "have been of good report since conversion, and who have done some Christian work", these indigenous women were vitally important to missions in terms of easing access to the wider community of women in India or China, for "while the native women have great respect for the foreign lady, her teaching may not always have its full effect from the fact that she is foreign".[16] But while invaluable as interpreters or mediators, racial inferiority placed them on some kind of middle ground on the spiritual hierarchy, somewhere above the rest of the "heathen", but with the potential to be more like western women. As Reverend William McMordie explained,

> These women have been lifted up from a slough of ignorance and superstition and low life, of which you can form no adequate conception. To train them, and make them true and pure and tender and loving, as Christian women ought to be, is a work worthy of all the consecrated energies that you can press into such noble service.[17]

There is no doubt that many women were horrified by the manifestations of some Asian customs: the "deified sin" of "temple girls", the "barbaric nature" of child marriage, but, as Carol Steedman points out, sympathy was often inappropriately expressed and an insufficient response given when "the alienness of that different experience . . . precluded understanding" (Cranny-Francis, 2002: 39). We should not, however, assume that the relationship was always entirely one-sided. As Kent (2004) points out, at the height of British colonialism, conversion could be a path to upward mobility, and Singh (2000), on the Asian experience, suggests that the interaction between missionary and "native" could have a positive impact on the latter's construction of identity. There were, therefore, many paradoxes and tensions in the attempts of white women to influence the lives of their Asian "sisters" and more work is required to tease out these complexities.

### New identities and careers

The remainder of this chapter focuses on missionary women's identity in the context of the white Christian community to which they belonged—in both foreign and domestic settings—for here too their role was somewhat anomalous. Whilst, as we have seen, these women had fully imbibed an ideology that placed their "devotional mission" within acceptable gendered boundaries they were, nonetheless, simultaneously treading new ground. Most had benefited from a higher than usual level of education and, increasingly, came from the early generation of female undergraduates who entered the teaching and medical professions.

Although the notion of female careers, particularly in medicine, was regarded in Ireland with suspicion, if not outright hostility, it took on a different meaning when couched in the language of service to God. So, while Margaret McNeill had to "fight opposition" in her wish for medical training, male missionary directors argued that since the desire for women doctors was "really catching on in India", they needed to urgently recruit women doctors themselves—to "move in and reap" as there was a "danger that the field will be seized by others".[18] Missionary work, therefore, provided real career prospects for those women wishing to move beyond the confines of domesticity and frustrated by lack of opportunities. For example, while women practising as physicians, surgeons or general practitioners do not appear on the Irish census until 1901, the Female Association had by that same date sent eight women to the Far East.[19] These women were able to give full reign to their professional skills while still maintaining the conventional gender identities of late Victorianism. Despite the challenges of their roles, the traditional humility of these Christian workers ensured they were largely unconcerned with drawing attention to anything other than the spiritual nature of their work. Their dedicated professionalism thus appears in the discourse as a mere means to an end, and provides us with few insights into an important aspect of their identity, though it seems reasonable to assume the significance of a well-salaried, high-status profession to individuals such as Margaret McNeill who used periods of furlough to take several higher degrees and whose experience in the removal of large tumours was written up in the *British Medical Journal*.[20]

In their relationships with male missionaries, however, these women were carefully supervised within familiar denominational structures which, whatever their professional expertise, located them well down the hierarchy. They had virtually no part in decision-making or senior levels of administration while, on a lighter note, one woman pointed out that "it need hardly be said that the rooms for the men are always the best in the house".[21] Discord or resistance to these arrangements was rarely recorded; particularly strong-minded individuals tended to work independently of established institutions and were rare indeed. One Irishwoman who did challenge male authority to forge her own distinctive identity was Amy Carmichael (1867–1951), whose "burning emotional responsibility" led her to reject institutional constraints, and eventually to found her own mission in South India.[22] A "down to earth mystic" who combined the conventional discourse of sacrifice and self-effacement with the spiritual arrogance of one who believed that all of her thoughts and actions were divinely guided, Carmichael used the moral power attached to the speaking of religious conviction—the language of certainty—to justify an independent stance, which the wider missionary family regarded with a distinct lack of enthusiasm (Sharpe, 1996).

The intensity of Carmichael's religious passion seems unusual (the subtitle of one biography, *The Story of a Lover and her Beloved*, captures the passion of her Christian faith) (Houghton, 1993) and it was rare for women to mount such direct challenges to male and institutional authority, but we should not underestimate the significance of religious conviction in the construction of identity, though it could be differently understood and expressed. Doing God's will, and "living for Christ" are dominant themes in the extensive writings of missionary women and provided them with a sense of personal fulfilment and membership of an exclusive group of like-minded individuals. The shared background, aspirations and experiences of these women, gathered together in the intimacy of mission compounds situated in alien and often hostile environments, enabled them to form close bonds, which seems to have been a particularly important factor in the construction of an identity both acceptable to the hierarchy and supportive of their individual and collective work. Moreover, their engagement in "the great battle of the faith" assured them an important status in the wider female Christian community with whom they were in regular contact.

Indeed, communication with the congregation at home was seen as a particularly vital aspect of missionary work, essential in ensuring its continuing high profile and to secure both financial and spiritual support. Letters from individual missionaries were regularly read out at the various meetings facilitated by the well-oiled machinery of the home base, staffed by teams of hard-working women keen to dedicate their energy, skills and talents to the moral imperative of sharing "the light of life" with their "dark sisters" in the east.[23] Those unable to travel abroad themselves were urged to answer the call "to be something for Him, to do something for Him" through service at home, and they responded enthusiastically.[24] The women of Belfast's Female Association, for example, formed forty-nine congregational and fourteen district branches within their first year of operation,[25] and within two years it was noted that the female auxiliaries were "contributing 2 or 3 times as much as the congregations they represent used to give to the foreign mission".[26]

Links between the women on the mission field and this home base were carefully developed by both missionaries and supporters; students' and children's auxiliaries were established with the aim of "kindling the missionary fire by knowledge".[27] In the Missionary Prayer Union, members' cards were printed with detailed information about individual missionaries, to make the connection "definite and personal".[28] Margaret McNeill noted the necessity of writing home often "to make them know they were partners".[29] A particularly successful means of bringing the work of foreign missionaries to the hearts and homes of church members, and of emphasising their mutually dependent relationship, was through the popular literature published by most societies. Papers such as the Female Association's *Women's Work*, containing missionary letters and articles and "pretty pictures of work", were both lighter in tone and more intimate in appeal than mainstream denominational literature, and had a much larger circulation.[30]

Within this discourse, missionary women were cast in the role of Christian heroines; in the course of the divinely-ordained task of "sharing with the peoples of that dark continent the light of life",[31] there was no shortage of martyrs. To quote just a few of many examples: Annie Gillespie, the first female medical missionary to China, died of dysentery after only eight months;[32] Miss Corothers suffered a similar early demise after contacting cholera;[33] Dr Mary McGeorge drowned when returning to China from her first furlough.[34] Margaret McNeill provided an account of persecutions and atrocities during her time in China at the time of the Boxer Rebellion.[35] In addition to tales of robbers, exotic customs and hair-raising travel adventures, this discourse served to reinforce the sacrifices made in the name of the "civilising" mission.

The relationships between missionaries and their ardent supporters at home were further strengthened by personal talks given to packed meeting halls when they were on furlough. Illustrated by lantern slides and delivered with passion, these talks appear to have been particularly effective in winning new recruits. Whether delivered in print or in person, these narratives, composed within the ideological context of western

Christianity, represented "versions of the self" through which missionary women could express their passionate religious fervour, pursue personal and professional fulfilment and win the support of male leaders and the esteem of their peers (Summerfield, 1998). On their eventual retirement these women continued to work energetically for the cause to which they had dedicated their lives, and this appears to be true also of missionary wives.

## Conclusion

Whether they married or remained single (and a large percentage of single missionaries married into service), this aspect of religious work provided women with a life-time's fulfilling occupation, although the records, particularly those of married women, conceal or misrepresent much of their experience. Indeed, that it gave them a "legitimate basis for enlarging their sphere of influence" (Starkey, 2006: 201), without transgressing social or religious conventions, reflects the flexibility of a dynamic religious culture which, particularly in "non-traditional" settings, could be manipulated and negotiated by both men and women. For while by its very nature the religious life appears one of submission and humility, the personal commitment involved in missionary vocation demanded high levels of independence and considerable strength of character. While many consciously perpetuated the conventional social image, others made use of the opportunities opened to them to underpin their own religiosity and to carve out professional and rewarding careers. Indeed, it is likely that their work proved of more benefit to themselves than to their "heathen sisters". Whether articulated in terms of devotional domesticity, maternal benevolence or as "Soldier of Christ", the identity of the female missionary was the product of a complex and often contradictory process of construction.

## Notes

1 *The First Annual Report of the Female Association for Promoting Christianity among the Women of the East*, p. 4.
2 *Centenary of Women's Work* (Belfast: Presbyterian Church in Ireland, 1973), p. 40.
3 Rev. A. Crawford, *Sketches of Missionary Life in Manchuria* (Belfast: R. Carswell & Son, 1899), p. 148. The pages of *Women's Work*, the magazine of the Presbyterian Female Missionary Association and the Annual Reports of all the missionary organizations are full of examples of the hardships suffered by missionary wives, with particularly poignant examples of the illnesses and deaths of children.

4 *Missionary Herald* (1 November 1898).
5 Mrs Lucy Jacobs was a rare exception, accepted by the Presbyterian Female Association after her missionary husband's death. The daughter of a missionary, for some years the Foreign Corresponding secretary of the mission, she was also able and willing to pay her own travel and work costs. *Report of the Female Association* (1892).
6 *Missionary Herald* (1 February 1892), p. 48.
7 *Missionary Herald* (1 February 1890), p. 120.
8 The records of the Female Association are held in Church House, Belfast, and those of the Hibernian Auxiliary of the Church of England Zenana Mission Society in the Representative Church Body Library, Dublin. The latter society also sent women to destinations such as Africa, Burma, Egypt, Persia, Palestine, Ceylon and Japan.
9 *First Report of the Female Mission* (1875), p. 6.
10 Obituary of Lucy Jacobs, *Bombay Guardian* (1910), p. 10.
11 D. A. Crawford, *Ruth H. Dickson: missionary to Manchuria, 1923–44* (Belfast: Presbyterian Church in Ireland, n.d.), p. 20.
12 *First Report of the Female Mission* (1875), p. 2.
13 James E. McWhirter, *Margaret E. McNeill: Medical Missionary to China 1899–1927* (Belfast: Women's Association for Foreign Missions, Presbyterian Church in Ireland, n.d.), p. 5.
14 *World Missionary Conference*, Vol. 5 (Edinburgh: Oliphant Anderson and Ferrier, 1910), pp. 153–4.
15 *Missionary Herald* (1 May 1890), p. 120.
16 *Women's Work* ( July 1894), p. 252
17 *First Report of the Female Association* (1875), p. 19.
18 *First Report of Female Association* (1875), p. 8.
19 Mary McGeorge (1885), Eleanor Montgomery (1895), I. Houston and A. Crawford (1900) Sara McElderry (1901) practised in India; Annie Gillespie, Sara McMordie (1896) and Margaret McNeill (1899) in China.
20 *The Fisherwick Messenger* (1944), p. 6.
21 *Hitherto: 1873–1923, Record of fifty years' work in connection with the Women's Association for Foreign Missions of the Presbyterian Church in Ireland* (Belfast: n.d.), p. 43.
22 Amy Carmichael's papers are held in the Public Record Office of Northern Ireland, D4061.
23 Such language is consistently used in the pages of *Women's Work*.
24 *Annual Report of the Female Association* (1897).
25 *Annual Report of the Female Association* (1875), p. 10.
26 *Annual Report of the Female Association* (1877), p. 5.
27 *Women's Work* (October 1907), p. 96.
28 *Hitherto*, p. 16.
29 McWhirter, *Margaret E. McNeill*, p. 12.
30 Copies held in Church House, Belfast.
31 *Report of the Female Association* (1879), p. 7.

32  *Report of the Female Association* (1898), pp. 14–15.
33  *Annual Report of the Female Association* (1897), p. 5.
34  *Report of the Female Association* (1893), p. 3.
35  *Dr Margaret McNeill, Medical Missionary of Manchuria* (Presbyterian Historical Society, n.d.).

## References

Addley, W. P. (1994) "A study of the birth and development of the overseas mission of the Presbyterian Church in Ireland up to 1910" (Unpublished PhD thesis, Queen's University Belfast).

Bowie, F., Kirkwood, D. and Ardener, S. (eds) (1993) *Women and Missions Past and Present: Anthropological and Historical Perceptions* (Oxford: Berg).

Boyd, R. H. (1908) *Manchuria and our Mission There* (Belfast: W. Strain & Sons).

Brouwer, R. C. (2002) *Modern Women, Modernizing Men: The Changing Missions of Three Professional Women in Asia and Africa, 1902–69* (Vancouver: UBC Press).

Collins, R. W. (2005) *Masculinities* (Cambridge: Polity).

Cranny-Francis, A., Waring, W., Stavropolous, P. and Kirby, J. (2002) *Gender Studies: Terms and Debates* (Basingstoke: Palgrave Macmillan).

Elliot, A. (1987) *A Chance to Die: The Life and Legacy of Amy Carmichael* (Carlisle: OM Publishing).

Flemming, L. (ed.) (1989) *Women's Work for Women: Missionaries and Social Change in Asia* (Boulder: Westview Press).

Haggis, J. (1998) "White women and colonialism: towards a non-recuperative history", in C. Midgley (ed.) *Gender and Imperialism* (Manchester: Manchester University Press), pp. 45–75.

Hill, M. (2005) "Women's work: the Presbyterian Zenana mission, 1874–1914", in R. Raughter (ed.) *Religious Women and Their History: Breaking the Silence* (Dublin: Irish Academic Press), pp. 82–97.

Hill, M. (2007) "Gender, culture and 'the spiritual empire': the Irish Protestant female missionary experience", *Women's History Review*, 16.2 (April): 185–208.

Houghton, F. (1993) *Amy Carmichael of Donhavaur, The Story of A Lover and Her Beloved* (London, Christian Literature Crusade).

Kent, E. (2004) *Converting Women: Gender and Protestant Christianity in Colonial South India* (Oxford: Oxford University Press).

Lee, J. (1996) "Between subordination and she-tiger: social constructions of white femininity in the lives of single, Protestant missionaries in China", 1905–1930, *Women's Studies International Forum*, 19.6: 621–32.

Ramusack, B. N. (1992) "Cultural missionaries, maternal imperialists, feminist allies: British women activists in India, 1865–1945", in N. Chaudhuri and M. Strobel (eds) *Western Women and Imperialism: Complicity and Resistance* (Indianapolis: Indiana University Press), pp. 119–36.

Rea, G. T. (1894) *A Broken Journey: Memoirs of Mrs Wm. Beatty* (London: James Nisbet).

Robert, D. (1993) "Evangelist or homemaker? The mission strategies of early nineteenth-century missionary wives in Burma and Hawaii", *International Bulletin of Missionary Research*, 17: 4–10.

Rowbotham, S. (2002) "Ministering angels, not ministers: women's involvement in the foreign missionary movement, *c.*1860–1910", in S. Morgan (ed.) *Women, Religion and Feminism in Britain, 1750–1900* (Basingstoke: Palgrave Macmillan), pp. 179–96.

Rutherdale, M. (2002) *Women and the White Man's God: Gender and Race in the Canadian Mission Field* (Vancouver, UBC Press).

Sharpe, E. J. (1996) "The legacy of Amy Carmichael", *International Bulletin of Missionary Research*, 20.3: 121–4.

Singh, M. C. (2000) *Gender, Religion and Power in Heathen Lands: North American Women in South Asia 1860s-1940s* (London: Garland).

Starkey, P. (2006) "Women religious and religious women: faith and practice in women's lives", in D. Simonton (ed.) *Women in Europe since 1700* (London: Routledge), pp. 177–215.

Summerfield, P. (1998) *Reconstructing Women's Wartime Lives* (Manchester: Manchester University Press).

# 8

# The Church of Ireland diocese of Ferns, 1945–65: a female perspective

*Catherine O' Connor*

## Introduction

This chapter explores Irish female Protestant identity in the Republic of Ireland between the years 1945 and 1965 in one local Church of Ireland community, the diocese of Ferns, in the south-eastern corner of the country. While concerns of identity appear to belie much of the historiography of southern Protestantism, to date, little historical attention has been focused on the female dimension of this community. Recent scholarship has addressed the history of social and cultural integration, as well as inter-community relations (Milne, 2003; Acheson, 1997; Gillespie and Neely, 2002; Megahey, 2000 and Bowen, 1983, among others), while the local studies of Dooley (2000) and Moffitt (1999) have examined Protestant rural and border society. Martin Maguire (2002) has identified the essential role played by women in parish life in Dublin, in his exploration of the world of the Protestant urban working class. However, no comprehensive study of rural Protestant female identity has been produced. Similarly, while many noted Irish historians have explored the gender identity of Irish women in the twentieth century, among them Cullen Owens (2005), Hill (2003) and Clear (2000), none has focused specifically on Protestant women.

This analysis of women's participation in the church community in the diocese of Ferns draws upon personal testimony as well as documentary material. The personal testimony was collected as part of an oral history of Anglican women who lived in the diocese in the twenty years after the end of the Second World War. These women's narratives provide valuable evidence of their activity and personal attitudes to their church. This testimony, together with the evidence provided by church records of the period, reveals the essential role played by women as actors in the shaping and preservation of rural Protestant society. As well as recording women's contribution in this way, this chapter provides a snapshot of life within a rural church community in these decades, highlights the social organisation of the church and uncovers issues relating to religious as well as gender identity.

## The diocese of Ferns

The geographical boundaries of the diocese of Ferns correspond to the county boundaries of Wexford, with the exception of one parish, Inch, together with the parishes of Carnew and Crosspatrick in county Wicklow, and Clonegal in county Carlow. The diocese was united with Leighlin in 1597 and Ossory in 1835 forming, in the period under review, part of the United Dioceses of Ossory, Ferns and Leighlin. In this chapter, as in Robinson (1973) census statistics for county Wexford are used to provide approximate demographic data for the diocese. The 1946 census returns for county Wexford recorded a Church of Ireland membership of approximately 4,000–4.4 per cent of the total county population. By 1961 this figure had decreased by about 400 hundred people.[1] A corresponding decline in church numbers throughout the Republic of Ireland, affected by emigration, reduced and delayed marriage rates and mixed marriage, threatened the survival of rural church communities. Indeed, declining congregational numbers and subsequent parochial reorganisation, together with the abiding financial difficulties posed by a scattered rural population, remained of enduring concern to the Church of Ireland hierarchy in the twenty years 1945 to 1965. This concern led to the establishment of the City and Town Parishes Commission in 1948 and, six years later in 1956, the Sparsely Populated Areas Commission, which reported annually to the General Synod from 1957 until 1965. In the diocese of Ferns the number of unions fell from 26 in 1945 to 20 in 1965.[2] While the reduction in church population in Ferns occurred most significantly in urban areas, some of which may be explained by suburbanisation, the rural farming communities remained the backbone of the Church in this period.

The female Church of Ireland population of county Wexford decreased slightly from 2,033 in 1946 to 1,821 in 1961. This decrease in numbers occurred most noticeably among single women aged 25–45, which may be explained by the increase in emigration among this age group. A similar anomaly occurred in the Roman Catholic female population in the county. Within that community there was a dramatic decrease of 2,557 in the numbers of single women aged 20–45, with the greatest reduction occurring in the age bracket 25 to 45.[3] Between 1945 and 1965, the majority of Anglican women aged 25 to 65 years in Ferns were married and listed in the census occupational classification of "non-gainful employment", in the category of "home duties". While apparently conforming to the societal norm of married women not working outside the home at this time, the exclusion of part-time and informal work in the census enumeration, together with the categorisation of farmers' wives as engaged in "home duties", does not provide a true representation of women's work. Indeed, in keeping with the occupational profile of the church community in Ferns, described as "typically rural, farm and trades based, with a small professional element" (Glenfield 1990: 252) the majority of the Church of Ireland female population would have been occupied, in the real sense of the word, in agricultural activity, as farmers' wives as well as farmers and farmers' daughters.

This demographic profile is represented in the oral histories of twenty-one respondents, aged between 60 to 86 years, which were collected over a three-year period, 2002–2005.[4] All of the women interviewed were married or widowed with children. The majority were farmers' wives or daughters, while two who were brought up in the diocese, were the widows of rectors who had ministered in Ferns. The resulting personal testimony discloses the significant role played by religion and their participation in church activity in these women's lives.

## Women as office holders

The structure of the Church of Ireland after disestablishment in 1869 was predicated upon such lay support and participation. From vestry to General Synod level, the laity occupied integral positions of responsibility in the administration and organisation of the church as well as possessing significant influence in the appointment of clergy and bishops. Until 1949, this involvement, with the exception of vestry membership at parish level, was confined to lay men. From 1949 onwards, women were allowed admission to all offices within the church. Nevertheless, only one woman was elected as a lay representative to the General Synod in 1951, with the numbers remaining in single figures until the end of the 1960s.[5] However, non-inclusion at General Synod level did not reflect non-participation at diocesan and parochial level. A minority of women appeared on vestries and also on diocesan synods, while large numbers of women served the church as Sunday school teachers, teachers in church primary and secondary schools, church organists, parochial treasurers and church wardens.

This pattern was replicated in the diocese of Ferns, where some, if few, women assumed positions of administrative responsibility in the period under review. A minority served on select vestries, and acted as parochial treasurers and secretaries. For example, in 1949 five women were elected to select vestries in the parishes of Ballycarney, Monart and Templescobin.[6] In 1945, three women served as parochial treasurers, with the numbers rising to five in 1950, and again three occupants of the same position in 1965. Two women were elected to the diocesan Synod in 1955 and 1960.[7] Women also sometimes acted as churchwarden or as sextoness. One respondent, Mary A., a farmer's wife in north Wexford, described how she assumed the role of church warden in her local parish in north Wexford in 1952 (a position she held for fifty years), when her father-in-law was unable to carry out this work due to ill health.[8] Longevity in such positions was common. For example, the work of Mrs Orr as sextoness in Killena church for "nearly half a century" was praised in the parish notes of March 1949 in the local *Diocesan Magazine of Ossory, Ferns and Leighlin*. While these records indicate some limited participation in church administration they fail to adequately represent female involvement in the life of the local church in Ferns during these years.

### Female church activity

Oral evidence recounts the dismissal of women's role in the church in these years as primarily a supportive one, in the provision of catering for parish functions. Jean A., born in 1933, described this perception as "we got the tea and washed up and were called on".[9] However, closer examination of the oral testimony reveals a much wider range of activity. For example, Yvonne C., in her reflection on women's activity in the church elaborated,

> Their [women's] participation consisted of putting the flowers in the church for all festivals, for every Sunday, fresh flowers and for the festivals of Christmas and Easter and Harvest Thanksgiving, for weddings, and they would also do all the catering for parish parties and then if the parish had bazaars or fetes, they worked very hard for those. They did a lot of sewing and knitting and they went with them and put up their stalls and put up all their goods and they collected jumble and they had book stalls and they gave teas at these events and it was an enormous amount of work and the women were involved in all that. The men did help, but most of it, I would say, was done by the women and that was how parishes financed themselves through these annual sales of work, and no sooner would one sale be over than they would start preparing and collecting for the next one, because there was a lot of hand knitting and sewing done and then there would be a children's party and they would, you know, do the catering at that at Christmas time.[10]

The social and fund-raising events described in this extract occurred with consistent regularity in the church calendar in all parishes in Ferns, with Harvest Festivals held in October, the Diocesan Choral Festival in June, fetes in the summer months and bazaars and jumble sales in November and early December. The proceeds of these sales of work were usually designated for some local parish need; for example, church repairs or support of the local school transport scheme. Indeed, fund-raising was a perennial feature of local church activity in these twenty years. Women bore the brunt of the labour involved in the organisation and conduct of these events. Very often work parties were organised by and for women of the parish to produce goods for sale. The Girls' Friendly Society and Mothers' Union meetings contributed enthusiasti-cally in the larger parishes to sewing meetings, knitting and making copious amounts of handcrafts for local as well as missionary fund raising. These get-togethers should not be underestimated in their con-struction of enduring social networks and intercourse in post-war Ireland, when the increasing usage of the motor car was only beginning to encourage social mobility in rural areas. Lesley J. remembered:

> Mother was always baking for different Church functions in nearby parishes and one day Margaret who was the maid at this time and was a bit fed up with all the washing up she had to do, water having to be heated in a big pot on the Aga or turf range when anthracite was scarce, said in a loud voice—can ye Protestants not pray without eating![11]

The parish notes of the *Diocesan Magazine* confirm the immense con-tribution made by women to the local church. In these notes, submitted in almost all cases by parish incumbents, the localism afforded by small parishes reveals in both tone and content, an intimate personal knowl-edge of community. The rectors recorded the most trivial events in their constituency in a paternal manner, documenting the illnesses and deaths of parishioners, engagements, marriages, the return of past parishioners to spend holidays with their families, the loss of parishioners through emigration, educational achievements and much more. Those women and men who contributed to parish activity were repeatedly thanked. Such continuous acknowledgement served to both affirm and promote lay and specifically female activity, and illustrated the dependency of the clergy upon the laity at local level during these years. Missionary fund raising was a huge part of the life of any Church of Ireland parish and again was led by women. Organisations that benefited from regular fund raising in Ferns, as elsewhere, included the Church Missionary Society and the Colonial and Continental Church. Some women served as members of the diocesan Board of Overseas Missions and acted as sec-retaries of missionary societies.[12] Missionary boxes, collected by women in many parishes, were returned and opened during Lent. Women also contributed financially through bequests made to the church—a useful source of income in struggling parishes.[13] Other material contributions to the church were also made by women, such as that from Miss Whitney from Kilmanagh Union who "kindly presented a set of books for use in Ballyhuskard Church as a memorial thank offering' in March 1949.[14]

Women contributed hugely to the provision of music in the church. Playing the organ was recognised as primarily a female role and many rectors' wives obliged. Indeed, the service of playing the organ was often passed from one generation to the next with daughters carrying on the family tradition. Elizabeth K.'s mother, a teacher, played the organ in her local church in north Wexford from the age of 17 to 96, when Elizabeth herself continued the role up to the mid-1970s. Lesley J. also described her mother playing the harmonium each Sunday "having rehearsed the hymns, psalms and chants the night before with the family around the piano".[15] Women in the diocese of Ferns participated enthusiastically in choral festivals and concerts. The Diocesan Church Music Committee was led by Miss Ellis in 1965, while at the annual choral festival held at St Mary's Church, Enniscorthy on 20 June 1965, "the music of the 1965 Festival book was sung by a choir of about fifty voices carefully trained during the preceding months by Miss Evelyne Miller".[16] In 1949 the Bishop of Ferns, Dr Phair, commented: "What happy functions these Diocesan Festivals are. Apart from their value in the training of parish choirs, they give our people a most valuable opportunity of meeting together in friendly fellowship. There is also the inspiration of numbers as we share in our common worship."[17]

Women played a vital role in the promotion of the community fellow-ship described by Bishop Phair. Their contribution at parish and diocesan level to religious sociability was essential to the preservation of a distinct religious identity by the church community. It is apparent from this brief examination of their participation at local level that member-ship of the church community in these decades implied subscription beyond devotional adherence. Strikingly, the oral history is devoid of any resentment among respondents towards this time-consuming church activity. Rather, these women viewed this work as an opportunity for social interaction and even entertainment. For many women in Ferns, church activity provided a respectable –and sometimes their only—social outlet. For example, one respondent Margaret G., after her marriage and relocation to north Wexford in 1943, became a very active member of her local church. She recalled:

> We would have bring and buy sales, a cake stand and that sort of thing. We built a new rectory at that particular time; I did a lot of collecting for that.

But that was all fun. That was all entertainment. We didn't want to go to the pictures or dance halls or anything.[18]

Such personal testimony is valuable in attempting to ascertain the attitudes of women to church membership.

### Female faith

Many respondents have testified to the central part played by religion in their lives, and the solace provided by their personal faith. Jean A. described:

> The Church and my faith mean everything to me and I am sorry for anyone who hasn't that to back them up in the trials and tribulations because there are plenty and I have always felt that God has helped me and still does and I could not exist if I didn't have that.[19]

Susan M., on the other hand, described what her religion meant to her as "I suppose it was sort of more a code of behaviour".[20] Devotional adherence was often secondary to family commitments, as in the case of Jean A. who had a deep personal faith, already described. She characterised her attendance at church in this way: "Well it wasn't easy the older we got, I went as often as I could but it wasn't just as easy, even like many a time like you know, you get everything done and old people and everyone seen to, it was difficult at times."[21]

Other respondents adopted a similarly pragmatic approach to church attendance. Margaret G. explained, "The church was very important but once I started on the guesthouse the church didn't come as important because if you have people you have to look after them."[22] Sarah W., who grew up on a small farm in south county Wexford in the 1940s, admitted: "we weren't great church goers, well it was a long ways I suppose and you'd have to yoke a horse . . . we went sometimes".[23] Victoria H., on the other hand, was more definite. After her marriage in 1958, she came to live on a large prosperous farm in county Wexford. In response to the question, "Was church important to you?" she replied, "It was, well not church, but belief . Do you know what I mean, the church as such wasn't, no, but I have a personal belief and it's very important to me."[24]

Brown (1981: 129) has described how "a devout attachment to orthodox religion was a central aspect of most people's lives, bound up with their sense of politics, economics and identity" at this time in Ireland. Religious faith, together with an active commitment to the conduct of church at parish level emerged in the oral history as deeply significant to these Church of Ireland women's daily lives. Another vital role played by women in the survival of Protestant identity lay in the transmission of this faith and community values. This inter-generational transmission was described and remembered fondly by many respondents. Susan M.'s recollections of her grandmother in this role exemplify this testimony. She recalled,

> My grandmother used to walk to early service. I have very early recollections of her coming round the corner over the road in her black coat, and we used to run, race over to see who would carry her prayer book, you know, and so that was . . . Although ours wasn't a religious house, we never prayed or sang hymns or did things like that, collectively. And there was, I suppose, a presence of it always. [25]

Later she confided that when her grandmother put her, and her sisters, to bed: "I would often say that still . . . that I can still almost feel, that I can get the smell of her apron, if I stop and think, when we would kneel down and say our prayers, you know."[26] In almost all cases women testified to their mother's role in ensuring that they said their prayers and attended church and Sunday school. Two of the respondent's mothers taught Sunday school themselves, and helped to prepare children for the annual diocesan scripture examinations, remembered fondly by all respondents, memories of the exam itself often overshadowed by memories of new clothes, a visit to town and ice cream!.

### Ensuring survival

Threats to the survival of rural church communities in the 1940s and 1950s resulted in diligent efforts being made to foster the identity of children with, and inclusion in, local church activities. Women at parish and diocesan level earnestly supported these efforts, led by the parish clergy. The local Mothers' Union and Girls' Friendly Society also sometimes contributed to the organisation of children's Christmas parties and outings. In unlucky smaller parishes this may have fallen to the hard-pressed rector's wife and Sunday school teachers—all women. The annual children's sports were usually held in the rectory grounds, often followed by an evening tea party, or dance, in later years. In the oral history, all of the women were conscious from an early age of their membership of a minority community. All attended Church of Ireland primary schools, often one or two-teacher schools, which were usually remembered with great fondness. In turn, the women were involved in the choice of exclusively Protestant schools, if at all possible, for their own families. As there was no Protestant secondary school in the diocese of Ferns prior to the introduction of free secondary education in the

Republic of Ireland in 1966, expensive boarding schools often necessitated a return to paid employment, the keeping of guests or the adoption of resourceful home and farm enterprises. The importance to respondents of Protestant education was linked to the desire to encourage the socialisation of young people within the church community. The women themselves recalled that their own social lives in the 1940s and 1950s revolved around family visiting and church-sponsored activities such as table tennis clubs, Young Women's Christian Association, Girls' Friendly Society, social activity such as playing tennis at the rectory, and the ubiquitous church "social".

While the oral evidence suggests much friendly social interaction with neighbouring Catholics, often occasioned by the nature of labour-intensive farming practices such as the threshing of corn, all respondents were acutely aware from a young age of the desirability of marrying within their own community. The Catholic *Ne Temere* decree of 1908 obliged Protestant partners in a mixed marriage to commit, in writing, to bring up any children of the marriage as Catholics. The rigid enforcement of the decree in this period caused much hurt, resentment and sometimes enduring family divisions, vividly recounted in the oral history. It was mothers, again, who particularly warned daughters of the dangers of marrying outside their own religious community. Hazel L. recalled her mother's advice to herself and her sister that "marriage is difficult enough as it is—why make it more difficult by marrying someone of a different religion?"[27] Meanwhile, in Susan M.'s home "it was a sense that you grew up with I suppose, you know. That was certainly the way it would have been in our particular family, and in a lot of similar, you know."[28] Church socials provided meeting places for prospective marriage partners and were widely attended in Ferns between 1945 and 1965. Yvonne G. described a typical social thus,

> But it was just very basic, you know, somebody playing the music in the corner and the supper, as I was telling you, and probably the women now might help in the parish to give the supper at this parish social. And they would travel, the young people would travel from the adjoining parishes to the social . . . And all the old tunes were played, the foxtrots, the Paul Jones, and they were the dances in those days, you see, and they would probably finish up with singing Auld Lang.[29]

Elizabeth K. explained that these socials were strictly confined to members of the Church of Ireland "They [Catholics] understood that they didn't come to our socials and they didn't hold it against us or anything you know. You see the *Ne Temere* decree would have been very much in force at that time."[30] While parish socials played an important

fund-raising role, evidenced in the Diocesan *Magazine*, Susan M. was in
no doubt as to their more urgent motivation. She described: "We did
have the Church of Ireland socials of course. But I mean the cause of a
lot of that was the *Ne Temere* decree in the Roman Catholic church,
because people were terrified that the church would become extinct altogether."[31]

Family censure of mixed marriage echoed communal censure in these
decades. The divisive Tilson case in 1950, together with the 1957
Fethard-on-Sea boycott in county Wexford, both concerning the
guardianship and religious education of children in a mixed marriage,
prompted a real sense of threat and isolation among the Protestant community in Ferns, as elsewhere. Mixed marriage, that might result in the
loss of children and sometimes adults (who converted to Catholicism on
the occasion of such a marriage) to the Church of Ireland community,
combined with the undermining of the rights of Protestants to the religious education of their children, underlined the vital importance of marriage to the Church of Ireland community.

One of the strongest commonalities to emerge in the married women's
oral history is the absorption of personal identity with that of the family;
in the role of carer for children, home and extended family. An understanding of this gender identity is essential to any consideration of religious identity. Indeed, for many of the respondents in this study, their role
within the church community could be described as an extension of their
familial role. Religious identity for women was rooted within the broader
mantle of family and community identity. However, it may be disingenuous to assume that women were simply conforming to a traditional role
ascribed to them. The wholehearted nature of female participation in the
local church community reveals a deep identification with, and desire for
continuation and survival of that community.

### Conclusion

Women's realm of activity within the rural church in the period 1945–65
went far beyond playing the organ and making the tea. They facilitated
the preservation and reproduction of religious community at parish level,
through financial support, committing their time to fund raising, the
socialisation of children, and the support and reinforcement of church
identity and interaction. Their interests and endless activity can be sum-
marised in concerns of preservation and welfare rather than concerns of
administration and doctrine. This role was not seen by Protestant women
in Ferns as in any way secondary, rather it was an essential contribution
to the welfare of their community. It is erroneous to confuse supportive

with inferior. Much has been written about the insular nature of the church in the Republic of Ireland in these years. This insular nature may have been essential in the social climate of the time, to the preservation of a small community buffeted by constant reminders of their minority, and even isolated, status in a confessional southern state. It is clear that the nature of this church at an economic and social as well as a religious level, while not constructed or administered by women, owed much to the energy and commitment of its female population. Religion played a defining role in the perception of women's personal, as well as social, identity. The study of their activity provides conclusive evidence of the inescapable inter-relationship of religious and social, as well as gender, identity in Ireland between 1945 and 1965. In turn, the exploration of the female contribution to the informal culture of the Church of Ireland diocese of Ferns has served to illuminate the social organisation of a minority religious community struggling to survive and preserve a distinctive religious identity.

## Notes

1 *Census of Population*, 1946, Vol. 3; 1961, Vol. 7.
2 *The Irish Church Directory*, 1945; 1965.
3 *Census of Population*, 1946, Vol. 3; 1961, Vol. 7.
4 Advertisements placed in the local Church of Ireland *Diocesan Magazine of Ossory, Ferns and Leighlin* and national newspapers in January 2003 elicited four candidates for the oral history segment of this study of Anglican women in Ferns, while a further seventeen were secured through personal contact. These contacts resulted in a total of fourteen taped interviews of one and half to two hour's duration. Notes were taken at four interviews in cases where respondents did not wish to be taped. (All interviews took place in the respondents' own homes). A further three respondents provided accounts of their lives in Ferns between the years 1945 and 1965 in lengthy written correspondence. Interviews were semi-structured, employing a combination of open questions such as, "Tell me about your life?" with direct questions such as "What did Church mean to you?" Interviews and written correspondence were directed along specific topics of home and family, education and work, community participation and church. To preserve anonymity all respondents quoted in this chapter have been accorded pseudonyms.
5 *Journal of the General Synod*, 1945–65.
6 *Diocesan Magazine*, June 1949.
7 Ferns Diocesan Synod, Reports to the General Synod, 1945–65.
8 Mary A., taped interview, 25 August 2003.
9 Jean A., taped interview, 26 August 2004.
10 Yvonne C., taped interview, 27 August 2004.
11 Lesley J., letter, 4 February 2004.

12  Ferns Diocesan Synod Report, 1950.
13  Ibid. 1965.
14  *Diocesan Magazine*, April 1949, p. 3.
15  Lesley J., letter, 12 February 2004.
16  *Church of Ireland Gazette*, 2 July 1965.
17  *Diocesan Magazine*, June 1949, p. 2.
18  Margaret G., taped interview, 22 September 2004.
19  Jean A., taped interview, 26 August 2004.
20  Susan M., taped interview, 11 February 2004.
21  Jean A., taped interview, 26 August 2004.
22  Margaret G., taped interview, 22 September 2004.
23  Sarah W., taped interview, 11 February 2004.
24  Victoria H., taped interview, 26 August 2003.
25  Susan M., taped interview, 11 February 2004.
26  Ibid.
27  Hazel L., interview notes, 5 August 2004.
28  Susan M., taped interview, 11 February 2004.
29  Yvonne G., taped interview, 27 August 2004.
30  Elizabeth K., taped interview, 28 February 2004.
31  Susan M., taped interview, 11 February 2004.

## References

Acheson, A. (1997) *A History of the Church of Ireland 1691–2000* (Dublin: Columba).

K. Bowen (1983) *Protestants in a Catholic State Ireland's Privileged Minority* (Dublin: Gill & Macmillan).

T. Brown (1981) *Ireland: A Social and Cultural History 1922–1985* (London: Fontana).

Central Statistics Office (1946) *Census of Population* (Dublin: CSO).

Central Statistics Office (1961) *Census of Population* (Dublin: CSO).

Church of Ireland Gazette (1945–65) Representative Church Body Library, Dublin.

Clear, C. (2000) *Women of the House Women's Household Work in Ireland 1922–1961* (Dublin: Irish Academic Press, 2000).

Cullen Owens, R. (2005) *A Social History of Women in Ireland 1870–1970* (Gill & Macmillan).

*Diocesan Magazine of Ossory, Ferns and Leighlin* (1945–65). A full back issue of this magazine is held at the Ferns Diocesan Library, St Canices, Kilkenny.

Dooley, T. (2000) *The Plight of Monaghan Protestants, 1912–1926* (Dublin: Maynooth Studies in Irish History).

Ferns Diocesan Synod, Annual Reports to the General Synod (1945–1965) Bound volumes held at Church of Ireland House, Rathmines, Dublin.

Gillespie, R. and Neely, W. G. (eds) (2002) *The Laity and the Church of Ireland, 1000–2000* (Dublin: Four Courts).

Glenfield, F. (1990) "The Protestant Population of South East Leinster, 1834–1981" (unpublished MLitt thesis, University of Dublin).

Hill, M. (2003) *Women in Ireland: A Century of Change* (Belfast: Blackstaff, 2003).

*The Irish Church Directory* (1945–65) (Dublin: Church of Ireland).

*Journal of the Proceedings of the General Synod of the Church of Ireland* (1945–65). Held at Representative Church Body Library, Dublin.

Megahey, A. (2000) *The Irish Protestant Churches in the Twentieth Century* (London: Macmillan).

Maguire, M. (2002) " 'Our people': the Church of Ireland and the culture of community in Dublin since disestablishment", in R. Gillespie and W. G. Neely (eds) *The Laity and the Church of Ireland, 1000–2000* (Dublin: Four Courts).

Milne, K. (2003) *A Short History of the Church of Ireland* (Dublin: Columba).

Moffitt, M. (1999) *The Church of Ireland Community of Killala & Achonry 1870–1940* (Dublin: Irish Academic Press).

Robinson, H. (1973) "A study of the Church of Ireland population of Ferns Diocese 1973". Held at the Representative Church Body Library, Braemor Park, Churchtown, Dublin.

# 9

# Assessing an absence: Ulster Protestant women authors, 1900–60

## Naomi Doak

### Introduction

Writing in 1931, leading exponent of the Gaelic League, Daniel Corkery, lamented the effects of what he regarded as a primarily English-centred literary education on the mind of an Irish boy:

> What happens in the neighbourhood of an Irish boy's home—the fair, the hurling match, the land grabbing, the *priesting*, the mission, the Mass—he never comes on in literature, that is, in such literature as he is told to respect and learn . . . In his riper years he may come to see the crassness of his own upbringing . . . but of course the damage is done: his mind is cast in an unnatural because unnative mould. (Corkery, 1931: 15, original italics)

For the critic J. W. Foster, what Corkery said about the estranging effects of a Catholic Irishman's literary schooling was also true of an Ulster Protestant some 30–40 years later. Foster states that he was in his 20s before he read a serious work by an Ulster writer, or a novel that was set in Ulster. To use Foster's words to summarise one of the potential psychological consequences of such a perceived sense of cultural alienation: "It was slowly I untaught myself that contempt for the imagination of one's own community which is a form of self-contempt" (Foster, 1991: 273).

Writing from a specifically female perspective, the Irish poet Eavan Boland has stated that for a writer like herself who began to work in a culture "inflected at every turn by male assumptions", as she describes it, the prior absence of a now esteemed author such as Kate O'Brien from the canon of Irish literature was an "important mystery" (Boland, 1993: 19). Referring to women living in the Irish Republic, the critic Geraldine Meaney corroborates Boland's contention, stating that "it may be shocking to some that the Irish woman reading finds in it [Irish literature] only a profound silence, her own silence" (Meaney, 1991: 17). Whether writing from a southern, Catholic, nationalist background or a northern,

Protestant, unionist one, what Corkery, Foster, Boland and Meaney share are feelings of estrangement and alienation in relation to their formal and informal encounters with Irish literature. The anxiety and frustration that they all express stem from a perception that somehow their own reality was not reflected in the fictional worlds that they encountered.

## A missing dimension

While the purpose of literature is not necessarily to hold a mirror up to reality, there is one other reader/writer category that is notably absent from this cross-section of Irish critical voices: that of the Ulster Protestant woman. Certainly, many Anglo-Irish Protestant writers from the so-called ascendancy class have received a considerable amount of critical attention. Most Irish literary anthologies pay homage to the esteemed works of Maria Edgeworth, Somerville and Ross, Elizabeth Bowen and Molly Keane, for example. Since the early 1980s researchers have also begun to unearth the names and novels of many hitherto neglected middle-class Catholic women writers who published from the end of the nineteenth, and well into the twentieth, centuries. Kate O'Brien, Mary Lavin and Kathleen Coyle are just some of the women who have recently come to light. Minor writers such as Rosa Mulholland, M. E. Francis, Attie O'Brien, M. E. Connolly and Katherine Roche have also emerged, thanks to the efforts of critics such as James H. Murphy (2000). In fact, as Joanna S. Wydenbach (2004) has highlighted, between the years 1900 and 1924 some 72 women published novels across the whole of Ireland. Foster (2006) has pointed out that the popular or mainstream novel is entirely missing from standard accounts of Irish fiction between 1890 and 1940. Overshadowed by the plays and poetry of the Irish literary revival, the cultural phenomenon of popular fiction and the leading role that women writers played in this remains a subject that has yet to receive critical attention.

James H. Cahalan has suggested that Catholic writers were prevalent during the first half of the twentieth century and that there are socio-political reasons for this. For Cahalan, the decline of the Anglo-Irish novel as written by members of the Protestant ascendancy directly corresponds to the rise of nationalism and the push towards Irish independence (Cahalan, 1988). To put this in simple terms, middle-class Catholic novels outnumber upper-class Protestant novels in a reversal of the ratio that was seen in the nineteenth century. At face value, this seems to be a logical conclusion. However, such an assertion tends to imply, directly or indirectly, that the only Irish Protestant women who were writing novels were members of an elite aristocracy. Indeed, whether for the interested

amateur perusing the Irish fiction section of his or her local library, or for
a professional academic scrutinising Irish anthologies or literary biographical sources, the conclusion that Ulster Protestant women writers
simply did not exist is not an extraordinary assumption to make. It is,
however, wrong.

### Unearthing the reality

Archive research has revealed that between 1900 and 1965, at least 23
Ulster Protestant women from middle- and upper-middle-class back-
grounds published novels with varying degrees of success throughout
Ireland and the United Kingdom. Among the names of these hitherto
neglected writers are: Eleanor Alexander, Margaret Barrington, Caroline
Blackwood, F. E. Crichton, Anne Crone, Vivienne Draper, E. R. Esler,
Olga Fielden, Lydia M. Foster, Beatrice Grimshaw, Margaret Hamilton,
S. M Harris (alias "Athene"), Violet Hobhouse, Maggie J. Houston,
Isabel Marshall, Louise McKay, Amanda McKittrick-Ros, Janet
McNeill, Moira O'Neill, Charlotte Riddell, Agnes Romilly-White, Helen
Waddell and D. G. Waring. This list is by no means definitive, but
includes only those women whose Protestant background has been
readily identifiable through biographical research.[1] As an eclectic cluster
of varying Protestant denominations, class, talent and political outlook,
the existence of this group of women writers goes some way to deconstructing the notion that the only Protestant women who wrote novels in
Ireland were members of the Anglo-Irish ascendancy.[2]

The absence of this lengthy list of women from the annals of
Irish/Ulster literary history is intriguing. It would be unfair to say that
they have been totally omitted from all of the most acknowledged
sources of Ulster literary biography, but certainly the details of their lives
and works are sketchy at best, even where they are included. Where the
lives and works of their male contemporaries, such as St John Ervine,
Shan Bullock, Michael McLaverty, Lynn C. Doyle or Sam Hanna Bell are
regularly and consistently catalogued, acclaimed reference sources are
unreliable where Ulster Protestant women's literary history is concerned.[3]

### Explaining the absence

Given the importance attributed to "minor" writing in Deleuze and
Guattari's groundbreaking study, *Kafka: Towards A Minor Literature*
(1986) not to mention the scholarly attention that "popular" culture
now receives at a critical level, the idea that these women are merely

"minor" writers who do not deserve critical attention, is no longer a viable one. Moreover, it would certainly be untrue to conclude that all of these women were simply "bad" writers.

One reason that so little research into Ulster Protestant women's fiction has been carried out may be due to the omnipotence that post-colonial theory has enjoyed across the globe since the early 1980s. This issue has not gone unnoticed by Irish feminist critics. In her essay, "The limits of 'Irish studies': Historicism, culturalism, paternalism", Linda Connolly argues that the term "Irish studies" has become almost exclusively associated with an identifiable group of literary critics associated with the Field Day publications and post-colonial criticism. Connolly asserts that as post-colonialism emerged as a critical orthodoxy during the 1980s and 1990s, it was quickly adopted and adapted by the Field Day critics, thus spawning a new wave of "Irish studies"—a wave in which the study of post-colonialism and "the Irish situation" were virtually synonymous and mutually reinforcing. For Connolly:

> The highly-ambitious three-volume *Field Day Anthology of Irish Writing* and associated publications . . . propelled postcolonial theory to the centre of Irish debate . . . Interventions by internationally celebrated theorists (such as Frederic Jameson, Terry Eagleton and Edward Said) were also commissioned in 1988 and reissued in one volume in 1990. In 1988, Cairns and Richards's landmark book *Writing Ireland: Colonialism, Nationalism and Culture*, inspired by the writings of Said, appeared, and other publications by Boylan and Foley (1992), Lloyd (1993, 1999), Kiberd (1995), amongst others consolidated Irish postcolonial studies as a distinct and comprehensive "paradigm". (Connolly, 2004: 140)

To write about culture in Ireland in a manner that seemed up to date in the 1980s and 1990s was to analyse writers whose work corroborated with the post-colonial paradigm. The result of such theory-driven criticism is that literary histories are carved out to suit the theory, rather than as true reflections of what is actually out there.

Moreover, if Irish studies and post-colonialism are to be equated, obvious problems arise for the study of literature from Northern Ireland. If, as many nationalist and/or post-colonial critics perceive it, Northern Ireland remains one of the last vestiges of the British empire and is, therefore, still in a colonial condition, then post-colonial criticism (with the emphasis on "post") is simply not applicable to Northern Ireland. Likewise, if Protestants, especially unionist Protestants are to be posited on the colonial side of the post-colonial binary then minority voices and differences of opinion within this community are in danger of being overlooked. The result of pushing those figures that are deemed to be marginal by post-colonial standards to the centre of critical debate is that other voices are silenced or overlooked in the process. Arguably, this is largely due to a tendency in post-colonial studies to align the politics of nationalism with a politics of oppression. As Colin Graham has pointed out, within the post-colonial paradigm, nationalism is posited as always subaltern and never hegemonic (Graham, 2003). This rather neatly suppresses any claim to subalternity that any non-nationalists living in Ireland might have.[4]

Although this may provide some explanation as to why so few efforts have been made to retrieve these writers from the archives, it does not explain why so many of them slipped into obscurity in the first place. Reasons for this may be closely linked to contemporary expectations of what women could or should do. Andrea Ebel Brożyna's 1999 study of Ulster women's religious writing between 1850 and 1914 suggests that if women wanted to write at all during this time, it was generally assumed (and encouraged) to be in the cause of propagating Christian ideals of how a woman should behave. Such expectations of female behaviour were in turn related to Victorian perceptions of womanhood, whereby women were thought to be more inherently pious than men. Interestingly, far from being different, Brożyna asserts that Catholics and Protestants shared very similar ideas about womanhood. For both denominations, traditionally, motherhood has been extolled as a sacrificial duty, and "the home" sanctified as the place wherein women should perform this virtuous duty. Although these ideas about women's roles emanate from patriarchal religious institutions, Brożyna's findings show that such beliefs were disseminated and reinforced by women themselves. In fact, during the late nineteenth century, a war-of-words ensued between Catholic and Protestant religious women writers to see who could be the most pious.[5] In the context of Ulster, where religious divisions were deeply politicised, the audience for novels exploring alternative perspectives on female subjectivity seems to have been limited.

As Elaine Showalter has said of nineteenth-century British women, in strict evangelical circles, all imaginative literature was suspect, and children were taught that storytelling could lead to transgressions and untruths (Showalter, 1977: 55). Certainly novels such as F. E. Crichton's *Tinker's Hollow* (1912) imply that the reading of novels was still frowned upon in certain Ulster Presbyterian circles at the beginning of the twentieth century. In *Tinker's Hollow*, the leading character Sally Bruce finds a clergyman's wife reading a book and feels as though she "had unwillingly detected the minister's wife in crime" (Crichton, 1912: 123).

If the reading of novels was frowned upon, the writing of novels was certainly not deemed to be a suitable female occupation. In an autobiographical radio play broadcast as part of Sam Hanna Bell's "I remember . . ." series in the 1950s, Olga Fielden described the shocked reaction of her parents to the publication of a poem in a London magazine without their having read it first, a reaction which led to the clandestine publication of her first novel, *Island Story* (1933).[6] Similarly, Lord Dunsany's biographer, Mark Amory, notes that apart from securing her a publishing contract, not the least of Dunsany's efforts were channelled into persuading Anne Crone's family that writing was a worthy career (Amory, 1972).

Until relatively recently, fiction written by women has also been regarded as writing for the consumption of a predominantly female readership. It has also largely been assumed that such writing is purely romantic in style and content. Although novelists such as Alexander, Crone, Fielden and McNeill have dealt with heterosexual relationships in their novels, this has usually been with a means to criticising conservative, patriarchal politics that govern women's lives within this relationship. Far from being simplistic romance novels, these fictional studies of family dynamics are in fact critical commentaries on the closed and hierarchical nature of the communities which produced them.

Late Victorian and Christian attitudes towards women's roles are only part of the reason that so many of these authors have fallen by the wayside. A closer examination of Fielden's *Island Story* (1933) will help to tease out other factors. *Island Story* tells the tale of leading female character, Jane M'Cormick's life on the imaginary island of Rathnaheena off the north-east coast of Ireland. Contrary to the codes of behaviour laid down by Christian morality, Jane has three illegitimate children born to three different fathers after various trips to the Scottish and Irish mainland. No weak, passive, angel-in-the-house figure, Jane is both physically and mentally strong; at odds with conventional expectations of femininity, Jane strides rather than walks, is described as having the strength of a man, and often uses physical violence against her children in order to make herself understood.

Like the character Grania in Emily Lawless's novel *Grania: The Story of an Island* (1892), Jane is likened to the island which she inhabits. After the birth of her first child (when she is only sixteen), Jane's mother approaches the local minister and begs him to persuade her daughter to stay on Rathnaheena. The clergyman's efforts, however, are in vain; when he speaks to her, the minister realises that "Jane was as Rathnaheena herself, vital, full-blooded devastating. His bodily frailty winced before her overpowering energy, and his sensitive mind shrank back into its cloistered study, away from the crass unconscious brutality of her force and mental hardihood" (Fielden, 1933: 37). Likewise, in *Grania*, Lawless writes of Inishmaan: "She [Grania] was a part of it, and it was a part of her . . . This tall, red-petticoated, fiercely-handsome girl was decidedly a very isolated, and rather craggy and unapproachable sort of island" (Lawless, 1979: 104). Strong, independent and intimidating, both Protestant Jane and Catholic Grania are characters who are clearly at odds with established notions of femininity. On the contrary, as Cahalan (2000) has said of Lawless, both *Grania* and *Island Story* look forward to eco-feminist ideas, which see the repression of women as intrinsically linked to patriarchal oppression of the natural world.

If Jane and Grania are forces of nature, likened to the islands on which they live, the choices that they make during their lives are individual ones based on their own instincts. In *Island Story*, it is only when Jane enters into a conventional marriage during her latter years that the autonomy she enjoyed as a single parent begins to be eroded. As her husband bullies her children, and expects to become the head of the household in accordance with patriarchal assumptions about marriage, Jane becomes a second-class citizen in her own home. If there is a didactic message in this novel, it is not that women should conform to Christian social expectations but that they would do well to maintain financial and emotional independence and to resist the social pressures exerted by the outside world.

Stories of life on Irish islands were a popular phenomenon among Fielden's contemporaries. Liam O'Flaherty's *Skerret* (1923) and Peadar O'Donnell's *Islanders* (1928) are just two examples. By far the most influential island stories of the era, however, were the Blasket autobiographies, oral and written histories composed by the inhabitants of the Gaelic-speaking Blasket islands situated off the most south-westerly point of Ireland.

During the Irish revival at the turn of the twentieth century, the Irish Ireland movement[7]—spearheaded by cultural activists such as Douglas Hyde,[8] Eoin MacNeill,[9] D. P. Moran[10] and Daniel Corkery—had preached a doctrine of national distinctiveness, where the only authentic Irish national life was certainly Gaelic and possibly Catholic as well. As texts by Gaelic-speaking, Catholic islanders, the appearance of the Blasket autobiographies seemed to provide confirmation of the Irish Ireland movement's assessment that the primal source of the nation's being was rooted in an ancient Gaelic oral tradition, which British colonialism had displaced. Indeed, for the critic Declan Kiberd, the Blasket writers possess what he describes as the "beautiful reserve and considered manners of real aristocrats" (Kiberd, 2000: 521). This is a description reminiscent of Corkery's celebration of the Irish peasantry whom he regarded as "the descendants of greatness, and of a cultivated greatness who were intrinsically linked to the noble Gaelic society of the past whose job it was to maintain supremacy of the countryside over the city" (Corkery, quoted in Ferriter, 2004: 521).

Yet, significantly, according to the doctrine of the Irish Irelanders, no such noble peasantry was to be found in the north of Ireland. In his oft-quoted lecture, "The necessity for de-Anglicising Ireland", Hyde claimed that Ulster, more specifically Ulster Protestants, were the bane of Irish purity:

> In two points only was the continuity of the Irishism of Ireland damaged. First, in the north-east of Ulster, where the Gaelic race was expelled and the land planted with aliens, whom our dear mother Erin, assimilative as she is, has hitherto found it difficult to absorb, and in the ownership of the land, eight-ninths of which belongs to people many of whom always lived, or live abroad, and not half of whom Ireland can be said to have assimilated. (Hyde, 1974: 127).

Clearly, according to this version of cultural nationalism, Ulster Protestants were to be regarded as non-Irish "aliens"—whom even the most familiar trope of Irish nationhood—the sacrificial mother—was unable to integrate. Understood in the light of this prevailing cultural nationalist attitude towards the north of Ireland, neither Fielden nor her northern, Protestant, English-speaking, fictional islander would have any claim to Irish authenticity in the way that authors such as O'Flaherty or O'Donnnell would.[11] Despite the fact that many of O'Flaherty's novels are considered to be artistically flawed, due to their status as "authentic" Irish literature they have received a considerable degree of critical attention throughout the years. Similarly, although O'Donnell and Fielden shared the same English publisher, the former's Irish-speaking background and Republican sympathies may have helped to secure his works a place in the annals of Irish literary history, whilst the latter's have simply vanished.[12]

If cultural nationalism placed restrictions on who or what was to be deemed authentically Irish literature, unionist culture in Northern Ireland also curbed women's writing but in a different way. Rosemary Sales has noted that whether it is the picture of men in bowler hats marching on the Twelfth of July, the archetypical Protestant worker (a skilled, male manual worker), the harsh fundamentalist rhetoric of Ian Paisley or of the balaclava-hooded Loyalist paramilitaries, the imagery within the Protestant community, as well as the face presented to the outside world, is predominantly masculine (Sales, 1997: 144). This perceptible gendering of unionism has been the result not only of a

conscious desire among some members of the unionist community to separate themselves from the feminised perceptions of Ireland previously
outlined in Hyde's description of "dear mother Erin", but has also
evolved as a consequence of the many complex layers of overlapping
patriarchal structures at work within church and family life.[13] If, as Edna
Longley has argued, the characterisation of Irish nationalism as arche-
typically female both "gives it mythic pedigree and exonerates it from
aggressive and oppressive intent" (Longley, 1990: 18) then the masculine
façade of unionism, veering as it does between militancy, paternalism and
pseudo-imperialism has had the opposite effect. Thus, Fielden's tale of a
woman's struggle for survival on an island ravaged not only by the
weather, but by economic hardship and patriarchal mores may have been
too potentially subversive for conservative unionist tastes in the 1930s.
Considering the tendency, especially in Anglo-Irish literature, to encode
political issues in gendered tropes of nationhood, despite removing her
character to an isolated imaginary island, there was always the chance
that *Island Story* could be read as an allegory of the struggle for Irish
independence. Not Irish enough according to the dictates of cultural
nationalism, potentially too Irish or at least too concerned with women's
issues within an Ulster unionist context, novels such as *Island Story* seem
to have made little impact on the Irish or Ulster literary scene.

## Conclusion

This chapter has highlighted the absence of Ulster Protestant women
from the annals of Irish/Ulster literary history. This has not been because
Ulster Protestant women writers did not exist. On the contrary, as the list
of names testifies, non-ascendancy women made up a considerable
portion of Ireland's literary output between 1900 and 1965. The reasons
for this literary hiatus include common assumptions about women's roles
and female reading habits; the growing strength of cultural nationalism,
including the ways in which tropes of nationhood were constructed as
female; the masculine structure of unionist culture in the North and necessary policing of female agency in order to preserve the traditional order
of the community. The predominance of post-colonial theory as well as
a tendency to maintain simple binary paradigms when discussing culture
in the North of Ireland, based on oversimplified versions of Catholicism
and Protestantism may have discouraged critics from retrieving these lost
voices from the archives. This chapter by no means proposes that these
are the only reasons for this cultural hiatus. If anything, the fact that
rather more questions than answers are raised here highlights the amount
of work that remains to be done on this subject.

Janet Madden-Simpson (1984) has already made the claim that Corkery's phrase, "the Hidden Ireland"—meaning Gaelic Ireland—could just as well be applied to Irish women writers. Referring to the Irish Republic, Gerald Dawe and Edna Longley (1985) have also argued that Corkery's phrase now has more cause to be applied to Irish Protestants. Taking the two together and making a geographical inflection towards the North it could be suggested that Ulster Protestant women writers have a special and complicated claim of their own to be the lost voices of hidden Ireland.

## Notes

1 Beatrice Grimshaw converted to Catholicism later in life.
2 Certainly Alexander, Crichton, Crone and Waring had unionist sympathies which are readily discernible from their texts. Fielden's father had a minor involvement with the UVF gun-running at Larne, which suggests a unionist background; St John Ervine's correspondence with White suggests strong affinities and sympathies with Ulster Protestants in particular.
3 Some of the acknowledged sources that were consulted during this research were: Stephen J. Brown, *A Guide to Books on Ireland: Prose, Literature, Poetry, Plays* (Dublin and London: Hodges Figgis and Longmans Green, 1912), Stephen J. Brown, *Ireland in Fiction: A Guide to Irish Novels, Tales, Romances and Folklore* (Shannon: Irish University Press, 1969) reissued by Royal Carbery in 1985; Anne M. Brady and Brian Cleeve (eds) *A Biographical Dictionary of Irish Writers* (Mullingar: Lilliput Press, 1985); Robert Welch and Bruce Stewart (eds) *The Oxford Companion to Irish Literature* (Oxford: Oxford University Press, 1996); Kate Newmann, *Dictionary of Ulster Biography* (Belfast: Queen's University of Belfast, Institute of Irish Studies, 1993); Ann Owens Weekes, *Unveiling Treasures: The Attic Guide to the Published Works of Irish Literary Women Writers* (Dublin: Attic Press, 1993), EIRDATA www.ricorso.org. Of the sources contained in this list, only EIRDATA and Kate Newmann's work contained an entry for Eleanor Alexander: F. E. Crichton's name was only quoted in one source. Anne Crone's name appeared in the first series of the *Dictionary of Irish Writers* but not in the second. It is the inconsistent and unreliable cataloguing of these women writers that I wish to draw attention to.
4 The suspected fusion between post-colonialism and nationalism has been commented on by several revisionist critics. See Edna Longley (1994) *The Living Stream: Literature and Revisionism in Ireland* and J. W. Foster (1991) *Colonial Consequences: Essays in Irish Literature and Culture*.
5 Brozyna's study surveys religious newspapers, pamphlets and periodicals that were in circulation in Ulster.
6 Queen's University, Belfast, Olga Fielden papers MS 25/11. In this play the narrator who was played by Fielden herself, also asks, "Why shouldn't boys do the same things as girls? That was a problem which puzzled me sorely."

7  "Irish Ireland" is used here as a generic term for cultural nationalism.
8  Douglas Hyde was the first President of Ireland and co-founder of the Gaelic League.
9  Eoin McNeill was the first Minister for Education in the Irish Free State, and co-founder of the Gaelic League.
10  D. P. Moran was editor of *The Leader* newspaper.
11  Namely as Irish-speaking Catholics from, and whose fiction was largely set in, the west coast of Ireland.
12  There is also a counter-argument that O'Donnell was a more prolific writer. However, newspaper archives demonstrate that Fielden enjoyed a degree of notoriety throughout Ireland during her writing career. My point is that whereas a writer such as O'Donnell now forms part of the canon of Irish literature, Fielden's name and excellent novel *Island Story* have slipped into obscurity despite her contemporary success.
13  The sacrifice made by many soldiers from Ulster during the Somme has also helped to strengthen unionist links with Britain that are based on an experience and a willingness to unite in combat.

## References

Amory, M. (1972) *Lord Dunsany: A Biography* (London: Collins).

Boland, E. (1993) "Continuing the encounter", in E. Walshe (ed.) *Ordinary People Dancing: Essays on Kate O'Brien* (Cork: Cork University Press), pp. 15–23.

Brozyna, A. E. (1999) *Labour, Love and Prayer: Female Piety in Ulster Religious Literature, 1850–1914* (Belfast and Montreal: McGill-Queen's University Press and Queen's University Institute of Irish Studies).

Cahalan, J. M. (1988) *The Irish Novel: A Critical History* (Dublin: Gill & Macmillan).

Cahalan, J. M. (2000) "Forging a tradition: Emily Lawless and the Irish literary canon", in K. Fitzpatrick (ed.) *Border Crossings: Irish Women Writers and National Identities* (Dublin: Wolfhound Press), pp. 38–57.

Connolly, L. (2004) "The limits of 'Irish studies': historicism, culturalism, paternalism", *Irish Studies Review* 12.2: 139–62.

Corkery, D. (1931) *Synge and Anglo-Irish Literature* (Cork: Cork University Press).

Crichton, F. E. (1912) *Tinker's Hollow* (London: Edward Arnold).

Dawe, G. and Longley, E. (eds) (1985) *Across the Roaring Hill: The Protestant Imagination in Modern Ireland* (Belfast: Blackstaff).

Ferriter, D. (2004) The Transformation of Ireland, 1900–2000 (London: Profile).

Fielden, O. (1933) *Island Story* (London: Jonathan Cape).

Foster, J. W. (2006) "The Irish Renaissance, 1890–1940: prose in English", in M. Kelleher and P. O'Leary (eds) *The Cambridge History of Irish Literature, Volume II 1890–2000* (Cambridge: Cambridge University Press), pp. 113–80.

Foster, J. W. (1991) *Colonial Consequences: Essays in Irish Literature and Culture* (Dublin: Lilliput).

Graham, C. (2003) "Subalternity and gender: problems of post-colonial Irishness", in C. Connolly (ed.) *Readers in Cultural Criticism: Theorising Ireland* (Basingstoke: Palgrave), pp. 150–9.

Hyde, D. (1973 [1894]) "The necessity for de-Anglicising Ireland", in *The Revival of Irish Literature: Addresses by Sir Charles Gavin Duffy, Dr George Sigerson and Dr Douglas Hyde* (New York: Lemington) (First published Dublin: T. F. Unwin).

Kiberd, D. (2000) *Irish Classics* (London: Granta).

Lawless, E. (1979 [1892]) *Grania: The Story of an Island* (London: Garland).

Longley, E. (1990) *From Kathleen to Anorexia: the Breakdown of Irelands* (Dublin: Attic Press).

Longley, E. (1994) *The Living Stream: Literature and Revisionism in Ireland* (Dublin: Bloodaxe).

Madden-Simpson, J. (1984) "Anglo-Irish literature: the received tradition". Introduction to *Women's Part: An Anthology of Short Fiction by and about Irish Women 1890–1920* (Dublin: Arlen House, 1984), pp. 1–19.

Meaney, G. (1991) *Sex and the Nation: Women in Irish Culture and Politics* (Dublin: Attic Press).

Murphy, J. H. (2000) " 'Things which seem to you unfeminine': gender and nationalism in the fiction of some upper middle class Catholic women novelists, 1880–1910", in K. Kirkpatrick (ed.) *Border Crossings: Irish Women Writers and National Identities* (Dublin: Wolfhound Press), pp. 58–78.

Sales, R. (1997) "Gender and Protestantism in Northern Ireland", in P. Shirlow and M. McGovern (eds) *Who are 'The People'? Unionism, Protestantism and Loyalism in Northern Ireland* (London: Pluto Press), pp. 140–57.

Showalter, E. (1977) *A Literature Of Their Own: British Women Novelists from Brontë to Lessing* (Princeton: Princeton University Press).

Wydenbach, J. S. (2004) "Women's writing in early twentieth-century Ireland". Paper presented to the New Voices conference, University of Ulster (February).

# Part IV
# Religion and identity

# 10

# Visible differences: the 1859 revival and sectarianism in Belfast

## Mark Doyle

### Introduction

It was a hot day in Belfast, on 29 June 1859. A few cynics would later mutter that it was the summer heat—and not some divine visitation—that produced the tremendous scenes of religious ecstasy that day, but true believers knew better. The place was the Botanic Gardens, a rare patch of green amidst the bustle and whirr of the dusty city, and the occasion was an unprecedented public prayer meeting hosted by ministers from each of Belfast's Protestant denominations. That morning, as dozens of Methodist, Baptist, Presbyterian and Anglican clergymen jostled each other on the wooden platform, at least 10,000 people (and possibly as many as 40,000) swarmed into the Botanic Gardens hoping to catch the "revival spirit" that had been sweeping through Ulster for the past two months. Some of the younger congregants climbed trees to get a better view; most, unable to hear the addresses on the platform, formed their own small groups on the grass. There they sang, preached, and prayed with one another, sharing the stories of their own "conversions" or pleading with the Holy Spirit to come down and absolve them, too, of their sins. Soon the cries of hundreds of sinners pierced the air, and many, overcome by the heat or the presence of the divine, collapsed to the ground, soon to be carried home to recover among family and friends. The scene, said one sympathetic reporter, resembled a Methodist camp meeting in America.[1] Another, even more enthusiastic observer, declared that the whole affair recalled no less than the seventeenth-century signing of the Solemn League and Covenant.[2]

The great Botanic Gardens prayer meeting was by no means the only public display of religious fervour in Belfast that summer. The Ulster Revival of 1859, as it has since become known, swept into Belfast with such force that the churches and meeting halls simply failed to contain the throngs clamouring for salvation. Vacant lots, public thoroughfares, even the textile mills and shipyards were pressed into service for weeks on end to accommodate this: the last great grass-roots revival in Ulster's history. Many historians have recognised the importance of 1859 in forging a distinctive Ulster Protestant identity. Working-class Protestants, they observe, emerged from the revival strengthened and emboldened, convinced of the divine favour with which their people were blessed and fired with an evangelical zeal that eventually found its way into the political ideology of Ulster Unionism (Hempton and Hill, 1992; Gibbon, 1975; Holmes, 2000).

But the 1859 revival was something else as well, and the exciting scenes in the Botanic Gardens hint at what that something else was: for revivalists and non-revivalists alike, the revival was a uniquely visible event. Prayer meetings, workplace "conversions", and other displays of evangelical fervour consumed the public spaces of Belfast that summer, sparking interest even among those who would never dream of attending a revival meeting themselves. The impact of these public displays spread well beyond the closed circle of revival participants, drawing responses from suspicious Protestant ministers, stolid middle-class industrialists and, not least, the city's growing number of Catholics. More than just a communal event, the 1859 revival was, in an important sense, a public event whose effects rippled through the whole of Belfast society.

In what follows, I argue that the 1859 revival was not merely a stepping stone in the construction of an Ulster Protestant identity, although it certainly was that. Just as importantly, the revival embodied and in many ways accelerated the processes of sectarian polarisation that were already under way in mid-Victorian Belfast. A few scholars have speculated that the revival may have had some such polarising effect, but how and why it should have done so has so far remained unclear (Hempton and Hill, 1992; Hirst, 2002; Wright, 1996). Part of the answer, I suggest, lies in the visible nature of the revival: in acting out their faith through public prayer meetings, demonstrations, and striking displays of "conversion", working-class revivalists performed their identities before themselves as well as others. In so doing, they inadvertently marked out one community from the other, highlighting not only the religious differences between Protestants and Catholics, but also the vastly different political and social positions of the two groups. During the revival, Belfast Protestants appeared bold and self-confident, asserting control over the city's contested geography and laying claim, physically as well as symbolically, to a central place in Belfast's urban culture. The response of Belfast Catholics, on the other hand, bespoke a deep demoralisation and vulnerability that served, in the long run, to strengthen the position of that community's most extreme elements. Before describing the revival's polarising effects, however, it is useful first to say something about the sort of place Belfast was in the summer of 1859.

### Belfast at mid-century

Mid-Victorian Belfast was a city in the process of inventing itself. Massive industrial expansion, driven by the mechanisation of the linen industry, was bringing tremendous wealth as well as tremendous difficulties to the city, much as it had to English and Scottish cities a generation earlier. As grand new buildings sprouted in the centre of town and along the busy riverbank, developers threw up ramshackle tenements in the city's western suburbs alongside hulking factories and polluted streams. Thousands of migrants, most of them from rural Ulster, made their way into these suburbs, pulled by the mills' decent wages and pushed by the collapse of the rural weaving economy. Overcrowding, disease, prostitution, casual violence—all the standard industrial-era ills intensified in Belfast during this decade, causing concern among middle-class inhabitants and calling forth a host of reforming societies designed to rescue the lower classes from their moral degradation. Most of these bodies were Protestant evangelical in persuasion and, as new churches, charities and domestic missions took root, the city acquired a formidable evangelical infrastructure that would serve as a vital conduit for the energies unleashed by the 1859 revival.

The other striking thing about mid-Victorian Belfast, apart from its rapid industrial expansion, was its increasingly severe sectarian violence. At least four times during this decade west Belfast shook with violence, usually for days on end and sometimes for weeks, and even months. One of the reasons for this surge in violence had to do with the city's patterns of migration. Drawn largely from the sectarian battlegrounds of rural Antrim, Down and Armagh, the workers who arrived in neighbourhoods like Sandy Row (home to working-class Protestants) and the Pound (home to working-class Catholics) brought with them a deeply engrained culture of violence that the conditions of urban life did little to erase (Farrell, 2000). The arrival of tens of thousands of Catholics during these years was particularly destabilising: long a self-consciously Protestant city, Belfast proved immensely inhospitable to Catholic migrants, most of whom clustered at the bottom of the city's economic and social ladder (Hepburn, 1996). A volatile political climate exacerbated local tensions. An increasingly assertive Catholic Church, led by Pope Pius IX in Rome, and Paul Cullen in Dublin, had in recent years triggered an anti-Catholic backlash among Belfast evangelicals, whose fire-breathing denunciations of "popery" frequently degenerated into violence. Belfast's most sustained period of rioting before the revival had occurred in 1857, when a string of Protestant demonstrations sparked street fights and home wreckings, which persisted for the better part of two months. These riots were minor compared to the titanic battles that engulfed the city in later decades, but they laid the groundwork for a tradition of violence that would persist well into the next century.[3]

## The revival and the Protestants

The flowering of an intense religious awakening under such circumstances was bound to have a profound effect on the city's emerging communal identities. This was particularly true given the boisterous, grass-roots character of the 1859 revival. Since its emergence in rural Antrim that spring, the revival had been propelled largely by lower-class Protestants who, having been overcome with the "revival spirit", sought to share their experiences with others through prayer meetings and other, less formal gatherings. The crucial moment during many of these meetings came with the so-called "strikings down"—emotional scenes in which worshippers cried out, fainted, or experienced religious visions which, they believed, came directly from the Holy Spirit. Many of Ulster's more sober churchmen dismissed the "strikings down" as disgraceful displays of ignorance and fanaticism, mere "enthusiasm" where there should have been religious knowledge and understanding.[4] For poor farmers and workers, however, the prospect of witnessing and possibly experiencing such heavenly visitations was difficult to resist, and lay-organised prayer meetings formed seemingly overnight across much of north-east Ulster. "It cannot be denied", remarked one Newry minister scornfully, "that, in some instances at least, the great attraction was a morbid desire of seeing physical manifestations—the smiting down of converts. Wherever this was anticipated, the multitudes flocked together."[5]

In Belfast, where large numbers of working-class people attended no church at all, the public nature of the revival was especially pronounced. Episodes of young women being "stricken" while sitting at home, walking down the street, or working in the textile mills were common. At one mill, some twenty female workers were "stricken" simultaneously before being carted away by sympathetic co-workers. At other mills, such as that belonging to Belfast mayor William Ewart, women established regular prayer meetings to sing, pray and, on occasion, receive visitations from the Holy Spirit. Other public prayer meetings, organised and attended solely by female converts, sprouted up in places like the Shankill Road, while on the Queen's Island the men of the shipyards and foundries held their own weekly revival meetings at dinner time. Often evangelical ministers were called upon to attend to the "stricken" at such meetings, but for the most part these scenes took place well outside churches and meeting houses.[6]

One of the most important revival centres was the working-class Protestant neighbourhood of Sandy Row, a place better known for its sectarian brawlers than for its evangelical zeal. "There", reported the *Belfast Weekly News*, ". . . the subject of religion engrosses the conversation, and after the labours of the day the people gather out into the streets to hear the Word of God read and expounded."[7] For the past several summers, Sandy Row had been at the centre of Belfast's most violent sectarian battles, its mill workers and artisans building up an intense rivalry with the Catholics of the nearby Pound that often took the form of massive street fights and frenzied bursts of residential purging. Now, in the same spots where they had formerly gathered to wage communal offensives or to fend off invasions, the people of Sandy Row joined one another in boisterous prayer meetings that, so one scandalised observer complained, continued until a very "late hour".[8] There was, these penitents knew, more than one way to act out one's Protestantism.

Another prominent revival spot was the new Custom House, and here, too, the sectarian associations were strong. In the summer of 1857, just months after it had been unveiled, the Custom House had found itself at the centre of a raging controversy between Protestants and Catholics over the practice of open-air preaching. A series of evangelical religious services held on the Custom House steps had escalated into violence in late August as Catholics, outraged at what they took to be a calculated insult to their religion, interrupted the preachers and assaulted their audiences. The conflict had come to a head on 6 September, when Hugh Hanna, an up-and-coming Presbyterian minister, held a service at nearby Corporation Square that set off a week of brawling, home wrecking, and assaults on police and property (Holmes, 2002). Now, in 1859, the Custom House again became the scene of evangelical demonstrations, as veteran preachers such as John Mateer (who had been attacked during the 1857 riots) led hundreds of worshippers in prayer services.[9] No violence accompanied these services, but the presence of great crowds of revivalists at this most resonant of sectarian landmarks served, in effect, to reclaim a vital piece of the city's contested geography for the Protestant people.[10]

Such scenes provoked intense discussion all over town. One observer remembered how "conversation upon religious topics was frequent everywhere—on steamboat, by rail, in the market-place, travelling by the road".[11] The *Banner of Ulster*, an organ of the Irish Presbyterian church, was unequivocal: "'The Revivals', to whatever side we turn, are the standing and universal topic of discussion."[12] Not all Protestants were so enthusiastic, however. One hostile Anglican minister likened the revival's public demonstrations to the monster meetings of the Repeal era, suggesting there was a whiff of the same "display, inducement, and menace" that the Repealers had employed. "Opposition to this movement was to be intimidated . . . At first, any one who ventured to say a word against the manifestations, the morbid excitement, or any other part of this movement was very freely and charitably described as an infidel."[13]

Reading through these sources, it is tempting to draw parallels between revivalism and other public displays of working-class Protantism, particularly Orangeism. Just as an Orange march relies for its meaning on visible signs of inclusion and exclusion—the flags, banners and regalia working together with the music to draw a line around those who are outside and those who are inside (Bryan, 2000; Jarman, 1997)—so, too, did the revival erect barriers between those who were saved and those who were not. Also like an Orange march, the revival allowed Protestants to display their Protestantism in public, to make the city's streets, public buildings and parks into venues for the demonstration of their people's special place in the eyes of God. At a time when Orange marches themselves were illegal (under the provisions of the Party Processions Act of 1850) and communal contests for control of urban space were intensifying, the revival acted as an alternative way for working-class Protestants to act out their identities and to do so in a way that emphasised the intimate relationship between Protestantism and the city itself.

It is possible to push this point too far, however, and I certainly do not mean to suggest that the revival was simply Orangeism by another name. If nothing else, the prominence of women in the revival should tell us that something subtly different was going on. In her study of female evangelicals in Leeds, Deborah Valenze has argued that revivalism was a way for working-class women to carve out spaces for themselves within the disorienting clamour of the industrial city, a way to resist the demands of middle-class "industrial religion", and to preserve something of the religious culture of the village (Valenze, 1985). In Belfast, where most of the revivalists had their origins in the countryside, a similar act of resistance seems to have taken place. Particularly for women, who were barred from the Orange Order and excluded from other male fraternal networks, the revival helped overcome the fractured and anonymous nature of industrial life restoring, for a time, a rural sort of religion that emphasised community, nurturing and direct communion with God. Just as the revival allowed working-class Protestants to perform their identities in a new and public way, so too did it help insulate Protestant women, in particular, from the disorientation and regimentation of urban life. At the most basic level, the revival helped make one's fellow Protestants visible again. As if in literal illustration of this idea, one scandalised observer reported that female converts were painting the words "Jesus Christ" on their breasts and claiming that it had come to them while under the spell of the revival.[14] The effect of all this was to bolster the confidence of working-class Protestant women at a time when such bolstering was badly needed, and to broaden as well as deepen the definition of what it meant to be a Protestant.

### Catholic responses

What, then, of the Catholics? If the revival had an essentially cohesive effect on working-class Protestants, what effect, if any, did it have on their communal rivals? The first thing to note is that many working-class Catholics would have found the revival quite difficult to ignore. Because the principal scenes of the revival were public spaces, and not indoor places like churches and lecture halls, many Catholics who had not previously encountered evangelical forms of worship would have done so in 1859 for the first time. Catholics living and working in mixed environments (and there were many more of these in 1859 than there would be in later years)[15] were especially likely to come into contact with the revival. Significantly, one of the most important revival centres was Hugh Hanna's Berry Street Presbyterian meeting house, a building that was a mere stone's throw from St Mary's Catholic Church, the main church of working-class Catholics. Hanna was already notorious among Catholics as an evangelical agitator and energetic proselytiser, and so the large crowds of anxious Protestants thronging his church that summer must have raised more than one Catholic eyebrow. Indeed, on at least one occasion the police were called to the area when the crowds of Protestants overflowed Hanna's church and spilled into the surrounding streets. The crowds dispersed peaceably, but it was clear that some magistrates, at least, recognised the potential for violence that such episodes carried.[16]

Unfortunately, there are very few Catholic sources directly conveying that group's response to the revival, and none at all from working-class Catholics themselves. Instead, we are left to rely on the revival stories told by evangelicals, in which Catholics play a substantial, if possibly exaggerated, role. If approached with sufficient caution, however, these sources paint a compelling picture of a community simultaneously intrigued and threatened by the strange occurrences sweeping through the city. One of the most persistent themes in the evangelical revival literature concerns working-class Catholics, usually women, who attended revival meetings and, convinced of the error of their faith, converted on the spot. One newly-converted Catholic woman, for instance, reportedly refused to kiss a crucifix offered her by a priest after attending a revival meeting. Another was said to have persuaded her father, mother and two brothers to convert along with her. A third reportedly cried out "No Virgin for me!" after her conversion at a revival meeting.[17]

It was not just individual Catholics who reportedly became swept up in the revival, however. In early June, the *Banner* reported that in the Catholic Pound neighbourhood, "the sounds of praise and prayer are now to be heard, evening after evening . . . from the hour when the din of the factory ceases until late in the night". According to a gentleman who was "well acquainted with the district", there had been some 60 conversions in the Pound, and at least half of the people of the neighbourhood could be heard singing and praying in their homes. These events, beamed the *Banner*, were "probably more remarkable than any other which we have had to notice".[18] The following week, the newspaper reported that a total of 140 conversions had taken place in the Pound, as a result of which the "character of the locality" had been greatly improved.[19]

Balanced against these exuberant tales of widespread Catholic conversions were a substantial number of stories of Catholic hostility to the revival. In fact, the two types of stories were often related, for the most frequent cause of anti-revival behaviour among Catholics, in these sources, was the anger of some Catholics at the conversions of their co-religionists. Thus, for instance, the *Banner* told of one Catholic convert who was placed under constabulary protection after her home was invaded by three Catholic men who abused her and "soiled" her Bible.[20] Another observer told of priests "distributing holy water, consecrated medals, and bottles of some medicinal preparation" to protect Catholics from the revival.[21]

While most Catholic anti-revival behaviour was directed against other Catholics, there were also reports of violence against evangelical ministers and other revivalists. Hanna complained to a friend in London, "I cannot traverse any of the streets without encountering insults, which evince the desperate demoralization of Belfast papacy. I believe it never was so bad."[22] The *Banner* alleged that revivalists in some city mills were enduring harassment from Catholic overseers and co-workers, and it told several stories of Protestant laymen and ministers coming under attack in Catholic areas. "We can point to localities", reported the paper, "to visit which is as much as a Protestant missionary's life is worth."[23]

Two important assumptions appear to be at work in these evangelical revival stories. The first has to do with the evangelicals' own understanding of the revival and of the place of Catholics in it. One of the most prominent strands of evangelical anti-Catholicism at this time was what John Brewer has called "pharisaic" anti-Catholicism, or that which seeks to engage Catholics in order to convert them (Brewer and Higgins, 1998). In this respect, the presence of Hugh Hanna at the centre of these stories is telling. Since arriving in Belfast in 1852, Hanna had undertaken energetic proselytising campaigns among working-class Catholics, leading "controversialist" lectures, at which he exposed the errors of Catholic doctrine, and hosting informal discussions between his Protestant congregants and the Catholics of the neighbourhood. For proselytisers such as Hanna, the revival was a heaven-sent opportunity to carry forward this campaign by attracting young, impressionable Catholics to revival services. "Roman Catholics are overtaken in the mercy of God, and God's grace proves itself stronger than controversy in the pulling down of strongholds", exulted Hanna to his London friend.[24]

A second, closely related assumption shaping these evangelical revival narratives was the expectation that some Catholics, especially priests and other "zealots", would oppose evangelicals' efforts to preach among poor Catholics. For many evangelicals, such "persecution" only helped to confirm the righteousness of their cause, solidifying a sense of embattlement that was deeply rooted in the Ulster Protestant identity. Hanna had expressed this idea succinctly a few years earlier when he explained to a parliamentary inquiry, "Our most valuable rights have been obtained by conflict, and if we cannot maintain them without that, we must submit to the necessity."[25] Given such attitudes, it is hardly surprising that the evangelical sources tended to stress Catholic opposition to the revival, as well as the success of some revivalists at winning Catholic converts.

All the same, these evangelical revival narratives probably contained some considerable truth. It seems likely that many poor Catholics were attracted to the exciting public displays of the revival and this, in turn, must surely have caused consternation among many other segments of the Catholic community. To understand why this would have been so, it is necessary to understand something crucial about Belfast Catholicism in the 1850s: that is, whatever the difficulties of industrial life for working-class Protestants, these challenges were magnified immensely for Belfast's Catholics. Shut out of political power, confined largely to the unskilled sectors of the textile industry, and frequently subjected to the angry tirades of highly placed anti-Catholic agitators, Catholics occupied an extremely precarious position at this time (Hepburn, 1996). The Catholic hierarchy, led by a strangely timid Bishop Cornelius Denvir, was hardly able to provide enough priests for the thousands of poor Catholics under its charge; much less could it mount any coordinated offensive against an evangelical revival (Macaulay, 1987). Nor could the tiny Catholic middle classes, struggling to achieve a measure of bourgeois respectability among their Protestant peers, muster enough influence among the lower classes to keep them from attending revival meetings. Abandoned by their own communal leaders and often unable to attend church themselves, many Catholics must have been attracted by the confidence and self-assuredness of the revival. Frank Wright, though conceding that Catholic conversions during the revival were probably rare, has speculated that "more [Catholics] were converted by this experience than by every effort at overt proselytization conducted before or since" (Wright, 1996: 232). This assessment seems broadly correct, and it suggests that, for some poor Catholics at least, sharp communal lines between the two religions were not yet fully drawn.

At the same time, the attraction of some Catholics to the revival helps to explain why other Catholics were hostile to it. Sheridan Gilley has noted that priests in London often acted as communal policemen to protect Irish Catholic immigrants from Protestant proselytism (Gilley, 1971). The handful of overworked priests in Belfast seem to have acted in a similar manner, but they were far too few to mount a coordinated counter-offensive in the Catholic neighbourhoods. Accordingly, many lay Catholics also adopted the role of communal policeman, responding rather more aggressively than their clerical counterparts to Protestant "aggression". The usual pattern, according to the evangelical sources, involved gangs of men intervening to "rescue" Catholic women from the revivalists.

Male vigilantism of this sort was not uncommon in Catholic Belfast: many of the city's riots were initiated, in part, by a sectarian hard core of Catholic men who attacked Protestant demonstrations that they deemed insulting, and they often did so in the name of defending Catholic women.[26] Such vigilantism was an endemic part of working-class Catholic life in mid-Victorian Belfast, a by-product of the inability of the Catholic clergy and middle classes to look after the interests of Catholic workers. In trying to prevent or reverse the conversion of Catholic women, these Catholic men were enforcing a strict code of behaviour and ensuring that communal boundaries remained rigid. That they felt the need to do so bespoke a deep demoralisation, born of vulnerability, among the Catholics of Belfast that stood in stark and telling contrast to the blustery self-confidence of the Protestant revivalists.

## Conclusion

Given the revival's tendency to highlight the differences between Protestants and Catholics, one might expect that communal violence became more frequent that summer. The truth is a little more complex. Nearly everyone in Belfast during the revival agreed that the summer of 1859 was the most peaceful in recent memory. The Anglican minister Charles Seaver, writing of the usually tense period surrounding the Twelfth of July, noted that "this year there was the greatest quietness and peace—no drunkenness, no party rioting, no quarrelling".[27] The *Belfast Morning News*, the city's sole Catholic newspaper, offered a similar assessment: "Mechanics and mill-workers of different persuasions, who in past years, during the entire month of July, seldom addressed each other except in terms of insult or provocation, pass along promiscuously to or from their work, chatting together as friends and acquaintances."[28] The revival, for all of its sectarian overtones, seemed to be having a most beneficial effect on the communal harmony of the city.

Or so many believed. At the time and in the years to come, the notion that the revival was responsible for cooling sectarian tensions became an essential part of how evangelicals, in particular, understood the event. For many revivalists, the absence of drunkenness, crime and rioting in 1859 was proof that the movement truly had been a divine event, and it demonstrated the great moral improvement that could come to the lower classes through a true knowledge of the Gospel.[29] Such claims, however, are dubious. County Antrim, the seat of the revival, actually saw a slight rise in the number of arrests for drunkenness between 1858 and 1859, and the number of convictions at Petty Sessions rose considerably.[30] It is true that the summer of 1859 saw little sectarian rioting, but the more likely explanation had to do with the large number of constables brought into the city to keep the peace around the Twelfth, as well as a certain exhaustion among the people of west Belfast after two intense summers of rioting in 1857 and 1858.

Whatever its cause, the lull in sectarian hostilities did not last long. The next major eruption came just a few years later, following an evangelical demonstration in the Botanic Gardens in 1862 and, after this, sectarian rioting continued to escalate through to the end of the century. In the long run, it seems, the most lasting legacy of the revival was not the momentary pause in sectarian violence it brought about, but the intensification and solidification of a sense of communal difference. In a society in which one normally could not distinguish one's communal rivals simply by looking, the revival served the important function of marking out one community from another. For this reason, the visible nature of the revival was crucial, for it allowed Catholics as well as Protestants to get a glimpse of what went on when evangelical Protestants communed with God. Among the Protestants, the net result was to strengthen communal cohesion by overcoming the anonymising effects of the city and also to reinforce Protestants' strong identification with the contested spaces of the city itself.

Among the Catholics, meanwhile, the revival promoted dissension, preying upon fears of evangelical aggression and giving strength to the hand of the most violent elements in the Catholic neighbourhoods. For many Catholics, whose only knowledge about the revival came from observing the movement at its most demonstrative and unusual, the idea that there were truly deep religious differences between them and the Protestants would also have been difficult to shake. For both groups, the revival solidified prejudices by publicly demonstrating differences, and in so doing it accelerated the communal polarisation that was driving Belfast's working-class people into two mutually suspicious camps

## Notes

1  *Belfast Newsletter* (30 June 1859).
2  *Banner of Ulster* (30 June 1859).
3  Mark Doyle, "Fighting like the Devil for the sake of God: Protestants, Catholics, and the origins of violence in Belfast, 1850–1865" (PhD dissertation, Boston College, 2006).
4  See, e.g., Isaac Nelson, *The Year of Delusion: A review of "The Year of Grace"*, third edition (Belfast, *The Advertiser* Office, 1861–66).
5  Francis King, *An Impartial View of the Revival in Ireland*, 3rd edn (Newry: James Burns, 1859), pp. 18–19.
6  *Banner of Ulster* (9 June and 9 July 1859); William Gibson, *The Year of Grace: A History of the Ulster Revival of 1859*, 2nd edn (Edinburgh: Oliphant, Anderson & Ferrier, 1909), p. 80.
7  *Belfast Weekly News* (2 July 1859).
8  Letter from Robert Workman, *Banner of Ulster* (5 July 1859).
9  *Banner of Ulster* (21 June 1859).
10 Stewart notes that, in later years, the Custom House became a regular platform for evangelical speakers, "Belfast's version of Speaker's Corner", A. T. Q. Stewart, *The Narrow Ground: Aspects of Ulster, 1609–1969* (Belfast: The Blackstaff Press, 1997), p. 146.
11 D. McMeekin, *Memories of '59* (Hull: M. Harland & Son, 1908), pp. 92–3.
12 *Banner of Ulster* (9 June 1859).
13 Richard Oulton, *A Review of the Ulster Revival in the Year 1859* (Dublin: Hodges, Smith, & Co., 1859), pp. 54–5.
14 Public Record Office of Northern Ireland D/1792/A2/1. J. B. Armour to John Megaw, 14 September 1859.

15 In the textile mills, for instance, the numerous reports of Protestant intimidation of Catholic workers during the riots of 1864 suggest that many mills were still communally heterogeneous before this date. See, e.g., the *Ulster Observer* (20 August 1864). A similar inference, drawn from reports of communal purging during the riots of 1864 and 1872, may be made about patterns of residential segregation in the 1850s.
16 *Banner of Ulster* (4 June 1859).
17 *Ibid.* (9 June, 18 June and 5 July 1859).
18 *Ibid.* (7 June 1859).
19 *Ibid.* (15 June 1859).
20 *Ibid.* (21 June 1859).
21 Quoted in George Salmon, *The Evidences of the Work of the Holy Spirit*, second edition, (Dublin: Hodges, Smith, & Co., 1859), p. 46.
22 Quoted in John Weir, *The Ulster Awakening: Its Origin, Progress, and Fruit.* (London: Arthur Hall, Virtue, & Co., 1860), pp. 123–4.
23 *Banner of Ulster* (21 June 1859).
24 Quoted in Weir, *Ulster Awakening*, 43.
25 Hugh Hanna's evidence, *Report of the Commissioners of Inquiry into the Origin and Character of the Riots in Belfast, in July and September, 1857; together with Minutes of Evidence and Appendix.* HC 1857–58 (2309) XXVI, 167.
26 See, e.g., the *Ulster Observer* (16 August 1864).
27 Quoted in Scott, *Revival in Ulster*, pp. 49–50.
28 *Belfast Morning News* (15 July 1859).
29 See, e.g., Gibson, *Year of Grace*, pp. 252–4.
30 *Tables showing the Number of Persons Committed or Held to Bail for Trial at the Assizes and Quarter Sessions in each County, in the Year 1859, and the Result of the Proceedings; with other Particulars.* H.C. 1860 (723) LVII, xxi.

## References

Brewer, J. and Higgins, G. (1998) *Anticatholicism in Northern Ireland, 1600–1998: The Mote and the Beam* (London: Macmillan).
Bryan, D. (2000) *Orange Parades: The Politics of Ritual, Tradition, and Control* (London: Pluto Press).
Farrell, S. (2000) *Rituals and Riots: Sectarian Violence and Political Culture in Ulster, 1784–1886* (Lexington: University Press of Kentucky).
Gibbon, P. (1975) *The Origins of Ulster Unionism* (Manchester: Manchester University Press).
Gilley, S. (1971) "Protestant London, no popery, and the Irish poor: II (1850–1860)", *Recusant History*, 11: 21–56.
Hempton, D. and Hill, M. (1992) *Evangelical Protestantism in Ulster Society, 1740–1890* (New York: Routledge).
Hepburn, A. C. (1996) *A Past Apart: Studies in the History of Catholic Belfast* (Belfast: Ulster Historical Foundation).

Hirst, C. (2002) *Religion, Politics and Violence in Nineteenth-Century Belfast: The Pound and Sandy Row* (Dublin: Four Courts Press).

Holmes, J. (2000) *Religious Revivals in Britain and Ireland, 1859–1905* (Dublin: Irish Academic Press).

Holmes, J. (2002) "The role of open-air preaching in the Belfast Riots of 1857", *Proceedings of the Royal Irish Academy*, 102C, 47–66.

Jarman, N. (1997) *Material Conflicts: Parades and Visual Displays in Northern Ireland* (Oxford: Berg).

Macaulay, A. (1987) *Patrick Dorrian: Bishop of Down and Connor, 1865–85* (Dublin: Irish Academic Press).

Valenze, D. (1985) *Prophetic Sons and Daughters: Female Preaching and Popular Religion in Industrial England* (Princeton: Princeton University Press).

Wright, F. (1996) *Two Lands on One Soil: Ulster Politics before Home Rule* (Dublin: Gill & Macmillan).

# 11

# Evangelicals and Irish identity in independent Ireland: a case study

*Patrick Mitchel*

## Introduction

The intention of this chapter is to describe and reflect critically upon the story of a historically marginal religious identity, that of Irish evangelicalism, within twentieth-century independent Ireland. It is a story that remains largely unexamined at an academic level.[1] This silence is quite understandable. Not only have evangelical Christians been numerically scarce within the Republic, they have also tended to be "hidden" within the broader Protestant denominations. However, the unfolding story of evangelicals in modern Ireland is not only a story of interest in its own right but also throws light on how religious identity can adapt to, and be influenced by, its changing political and social context.

## Defining evangelicalism

As a dynamic religious phenomenon, some subtlety is required in unpacking the movement's ideological and cultural strands. Defining evangelical Christianity has been light-heartedly described as to trying to nail jelly on the wall. Just when you think you have it neatly pinned down, it slips off, defying tidy categorisation. The analysis of evangelicalism is a growth industry, a prolific output of articles and books continues apace (e.g. Noll, 2004; Bebbington, 2005; Wolffe, 2006, and future volumes in this series). The intention here is not to enter into a maze of theoretical detail surrounding evangelical identity, but simply to outline three broad themes that are of particular relevance when it comes to understanding evangelical attitudes and priorities.

The first is a shared identity across denominational boundaries. To "be evangelical" is to share, even if diffusely, a common historical and theological heritage. Alister McGrath lists six widely accepted defining themes of evangelicalism as:

1  The supreme authority of Scripture as a source of knowledge of God and a guide to Christian living;
2  The majesty of Jesus Christ both as incarnate God and Lord and as the saviour of sinful humanity;
3  The Lordship of the Holy Spirit;
4  The need for personal conversion;
5  The priority of evangelism for both individual Christians and the church as a whole;
6  The importance of the Christian community for spiritual nourishment, fellowship and growth. (McGrath, 1994)

Evangelicals in Ireland today are found in varying strength, within all the following denominations and groupings: Anglicans, Baptists, independent churches, Pentecostals, Mennonites, Methodists, Brethren, Presbyterians, charismatics, ethnic churches and the Roman Catholic Church. It is only common assent to a mutual set of beliefs and their practical implications that binds such a spectrum of Christians together. They share, however broadly, a common experience and understanding of being a Christian. This is why evangelical Christians of many different hues can feel a sense of collective identity. It flows out of their communal assent to, and experience of, core theological doctrines. Thus, though the picture is certainly not tidy, it is possible to talk of an "evangelical Christian community" within the Irish Republic.

The second theme is the importance of religious motivation. It is a curiosity of political analysis of the Northern conflict that the role of religion has often been dismissed as an irrelevant factor. Steve Bruce has often stood as a lone figure in this regard (Bruce, 1986), with differently nuanced analysis recently emerging, for example, from the pen of Claire Mitchell (Mitchell, 2005, 2006). Others, for a mixture of ideological and methodological reasons, have been unreasonably dismissive of the importance of religion (O'Leary and McGarry, 1995). If one is to discuss the political and social policies of evangelical Christianity, one would do well to take religion seriously as a motivating factor because it is committed religious belief that is at the heart of evangelical self-understanding.

The third theme is the adaptability of evangelical identity to changing social contexts. In the words of evangelical historian David Bebbington, "Nothing could be further from the truth than the common image of Evangelicalism being ever the same" (Bebbington, 1989: 271). While the movement's core characteristics may have remained relatively consistent, during the period from the 1730s to the 1980s, evangelicalism in Britain evolved both outwardly in terms of social structure and political orientation and inwardly in terms of theology and behaviour. As we shall see, his conclusions have resonance for interpreting the story of Irish evangelicalism.

Recent work by Irene Whelan and others (Whelan, 2005; Murphy, 2005; Brown et al., 2005; Gribben and Holmes, 2006) has built on the earlier work of Desmond Bowen (1978, 1985) and refocused attention on the extraordinary period of evangelical influence in nineteenth-century Irish life. Space permits only a short visit to this era, but it is one worth making in that it provides a useful backdrop with which to compare and contrast not only the fortunes, but also the evolving theological and political priorities of evangelicals in the two radically different political contexts of "then" and "now". Three characteristics of nineteenth-century evangelicalism are of particular relevance.

### A Protestant identity

It was the extraordinary impact of John Wesley and the Methodist movement in the eighteenth-century that provided a catalyst for later evangelical advance within the wider Protestant population. Despite initial distain from the establishment, Alan Acheson concludes that by the 1830s evangelicalism had moved from the margins to an influential and central place within Anglicanism (Acheson, 1997). This development was part of wider "evangelical revival" which witnessed "vital religion" vigorously making inroads into British and Irish public life. The reach of evangelical vibrancy in Ireland was remarkable in that it penetrated the highest echelons of Protestant society (Whelan, 2006) as well as commerce and the professions of banking, law, medicine, politics, the armed services and university education (Acheson, 1997). An evangelical presence in the aristocracy, church, government and business constituted a formidable source of political and economic capital which was used to fund and facilitate rapid evangelical expansion including for example the building of several "trustee churches" for popular preachers within the Church of Ireland.[2]

### Political and religious synthesis

There is strong evidence that the political context of the minority Protestant ascendancy profoundly shaped the character and specific ambitions of Irish evangelicals in this period. The French revolution and the apocalyptic scenes of the 1798 rebellion had deeply shaken the established order, a fear that the 1801 Act of Union had done little to assuage. Protestants also were facing the threat of an increasingly numerous and disaffected Catholic peasantry and the rising assertiveness of political Catholicism, particularly in the form of O'Connell's campaign for Catholic emancipation. Earls (2007) argues that Irish Protestantism was in need of a "big idea".

The idea that emerged was that of the advance of evangelical Christianity. This move was grounded in the widespread belief that "moral reform grounded in biblical Christianity was the most effective guarantor of social and political stability" (Whelan, 2005: xvi) and that it had been Protestant religion and constitutional government that had saved Britain from the terrors of revolution that had overtaken France. Peter Roe, a well-known evangelical preacher from Kilkenny, encapsulated this thinking,

> Those who are most under the influence of the word of God are most anxious that its [government] administration should proceed steadily and uninterrupted—while, on the contrary, those who are unacquainted with, or neglect, or oppose that word, are dissatisfied, turbulent and rebellious. (Liechty, 1993: 31)

If the goal was to ensure the future of Irish society as peaceful, industrious and loyal, the means that emerged was an extraordinary educational evangelistic campaign, unheralded in its scope, vigorousness and strategy, to persuade the Catholic population to embrace the purity and freedom of biblical Christianity and thus, as a natural consequence, come to see the benefits of Protestant constitutional government. For it was clear that without a dramatic shift of allegiance within the Catholic population, the future of established Protestantism in Ireland was bleak. Lord Farnham, a leading evangelical responsible for founding the Cavan Association for promoting the Reformation, prophetically argued this way:

1  The claims of Irish Catholics must be conceded if they continue in their present strength of numbers.
2  If conceded, the Church Establishment must fall.
3  The separation of Ireland and Britain would follow. (Liechty and Clegg, 2001: 89)

An implication of this type of thinking was that maintenance of the political status quo depended upon converting Catholics to Protestantism. The shape of subsequent evangelical policy is described by Whelan:

> With the strength of the United Kingdom and its immense commercial empire at their back, and the global imperative of awakened Christianity to provide wind for their sails, they were now emboldened to launch an

ideological crusade to undermine the threat to their liberty from the forces of Catholic subversion. (Whelan, 2005: 268).

Desmond Bowen concludes, "Evangelical tactics called for unrelenting proselytising" (Bowen, 1978: 83).

## Opposition to Catholicism

A final characteristic of evangelicalism of this era was its reactive and deep-seated theological opposition to the errors of Rome. In this, Irish evangelicals were not unique; uncompromising rejection of the dangerous errors of Catholicism was a hallmark of evangelicalism during a polemical age (Bebbington, 2005). In Ireland, the twist was, of course, that evangelical Protestants were surrounded by an overwhelming Catholic majority. At first, Protestant attitudes tended to take the form of paternalistic benevolence. The Catholic hierarchy's attitudes ranged from a degree of cautious cooperation in educational initiatives to resistance to the dangers of unrestricted Bible distribution (Whelan, 2005). But a more formidable anti-Catholicism emerged in the period after Archbishop of Dublin William Magee's famous sermon preached at St Patrick's Cathedral in October 1822, in which he claimed that the Church of Ireland possessed sole ecclesiastical legitimacy. The subsequent "Bible War" acted to intensify religious identities on both sides, fuelled by large public meetings (or "Contros") debating the merits of evangelical or Catholic beliefs. Later evangelistic campaigns of the Irish Church Missions such as those in Dublin (Prunty, 2006) and Edward Nangle on Achill Island (Kelly, 2006) progressed in a bitterly polemical atmosphere. Thrown into this mix is strong evidence that part of the urgency behind nineteenth-century evangelical mission lay in a fusion of millennialist theology and a deep conviction that resurgent Irish Catholicism represented the forces of Antichrist (Gribben, 2006). The title of a lecture by Nangle typifies this interpretive mindset: "The Church of Rome the foretold apostasy: the substance of lectures delivered in Dublin, Ballinasloe, Portarlington, and Cork" (Nangle, 1850).

As the century progressed it became clear that the evangelical campaign to convert the Catholic population had not only failed but had profoundly unwelcome and unforeseen consequences. Liechty (1993) concludes that by 1861, the Protestant campaign of conversion had left Ireland's demography essentially unchanged and had actually only intensified sectarian animosity. Mounting political and religious radicalism marked a process of modernisation of the Catholic population whereby religion and national identity became virtually indistinguishable. Not only was the Catholic Church strengthened by its oppositional defensive role of Catholic political and spiritual rights against Protestant hegemony, but the "hardened antagonism" that came to define relations between Protestants and Catholics in the 1800s was to become a "permanent feature of the Irish political landscape" (Whelan, 2005: xix). The "evangelical moment" had passed. It is symbolic that Merrion Hall in central Dublin appears in Joyce's *Ulysses* during its prime as a 2,800-seat Brethren assembly, but by the end of the twentieth century it had been sold to become the Davenport Hotel, demonstrating how nineteenth-century evangelical fortunes withered in the increasingly inhospitable climate of full-blown twentieth-century Catholic nationalism.

## The twentieth-century: high walls and impermeable barriers

Terence Brown writes that "the history of Protestantism in independent Ireland from 1922 to the late 1960s is a history of decline and isolation" (Brown, 1996: 226). A 25 per cent minority over time became a 5 per cent minority. Between 1911 and 1926 the Anglican population declined by 34 per cent, mainly due to partition, the articulation of triumphalist Catholic identity at all areas of life and the withdrawal of the imperial power. Martin Maguire has shown that, up to this time, despite common perceptions of "big house" gentry, Protestants in Ireland had primarily been an urban rather than a rural population. Prior to independence, Dublin had a Protestant working class of about 10,000 men and their families. The decline in the Protestant community after partition was primarily a decline in the urban working class. Research has suggested that reasons for this haemorrhage of people include industrial collapse during the 1914–18 war; acts of violence against the Protestant population; and the *Ne Temere* decree which had its greatest effect on the working class (Maguire, 1995). The significance of the decline within this strand of Protestantism is that it was here that evangelicalism had its strongest presence (Brown, 1996). The virtual disappearance of this community had several effects, but one is of particular relevance.

Over time robust evangelicalism became associated with the "sectarian" North rather than the "moderate" and "genteel" middle-class world of southern Protestantism. These two types of Protestantism drifted apart after partition. Evangelicalism's deep roots in the South were largely forgotten within Anglicanism. The small remnant of clergy and lay people committed to evangelical truths were largely marginalised at official level and seen as proponents of "overly enthusiastic" beliefs that could threaten the delicately balanced status quo between Ireland's two ethno-religious communities. In radical contrast to glorious nineteenth-century visions of spiritual advance, the priority now was communal and ethnic survival. Successful propagation of identity depended on maintaining borders and resisting assimilation. Even as late as the 1980s, the sociologist Kurt Bowen, was debating whether the future of the Protestant minority would be integration (and survival) or assimilation (and disappearance) (Bowen, 1983). It was in this context that the evangelical heritage of the church was, by and large, repudiated by the church establishment.

Evangelicals, however, tended to have more explicitly spiritual priorities. Acheson records examples of evangelical frustration within the Church of Ireland:

> Bishop W. S. Kerr of Down (1945–56) thus expressed his exasperation after a service . . . "The Church! The Church! When are we going to hear a sermon on the Church's Lord?' Herbert O'Driscoll, a native of Cork diocese who became Dean of Vancouver . . . referred to conversion—"that word that sends shivers up and down the spines of loyal Anglicans'. (Acheson, 1997: 231)

Not content with mere maintenance, many evangelicals found sources of Bible teaching and fellowship elsewhere. Most remained within the Anglican Church, but some left to join more explicitly evangelical groups. Numbers of accomplished clergy left for the Church of England (Acheson, 1997). Others focused on the need for spiritual revitalisation both within Anglicanism and beyond. But stepping outside ring-fenced identities was a hazardous business. In divided states (with more than one identity) a high degree of mental, if not also physical, segregation is likely to occur (Douglas, 1997). This is precisely what happened in the Free State and later the Republic. The "identity gulf" between the two communities was not just religious, or political or cultural. It went to a deeper and rawer emotional level than a mere difference of values.[3] Leaving one's identity was, therefore, tantamount to being perceived as betraying not only the cause of the nation, but your church, your family, even yourself. While from an evangelical perspective, preaching the gospel was not a political act but "simply" a message of justification by faith alone, for a Catholic to become an evangelical Christian was indistinguishable from becoming a Protestant and tantamount to "taking the King's shilling". Few other actions could be as shockingly counter-cultural as choosing to become the "Other". As a consequence, evangelical identity, even up to the 1980s, operated in a context of negative opposition to Irish Catholic identity as the following examples illustrate.

T. C. Hammond, superintendent of the Irish Church Mission (ICM) from 1919 until 1936, author of the highly influential evangelical textbook *In Understanding be Men*, and later Principal of Moore Theological College in Sydney, saw over five hundred people converted during his tenure. The circumstances surrounding this evangelistic endeavour are recounted by Nelson.

> Each person signed a register in the Mission declaring that he or she was acting freely and out of personal conviction, and each signature was witnessed by two people. Such a safeguard was needed since the Mission was always open to hostile criticism and charges of fraudulent proselytising. Sometimes it was necessary to see that new converts had an escort in case they were spirited away. (Nelson, 1994: 86)

These were the days of "zero-sum" religious conflict. Success for one identity was defeat for the other. On Hammond's departure for Australia, *The Irish Catholic* articulated its hostility to evangelical Protestantism. "We cannot congratulate Australian Protestants on the acquisition . . . the notorious chief of Soupers . . . he will carry with him the curses of many a drunken mother and father whose children's souls were lost through the devilish work of the spiritual harpies of whom Rev Hammond was chief" (Nelson, 1994: 90).

It took some strong-willed characters to engage in open-air preaching, door-to-door evangelism and Bible distribution, especially in rural areas. Determining motivation of others is a notoriously imprecise business, but to understand such actions it is best to recall how evangelicals are generally highly motivated by a religious desire to share the "good news" of God's self-giving sacrifice on the cross rather than a temporal political agenda. Johnny Cochrane (1900–71), appointed an evangelist with the Dublin YMCA in 1933, developed an open-air evangelistic ministry at fairs and markets throughout the country. Such activities frequently attracted hostility. He wrote of one such occasion at Ballinrobe, Co. Mayo, "Just before train time we were attacked and beaten up by 30 or 40 men, our Bibles thrown into the river. We were then kicked to the railway station, packed like cattle into the train and warned never to come back" (Dunlop, 2004: 195). Such stories were not uncommon among Presbyterian Irish Mission colporteurs, street preachers or itinerant evangelists. Some Protestant locals cooperating with such men had to do so with discretion because "if they identified too closely . . . there was the distinct possibility that their livestock would remain unsold" (Dunlop, 2004: 228).

Even during the 1970s and 1980s many Irish evangelicals continued to encounter a considerable degree of hostility and exclusion from their communities if they left the all-embracing fold of the Catholic Church. New groups trying to find a place to worship in their towns faced a blanket of exclusion, sometimes being forced to find a location some distance away. At an individual level, new believers faced the sudden shock of exclusion from the secure experience of belonging to a majority identity. Some were disinherited and others disowned by their families. In the 1970s, a friend of this writer received a letter from his uncle to announce the ending of their relationship. In it he was addressed with the Anglicised name "John" rather than his real name, Sean. The message was unambiguous; he had betrayed his Irish identity, an unforgivable act. The Irish Catholic ethos provided a powerful sense of cohesion. Life's seminal moments were all included within a religious communal identity, birth, baptism, first communion, confession, marriage and death all formed part of an all-embracing programme of ritual within the church. A person "cut adrift" from this experience suddenly faced such unsettling questions as "where will I get married?" or "where will I be buried?" even to existential questions like "who am I?" and "where do I belong?"

In the 1980s the initial response of some within the Catholic Church to the beginnings of evangelical development tended to be hostile. Some evangelicals were denounced from the pulpit. The work of Michael Tierney, then Director of the Catholic Communications Institute, while perceptive in many ways, managed to lump the Elim Pentecostal Church with, for instance, cults such as the Moonies and the Hare Krishna Movement (Tierney, 1985). The Irish media, unused and unable to think in categories outside the simple duality of "Catholic" and "Church of Ireland" demonstrated how the wider society was ill-equipped to deal with alternative religious identities. One of the most significant examples of this was the 1982 "Ballaghaderreen affair", which was widely reported in the Irish media (Wilson, 1985). When a charismatic group[4] broke away from the Catholic Church and began baptising its members, the Western Bishops were prompted to publish a pastoral letter. This talked of how some "non-denominational Christians" had established "missions" through which people leaving the Catholic Church "in many cases . . . begin to seem like different people" to such a degree that "they have been, not so much converted as taken over" (Western Bishops, 1983). The media perception of the new fellowship was overwhelmingly negative, mistakenly associating evangelicals as synonymous with cults such as the Jehovah's Witnesses or Mormons, rather than as orthodox Christians (Cook, 1991). Christians who were neither Catholic nor Protestant did not fit (and often still do not fit) in any known category.

### Twenty-first-century Ireland: crumbling walls and permeable barriers?

By the late 1960s Irish evangelicalism had, despite all efforts, made little or no impact on the wider Catholic nationalist population. Even where vibrant, it remained largely trapped within the confines of a declining Protestant ethnicity.

This picture of stagnation has been transformed with the modest but significant growth of the evangelical community throughout the Republic since the late 1970s. Figures from a recently compiled Evangelical Alliance Ireland (EAI) database of evangelicals in Ireland show that fewer than 150 evangelical congregations existed in 1980 compared with over 400 today, reflecting a total attendance growth from less than 10,000 in 1980 to over 30,000 (EAI, 2006). However, despite such relatively rapid expansion, evangelicals still constitute less than 1 per cent of the population and remain a marginal religious identity within Irish society.

As elsewhere, these evangelicals have not chosen to organise themselves within one church. Instead, they have divided according to their preference, for example, on style of worship, structure of church government, understanding of baptism or practice of spiritual gifts and so on. Such churches are now found in practically every town all over Ireland. As a result, in contrast to the predictable bi-polar boundaries of the past, contemporary Irish evangelicalism consists of a disorganised spectrum of churches and fellowships made up of three distinct streams. The largest consists of individuals from a Catholic and nationalist cultural identity who usually find homes in a variety of independent new churches and fellowships. This has been supplemented by growth in numbers of evangelicals within some denominational churches[5] and the arrival of considerable numbers of ethnic Christians, a significant proportion of whom are evangelicals, usually of Pentecostal persuasion.[6] The launch of EAI in May 2004 demonstrates that significant numbers of these Christians find a common identity under the term "evangelical" rather than any other descriptor.

This description of change, of course, begs the question, "Why?" Certainly there is room here for further research on how religious ideas and practices affect people's political attitudes and vice versa, but two broad reasons can be suggested. The first lies in the radically altered landscape of Irish identity. The second is located within the nature of evangelicalism itself.

Much ink has been spilled recently on the remarkable transformation in Irish society. Social psychologist Michael O'Connell concludes, after lengthy analysis of a wide variety of data, that antonyms seem most appropriate to compare even the 1980s with the 2000s: "So while one might have described the Ireland of the past as stagnant, poor, religious, traditional or withdrawn, now opposing adjectives spring to mind—dynamic, wealthy, secular, brash, vulgar" (O'Connell, 2001: 6). Whatever the fairness or not of his comparisons, few would disagree that "old Ireland" and the "new Ireland" seem two different worlds. The ideological structure of classic Irish nationalism formed during the nineteenth century—a cohesive sense of Gaelicism intertwined with Roman Catholicism—appears increasingly obsolete in a globalised society. Commentators agree that Ireland is gradually moving towards the increasingly secular norms of European social and religious values (Hornsby-Smith and Whelan, 1994). If de Valera's Ireland was characterised by a monolithic Catholicism that allowed little room for alternative beliefs, the loss of that secure feeling of unanimity has provided a new sense of individualised "religious space". It is in this context that there is even talk of Ireland's "Protestant moment".

A second reason for the broadening and growth of the evangelical community lies in the nature of evangelicalism itself. Historically, evangelical faith has generally been differentiated from fundamentalism by its desire to engage with contemporary culture and has demonstrated a high degree of flexibility in response to changing political, cultural and social environments (Bebbington, 1989; Noll, 2004). This is most clearly exemplified by the theme of EAI, which is "Christianity engaging". Sean Mullan, its director, articulates six ways in which he argues that the message of evangelical Christianity is particularly suited to religious needs in contemporary Irish culture. These are:

1  its personal, experiential and inherently anti-institutional nature;
2  the communal character of biblical Christianity that embraces all equally regardless of race, gender, religious background;
3  an ethical framework drawn from a personal response to God of thankful service, which provides an alternative to the straitjacket of "past traditional moralism" and the "destructive moral relativism of liberal individualism";
4  a future orientated supernaturalist hope that also "provides a paradigm for action in the present";
5  the life-affirming libertarian nature of authentic Christianity that understands the moral guidelines of Scripture neither as the life-denying asceticism of authoritarian religion nor a self-centred pursuit of pleasure, but "a prescription for life that can be lived fully and enjoyed fully";
6  an experience on the margins of Irish identity that can serve to protect from the temptation to attempt to enforce religious values on wider society. (Mullan, 2004: 231–7).

It is surely significant that, at each stage, this articulation of contemporary evangelical priorities is shaped by contrast with past authoritative Irish Catholicism and contemporary liberal secularism. The resultant "shape" of this modern evangelicalism, while continuing to exhibit the movement's traditionally strong activism and wishing to maintain its core theological identity,[7] nevertheless, stands in stark relief when set against the priorities and theological agendas of nineteenth-century evangelicals outlined earlier. Gone is any vestige of a religio-political agenda of securing Protestant interests. Indeed, the term "evangelical" actually functions as a replacement identity to that of Protestantism. The Christian life is described in terms of personal fulfilment functioning within an egalitarian community entered into by personal faith rather than as part of any institutional identity structures. Far from operating from a position of social privilege and political influence, modern Irish evangelicals form a minor religious identity on the fringes of popular consciousness. A rigorous opposition to Catholicism is softened by a positive emphasis on religious freedom compared to either legalistic, authoritarian religion or liberal pluralism. I would argue that this is an example of how identity is continually adapting to and proactively interacting with its fluid social, political and religious context.

## Conclusion

Today, no longer are evangelicals confined within a Protestant elite. It is noteworthy that most Irish evangelicals feel little, if any, affinity for the unionist politics and Protestant cultural identity of their fellow evangelicals north of the border (or with the story of nineteenth-century evangelicals either, for that matter). While Irish evangelicals will agree that in Christ all other loyalties, whether cultural or political, are relativised under his Lordship, many will resist any (perceived or real) requirement to leave their national identity by "becoming" a Protestant, with all the alien cultural and political implications associated with that word.

Modern Irish evangelical identity has been, and continues to be, deeply influenced by its evolving social and political environment and cannot be properly understood apart from its particular historical relationship with Irish national identity. The content, character and membership of the contemporary Irish evangelical community are all significantly distinct from that of nineteenth-century Irish evangelicalism. Arguably it represents a genuinely new expression of religious identity in Ireland. For, while it claims to stand in theological continuity with historic evangelical Christianity, many of its members are only loosely associated with, and in most cases are strongly detached from, a Protestant, much less a unionist, identity. In the new pluralist Ireland, evangelicals are perhaps re-emerging, this time not as alien "outsiders", but as one of a diverse range of minority communities existing within a broader and more inclusive Irish identity than that of the past.

## Notes

1  A recent popular level contribution is Dunlop, 2004. My study on evangelicalism and national identity focused on Ulster rather than an all-Ireland approach (Mitchel, 2003).
2  Examples were the evangelical preaching station Bethesda Chapel in Dorset Street (founded in 1786 and formerly licensed in 1825), Crinken, near Bray, built in 1840 and still a lively evangelical Anglican church, and Trinity Church, Gardiner Street built in 1839 and recently purchased and being restored as a centre of evangelical life and witness by Trinity Church Network, a large charismatic fellowship in Dublin.
3  For a revealing insight into Protestant experience within the full force of Catholic nationalist identity, see C. Murphy and L. Adair (eds) (2002) *Untold Stories: Protestants in the Republic of Ireland 1922–2002* (Dublin: Liffey Press). Edith Devlin's article poignantly captures the mood as perceived by a child, "Catholic blood seemed to flow in every vein but ours . . . we knew that in a vague sort of way that we were not considered 'the real thing', for we were Protestants and must only be playing at being Irish . . . A mental barrier was erected which separated those who naturally belonged together. The version of Christianity in which I had been brought up was, it seemed, tainted and unacceptable. I wish it had been otherwise" (see pp. 69–70).
4  Charismatic Christianity began to impact Ireland in the 1960s and now represents a significant proportion of evangelicalism in Ireland. Five distinctive characteristics of what is now a global movement are: (i) a major post-conversion enriching of personal Christian experience; (ii) speaking in tongues (for some); (iii) the use of all the spiritual gifts described in the New Testament; (iv) the importance of expressive worship; (v) a particular understanding of God's strategy of renewal.
5  Statistics from the 2002 Census compared to 1991 indicate increases in the following populations: Church of Ireland (including "Protestant") from 89,187 to 115,611; Presbyterian from 13,199 to 20,582; Methodist from 5,037 to 10,033; and Other Stated Religions from 38,743 to 89,223. It is highly probable that evangelical increases are included within all these categories—including "Other Stated Religion" because some evangelicals used the term "evangelical" in the Census as a self-designation rather than the term "Protestant". See www.cso.ie/census/documents/vol12_entire.pdf.
6  One of the most influential ethnic church networks is the Redeemed Christian Church of God. Informal research suggests that there are nearly fifty churches belonging to this denomination meeting all over Ireland, some of which in Dublin have over 600 people attending.

7   EAI has articulated a theological position that stands in close continuity with other "statements of faith" within global evangelicalism (Mitchel, 2005).

## References

Acheson, A. (1997) *A History of the Church of Ireland 1691–1996* (Dublin: Columba Press).

Bebbington, D. (1989) *Evangelicalism in Modern Britain: A History from the 1730s to the 1980s* (London: Unwin Hyman).

Bebbington, D. (2005) *The Dominance of Evangelicalism: The Age of Spurgeon and Moody* (Leicester: Apollos).

Bowen, D. (1978) *The Protestant Crusade in Ireland 1800–1870* (Dublin: Gill & Macmillan, 1978).

Bowen, K. (1983) *Protestants in a Catholic State: Ireland's Privileged Minority* (Montreal: McGill/Queen's University Press).

Bowen, D. (1985) *The History and Shaping of Irish Protestantism* (New York: Peter Lang).

Brown, M., McGrath, C. I. and Power, T. (eds) (2005) *Converts and Conversion in Ireland 1650–1850* (Dublin: Four Courts Press).

Brown, T. (1966) "Religious minorities in the Irish Free State and the Republic of Ireland (1922–1995)", in *Building Trust in Ireland: Studies Commissioned by the Forum for Peace and Reconciliation* (Belfast: Blackstaff), pp. 215–53.

Bruce, S. (1986) *God Save Ulster! The Religion and Politics of Paisleyism* (Oxford: Oxford University Press).

Cook, A. (1991) "News coverage of Irish evangelicalism 1978–1991: a case study of ideology in the media" (unpublished MA thesis, National University of Ireland, Maynooth).

Dunlop, R. (ed.) (2004) *Evangelicals in Ireland: An Introduction* (Dublin: Columba Press).

Douglas, J. H. N. (1997) "Political structures, social interaction and identity change in Northern Ireland", in B. Graham (ed.) *In Search of Ireland: A Cultural Geography* (London: Routledge), pp. 151–73.

Earls, M. (2007) "The politics of assimilation" in *Dublin Review of Books* website at www.drb.ie/fa_thepolitics.html (accessed on 1 February 2007).

Evangelical Alliance Ireland (2006) National Survey Results, available at www.evangelical.ie/pages/press/national%20survey.html.

Gribben, C. (2006) "Antichrist in Ireland—Protestant millennialism and Irish studies", in C. Gribben and A. Holmes (eds) *Protestant Millennialism, Evangelicalism and Irish Society 1790–2005* (Basingstoke: Palgrave), pp. 1–30.

Gribben, C. and Holmes, A. eds (2006) *Protestant Millennialism, Evangelicalism and Irish Society 1790–2005* (Basingstoke: Palgrave).

Hornsby-Smith, M. P. and Whelan, C. T. "Religious and Moral Values", *Values and Social Change in Ireland* (Dublin, Gill & Macmillan).

Kelly, T. J. (2006) " 'Come Lord Jesus, quickly come!': The writing and thought of Edward Nangle, 1828–1862", in C. Gribben, and A. Holmes (eds) *Protestant Millennialism, Evangelicalism and Irish Society 1790–2005* (Basingstoke: Palgrave).

Liechty, J. (1993) *The Roots of Sectarianism in Ireland* (Belfast: Irish Inter-Church Meeting).

McGrath, A. E. (1994) *Evangelicalism and the Future of Christianity* (London: Hodder & Stoughton).

Maguire, M. (1005) "The Church of Ireland and the problem of the Protestant working-class of Dublin", in A. Ford, J. Maguire and K. Milne (eds) *As by Law Established: The Church of Ireland Since the Reformation* (Dublin: Lilliput Press), pp. 195–203.

Mitchel, P. (2003) *Evangelicalism and National Identity in Ulster, 1921–1998* (Oxford: Oxford University Press).

Mitchel, P. (ed.) (2005) *A Common Faith, A Common Purpose* (Dublin: Evangelical Alliance Ireland).

Mitchell, C. (2005) "Behind the ethnic marker: religion and social identification in Northern Ireland", *Sociology of Religion*, 66.1: 3–21.

Mitchell, C. (2006) *Religion, Identity and Politics in Northern Ireland: boundaries of belonging and belief* (Aldershot: Ashgate).

Mullan, S. (2004)"The way ahead", in R. Dunlop (ed.) *Evangelicals in Ireland: An Introduction* (Dublin: Columba Press).

Murphy, J. H. (ed.) (2005) *Evangelicals and Catholics in 19th Century Ireland* (Dublin: Four Courts Press).

Murphy, C. and Adair, L. (2002) *Untold Stories: Protestants in the Republic of Ireland 1922–2002* (Dublin: Liffey).

Nangle, E. (1850) "The Church of Rome the foretold apostasy: the substance of lectures delivered in Dublin, Ballinasloe, Portarlington, and Cork" (Dublin).

Nelson, W. (1994) *T. C. Hammond, Irish Christian: His Life and Legacy in Ireland and Australia* (Edinburgh: Banner of Truth).

Noll, M. A. (2004) *The Rise of Evangelicalism* (Leicester: Apollos).

O'Connell, M. (2001) *Changed Utterly: Ireland and the New Irish Psyche* (Dublin: Liffey Press).

O'Leary, B. and McGarry, J. (1995) *Explaining Northern Ireland: Broken Images* (Oxford: Blackwell).

Prunty, J. (2006) "Battle plans and battlegrounds: Protestant mission activity in the Dublin slums, 1840s–1880s", in C. Gribben and A. Holmes (eds) *Protestant Millennialism, Evangelicalism and Irish Society 1790–2005* (Basingstoke: Palgrave).

Roe, P. (1858) Sixth Annual Address to the Parishioners of St Mary's Kilkenny, Kilkenny.

Tierney, M. (1985) *The New Elect: The Church and New Religious Groups* (Dublin: Veritas).

Western Bishops' Lenten Pastoral (1983) *Renewing our Faith in the Church* (Ireland).

Whelan, I. (2005) *The Bible War in Ireland: The "Second Reformation" and the Polarization of Protestant-Catholic Relations, 1800–1840* (Dublin: Lilliput Press).

Whelan, I. (2006) "The Bible gentry: evangelical religion, aristocracy, and the new moral order in the Early Nineteenth Century", in C. Gribben and A. Holmes (eds) *Protestant Millennialism, Evangelicalism and Irish Society 1790–2005* (Basingstoke: Palgrave), pp. 52–82.

White, J. (1974) *Minority Report: The Protestant Community in the Republic of Ireland* (Dublin: Gill & Macmillan).

Wilson, D. (1985) *A New Breed of Irishman* (Dublin: Merrion Press).

Wolffe, J. (2006) *The Expansion of Evangelicalism: The Age of Wilberforce, More, Chalmers and Finney* (Leicester: Apollos).

# 12

# "No, we are not Catholics": intersections of faith and ethnicity among the second-generation Protestant Irish in England[1]

*Sarah Morgan and Bronwen Walter*

## Introduction

Protestants remain largely invisible in the growing body of work on Irish migrants to England (Hickman and Walter, 1997; Dunne, 2003), although there are exceptions (Kells, 1995a, b; McAuley, 1996). In part this reflects their smaller numbers. Until recent decades fewer Protestants needed to leave Northern Ireland to find employment (Compton, 1992), while the numbers of Protestants in the Republic fell very sharply in the years immediately following the establishment of the Free State, and have constituted less than 5 per cent of the total for the past fifty years (Kennedy, 1973: 112; CSO, 2002).

However their absence from public view also reflects differences in the experiences, positioning and identities of Protestant migrants and their descendants from those of the more recognised Catholic populations. These include lower levels of residential and social clustering—the occupation of distinctive neighbourhood and institutional participation, for example, have often been often linked to churches and schools for the Catholic population (Walter, 1986)—limited overlap of family and social networks and, for those from Northern Ireland, inclusion within a British national identity.

In addition, there is no specific label available to distinguish a population of Protestant background from the blanket description of "Irish", which carries a very specific set of understandings in England—Catholic, nationalist and often "paddies" (Hickman and Walter, 1997; Morgan, 1997). Irish Protestant migrants in England are generally assumed to be Irish and (therefore) Catholic. While some choose to embrace Irishness, and its inherent contradictions for people from their background (Hyndman, 1996),[2] for others it is an alienating experience, which questions their relationship with Britain and Britishness (McAuley, 1996).

The situation in England contrasts with other Irish diasporic locations where significant numbers of Northern Irish Protestants, in particular, have been identified (Walter et al., 2000a), notably Canada (Jenkins, 2003) and New Zealand (Patterson, 2002) so that such identities are more readily claimed. Much closer to home, there is a more visible Irish Protestant population in Scotland, which reproduces the high profile ethnic divisions in Northern Ireland. On a longer historical timescale, over 40 per cent of those now claiming Irish ancestry in the USA are believed to have a Protestant background, reflecting their greater proportion in the eighteenth-century Ulster migrations from whom many are descended (Akenson, 2000). Such identities have been differentiated by the label "Scots-Irish" (Miller, 2000; Leyburn, 1962).

For those in the second generation, born in England to one or two Protestant Irish-born parents, such identities may become even more submerged. This chapter explores intersections of faith with ethnicity, drawing on a subset of interviews from a large-scale study of second-generation Irish people in Britain.[3] In particular, we trace how and to what extent the Irish Protestant[4] background of interviewees' parents has influenced their own senses of identity. Differences and convergences with interviewees from an Irish Catholic background are noted. We also examine interviewees' narratives of their parents' relationships to Irish Catholicism, including sectarianism, and the importance of the context of parental migration to England in relation to interviewees' understandings of their parents' anti-Catholicism.[5]

Importantly, interviewees include both those whose parents are from the Republic of Ireland and those with a Northern Irish background. Frequently studies of Irish Protestants focus on the majority population in Northern Ireland (see, for example, Shirlow and McGovern, 1997; Hyndman, 1996): "we Protestants in the Irish Republic are no longer interesting to anyone but ourselves" (Butler, cited in Tobin, 2005: 171). In the decades when the parents of our interviewees migrated to England, numbers of Protestants in the Republic were small (Tobin, 2005; CSO, 2002; Kennedy, 1973); in the North Protestants remain the majority although there has also been a decline over time.[6]

### Locating the Protestant second generation

The interviews that provide the empirical evidence for this chapter were conducted as part of a large-scale study, which aimed to examine the identities and social positions of the children of Irish migrants in England and Scotland. A non-random stratified quota sampling approach was employed for the project, drawing on a statistical profile of second-generation Irish people (Hickman et al., 2001). The aim was to ensure that important variations in the profile were represented in the overall sample, rather than to produce statistical representation. Although it was difficult to define, in any meaningful way, what might constitute a representative sub-sample in an English context, it was important that second-generation Irish people of Protestant heritage were represented in the overall sample. An additional barrier was the lack of avenues through which to contact or reach Irish Protestants in England, first and second generation, as a specific element of the Irish population. Contacting specific graduate, sporting and political groups with links to Irish Protestants failed to produce participants for the study. Two methods led to recruitment of seven interviewees with Irish Protestant backgrounds in two locations, Banbury and London: articles in the press (four) and, as with participants from a mixed heritage background (Walter, 2005), personal contacts (three). However, it should be noted that in Banbury, where four of the Irish Protestant interviewees were located, the most effective tool for recruiting respondents *overall* was an article in the local press, which highlighted that lack of strong affiliation with Irishness was an important element of the study (Walter et al., 2002b).

The sample comprised five women and two men. Two participants, both women, had Republic Protestant backgrounds. Tara's parents were both Church of Ireland adherents who came from Dublin, while Yasmin, who was of mixed race, had a Protestant mother from Co. Meath in the Irish Midlands, and a Pakistani father. The five participants with Northern Irish Protestant family background included only one with both parents Irish born, Linda, whose parents were of working-class Protestant background from Belfast. Of the remaining four, two had Irish Protestant fathers (Kevin and Terry) and English mothers, while two (Emily and Shona) had Irish Protestant mothers and British fathers.[7] Kevin was the only participant whose parents crossed the Protestant/Catholic divide. His mother was an "English" Catholic of Irish descent. The high level of intermixing between Irish-born and non-Irish-born parents contrasted with the remaining sample of people with a Catholic Irish background (80 people), which included a much larger proportion with two Irish-born parents.

The Irish-born parents occupied varied social class positions in England. Four fathers (Tara, Emily, Shona, Terry) had middle-range professional jobs, mainly connected with education, whilst three (Kevin, Linda, Yasmin) had manual, factory occupations. At the time of the interviews all their children were in white-collar/blouse or professional occupations. Five of the interviewees were in their 30s, one (Terry) in his 20s and one (Shona) in her early 50s, mirroring the age distribution of the second generation as a whole. We have tried to indicate parental choice of first names in our allocation of pseudonyms, only two of those in the sample being distinctively Irish.

## Religious and ethnic affiliations

Prior to interview, each participant was sent a blank "Family Tree" recording instrument in which they were asked them to complete information about themselves and family members in the first, second and third generations. This had the advantage of allowing interviewees to select religious and ethnic affiliations prior to interview. In the Protestant group, four people identified themselves as having a religion as an adult but only two (Yasmin and Kevin), both converts to the Church of England, attended church regularly. The other two (Tara and Linda) occasionally attended their local church, but were not in any meaningful sense members of the congregation. Of the remaining three interviewees, none had been brought up within a faith, and none identified with any religion or faith group at the time of interview.

In terms of ethnic affiliation, three used labels on their family tree reflective of their Irish roots: Irish (Tara), British Celtic (Shona) and Ulster British (Kevin). In each case, there were specific reasons for choosing these ethnic identifiers, which were discussed at length in the course of the interview. Of the remaining four participants, three wrote "British" and one "mixed race". Linda, whose parents were both from Belfast, was pressed to specify her non-Irish sense of identity as precisely as possible:

> *Linda*: British probably I would say I was [. . .] British because nowadays they have changed what ethnic origin you are, if you are filling out forms, the choice you get is British, isn't it? If English is a choice, I would be happy to put English. The forms these days put British.

For Linda there was no question that she was now part of the mainstream white "English" culture of the town in which she had been born and raised. However, this was a personal choice, part of a shift over the life-cycle rather than an identity inherited from her Irish-born parents. The next section examines in greater depth interviewees' reasons for choosing their specific identities as well as their relationships to Irishness and Catholicism.

## Relationships to Irishness

### Childhood

The extent to which interviewees in the study felt their childhood and upbringing was, or was not, particularly "Irish" was explored at length.

None of the Protestant interviewees felt that their early years had been especially "Irish". Within the home, religious iconography had not marked out Protestant households as different, and neither was there discussion of different attitudes towards hospitality, music, sporting affiliations or Irish history (see Walter et al., 2002b; Hickman et al., 2005). Moreover the wealth of detail, obtained from other interviewees who had typically (but not all) grown up in Irish neighbourhoods and gone to Catholic schools, was absent. Only Kevin, who was raised as a Catholic and attended a Catholic boys' school, experienced any level of visibility of his Irishness during his childhood.

There were two aspects of childhood shared by Protestants and Catholics. Both commented that they were marked out from their English childhood peers by a higher level of religious practice: Tara and Linda remarked that the requirement to attend service on Sundays, unlike their English peers, was distinctively Irish. Linda said: "That was it, you went to Sunday school whether you wanted to or not. I can't remember the other kids in the street going to church."

A second common feature was memories of English people's reactions to their parents' unfamiliar ways of speaking. Accent is a key signifier of Irish ethnicity in England (Walter, 2000). In contrast to Catholic interviewees, however, their Protestant children's recollections were of misidentifications, with parental accents being mistaken for Scottish or American or simply being incomprehensible to English people. Shona spoke about her mother's Northern Irish accent:

> I remember somebody saying to her,, "Are you American, where are you from?" She said to this person, "Wisconsin." She told a bare-faced lie, and it was slightly contemptuous—"If you can't tell where I am from, then sod you"—basically.

None of our interviewees recalled their Irish Protestant parents being identified as Irish. Unless their Irish Protestant parents disclosed their ethnic background, English people would not discern it. In this way, the Irish background of these interviewees has been invisible since childhood.

### Transitions to adulthood

In common with a number of Catholic interviewees, the transition to adulthood, often signified by key moments such as leaving home or getting married, also involved interviewees choosing their identity— sometimes quite deliberately (Song, 2005). Four interviewees in particular from this cohort—Tara, Linda, Shona and Kevin—reflected on how their chosen identities signified achievement of adulthood. Both Linda and Shona saw their affiliation to Irishness belonging to the past. Linda explained her shift away from Irishness as part of her transition to adulthood: "Probably I thought I was Irish up until my 20s then I thought, 'No, I am not.'" As she explained:

> I don't know that it was living with my parents, but when you are younger you tend to think what other people think, or make you believe. My mum would be horrified that I said I thought I was English. "You are Irish", she would say to me. I suppose you are brought up like that, until you get to a stage where you think, I am not Irish, I wasn't born there.

It is interesting that Linda's working-class Protestant parents from Northern Ireland, who might have been expected to identify as British in the unionist tradition, in fact saw themselves as Irish.

Shona, who described herself as British, also described her Irishness as belonging to her childhood: "At primary school I had a bit of an Irish identity. I do remember my mum on St Patrick's Day—she gave me a bit of shamrock to pin on me, and I was quite proud about that." Her mother had an extremely conflicted sense of identity, which changed sharply over time and by context, from accepting being labelled as Irish during the war, to calling herself a "North Ireland Prod" and then "she seemed to get more rabid when she got back there . . . She wouldn't identify as Irish, that was a "no no", settling in the end on "Ulster Scots".

The other two interviewees who discussed their relationships to Irish identities both had an affiliation with their Irish background, which reflected the importance to them of maintaining family relationships. Like Linda and Shona, Tara felt that being English was symbolic of maturity. It was, she said, "a natural progression from childhood". But the desire to maintain links to her family, current and future, meant that she chose to retain an affiliation with Irishness. For example, she described how a ceilidh band was booked for her wedding reception as a way of showing her relatives that she had not forgotten her Irish background, even though she was marrying an English man. Tara chose to identify herself as Irish in the 2001 census because she believed it would have a practical application for future genealogical searches by any future descendants because: "They are going to have to go to Ireland [. . .] so they need to know."

Kevin identified as "Ulster British" and wrote this on his family tree. Indeed, a desire to have this particular identity included in the project motivated Kevin to participate. When first asked about his identity, Kevin's response was to talk about his family name which, he said, "goes back fifth or sixth century". Kevin had been raised as a Catholic by his adoptive mother, but following a period living with his father's relatives in Portadown, County Armagh, in his late teens he chose to identify as Ulster British. However, he had kept the fact of his adoption, and his Irish Catholic birth mother, from his Northern Irish relatives.

Although quite different stories, Tara's and Kevin's discussions of their current relationships to Irishness, and what it meant to them as adults, had in common the importance of family and the use of ethnic affiliation to signal that relationship. Tara wanted to indicate to relatives, present and future, her Irish background. Kevin's identity furnished him with a link of authenticity to his relatives in Portadown, which his nativity (unknown to them) and upbringing did not. Their strategies for maintaining Irish family links reflect the entangled genealogies of second-generation Irish people (Walter, 2005). Other interviewees in our sample similarly commented on the role of Irish identities in maintaining family links (Hickman et al., 2005).

### Relationships to Catholicism

A feature of Irish Protestant identities, and one which is most readily associated with Northern Protestants, is their oppositional relationship to Catholicism. This is apparent in narratives of Northern Protestant identities, which constantly and consistently take up the theme of being defined by not being Catholic (see Hyndman, 1996; Logue, 2000, various contributors; and "Anne" in Walter, 2001: 251–5). This oppositional relationship also holds true for Irish Protestants in the Republic, where antipathy to Catholicism is, according to one commentator "an essential mark of Protestant identity, a sign of God's chosen people" (Sloane, 1993: 40).

Catholicism, and parental attitudes towards it, arose unprompted in the course of these interviews. Not all Irish Protestant parents were described as having sectarian beliefs, but all seven interviewees were aware (in some instances acutely so) of the dividing lines between Irish Catholics and Irish Protestants. In particular, two interviewees with Northern Protestant parents (Linda and Terry) recounted stories of visiting Northern Ireland, which illustrated their knowledge of the importance of these divisions and the geographic boundaries associated with them. Interviewees with Northern Catholic parents often had similar stories.

Apart from Kevin's story, the narratives of anti-Catholicism all involved Irish Protestant mothers, and were recounted by their daughters. This is not to say that Irish Protestant fathers did not hold such views; rather the stories reflect interviewees' close relationships with their mothers, and women's roles in passing on cultural beliefs and practices. The stories these women shared with us revolve around maintaining and monitoring the cultural, political and social divides between Irish Catholics and Irish Protestants in both parts of Ireland.

One mother, originally from County Meath in the Irish Republic, was especially anti-Catholic. Yasmin's mother forbade her children from having Catholic friends in London: "We weren't allowed to play with their kids either, they were demons." Her mother even ended one of her own friendships when she discovered the friend's Catholicism. Such a virulent hatred of all Catholics was an emotion and prejudice which her daughter could not comprehend at all as an adult and from which she distanced herself, although it had impacted directly on her childhood:

> With Catholicism, it was a "no-no" and you didn't mix with those people because they were bad. Obviously, we believed it, at the same time it was very hard. People didn't come into the house, they didn't socialise, it was hard [. . .] "Never trust a Catholic" and all that stuff, "They will stab you in the back as soon as you see them", she would say in her Irish accent.

Her mother's family in County Meath also shared this antipathy, tinged with fear: " 'Bloody Catholics', they were always there, all supporting one another. Growing up as a child you would be fearful of a Catholic." In Tara's middle-class family, also from the Republic of Ireland, maternal anxieties were more controlled, but nevertheless deep-seated. Tara told us that she had a Catholic boyfriend from Derry when she was a student at an English university. This relationship highlighted class (signified via accent) as well as religious differences. Her boyfriend's aunts "constantly mocked the way I spoke, made references to the fact that I wasn't Roman Catholic".

Tara was relieved when the relationship ended and her mother then revealed her own fears. She had been concerned that the young man belonged to "a strong Irish family, with strong religious and political opinions" as well as "how any children we had would be brought up".

Shona recalled an incident from her childhood when her mother had asked whether a schoolfriend was Catholic. Although this was true, the friendship continued—but Shona particularly recalled her sense of bewilderment at her mother's question. This resurfaced when her parents moved to Bangor, County Down, her mother's hometown, and her mother's anti-Catholicism became apparent. Shona visited regularly but found her mother's antipathy to Catholics and re-embracing of unionism alien, and a source of frequent arguments between them.

In each of these three examples, Irish Protestant mothers were actively monitoring their daughters' relationships with Catholics. Ranging in tenor from concerns about a daughter's future if she married an Irish Catholic to strict policing of the Protestant/Catholic divide, they can all be placed on a continuum where Catholicism, and Irish Catholicism in particular, is viewed with concern if not outright hostility. A further example of this maternal monitoring was provided by Linda who, when we mistakenly asked her whether she had attended Catholic school, said, "No, we are not Catholics" and, then, discussing how people always assumed she was Catholic if she mentioned her Irish background, said that her mother was "terrible for Catholic and Protestant".

The final example of familial anti-Catholicism comes from Kevin. In this case, it was his family in Portadown who exhibited anti-Catholic attitudes. Kevin's father was disinherited when he married a Catholic. Although attitudes softened after the Portadown family had met Kevin's mother, an English Catholic (but with Irish grandparents), and "particularly when the children came along" (ironically given the fact that Kevin—the eldest in his family—was adopted), his father remained disinherited. Later on in the interview, Kevin was at pains to illustrate the non-sectarian nature of his relatives: "they were strong Unionists, on the whole they were very tolerant [. . .]. My uncle Jack had the Lambeg drum in the back shed, he can remember lending it to the Hibernians". This ties in with Todd's typology, in which those who subscribe to Ulster Britishness "*largely* disapprove of sectarianism and *overt* anti-Catholicism" (McAuley, 1996: 61, emphasis added).

In contrast, neither Terry nor Emily said they had experienced any parental expressions of sectarianism. Nevertheless, it had been a powerful factor in their families' recent histories, motivating their parents' migration to England. Emily described how her Protestant mother's sympathy with Catholics was a reason for her leaving Northern Ireland and her estrangement from her family there, who, with the exception of one sister, did not share her views. Although Terry's father did not appear to have commented at all on anything to do with Northern Ireland, as a child Terry was acutely aware of the need to stay within particular boundaries when visiting his grandmother who lived in the Shankill (Protestant area of Belfast). Again, this resonates with Walter's interviewee "Anne's" desire to escape her past through the transformative act of migration (Walter, 2001: 251–5).

What emerges strongly from these accounts of parental anti-Catholicism is the lack of context which our interviewees had available to them to understand their parents' attitudes. It is quite clear that Yasmin and Shona in particular had no frame of reference through which they could even begin to comprehend their mothers' sectarian outbursts, and that it had damaged their relationships with them. Even for Linda, who was quite adamant that she was not Catholic, it was her mother who was identified as the keeper of this divide. For our other interviewees, parental comments and attitudes were less of an issue. But for all our Protestant interviewees, their parents' sectarianism was out of context with their lives in England, where overt anti-Catholicism is largely subsumed into historical discourses, although latent antipathy to Catholicism in England continued in the second half of the twentieth century. Thus, for our interviewees, growing up and living in late twentieth and early twenty-first century England, parental expressions of anti-Catholicism and sectarian attitudes were strange and bizarre.

The specificity of the English experience is underlined by comparison with the accounts of the Scottish sample, who also had Irish Protestant heritage. With the exception of Kevin, who as an adult deliberately chose to embrace this part of his cultural background, interviewees in England with Northern Irish Protestant parents had little or no understanding or knowledge of unionist politics or Orange traditions. Some interviewees in Scotland described lived experiences of these cultures and traditions, usually as a child, and occasionally continued into adulthood. This involved participation in Orange ceremonies, bands and traditions, including travel to Northern Ireland to participate in parades and events. In addition, there were sporting affiliations, which resonated with and affirmed Orange identities. Similar sporting affiliations were mentioned only briefly by the male interviewees, Terry and Kevin, who supported Rangers (Glasgow) and Glenavon (Belfast), respectively. While the lives of participants in Scotland from Irish Protestant backgrounds were not entirely under an "Orange banner" (McAuley, 1996), they did understand its resonance and what, in terms of cultural practices and attitudes, fitted under that banner.

Divergences in experience between interviewees located in England and Scotland highlight the differing legacies of migration to Scotland and England from Northern Ireland. Migration to Scotland facilitated the maintenance of links with unionist and Orange culture and traditions, and enabled the induction of children, the second generation, into these cultural values and norms (see Bradley, 1995, 1996). This could be achieved through the network of Orange Lodges in Scotland, as well as the transport (the Stranraer–Larne ferry) and family links with Northern Ireland. Scotland also has its own continuing tradition of sectarianism, in which anti-Catholicism and anti-Irishness are intertwined (Walls and Williams, 2005).

## Conclusion

These seven participants were unknown to the recognised Irish communities and networks in the four English locations where the fieldwork was carried out. This reflects observations made elsewhere that Irish Protestants do not, in general, identify with the imagined community of the Irish abroad and do not participate in community associations and networks (McAuley, 1996; Devlin Trew, 2005).

In his reflection on the emigration experiences of Northern Irish Protestants to Britain, McAuley (1996) highlights the profoundly alienating experience of migration. Outsiders to both the emigrant Irish community and mainstream British society, they are, to use McAuley's phrase "double migrants"; he also notes the centrality of sectarianism and social division to the experiences of migrant Northern Irish Protestants (1996). Similarly, Devlin Trew noted that many Northern Irish Protestant emigrants narrated their frequent sense of alienation from Irish communities and networks (2005).

This examination of the narratives of the children of Irish Protestant migrants (from the Republic of Ireland as well as Northern Ireland) illustrates the impact of this alienation and sectarianism on the next generation. None of the interviewees from Irish Protestant backgrounds had particularly Irish childhoods nor did they have strong Irish/Northern Irish senses of identity. Their distance from the Irish community in Britain was underlined by the snowballing methods used to locate these interviewees. But all acknowledged that there were elements of their life stories reflective of their Irish backgrounds and which motivated their participation in this research. In common with much of the broader cohort, their interview was the first time they had discussed their Irish background with anyone outside of their immediate family.

In particular, parental expressions of anti-Catholicism posed profound difficulties for some of the interviewees, as they lacked the cultural knowledge and experience which might have provided an explanatory framework. They were also aware of sectarian fault lines in Ireland, and particularly Northern Ireland. These experiences and knowledge marked an important dimension of difference between themselves and their peers (Irish or otherwise), albeit one which they struggled to understand in a contemporary English cultural and political context.

### Notes

1 The authors would like to thank Mary J. Hickman and Joseph M. Bradley for their comments on the paper.
2 In particular, the section "Leaving Ireland" in Hyndman, 1996.
3 This project, "The second-generation Irish: a hidden population in multi-ethnic Britain", was funded by an ESRC grant (R000238367), and directed by Professor Bronwen Walter. Co-researchers were Professor Mary J. Hickman,

Dr Joseph Bradley and Dr Sarah Morgan. "The Irish2 Project" was the name used when recruiting participants. Fieldwork locations were Banbury, Coventry, London and Manchester in England, and Strathclyde in Scotland.

4 Throughout, we use the term "Protestant" in its widest sense, to include dissenter denominations as well as Church of Ireland.

5 This paper deals with interviewees in England only, although some comparisons with interviewees in Scotland with Irish Protestant backgrounds are drawn. The situation in Scotland is quite different from England, and merits a separate discussion.

6 The proportion of people identifying as Church of Ireland (including Protestant), Presbyterian and Methodist in relevant Republic of Ireland Censuses was as follows: 1946, 5.3%; 1961, 4.6%; 1971, 4.0%. Equivalent proportions for Northern Ireland are: 1951, 60.6%; 1961, 58.2%; and, 1971, 53.4%. See CSO, 2003 and NISRA, 1993.

7 In this instance, we use the term *British*, since not all the fathers concerned were born in England.

## References

Akenson, D. H. (2000) "Irish migration to North America, 1800–1920", in A. Bielenberg (ed.) *The Irish Diaspora* (London: Longman), pp. 111–38.

Bradley, J. M. (1995) *Ethnic and Religious Identity in Scotland: Culture, Politics and Football* (Aldershot: Avebury).

Bradley, J. M. (1996) "Football, religion and ethnicity: Irish identity in Scotland", *Irish Studies Centre Occasional Papers Series*, 9, University of North London.

Central Statistics Office (2002) *Census of Population, volume 12—religion* (Dublin: CSO). www.cso.ie/census/Census2002Results.htm

Compton P. (1992) "Migration trends for Northern Ireland; links with Great Britain", in J. Stillwell, P. Rees and P. Boden (eds) *Migration Processes and Patterns: Volume 2 Population Redistribution in the United Kingdom* (London: Belhaven).

Devlin Trew, J. (2005) "Irish Protestant migration in the late 20th century". Paper presented at conference on Irish Protestant Identities, University of Salford, 16–18 September.

Dunne, C. (2003) *An Unconsidered People: The Irish in London* (Dublin: New Island).

Hickman, M. J. and Walter, B. (1997) *Discrimination and the Irish Community in Britain* (London: Commission for Racial Equality).

Hickman, M. J., Morgan, S. and Walter, B. (2001) *Second-Generation Irish People in Britain: A Demographic, Socio-economic and Health Profile* (London: University of North London).

Hickman, M. J., Morgan, S., Walter, B. and Bradley, J. (2005) "The limitations of whiteness and the boundaries of Englishness: second-generation Irish identifications and positionings in multiethnic Britain", *Ethnicities*, 5.2: 160–82.

Hyndman, M. (1996) *Further Afield: Journeys from a Protestant Past* (Belfast: Beyond the Pale).

Jenkins, W. (2003) "Between the lodge and the meeting-house: mapping the identities and social worlds of Irish Protestants in late Victorian Toronto", *Social and Cultural Geography*, 4: 75–98.

Kells, M. (1995a) *Ethnic Identity Amongst Young Irish Middle Class Migrants in London*, Irish Studies Centre Occasional Papers Series 4, University of North London.

Kells, M. (1995b) " 'I'm myself and nobody else': gender and ethnicity among young Irish middle-class women in London", in P. O'Sullivan (ed.) *Irish Women and Irish Migration Volume 4: The Irish World Wide: History, Heritage, Identity*, (Leicester: Leicester University Press), pp. 201–34.

Kennedy, R. (1973) *The Irish: Emigration, Marriage, and Fertility* (Berkeley, CA: University of California Press).

Leyburn, J. G. (1962) *The Scotch-Irish: A Social History* (Chapel Hill: University of North Carolina Press).

Logue, P. (ed.) (2000) *Being Irish* (Dublin: Oak Tree Press).

McAuley, J. (1996) "Under an Orange banner: reflections on the northern Protestant experiences of emigration", in P. O'Sullivan (ed.) *The Irish World Wide, Volume Five: Religion and Identity* (Leicester: Leicester University Press), pp. 43–69.

Miller, K. A. (2000) " 'Scotch-Irish', 'Black Irish' and 'Real Irish': emigrants and identities in the old South", in A. Bielenberg (ed.) *The Irish Diaspora* (Harlow: Longman), pp. 139–57.

Morgan, S. (1997) *The Contemporary Racialization of the Irish in Britain* (unpublished PhD thesis, University of North London).

Northern Ireland Statistical Research Agency (1993) *The Northern Ireland Census Report 1991* (Belfast: NISRA).

Patterson, B. (ed.) (2002) *The Irish in New Zealand: Historical Contexts and Perspectives* (Wellington: Stout Research Centre for New Zealand Studies).

Shirlow, P. and McGovern, M. (eds) (1997) *Who are the "People"? Unionism, Protestantism and Loyalism in Northern Ireland* (London: Pluto).

Sloane, B. (1993) "Sectarianism and the Protestant mind: some approaches to a current theme in Anglo-Irish drama", *Études Irlandaises*, 18.2: 33–43.

Song, M. (2005) *Choosing Ethnic Identity* (Cambridge: Polity).

Tobin, R. (2005) " 'Tracing again the tiny snail track': Southern Protestant memoir since 1950", *Yearbook of English Studies: Irish Writing Since 1950*, 35: 171–85.

Walls, P. and Williams, R. (2005) "Religious discrimination in Scotland: a rebuttal of Bruce et al's claim that sectarianism is a myth", *Ethnic and Racial Studies*, 25.4: 759–67.

Walter, B. (1986) "Ethnicity and Irish residential distribution", *Transactions of the Institute of British Geographers*, 11: 131–46.

Walter, B. (2000) "Shamrocks growing out of their mouths: language and the racialisation of the Irish in Britain", in A. Kershen (ed.) *Language, Labour and Migration* (Ashgate: Abingdon).

Walter, B. (2001) *Outsiders Inside: Whiteness, Place and Irish Women* (London: Routledge).

Walter, B. (2005) "Exploring diaspora space: entangled Irish/English genealogies", in L. Harte, Y. Whelan and P. Crotty (eds) *Ireland: Space, Text, Time* (Dublin: Liffey).

Walter, B. with Gray, B., Almeida Dowling, L. and Morgan, S. (2002a) *Irish Emigrants and Irish Communities Abroad: A Study of Existing Sources of Information and Analysis for the Task Force on Policy Regarding Emigrants* (Dublin: Stationery Office).

Walter, B., Morgan, S., Hickman, M. J. and Bradley, J. (2002b) "Family stories, public silence: Irish identity construction amongst the second-generation Irish in England", *Scottish Geographical Journal*, 118.3: 201–17.

# Part V
# The overseas context

# 13

# Ulster Presbyterian immigration to America

*James E. Doan*

## Introduction

This chapter deals with the immigration of Ulster Presbyterians to America over a 100–year period, from the late seventeenth to the late eighteenth century. During this period, they formed one of the major groups of immigrants to the American colonies, and their influence both then and subsequently in American culture has been of major importance. This chapter examines the reasons for their emigration from Ulster, the times and locations of their settlements in America, and their relationship with the colonial authorities, with other Protestant groups in the American colonies and with the indigenous peoples they encountered.

## The first phase: 1680–1720

Throughout the eighteenth century, Ulster-Scot Presbyterians formed one of the major groups immigrating to the American colonies. As early as the 1680s Ulster Scots, or "Scotch-Irish", were settling in the Chesapeake Bay region of Maryland. In a report dated 25 June 1695, for example, Sir Thomas Laurence, Secretary of Maryland, states:

> In the two counties of Dorchester and Somerset, where the Scotch-Irish are most numerous, they almost clothe themselves by their linen and woolen manufactures and plant little tobacco, which learning from one another, they leave off planting. Shipping, therefore, and the bringing in of all manner of English clothing is to be encouraged, and if they be brought in at easy rates, the planter will live comfortably and will be induced to go on planting tobacco. (Ford, 1915: 180)

This mention of the "Scotch-Irish" (more common, by far, in American parlance than the now more politically correct "Scots-Irish") indicates that they were a community already well established in which linen and wool manufactures had attained considerable development. By this time the community had called for ministerial support, with clergy eventually coming from the Laggan Valley in east Donegal to serve Maryland's eastern shore (Griffin, 2001: 89, 114).

No other record exists of a specifically Scotch-Irish settlement in America at this point. For instance, on 18 May 1680, Governor Bradstreet of Massachusetts wrote that very few English, Scots, Irish, or foreigners had arrived within the past seven years, though many Scots and Irish had been brought there as indentured servants during the Cromwellian period (Ford, 1915: 181). Numerous Anglo-Irish and Scotch-Irish may have emigrated to the American colonies during the disturbances of the mid- to late 1680s, for we read in the memoranda of Sir Paul Rycaut, the English Royalist who served as secretary to the Irish Lord Lieutenant: "Those who can fly out of the country, either to Pennsylvania, Virginia or other places, hasten away" (Patrick, 1972: 123–82, cited in Connolly, 1992: 37).

At any rate, the Maryland settlement had little influence on the overall development of a Scotch-Irish presence in America, though it was important in terms of the establishment of the Presbyterian Church. Francis Makemie, who came to Maryland in response to the initial call for support, organised the first American Presbytery. In the early 1700s the Anglican Church was trying to build up membership in the American colonies. Makemie went to London in the summer of 1704 and appealed to both Presbyterian and Anglican leaders for men and funds to sustain them. Support was pledged for missionaries for two years, and Makemie returned to America with two young clergymen, John Hampton (who, like Makemie, had prepared for the ministry under the supervision of the Laggan Presbytery) and George McNish, the latter probably a Scotsman. The three arrived in Maryland in 1705, and in the spring of 1706 they united with Jedediah Andrews, John Wilson, Nathaniel Taylor and Samuel Davis, four clergymen already working in Pennsylvania, Delaware and Maryland, to form the Presbytery of Philadelphia (Ford, 1915: 331).

Antagonism between the settled colonists and the Scotch-Irish newcomers, particularly over religious matters, may be seen from the fact that Makemie incurred the wrath of the Anglican Governor of New York and New Jersey, Edward Hyde Cornbury, by not gaining his permission to preach, which he would have undoubtedly refused since he was opposed to dissenters. Though ultimately acquitted of "preaching without a license", Makemie still forfeited £83 to the legal system to be rid of his problems (Bolton, 1989: 269, and Jackson, 1993: 44).

The large-scale exodus from Ulster beginning in the early eighteenth century was a direct result of the English attempts to control industry and trade in Ireland, Scotland and the American colonies. "Colonies and plantations were valued simply as a convenience to home interests and it was considered intolerable that they should develop industries of a competitive character" (Ford, 1915: 182). After the Restoration, when Ireland was beginning to recover from the effects of the Cromwellian wars, Irish exports of cattle so alarmed English landowners who claimed that Irish competition was lowering English rents that laws were enacted in 1665 and 1680 prohibiting the importation into England from Ireland of all cattle, sheep and swine, beef, pork, bacon, mutton, butter and cheese (Ford, 1915: 182). The Scottish government also complained of the restrictive effects of English law on Scottish industry and obtained some relief, at the same time subjecting Ireland to worse treatment. In February 1667, an embargo was placed on the importation of Irish cattle, salt beef, meal and all kinds of grain; and subsequently horses were added to the list. This embargo was probably more injurious to Ulster than the earlier English prohibition, and explains "the general poverty abounding in those parts" mentioned as one of the reasons that in 1684 there was a general disposition toward emigration among the clergy of the Laggan Presbytery (Ford, 1915: 183).

In addition to prohibiting Irish importation to England and Scotland, the government also passed laws in 1663, 1670 and 1696 excluding Irish vessels from the American trade and prohibiting any importation directly from the colonies to Ireland. These protectionist acts were aimed particularly at the Irish woollen industry, which directly threatened English manufacturers. In 1699 the exclusionary policy was confirmed by a law (the Woolen Act) passed by the English Parliament prohibiting the Irish from exporting manufactured wool to *any* country whatsoever. The main Irish industry was thus destroyed and it was not until 1705 that, at the urgent petition of the Irish Parliament, the Irish were allowed to export white and brown linens to the American colonies; but checked, striped and dyed linens were absolutely excluded, and no colonial goods could be brought directly to Ireland (Ford, 1915: 184–5).

After the Glorious Revolution in 1688 Scottish migration to Ulster greatly increased. Land was offered on long lease at low rents, and for several years a steady stream of Scottish Presbyterians entered the country. In 1715 Archbishop Synge estimated that no fewer than 50,000 Scottish families had settled in Ulster since the Revolution. In 1717 and 1718, as the leases began to fall due, the landlords doubled and tripled the rents, so that smaller farms actually passed from Protestant to Catholic tenants who were ready to pay higher rents. While both Catholic and Presbyterian tenants were being rackrented by their land-lords, they were also forced to pay tithes to an established Anglican

Church. Moreover, fresh legal disabilities were placed on both religious groups. The penal act of 1704 against Roman Catholics had a test clause aimed at Presbyterians as well, unless they received communion in the Anglican Church, which most refused. Presbyterian clergy had now no official standing and marriages performed by them were considered null and void. To the High Churchmen they were actually inferior to Catholic priests, who were considered lawfully ordained in the line of apostolic succession. Presbyterians and other dissenters could not serve in the army, the militia, the civil service, the municipal corporations, the teaching profession or the commission of the peace. In Belfast, the entire corporation was expelled, and Derry lost ten of its twelve aldermen (Adamson, 1994: 1–21).

Meanwhile, the New England colonies had begun soliciting immigrants from Scotland and Ireland. The Reverend Cotton Mather, the leading Congregationalist clergyman in a colony (Massachusetts) where religion was the principal force in education, society and official life, was in close touch with religious and political affairs in both countries. His father had received his Master of Arts from Trinity College, Dublin, and his two uncles, Nathaniel and Samuel, were well-known preachers in Dublin. He sent books and pamphlets to Glasgow University from time to time, and had received the honorary degree of Doctor of Divinity there in 1710. On 20 September 1706, he recorded:

> I write letters unto diverse persons of Honour both in *Scotland* and in *England*; to procure Settlements of Good *Scotch* Colonies, to the Northward of us. This may be a thing of great consequence. (cited in Bolton, 1989: 17)

Mather's plan was to settle hardy Scots families on the frontiers of Maine and New Hampshire to protect the settled towns of Massachusetts from the French and native tribes. In his *Memorial of the Present Deplorable State of New England* he also suggested that a Scots colony might be of good service in getting possession of Acadia (Nova Scotia) (Bolton, 1989: 17). A final, and perhaps most important, reason for moving the Scotch-Irish to the frontier was that there was insufficient good farm land in eastern Massachusetts, which also explains why the indentured labour system was less popular here than in the middle and southern colonies (Jackson, 1993: 58).

In response to these calls and to escape from the harsh religious and economic conditions being imposed, people began to flee Ulster, frequently accompanied by their clergy. Among those emigrating were the Rev. William Homes and his brother-in-law, the Reverend Thomas Craighead, who sailed from Derry on the ship *Thomas and Jane*, arriving in Boston during the first week of October 1714. The settling of these two clergymen in New England provided a conduit for the subsequent emigration. Homes's eldest son, Robert, became captain of a ship engaged in transporting emigrants to America. Married to Mary Franklin, sister of Benjamin Franklin, Captain Homes appears to have been the agent through whom people in Strabane, Derry, Donoghmore (Co. Donegal) and Donegal town learned of opportunities to leave for New England. On 13 April 1718, he sailed for Ireland and his ship returned "full of passengers about the middle of October" (Ford, 1915: 189–90). During this first phase of Scotch-Irish immigration (1714–20, inclusive), fifty-four ships arrived in New England from Ireland (Ford, 1915: 192). Some 5,000 Ulstermen, women and children sailed to America in 1717 and 1718 alone—a highly risky journey taking anywhere from 42 to 90 days. By July 1728, seventeen ships were in Northern Irish ports waiting to take passengers to North America (Jackson, 1993: 45), and during the summer some 3,000 persons left for New England and Pennsylvania. A year later the number had increased. Robert Gambie, a Derry merchant, reported in July 1729: "There is gone and to go this Summer from this Port Twenty-five Sail of Ships, who carry each from One Hundred and forty passengers to America; there are many more going from Belfast; and the Ports near Colrain" (Jackson, 1993: 46). At this time, Belfast was the usual port of embarkation, with New Castle, Delaware, and Philadelphia the usual destinations. Larne, 30 miles from Belfast, was the second largest, with many of its departing ships headed for New York, and Derry was third, with additional ships sailing from Portrush (Coleraine) and Newry.

A decade after these first general sailings, the English authorities began investigating why so many Ulster folk were leaving. A commission was appointed and, on 26 June 1729, it sent its findings to the Privy Council. The reasons that emerged were the bad harvests in the late 1720s, which produced multiple hardships, including the rise in the price of corn and the disastrous drop in the price of linens. Rackrenting had continued unabated and clergy had pushed steadily, even bringing suit in some cases, to collect tithes from farmers whose income had declined on a daily basis. Despite these reasons the commissioners felt that the people from Northern Ireland left for purely "selfish" reasons. Like their nineteenth-century Irish counterparts, they expected to find "great advantages in New England and Pennsylvania", and had been led to these conclusions by rosy, "unrealistic" letters from those who had preceded them. Shipping companies and ship captains were most to blame, giving idyllic pictures of the New World and frequently offering free passage to the head of a household. The report asserted that these shipping companies had become large landowners in

America and it was in their interest to bring people over to settle on their lands. Finally, in a jab at the Ulstermen's probity, the Commission claimed that "many dishonest and ill-designing people, to avoid payments of their just debts get on board ships . . . [whose captains] . . . conceal them from their creditors by refusing to let any persons see who is on board" (cited in Jackson, 1993: 46–7).

The General Synod of the Presbyterian Church in Ulster was closely connected with the emigration in this early period. The Synod of 1717 is particularly interesting for its long and important sessions, in which the Reverends William Boyd of Macosquin, James McGregor of Aghadowey and Cornwall of Augher (near Clogher) and others interested in America took part. Nine presbyteries were represented: Down, Belfast, Antrim, Tyrone, Armagh, Coleraine, Derry, Convoy and Monaghan. One hundred churches sent their clergy and usually also a ruling elder to the Synod.[1]

In 1718 the Reverend William Boyd of Macosquin was sent to New England to see what arrangements could be made for settling a group of Presbyterians there. Boyd had brought with him a petition signed by 322 persons, many of them clergy, addressed to Governor Shute of New England, certifying that he (Boyd) had been appointed "to assure his Excellency of our sincere and hearty Inclinations to Transport ourselves to that very excellent and renowned Plantation upon our obtaining from his Excellency suitable incouragement" (Ford, 1915: 190–1). Shute agreed to let them settle on the frontier. One of the groups, led by Reverend James McGregor of Aghadowey, established the town of Londonderry, New Hampshire (Doan, 2000: 1–17).

Despite his seeming receptiveness on the part of the New England authorities, the Scotch-Irish immigration was from the first viewed with doubts and suspicion. Despite their shared Calvinist beliefs, the New England Puritans did not welcome the immigrants, possibly reflecting an English distrust of the Scots and Irish. The New Englanders considered the Ulstermen to be rough of speech, hard drinkers, poorly dressed and illiterate, although Boyd's petition shows that 97 per cent (311 out of 322) of these immigrants could write their own names—the test of literacy at that time. A letter from Thomas Lechmere to John Winthrop mentions Irish immigration in 1718 with the remark: "20 ministers with their congregations in general, will come over in Spring; I wish their comeing so over do not prove fatall in the End" (Ford, 1915: 193).

Among the various early Ulster Scot colonies established in New England, in 1718 a party of settlers from western Co. Derry established a settlement at Casco Bay in modern Maine, though this colony disappeared after four or five years of severe winters and hostile native

Americans. Another group in Maine, led by David Dunbar, attempted to become a colony independent of the Puritans, though the Massachusetts magistrates would have none of this and, in 1732, persuaded parliament to disavow Dunbar, who had returned to England. He was imprisoned for debt and later released and appointed Governor of St Helena in the South Atlantic. The "Irish" potato (still so-called in much of America despite its actual New World origins) was introduced to Maine from Ireland during this period, where it flourished. In addition, the Scotch-Irish are credited with introducing the spinning wheel and the manufacture of linen products to the British American colonies in the early eighteenth century, not to mention "moonshine" (comparable to their *poitín*) (Jackson, 1993: 59).

The arrival of hordes of poverty-stricken Ulster immigrants, foreshadowing the arrival of their equally destitute countrymen during the famine some 130 years later, must have sent shivers down the spines of the more proper Bostonians. Very few were allowed to remain in Boston, and the majority were diverted to settlements in central Massachusetts (Worcester Co.), and the frontier regions of New Hampshire and Maine. As the influx had increased by 1718 (fifteen ships from Ulster arriving in the American colonies in that year alone), the authorities were becoming more and more nervous about the situation. During that winter many were warned to leave Boston, including: Thomas Walker, John Rogers, James Blare (Blair), with Elizabeth and Rachel, who had come from Ireland in August; Anne Hansom who came down from Casco Bay, and Mehitable Lewis from Piscataqua; Robert Holmes and wife, William Holmes and child, also from Casco Bay; and Alexander McGregory, lately from Ireland with his family. All were asked to leave or provide sureties (Bolton, 1989: 157).

It soon became clear to the Scotch-Irish that these descendants of the early English setters were, if anything, less tolerant than the Anglicans they had fled in Ulster. The conflict between Puritan (Anglican or Congregationalist) and Presbyterian was, as historian Maury Klein put it, a "confrontation between marble and granite" (Jackson, 1993: 58). They were alike in their religious rigidity and their unwillingness to have anything to do with other creeds. The Congregationalists expected the Presbyterian Scotch-Irish to support the established church if they wanted to remain in Massachusetts.

### The second phase: Pennsylvania and points south-west

The earliest Irish settlement in modern Pennsylvania was in the triangular projection between Delaware and Maryland now belonging to

Chester Co., Pennsylvania. In 1683 a tract on the east side of Elk Creek, Cecil Co., Maryland, was surveyed for Edwin O'Dwire and "fifteen other Irishmen". This tract became known as New Munster, suggesting that the original group of settlers came from the south-west region of Ireland. However, the district received so many settlers from Ulster that they founded two Presbyterian churches, "Head of Christiana" and "The Rock". This region was claimed by both Maryland and Pennsylvania, and the boundary lines were not resolved until 1774. The Scotch-Irish settlers generally entered through the port of Newcastle (Delaware) thirteen miles away, hoping to settle on lands claimed by William Penn, thus avoiding Maryland and its tithes.

In 1720, James Logan (1674–1751), the Colonial Secretary of Pennsylvania, was extremely worried by the aggressive movements of native tribes on the borders of the Quaker and German settlements. He wrote to a friend, "I thought it might be prudent to plant a Settlement of those who had so bravely defended Derry and Inniskillen as a frontier in case of any Disturbance" (cited in Fitzpatrick, 1989: 73). As in Massachusetts the Ulster Scots were being cast in the role which they had provided in Ulster, as defenders of the English Establishment against the rebellious natives. Because of disputes within the Penn family, Logan allowed few grants in any one place after 1720, except to the Scotch-Irish, who established settlements such as Donegal, in Lancaster Co. (at that time part of Chester Co.). Place names such as Toboyne (from Taughboyne) suggest that many of the early emigrants came from west of the River Foyle, once again, the Laggan region (east Donegal).

Logan was not prepared for the consequences of his invitation. In a letter to the Penns in 1724, he referred to the new immigrants as "bold and indigent strangers, saying as their excuse when challenged for titles, that we had solicited for colonists and they had come accordingly" (Ford, 1915: 264). In a letter of 23 November 1727, he wrote: "The Irish settle generally toward the Maryland line, where no lands can honestly be sold till the dispute with Lord Baltimore [Governor of Maryland] is decided." He continues with some particulars about the great volume of migration from Ulster to Pennsylvania: "We have from the North of Ireland great numbers yearly. Eight or nine ships this last Fall discharged at Newcastle." Obviously more concerned two years later, in 1729 he wrote: "It looks as if Ireland is to send all its inhabitants hither, for last week not less than six ships arrived, and every day, two or three arrive also" (Ford, 1915: 264). Between December 1728 and December 1729, the immigrants numbered 6,208, of whom 5,605 were Scotch-Irish. Later, the arrivals exceeded 10,000 a year, close to the 12,000 German immigrants a year arriving at the same time. By 1749, it was estimated that the Irish and Scotch-Irish formed one quarter of Pennsylvania's population (62,000 out of 250,000), and in 1774 Benjamin Franklin estimated the proportion as one-third (116,000 out of 350,000), including descendants of the original settlers.

In 1715, the population of Ulster was about 600,000, including 200,000 Scottish-descended Presbyterians, 130,000 Anglicans and 270,000 Irish Catholics (Doyle, 1981: 58). As many as 250,000 to 300,000 Ulster men, women and children came to America by 1776, mainly Presbyterian, though also including Anglicans, Quakers and other Protestants (possibly comprising 20,000 of the total). The immigrants included Catholics as well, perhaps as many as 30,000–40,000, many of whom later converted to their neighbours' religions in predominantly Protestant colonial America, perhaps when they married Protestant women (Doyle, 1981: 69–70, 74). In 1755, William Douglass wrote that the fall-in of leases "occasioned an emigration of many north of Ireland Scotch Presbyterians, with an intermixture of wild Irish Roman Catholicks" (Doyle, 1981: 57). Wealthier immigrants, including Irish Quakers in Philadelphia and prosperous Scotch-Irish farmers, probably brought northern Irish Catholic servants with them (Doyle, 1981: 57, 94–7). Up to 100,000 southern Irish (mainly Catholics, but including perhaps 10,000 Anglicans and other Protestants), as well as a number of Irish inhabitants of the West Indies, migrated to America before the Revolution (Doyle, 1981: 61, 70–1, 74).

The immigrants generally followed the river valleys. One stream moved up the Delaware River, and not long after 1720 a group of Scotch-Irish settled in Bucks Co., with an early monument being Neshaminy Presbyterian Church, established about 1726 in Warwick township. The principal and most desirable area of occupation, however, was the Susquehanna Valley. From the original settlements on the Maryland border, the Scotch-Irish moved into the interior along the east side of the Susquehanna, settling by sides of creeks, using the water for mills. Signs of these early settlements are Upper Octorara Church (1720), Donegal (1721), Pequa (1724), Middle Octorara (1727), Derry (1729) and Paxtang (1729). Thus, large Scotch-Irish settlements were made in Chester, Lancaster and Dauphin Cos in the first third of the century.

Partly as a result of James Logan's plan and partly because the frontier drew the Ulster settlers like a magnet, the Scotch-Irish townships had formed a protective circle around the old Quaker farmlands. Once the newcomers were established in force, though, there was continual friction between them and the indigenous peoples. Probably their experience in Ireland had conditioned them to conflict with a native population, particularly one they considered "heathen". As early as 1729, Logan had

**Figure 13.1** Ulster Presbyterian settlements in colonial North America to 1776

written that "the Indians themselves are alarmed at the swarms of strangers and we are afraid of a breach between them, for the Irish are very rough to them" (Ford, 1915: 291). The Ulstermen generally ignored treaties setting limits to white expansion, which the Quaker authorities had made hoping to maintain peace with the native population. The Scotch-Irish had little regard for either provincial laws or native rights. They moved into native-designated lands and were quick to resort to violence if any attempt were made to stop them (Fitzpatrick, 1989: 73). Whenever they took land from the indigenous peoples, they did so because they felt they could "do what God wanted" with it better than the natives (Jackson, 1993: 112). Complicating matters was Pennsylvania's long-standing border dispute with Maryland "which was willing to legitimate its claims to the Susquehanna country by issuing titles to the immigrant squatters and endorsing armed resistance to Pennsylvania officials" (Richter, 1992: 274).

When the indigenous tribes, including Delawares, Conestogas and Shawnees, refused to sell their land, Logan found a solution through the exploitation of Iroquois claims to possession of the Susquehanna watershed. He wrote to John Penn in 1731: "There will be an absolute necessity of treating with the Five Nations [Iroquois] and securing their friendship more effectually" (Richter, 1992: 274). In a series of shady transactions ending in the "Walking Purchase" of upper Delaware lands in 1737, Logan worked closely with the Iroquois leaders, which led to the transfer of Susquehanna and Delaware Valley lands to the province and a forced removal of the indigenous peoples to new homes in the Ohio country (Richter, 1992: 274).

These actions resulted in bands of displaced native groups (like the seventeenth-century Irish woodkerns in Ulster) roaming through the frontier areas, becoming increasingly bitter and hostile towards the white man. In 1737 John Craig wrote about natives travelling in western Pennsylvania, in groups of twenty to fifty. They were "generally civil", but when they arrived at a household, they had to be fed "or they become their own stewards and cooks sparing nothing" (Diary, Historical Foundation, Montreat, North Carolina, cited in Jackson, 1993: 112). Roving native Americans also killed white men's cattle for food, and whole communities would build fortifications to which they would retreat whenever it would appear that unfriendly natives were around.

The "Indian problem" was one reason why Parliament raised no strong objections to increased Scotch-Irish immigration to America in the 1740s and 1750s. At the same time, England's great competitor for the North American continent, France, was enlisting the support of numerous native tribes against the English, so that Parliament was actively encouraging immigration. Thus, throughout the 1750s the owners of at least a dozen ships advertised in the *Belfast News-Letter* for passengers bound for America, frequently offering financial assistance to those who needed it (Jackson, 1993: 113). The first colonial war in which the

Scotch-Irish played a role was King George's War (1744–48), known in Europe as the War of the Austrian Succession (which had begun in 1740). Most of the action took place in New York and New England; the war ended in 1748 with England returning Louisburg to France without consulting the colonial forces, an action which led to resentment on the part of the colonists towards the mother country.

By the 1730s the Scotch-Irish began moving west along the Schuylkill and Susquehanna rivers, crossing the Blue Ridge mountains and turning southwards along the rich Cumberland Valley. As the Scotch-Irish moved down along the east side of the Susqehanna, no doubt they lusted over the native lands across the river, known as Kittochtinny, a beautiful valley lying between the Susquehanna and the Tuscarora Mountains, extending into western Maryland and Virginia. This is a natural thoroughfare between the north and the south, a fact made clear during the Civil War in the series of battles leading up to Gettysburg. The colonial authorities agreed to Scotch-Irish occupation after title was obtained from the native peoples in 1736. From here migration moved southward, with Cumberland Co. being organised in 1750; Franklin Co., to the south-west, in 1764; and Adams Co., to the south-east, not until 1800. By the 1750s, Scotch-Irish were also filling up the back country of North Carolina, and by the 1760s they had pushed south into the Carolina Piedmont, joined by new Ulster immigrants coming through the port of Charleston. At the same time, they began moving south-west along the mountain ranges into what became West Virginia. In the 1780s they went through the Cumberland Gap, settling in Kentucky and Tennessee, though this was primarily a second-generation movement (Doyle, 1981: 56). These later settlers were accompanied by Baptist clergy, more willing to face the rigours of frontier living than the more settled Presbyterians. "Less encumbered by formalities than the Presbyterian Church, the Baptist Church proved the ideal religious institution for the frontier' (Griffin, 2001: 165). Hence, we see the gradual disappearance of the strong link between the early Ulster Scot immigrants and Presbyterianism in what was to become the United States, replaced by a link with the Baptists and other more evangelical faiths among the descendants of the Ulster Scots even today.

## Conclusion

Probably as a result of their success in acting as a buffer between the settled English colonists and the native Irish in Ulster, the Scottish immigrants had provided an invaluable service in the colonisation and subjugation of that province. Similarly, at least initially, their descendants provided the same service in the American colonies, but as their desire for land outpaced the supply, they helped spark the revolt leading to the end of British rule. Their spirit of independence and even anti-authoritarianism continues even to this day among their descendants today, the Scotch-Irish, particularly in the American South.

## Note

1 The Synod records from this time also show a considerable interest in the Irish language, some clergy being able to read and others to preach in Irish. In 1710 the Synod sent six clergy and three probationers (including McClean of Markethill, Thompson of Ballybay, McGregor of Aghadowey, Dunlop of Letterkenney, Wilson of Carlingford, Boyd of Maghera, Higginbotham of Coleraine, Plunkett of Glasslough and Dunlop of Derg) to preach in Irish (Ó Snodaigh, 1995: 49), probably to minister to Irish- and perhaps Scots Gaelic-speaking Protestants as well as to convert Roman Catholics (which became more of an impetus during the nineteenth century). As late as 1716 some 10 per cent of the Presbyterian clergy in Ulster could speak and preach in Irish.

## References

Adamson, I. (1994) "The Ulster-Scottish connection", in I. S. Wood (ed.) *Scotland & Ulster* (Edinburgh: Mercat Press), pp. 1–21.

Bolton, C. K. (1989[1910]) *Scotch-Irish Pioneers in Ulster and America* (Bowie, MD: Heritage).

Connolly, S. J. (1992) *Religion, Law and Power: The Making of Protestant Ireland 1660–1760* (Oxford: Clarendon).

Doan, J. E. (2000) "The *Eagle Wing* Expedition (1636) and the Settlement of Londonderry, New Hampshire (1719): Two Episodes in Ulster-Scots/Scotch-Irish History", *Journal of Scotch-Irish Studies*, 1.1: 1–17.

Doyle, D. (1981) *Ireland, Irishmen and Revolutionary America, 1760–1820* (Dublin and Cork: Mercier).

Fitzpatrick, R. (1989) *God's Frontiersmen: The Scots Irish Epic* (London: Weidenfeld & Nicolson).

Ford, H. J. (1915) *The Scotch-Irish in America* (Princeton: Princeton University Press).

Griffin, P. (2001) *The People with No Name: Ireland's Ulster Scots, America's Scots Irish, and the Creation of a British Atlantic World, 1689–1764* (Princeton: Princeton University Press).

Jackson, C. (1993) *A Social History of the Scotch-Irish* (London: Madison).

Ó Snodaigh, P. (1995) *Hidden Ulster: Protestants and the Irish Language* (Belfast: Lagan).

Patrick, M. (1972) "Sir Paul Rycaut's Memoranda and Letters from Ireland 1686–1687", *Analecta Hibernica*, 27: 123–82.

Richter, D. K. (1992) *The Ordeal of the Longhouse: The Peoples of the Iroquois League in the Era of European Colonization* (Chapel Hill: University of North Carolina Press).

# 14

# Ulster transplanted: Irish Protestants, everyday life and constructions of identity in late Victorian Toronto

*William Jenkins*

## Introduction

The city lives of Irish Protestants and their descendants remain a neglected feature in the historical geography of Irish migration. This is especially true in North America, the "big case" Irish diasporic location, according to Akenson (1996). There, predominant images of Protestant Irish settlement remain centred largely on the wilderness-clearing exercises of pre-famine migrants in areas as far apart as the Old South and Upper Canada. While more recent Canadian literature has been noteworthy for providing insights on this "Protestant contribution", its emphasis, so far, on nineteenth-century rural environments has also served to draw attention to, and challenge, a more general historiographical orientation towards the settlement of Irish Catholics in American cities in the decades after 1845, and the senses of "exile" and alienation felt by many among them (Akenson, 1984, 1996; Miller, 1985; Elliott, 1988; Houston and Smyth, 1990; Wilson, 1994). It is, therefore, clear that more work is required to establish how Protestant Irish migrants experienced North American cities in the pre- and post-famine eras. While such encounters are not entirely absent from the Canadian historical literature, these studies have focused for the most part on the Orange Order and the dramatic yet unlovely issue of sectarian rioting (Houston and Smyth, 1980; Kealey, 1980; See, 1993; Winder, 2000; Clarke, 2007).

With its focus on late Victorian Toronto, this chapter suggests some additional avenues in which Irish Protestants' lives might be studied. One area that remains surprisingly unclear is the timing and provincial origins of Irish Protestant migration to urban North America. Though the role of migration from Ulster has been shown to be pivotal in the settlement of nineteenth-century Upper Canada/Ontario generally, its imprint in Toronto has been assumed rather than quantified. The city's label as the "Belfast of North America" provides suggestive, but hardly sufficient, evidence for this, though it does invite exploration of a second area of enquiry, namely, the social networks shaped by Irish Protestant migrants within Toronto and their impact in navigating these migrants (and their descendants) between the worlds of the "ethnic group" and the "host culture" at various stages of their lives. In Toronto, like Belfast, a majority "Protestant host culture" took form while the energies of its more evangelically-minded residents inspired another nickname for the city— "Toronto the Good". Ulster Protestant migrants were influential in giving legitimacy to this second nickname as well. A third and final area concerns the fate of the "Irish" portion of these migrants' identities in the making of such a "host culture". Given the extent to which senses of Irishness have endured and become reinvigorated at various times among the Catholic Irish in North America, and the United States in particular (Byron, 1999; Kenny, 2000), it is all too easy to overlook the elements of Irish identity that Irish Protestants might have retained and consider how these could be mobilised among both migrant and later generations. Through the use of quantitative and qualitative materials in a selected number of social and spatial contexts, this chapter uses the case of Toronto to illuminate these three avenues of enquiry about Irish Protestants in urban North America. With much of the ensuing discussion revolving around Toronto's public life, an emphasis on the lives of men is evident. Research that clarifies the experiences of Protestant Irish women in urban North America remains a largely open field.

### Irish Protestant immigration to Toronto in the nineteenth century

If one is to consider the possibility of a global "Irish Protestant diaspora", or even an "Ulster diaspora", Toronto emerges as a location of some significance. Through the cross-linking of different source materials, the immigration stream between Ireland and Toronto can now be established with more clarity than previously. Table 14.1 indicates that Ulster migrants have been prominent in both a materially "comfortable" group of Irish Protestants as well as their "needier" counterparts in late Victorian Toronto.[1] To take the more affluent portion first, the biographies of 138 Irish-born men were derived from the two-volume *History of Toronto and the County of York* (Mulvany and Adam, 1885). Given certain inconsistencies of detail for variables such as birth year and religion, a cross-linking exercise was performed to enhance the profiles, using the indexes to the Ontario censuses of 1871 and 1881.[2] The Irish provincial origins of 78 men of known Protestant denomination were thus derived and 69.2 per

Table 14.1 The provincial origins of two groups of Irish-born Protestants in late Victorian Toronto

| Province of birth | "Comfortable" (c.1885) | | "Needy" (March, 1872) | |
|---|---|---|---|---|
| | Number | % | Number | % |
| Ulster | 54 | 69.2 | 44 | 50.6 |
| Leinster | 10 | 12.8 | 22 | 25.3 |
| Connaught | 9 | 11.5 | 8 | 9.2 |
| Munster | 5 | 6.4 | 13 | 14.9 |
| Total | 78 | 100.0 | 87 | 100.0 |

*Sources*: C. P. Mulvany and G. M. Adam, *History of Toronto and County of York*, 2 volumes (Toronto, 1885) and subsequent cross-linkages (see note 2); IPBS annual report 1872, Metropolitan Toronto Reference Library. Percentages are rounded.

cent were of Ulster birth. Evidence from the volumes also supports the impression of Protestant dominance and Catholic under-representation within the city's Irish middle-class that the "Belfast of Canada" label suggests (Hepburn, 1996). Of the 120 "comfortable" individuals for whom religion could be traced, only twenty were Catholics. Though this source is clearly partial in terms of who was selected from the various branches of Toronto's commercial and public world and includes a wide range of occupations, the image of a Toronto Irish middle-class with a significant cohort of Ulster Protestants becomes very clear.

Like Belfast also, Toronto had its less well-off Protestant Irish individuals and families who drew assistance from both public and private sources in hard times. Table 14.1 includes the provincial origins of such "needy" male and female recipients of financial assistance as reported in the balance sheet of the Irish Protestant Benevolent Society (IPBS) for the year ending 31 March 1872.[3] While some of these were likely to be recently arrived migrants, there is no reason to believe that all were. While a more variegated geography of Irish provincial origins is observable here, Ulster's prominence remains clear with just over half the recipients hailing from Ireland's northernmost province.

Though the numbers of individuals are relatively small, these breakdowns provide a valuable insight into the provincial sources of Toronto's Irish Protestants. They also shatter any illusions of an Irish group in the city neatly divided between comfortable Protestants and impoverished Catholics, supplementing recent analyses from census sources. For example, in a 10 per cent sample of all households of Irish ethnic origin from the 1881 census manuscripts of Toronto and its suburbs, Jenkins (2001) found 18 per cent of Irish-born Protestant household heads with a stated occupation to be engaged in unskilled labour; the proportion for more skilled and semi-skilled manual pursuits was almost 24 per cent, while a further 20 per cent were self-employed.[4] Protestant Irish migrants and their descendants evidently lived in varying material circumstances in late Victorian Toronto. The very existence of an organisation concerned with offering financial support to a clearly-defined "Irish Protestant" group, however, says something about the sectarian lenses through which Irishness was being viewed in the city in the early 1870s. The activities of the IPBS are discussed later in the chapter.

As with Upper Canada in general, the migratory flow of Irish Protestants to Toronto both pre-dated the mid-century influx of famine refugees and continued in its wake. For 90 Protestant male migrants identified in the *History of Toronto* for whom the year of departure from Ireland was provided, 52 (57.7 per cent) departed before 1848. The traces of these pre-famine arrivals were also evident in Toronto's evolving urban landscape. The streets provided the venue for both St Patrick's Day and Orange Order parades in the 1830s, the latter spectacles featuring predictable banners such as "No Surrender" and "No Repeal for Ireland" and often concluding in a less-than-respectable fashion (Goheen, 1992). In what was a medium-sized frontier town whose muddy streets were quickly traversable on foot, taverns with distinctively Irish and Ulster names greeted traveller and newly-arrived migrant alike. The 1843 city directory lists venues such as the Cavan Arms Inn, the Derry Inn, the Erin-go-Bragh Inn, the Fermanagh Inn, the Londonderry Inn and the William III inn (Lewis, 1843).

This emerging ethno-religious character of Toronto appealed to more than a few Irish Protestants contemplating migration in the post-famine period. In the new era of passenger steamships, Irish emigration agents, and those in Belfast in particular, worked hard to channel Protestants into the newly-established province of Ontario and its capital (Houston and Smyth, 1990). While the bulk of Irish emigration to North America in the post-famine era was Catholic, the majority of Irish arrivals to Toronto during these decades were Protestant, reflecting specific channels from Ireland to Canada (Fitzpatrick, 1989; Doyle, 1996). Table 14.2 indicates as such, cross-tabulating a sample of the Irish-born in the city in 1901 by year of immigration to Canada (Sager et al., 2002). Although not all of these migrants may have chosen Toronto as their initial destination, these calculations, nevertheless, suggest Catholics to have comprised just under one-third of Irish migrants settling in Toronto between 1825 and 1900. While Toronto could not compete with the labour opportunities

Table 14.2 Irish-born in the City of Toronto by year of immigration, 1901

| Year of immigration to Canada | Total number of Irish-born | % | Total number of Irish-born Catholics | % | Catholics as a % of the total for each immigration period |
|---|---|---|---|---|---|
| 1825–1855 | 93 | 16.8 | 32 | 18.1 | 34.4 |
| 1856–1870 | 128 | 23.2 | 43 | 24.3 | 33.6 |
| 1871–1880 | 106 | 19.2 | 34 | 19.2 | 32.1 |
| 1881–1890 | 170 | 30.8 | 60 | 33.9 | 35.3 |
| 1891–1900 | 55 | 10.0 | 8 | 4.5 | 14.5 |
| Total 1825–1900 | 552 | 100.0 | 177 | 100.0 | 32.1 |

*Source*: Canadian Families Project 5 per cent sample (Sager et al., 2002). Percentages are rounded.

presented by American cities such as New York and Chicago, its reputation as a Protestant and Orange citadel was hardly appealing to Irish Catholics either. Of those Irish-born individuals resident in the city in 1881, just over 40 per cent were estimated to be Catholic (Jenkins, 2001), a credible proportion in light of the evidence presented in Table 14.2. In the context of nineteenth-century Irish emigration, then, Toronto became a distinctive northern branch of "a complex network of distinct streams" flowing between specific Irish source regions and certain North American destinations (Fitzpatrick, 1996: 612).

For those Catholics living in Toronto during the late Victorian period, the vast majority of whom were of Irish birth or ancestry, it was all but impossible to ignore the economic, political and institutional power held by Protestants of various denominations. By 1881, Catholics made up less than one-fifth of the city's population (Canada, 1882) and Catholic editors such as the *Irish Canadian*'s Patrick Boyle repeatedly condemned what they regarded as the socio-political exclusion of their co-religionists. Of the twenty-nine mayors who served Toronto between 1837 and 1899, six were Irish-born Protestants (Russell, 1982) while many others served on city council as aldermen. In colonial and later provincial and dominion politics, Protestant Torontonians of Irish background such as Robert Baldwin, James Beaty, Edward Blake, and William McMaster represented a range of political opinions. The city's fiercely partisan newspaper industry also received input from Irish Protestant publishers, editors, and journalists. In the 1880s, Limerick-born Christopher Bunting's *Mail* emerged as a powerful Conservative organ, while the Orange Order's *Sentinel* newspaper was edited by the Clarke brothers from county Cavan one of whom, Edward or "Ned", would achieve prominence as city mayor and Conservative politician (Russell, 1982). The Methodist *Christian Guardian* was edited by another Cavan-born migrant, Reverend Edward H. Dewart. Toronto's police force, criticised in mid-century for its overly Orange cast, was remodelled in the 1860s along the quasi-militaristic lines of the Royal Irish Constabulary (RIC). By 1881, 75 (or 56.8 per cent) of the personnel employed on the force were Irish-born aside from the chief and his deputy, and there was a noticeable presence of ex-RIC Protestants from Ulster (Jenkins 2002/2003).

There were also alliances of evangelical Protestant clerics and lay persons whose persistent campaigns aimed at structuring Toronto into a city whose population would pursue lives consistent with what the reformers considered to be "correct" forms of morally righteous conduct. Prominent temperance men in the 1870s, for example, included Reverend Dewart, Fermanagh-born Methodist Reverend John Potts, the county Tyrone-born Baptist city treasurer, Andrew Taylor McCord, and Samuel Hume Blake, an Anglican lawyer and pamphleteer, born to Wicklow parents. All these men were involved in the IPBS at various times while their middle-class Liberal politics put them in a different social and political space from the city's Orangemen. By the end of the century, Donegal-born Francis Stephens Spence, a teacher, lay Methodist preacher, journalist and city alderman, was the driving force behind prohibition interests in both the city and province via the Dominion Alliance for the Total Suppression of the Liquor Traffic, and while a dramatic reduction in the number of tavern licences in both Toronto and Ontario had taken place since the mid-1870s, the work of Spence and his associates was anything but finished (Spence 1896; Hallowell, 1972). In 1894, a city plebiscite resulted in a majority vote for prohibition, but the measure would not arrive in the city until 1916. Protestant men of Irish background such as the above thus played an important role in ongoing attempts to make Toronto "good" throughout the Victorian period. They were not only enforcing the laws of the land, they were also instrumental in making and modifying them, and their effects could be felt in the streets and atmosphere of the city, not least on the quiet Sabbath.

If it were possible for some observers to detect a specifically Irish component to the various manifestations of "Protestant power" in Toronto, others went further in pinpointing its provincial source. With the Orangeman Ned Clarke campaigning for a third year in the mayor's seat, a correspondent named "Iroquois" complained to the *Toronto World*:

> Look at City Hall. From the Mayor down to the street scavenger it is nothing but North of Ireland "phizes" that greet you . . . the police force, the fire brigade and, to a certain extent, the public school department, is

equally overrun with North of Ireland men. North of Ireland should take a back seat for a few years. They have had more than a fair innings.[5]

Given Clarke's birthplace and fraternal affiliation, it was usual for such accounts to equate "north of Ireland" influence with that of Orangeism. But while there was more to Toronto's Ulstermen than Orangeism, so it was also true that the city's lodges had outgrown their Irish roots. Men of English and Scottish background were now present within a fraternity that bridged sections of the city's working- and lower-middle classes (Houston and Smyth, 1980; Kealey, 1980). By mid-1899, Toronto's "county" division contained fifty-eight local (primary) lodges with a membership of more than 4,000.[6] Toronto Orangeism had also largely discarded its abrasive reputation and, taking its cues from the social atmosphere around it, embraced a more "respectable" public image while continuing to grow in strength, numerically and politically, into the twentieth century (Jenkins, 2007). Toronto's "Irish Protestant world" overall was a far from homogeneous entity.

## Micro-geographies of everyday life

Despite comparisons with Belfast, tightly-defined pockets of segregated Protestants and Catholics were not typical of nineteenth-century Toronto. By the early 1880s, people of Irish birth and ancestry lived in all parts of the city (Figure 14.1).[7] Households of Irish ethnic origin ranged from a minimum of 20.3 per cent of all households in the affluent northern section of St Thomas' Ward, to a maximum of 49.3 per cent in its heavily working-class southern section. Figure 14.2 builds on these spatial distinctions, mapping Irish Protestants as a proportion of all those of Irish ethnic origin on a ward subdivision basis. Though Irish Protestants resided all over Toronto, the eastern neighbourhood of Cabbagetown emerged as a key focus for their working-class portion, with their middle-class counterparts more likely to be found in the northern subdivisions of the city. In both of these areas, it was unusual for more than one-fifth of those of Irish ethnic origin to be Catholic.

Modest single-family homes clustered along geometrically-aligned streets with a scattering of corner stores and Protestant churches summarises Cabbagetown's working-class landscape. There were also more than a few members of Orange lodges present in the neighbourhood (Houston and Smyth, 1980; Careless, 1985). Using it as the base for his novel *Cabbagetown*, Hugh Garner later described the district as the "the largest Anglo-Saxon slum in North America" (1968: vii). For journalist John V. McAree (1876–1958), the son of Ulster immigrants, who spent

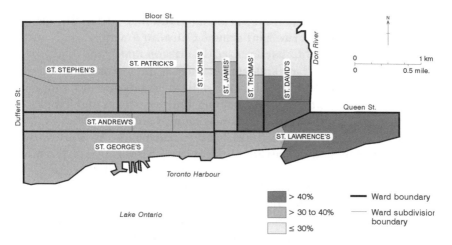

**Figure 14.1** Percentage of households of Irish ethnic origin by ward subdivision, Toronto 1881

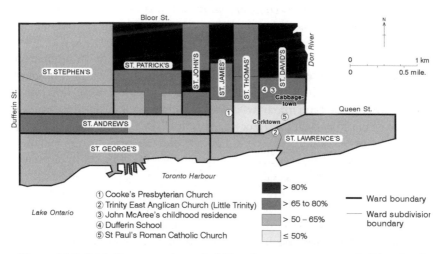

**Figure 14.2** Irish Protestant household heads as a percentage of all heads of Irish ethnic origin by ward subdivision, Toronto 1881
*Source*: see note 7. (This applies to both Figures 14.1 and 14.2)

his formative years in Cabbagetown, the "upstarts and dudes" living in the city's west end could not compare with the east end's "old history . . . especially the North of Ireland traditions which had developed there" (McAree, 1953: 92, 2).

There was more to this statement than mere nostalgia, however. As the earlier tracings of provincial origin in Table 14.1 indicate, material and imaginative links between Ulster and Toronto were forged from the 1830s onwards, and the Protestant "traditions" these engendered remained into late Victorian times. Cultural practices and social values self-consciously characterised as "Protestant" and sometimes "Irish" or "northern Irish" would continue to be identified and transmitted through routine interactions in local spaces such as churches, homes, workplaces, taverns and schools, touching males and females of all ages in different ways and with varying intensities. Identities became steadily shaped through such everyday engagements. As Shirlow and Murtagh usefully put it: "Identity is infused with imagination, but more important than that is [its] functioning . . . within defined material, social and cultural practices" (2006: 28). Likewise, the structuring of social lives around particular spaces and venues in which these practices become normal, acceptable and habitual is an important part of the story. Churches provide a good first example of these points.

The strong tradition of self-government within nineteenth-century Ulster Presbyterianism, as well as its growing evangelical component, made its Canadian counterpart receptive to the expectations of its immigrant faithful. The institutional coherence of Canadian Presbyterianism, facilitated by the uniting of its various denominations in 1875, was familiar to Ulster migrants for whom a "general tightening-up on regulations and behaviour" was par for the course in the second half of the nineteenth century (Hill, 1997: 501; see also Grant, 1988). Even more familiar to them, though, was the church named after Henry Cooke, perhaps the most outspoken cleric of their province until his death in 1868. Cooke's Church, originally the Second Presbyterian Church (the first was the aptly-named Knox church), was established in a schoolhouse in 1851 before a permanent church was erected in 1858; an anniversary booklet modestly referred to it as "the most pretentious structure in the city [with] its lofty twin towers pointing heavenward".[8] One generation after its establishment, a decidedly "northern Irish" ambience could still be detected at the services, sermons and meetings held within the walls of Cooke's Church.

Given the impact of evangelicalism in the nineteenth-century Church of Ireland, Irish Anglican migrants were more than likely to be present within those circles in Toronto. As Alan Hayes has noted, their evangelicalism routinely clashed with the high-church approach of a clergy "imported from Anglo-Catholic English colleges" that sought to re-infuse Medieval-era rituals into the celebration of services (Hayes, 1989: 45). This split, at its height in the 1870s, was expressed with separate newspapers, hymn books, Sunday school curricula, and even theological colleges for both branches of Anglicanism, producing a "great liturgical variety among [Anglican] parishes" in the city (Hayes, 1989: 54).

Trinity East, known as "Little Trinity", opened in 1844 as the second Anglican parish in Toronto. Known as the "Poor Man's Church" in comparison to St. James' Cathedral, its congregation was drawn mainly from the working-class district south of Cabbagetown. The short walk to the Catholic church of St. Paul's, serving the Corktown neighbourhood (Figure 14.2), suggests a more subtle sense of "Catholic" and "Protestant" territoriality than existed at the time in working-class Belfast (Baker, 1973; Hirst, 2002). Tellingly, Little Trinity's spireless Gothic façade was compensated for by having a Union Jack raised on its tower while its pastor, the Scottish-born Rev. Alexander Sanson, was an active chaplain in the Orange Order in the late 1870s (Hayes, 1991). Sanson's "audience" was thus not restricted to those who chose to patronise his church; he served the Toronto county lodge, the city's Centre District lodges, Enniskillen primary lodge 387, and was not the last pastor from Little Trinity to have direct Orange links.[9]

The evangelical Protestants of Cooke's and Little Trinity, Irish or otherwise, cared deeply about their spaces of worship. Their church interiors communicated a preference for simplicity and a dislike of objects or symbols that leaned too much towards "Romish ritual". Little Trinity was described upon its opening as "chaste and seemly in all its fittings and simple decorations".[10] Issues surrounding music and altar objects also mattered in the production of pious evangelical space. In December 1880, a meeting of the Cooke's music circle was angrily interrupted by six congregation members who forcibly removed the circle's recently-purchased organ. Testifying in court, Cooke's Antrim-born minister Reverend J. Kirkpatrick admitted that "for several years there has been a difference of opinion as to the introduction of music"; four of the interrupters were subsequently given options of fine or jail time in what one newspaper termed the "kist o' whistles" case.[11]

Issues of remaining true to particular practices of Protestant Christianity were often taken very seriously. The Anglican Church of the Ascension was established in 1875 after a split in the St George the Martyr congregation; the departing evangelicals would scarcely have remained in a church described less than a decade later as "one of the few Anglican churches in the city (to) possess a surpliced choir" (Mulvany and Adam, 1885: 311). Of the 274 burials listed for Ascension between 1875 and 1890, 36 or 13 per cent were for Irish-born individuals, though there were doubtless others born to Irish parents.[12] One of the church's more prominent members was Robert Bickerstaff, the Armagh-born Master of Armstrong Orange lodge 137.[13] Deeded to its trustees on condition that it remained "always strictly Protestant and evangelical", such vigilant words were strongly endorsed by Orangemen like Bickerstaff

(Hayes, 1989: 70). Indeed, as far as the forms of Protestant worship went, the latter association occasionally sought to uphold an evangelical status quo of sorts. A retrospective examination of Toronto's lodges recalled how a stress on "the purity and simplicity of religion" led to the passing of the following resolution at the annual County Lodge meeting in 1871:

> that this County Lodge cannot too highly censure the ritualistic practices and Popish tendencies in the (Anglican) Church of the Holy Trinity, Toronto, and hereby caution the members of this lodge against the danger of permitting their families to attend the church.[14]

Strictures from the pulpit found their way into the domestic spheres of Toronto's Irish Protestants. John McAree described his early years in a "pious but hard-headed household" shaped by Anglicanism and Methodism whose traditions were "imported from Down and Armagh" (1953: 26, 2). It was not so difficult to reconstitute such outlooks and practices from Ulster, given the overall tone of "Toronto the Good".

If the churches frequented by Irish Protestants were to remain unsullied from the inside by the ritualism of Rome or high-church Anglicanism, it was the wish of at least some of the city's clergy that similar standards extend to home life. Intra-denominational marriages were an important area of concern in this regard and the Irish precedent, on both the Catholic and Protestant side, was telling. Addressing the Irish Protestant Benevolent Society in 1889, the Dublin-born Anglican Bishop of Algoma, Edward Sullivan, described "mixed marriages between Protestants and Roman Catholics as prolific sources of mischief and misery, domestic, social and religious" while decrying those Protestants who sent their children to "Romish schools and convents".[15] These standards cut both ways, however, since Sullivan's Catholic counterpart in Toronto, Archbishop John Joseph Lynch, who was rarely short of a few words on the "errors of Protestantism", expressed his own hostility to "mixed" marriages. While Lynch's successor, Archbishop John Walsh, took a more liberal line on providing dispensations, the following incumbent, Denis O'Connor, did not. By the early 1900s, therefore, the share of dispensed interfaith marriages within all church marriages in Toronto's English-speaking Catholic parishes rarely rose above 7 per cent (McGowan, 1999).

Religious sensibilities also shaped another arena of Protestant "inter-mixing", that is, Toronto's public school system. Robert Stamp's comment about "an omnipotent and omniscient God" permeating the pages of school textbooks in late Victorian Ontario speaks to the designs of educators to mould children from various denominations into young and moral Christian Canadians (Stamp, 1982: 11). Sunday schools performed a similar function at denominational level; for example, one Monaghan-born shoemaker, Samuel Hanna, handled more than two hundred students in the Metropolitan Methodist Church's Sunday school by the end of the century (Champion, 1899: 136–7). While Catholics were clearly absent from the latter venues, they were seemingly quite rare in the city's public schools if John McAree's experience of the Dufferin school in Cabbagetown (Figure 14.2) is in any way indicative of general city trends: "Mike Kennedy was the only Catholic neighbour of my age, and of course I met no Catholics at school. So it happened that I made no Catholic friends until I had almost grown up" (1953: 92). This inter-action pattern was mirrored in other aspects of McAree's boyhood; though living less than a half-mile north of the Catholic neighbour-hood of Corktown, he had little occasion to venture into its streets (Jenkins, 2003). McAree later acknowledged his schooldays to have shaped an "unreasonable prejudice . . . it makes boys conscious of reli-gious differences when they are far too young to understand much about religion . . . (such prejudice) would not have existed, I think, had it not been for Separate Schools" (1953: 93). Institution- and network-building on both sides contributed to these fissures, as did contested notions of "Irishness".

## Loyalty, industry and virtue: the "ethnic" imaginations of Irish Protestants

Toronto's Irish Protestants possessed a clear sense of their social and cul-tural location at the centre of an emergent Anglo-Canadian society, with their Orange portion in particular seeing themselves at the front line of those holding true to the new dominion's "loyal" ideals. Given the newness of the state, however, the personal and group identities of Irish Protestants were not easily collapsed into an undifferentiated "Canadian" whole. "British North America" disappeared from maps, but not from minds. Confederation represented little more than a polit-ical deal "born in pragmatism" and was carried out without a great deal of fanfare or any grand pronouncements on the nature of "Canadian" identity and citizenship (Watts, 1987: 769–1). Like their English and Scottish counterparts, these Irish remained British subjects, and within the city's Protestant circles at least, to declare oneself Irish, British and Canadian simultaneously was not a controversial gesture. In claiming and celebrating British citizenship in North America, Irish Protestants were under no obligation to rapidly shed their "ethnic baggage".

The role of Orange lodges in promoting Britishness and loyalty in pre-Confederation Canada has been well documented (Houston and Smyth,

1980; Goheen, 1993; Radforth, 2007). Though previously mentioned tavern names such as "William III" clearly referenced the Irish roots of the organisation through the Dutch king's victory over the Catholic King James II at the Boyne in 1690, some Irish Protestant migrants were active in building a history and memory of loyalty in their new place of settlement in the most overt way possible: by taking up arms in its defence. Two events stand out: the Upper Canadian republican rebellion of 1837 and the Fenian border raid of 1866. The *History of Toronto* (Mulvany and Adam, 1885) contains accounts of Irish-born Protestants who took up arms on these occasions. In 1827, for example, Ulsterman Samuel Platt emigrated with his family at fifteen and acquired work as a wood-chopper and clerk in Toronto; he took charge of two companies of militia in the rebellion before later establishing himself as a distillery owner and politician.[16] Not long after arrival in Toronto, such Irish Protestants, not all of them Orangemen, became acutely aware of the fragile political status of their new colonial setting. Now veterans as much as they were settlers, their senses of territory and loyalty were taking form, shaping the future Ontario province and its capital of Toronto into places whose loyal British values would be remarked upon by later residents and visitors (Jenkins, 2003).

Less than thirty years later, in July 1866, a new generation of Irish-born Protestants shared volunteering activities in the showdown with the Irish republican Fenians at Ridgeway, close to the American border at Buffalo. Toronto's Orangemen were particularly to the fore on this occasion (Senior, 1991), putting their mantra of "No Surrender" into practice, and it is worth speculating on the sorts of local impact that the Ridgeway veterans could have had in Toronto's Protestant social circles in the succeeding decades. Fermanagh-born Frank Somers, for instance, brought the bodies of three fallen comrades back to Toronto, later rising to become Orange county Master of Toronto and a member of the city's public school board. Described as "one of the best known men in the Grand Lodge", Somers' activity at Orange meetings was noted in the *Sentinel* right up to his death in 1917 at the age of eighty-three.[17]

Somers and other Orange veterans doubtless had their admirers among the association's younger cohorts in the decades following Ridgeway, and outlets existed to channel these youngsters into its ranks prior to formal initiation into primary lodges. In the 1870s, the Orange Young Britons (OYB) and the 'Prentice Boys were the organisations providing such channels for the sons and grandsons of Irish migrants, the latter group's name recalling the apprentice boys responsible for the lock-out of King James II from Derry in 1688 that prompted the famous siege. Never noted for patronising Toronto's temperance lodge rooms, the less-restrained members of the OYB clashed regularly in the 1870s and 1880s with other young men they were unlikely to encounter in a social context—Catholics (Clarke, 2007). Acutely aware of the Catholic geography of Toronto, the OYB were blamed for violent activities in the western parish of St Patrick's on St Patrick's night in 1889 "where church and school-house were filled with stones" by a group later witnessed returning to their east end base "with their fifes and drums".[18]

Identities that were specifically "Irish" could exist within these loyal visions. Somers was also involved in the Irish Protestant Benevolent Society, as were Orange-Irish mayors such as Ned Clarke and Warring Kennedy. The IPBS challenged what its members would have considered a Catholic-centred and "disloyal" conception of Irishness in Toronto at the time of its inception in 1870. The *Irish Canadian*, after all, enjoyed a mostly Catholic readership and was sympathetic to the cause of Irish nationalism (Clarke, 1993; McGowan, 1999). Article 2 of the IPBS constitution stated its aim as providing "advice and information to those Irish Protestants who arrive as strangers in our midst, and encourage their settlement in the Province of Ontario; to assist those of them who . . . stand in need of pecuniary aid, and to promote the welfare of Irish Protestants generally".[19] By so restricting its financial disbursements to the "deserving poor", the IPBS reinforced Victorian conceptions of Protestant Christianity as a morally righteous and civilising enterprise.

Widows and the infirm were important groups of recipients. In January 1871, the society's Charitable Committee recommended relief to eight "sober and respectable" female applicants who were "unable from age or sickness to do much for themselves".[20] Such self-conceptions also served, directly or indirectly, to reproduce unflattering associations between Roman church doctrine and the material conditions of Toronto's Catholics. Though the latter group's middle class grew steadily throughout the period, their over-representation in lower classes of work and enduring prominence in the registers of those seeking financial assistance reinforced Protestant views of them as social inferiors lacking a sense of individual responsibility (Houston and Laskin, 1993; Jenkins, 2001).

Qualitative differences between the Protestant and Catholic poor were highlighted on a number of occasions that also betrayed an Irish twist. At the founding of the IPBS, Dr Dewart remarked that: "Indiscriminate charity rather tended to increase rather than ameliorate the evil of begging" claiming that "only the minority and a very small minority of the poor who applied for aid were Protestants".[21] Alexander Hamilton was more blunt with his claim that it was "rarely indeed that Protestants begged for assistance. They would rather perish than beg, but it was not so with the Roman Catholics. No doubt the majority of beggars in the city were Irish, but they were not Protestants".[22] Under this array of self-images, Protestants understood their role as resourceful institution builders within the state, with working-class Catholics in contrast doing little other than drawing from the resources of that same state. At another level, the Catholic hierarchy was accused of undermining the state through its insistence on separate schools. As in Ireland and Britain, the line between religion and politics was often blurred.

These Protestant claims to the higher ground of piety, self-sacrifice and loyalty were not simply traced back to Ireland, but to Ulster in particular. John McAree's Uncle Aleck apparently "had the Ulsterman's shrewdness and thrift" while being as "tight-fisted a curmudgeon as ever came out of Ulster"; Aleck's friend William was another "shrewd Ulsterman" (McAree, 1953: 20–6). Delivering an argument that was now well-rehearsed in the Ulster he left, Reverend William Patterson of Cooke's Church explained to the IPBS in 1888 how "unselfishness, independence and self-reliance characterized the Irish Protestant . . . They did not seek relief if they could help it and, during a Famine in Ireland the poor in Ulster had to be searched for in their homes and supplied with food or money by the distributors."[23] These Protestant Irish were not victims at home, and neither were they exiles in Canada. Already armed with the superior certainties of Christianity and progress received through the voluntary agencies of "bureaucratised evangelicalism" prior to departure from Ulster (Hempton and Hill, 1992: 61), they were now active contributors in the shaping of a "British-Canadian" social and moral landscape in rural and urban Ontario.

The annual services, St Patrick's Day dinners and other events of the IPBS provided occasions for these Irish Protestants to recognise and preserve the intertwined nature of Irish and Canadian identities in a context supportive of Britain's empire and Protestant tradition. In 1876, the sermon by Belfast-born pastor J. Gardner Robb of Cooke's Church requested that the audience "vindicate their national evangelical Christianity before those who never yet acknowledged what the Empire and its evangelical churches owed to Irish Protestantism", while concluding that they "be faithful to God, their country and to ever hold the sentiment 'Erin mavourneen, Erin go bragh' ".[24]

The dinners of the mid-1880s extended these assertions of Irish identity into the public domain. Promoted by *Mail* editor Bunting, the dinners brought together not only society members but a respectable middle-class axis of clergymen, intellectuals, newspaper and magazine editors, businessmen, local politicians and some of Queen Victoria's Canadian representatives. Delegates from Irish Catholic societies were not present, unlike their St George's and St Andrew's counterparts. Dining on delicacies such as green turtle soup and oyster patties, they listened to speeches recounting the achievements of Irish Protestants in building Britain's empire through industry, sacrifice and courage. On more than one occasion, the victories of the century's military icons such as Wellington, Wolseley and Roberts were claimed as distinctive Irish contributions to the empire alongside those of intellectuals such as Edmund Burke (Jenkins, 2005). Toasts to the Queen, the army and navy, and the various institutions of Canadian government were a staple of these affairs, such gestures reminding participants of the place of the new dominion within Britain's global imperial geography.

Yet even here we should not overstate a cohesive and consensual way of imagining Ireland among these Protestants, as reactions to the absorbing issue of granting Home Rule to Ireland in the 1880s and 1890s testify. Edward Blake was the son of Anglican migrants from Wicklow who led the Liberal party in both the provincial and dominion legislatures. Emerging as a key supporter of Irish Home Rule in the city, Blake made a well-publicised return to his ancestral land in 1892 where he successfully won election to Westminster (Banks, 1957).[25] It was, in contrast, unlikely that Toronto's Orangemen would deviate from the Irish brethren's script of "no Home Rule". Championed in the cause by Toronto's most well-known Oxonian resident, Goldwin Smith, the Order welcomed one of Ulster's more vociferous opponents of Home Rule, Rev. Robert Kane, in 1886. His welcoming party included the previously-mentioned Orangemen Ned Clarke, Frank Somers and Robert Bickerstaff.[26]

## Conclusion

The parallels drawn between Toronto and Belfast in the nineteenth century were no accident. This brief discussion has attempted to broaden the perspective of these parallels beyond Orangeism and sectarian violence. In terms of migration paths, a strong case can be made for ongoing links between Toronto and Ulster in both the pre- and post-famine decades. At the same time, these migrants' religious and fraternal institutions became influential shapers of Toronto's social, cultural and political landscapes in addition to those of Upper Canada/Ontario in general. Many were instrumental in attempts to make the city and its citizens into morally "good" subjects and their efforts did not pass without comment. There were fractures within Toronto's Irish Protestant circles, of course. The fault line of class was the most noticeable of these, roughly dividing those active within Orange ranks from more middle-class elements who had little interest in the donning of sashes and parading of streets. These divisions could in turn be party-based. While the Orangemen aligned themselves closely with Conservative interests throughout the period, Toronto was also home to prominent Liberals of Irish birth or ancestry. At a different level, and influenced by everyday social circulations as well as intermittent political-religious debates within the dominion, Protestant identities were often regularly constructed relationally against those of Catholics.

David Doyle's claim that the famine and its aftermath represented "a final flourish of immigrant protestant solidarity with the old country" in the United States cannot be extended to Toronto's Irish Protestants (1996: 730). The range of identities expressed and preserved by these immigrants and their descendants adhered broadly to a loyal British-Canadian sensibility in which an Irish dimension remained relevant and usable at different times. Though the case of Victorian Toronto illustrates well the transplantation of an ensemble of outlooks and convictions from Protestant Ulster to urban North America, such values were not simply open to elaboration and modification by the experience of a new location. They also remained informed by the divisive politics of Ireland and Ulster as well as the value accorded to diasporic audiences by political and religious actors from the "homeland". While the Kane visit provides one dynamic instance of this Ulster–Toronto transatlantic connection, it is clear that further investigations are needed to clarify how events in Ireland were responded to and given meaning in other spaces and at other times, informing Protestant diasporic identities with various mixtures of Irishness, Orangeism, nationalism, and imperialism.

## Notes

The author thanks Taylor and Francis Journals for their permission to reproduce Figure 14.1, a previous version of which appeared in William Jenkins, "Between the lodge and the meeting-house: mapping Irish Protestant identities and social worlds in late Victorian Toronto", *Social and Cultural Geography*, 4 (2003), 75–98. The latter article also featured the evidence of John McAree used in the present chapter.

1 "Comfortable" and "needy" are used here as summary descriptions of the material conditions in which certain Ulster Protestant migrants found themselves by the 1870s and 1880s. These two labels are applied purely for their heuristic value; "comfortable" did not necessarily imply the possession of an excessive amount of wealth.

2 The Programme de Recherche en Démographie Historique at the Université de Montréal have made the complete 1881 census manuscript returns available at www.prdh.umontreal.ca/1881Browser/en/home.aspx, while Library

and Archives Canada have an online database containing the heads of house-holds counted in Ontario in the 1871 census at www.collectionscanada.ca/02/020108_e.html. Both websites were accessed in August 2006.

3 Annual report of the Irish Protestant Benevolent Society for the year ending 31 March 1872, contained in minute book: March 4 1872, Irish Protestant Benevolent Society folder, Baldwin Room, Metropolitan Toronto Reference Library.

4 "Ethnic origin" was often measured in the nineteenth-century Canadian censuses in paternal terms. In the case of Toronto (and Ontario) families with parents of different ethnic origins, for example, the children were assigned the ethnic origin of the father. See Curtis (2001) for a fuller discussion of this phenomenon.

5 *Toronto World*, 8 December 1890.

6 *Sentinel*, 27 July 1899.

7 The sampling procedure is outlined in detail in Jenkins (2001). Briefly, 10 per cent of households with a head of Irish ethnic origin were drawn in systematic fashion from the 1881 census manuscripts for the City of Toronto and the three suburban villages of Brockton, Parkdale and Yorkville.

8 See the undated pamphlet "Annals of sixty years: Cooke's Presbyterian Church, Toronto, 1851–1910", Metropolitan Toronto Reference Library.

9 *Sentinel*, 28 February 1878. Between 1906 and 1926, the Trinity East rectorship was held by Rev. Hillyard Cameron Dixon, a third-generation Irishman, First World War chaplain, and passionate Orangeman (Hayes, 1991).

10 *The Church*, 23 February 1844.

11 *Globe*, 18 December 1880.

12 Church of the Ascension Parish Register, Births, Marriages, Burials *c.*1875–92, Toronto Diocesan Archives, Anglican Church of Canada, were cross-listed with the online sources provided in note 2.

13 *Sentinel*, 1 May 1913.

14 *Sentinel*, 27 July 1899.

15 *Toronto Mail*, 18 March 1889.

16 See www.historyoftoronto.ca/history/bios/torP.html for a short biography of Platt, originally published in the second volume of Mulvany and Adam (1885), p. 130.

17 *Sentinel*, 11 January , 26 April 1917.

18 *Irish Canadian*, 21 March 1889.

19 Irish Protestant Benevolent Society constitution, Irish Protestant Benevolent Society folder, Baldwin Room, Metropolitan Toronto Reference Library.

20 Irish Protestant Benevolent Society minute book, January 6, 1871, Irish Protestant Benevolent Society folder, Baldwin Room, Metropolitan Toronto Reference Library.

21 *Globe*, 18 March 1870.

22 Ibid.

23 *Toronto Mail*, 12 March 1888.

24 *Toronto Mail*, 20 March 1876.

25  This was not the first time Blake had visited Ireland. He had been at least once
    before in 1887, where "having gone with some of the Irish Nationalist leaders
    to witness an eviction, he had expressed sympathy with the sufferings of the
    tenants" (Banks, 1957: 12). No source recording this event is given by Banks.
26  *Globe*, 9 September 1886.

# References

Akenson, D. H. (1984) *The Irish in Ontario: A Rural History* (Montreal and
    Kingston: McGill-Queen's University Press).

Akenson, D. H. (1996) *The Irish Diaspora: A Primer* (Toronto: Meany, 1996).

Baker, S. E. (1973) "Orange and Green: Belfast 1832–1912", in H. J. Dyos and M.
    Wolff (eds) *The Victorian City: Images and Realities, Vol. 2* (London: Routledge
    & Kegan Paul), pp. 789–814.

Banks, M. A. (1957) *Edward Blake, Irish Nationalist: A Canadian Statesman in Irish
    Politics* (Toronto: University of Toronto Press).

Byron, R. (1999) *Irish America* (Oxford: Clarendon Press).

Careless, J. M. S. (1985) "The emergence of Cabbagetown in Victorian Toronto", in
    R. Harney (ed.) *Gathering Place: Peoples and Neighbourhoods of Toronto*
    (Toronto: Multicultural History Society of Ontario), pp. 25–46.

*Census of Canada 1881: Vols 1 and 2* (Ottawa: S. E. Dawson, 1882).

Champion, T. E. (1899) *Methodist Churches in Toronto: A History of the Methodist
    Denomination and its Churches in York and Toronto, with Biographical Sketches
    of many of the Clergy and Laity* (Toronto: G. M. Rose).

*The Church*, 23 February 1844.

Clarke, B. P. (1993) *Piety and Nationalism: Lay Voluntary Associations and the
    Creation of an Irish-Catholic Community in Toronto 1850–1895* (Montreal and
    Kingston: McGill-Queens University Press

Clarke, B. P. (2007) "Religious riot as pastime: Orange Young Britons, parades, and
    public life in Victorian Toronto", in D. A. Wilson (ed.) *The Orange Order in
    Canada* (Dublin: Four Courts Press), pp. 109–27.

Curtis, B. (2001) *The Politics of Population: State Formation, Statistics and the
    Census of Canada 1840–1875* (Toronto: University of Toronto Press).

Doyle, D. N. "The remaking of Irish America, 1845–80", in W. E. Vaughan (ed.) *A
    New History of Ireland, Vol. VI: Ireland under the Union II* (Oxford: Oxford
    University Press), pp. 726–63.

Elliott, B. S. (1988) *Irish Migrants in the Canadas: A New Approach* (Montreal and
    Kingston: McGill-Queen's University Press).

Fitzpatrick, D. (1989) "Irish emigration 1801–70", in W. E. Vaughan (ed.) *A New
    History of Ireland, Vol. V: Ireland under the Union I* (Oxford: Oxford University
    Press), pp. 562–622.

Fitzpatrick, D. (1996) "Irish emigration 1871–1921", in W. E. Vaughan (ed.) *A New
    History of Ireland, Vol. VI: Ireland under the Union II* (Oxford: Oxford
    University Press), pp. 606–52.

Garner, H. (1968) *Cabbagetown: A Novel* (Toronto: Ryerson Press).

*Globe*, 18 March 1870.

*Globe*, 18 December 1880.

Goheen, P. G. (1992) "Parading: a lively tradition in Early Victorian Toronto", in A. R. H. Baker and G. Biger (eds) *Ideology and Landscape in Historical Perspective* (Cambridge: Cambridge University Press), pp. 330–51.

Goheen, P. G. (1993) "The ritual of the streets in nineteenth century Toronto", *Environment and Planning D: Society and Space*, 11: 127–46.

Grant, J. W. (1988) *A Profusion of Spires: Religion in Nineteenth-Century Ontario* (Toronto: University of Toronto Press).

Hallowell, G. A. (1972) *Prohibition in Ontario 1919–1923* (Ottawa: Ontario Historical Society).

Hayes, A. L. (1989) "Repairing the walls: church reform and social reform 1867–1939", in A. L. Hayes (ed.) *By Grace Co-workers: Building the Anglican Diocese of Toronto* (Toronto: Anglican Book Centre), pp. 43–95.

Hayes, A. L. (1991) *Holding Forth the Word of Life: Little Trinity Church 1842–1992* (Toronto: Corporation of Little Trinity Church).

Hempton, D. and Hill, M. (1992) *Evangelical Protestantism in Ulster Society 1740–1890* (London: Routledge).

Hepburn, A. C. (1996) *A Past Apart: Studies in the History of Catholic Belfast 1850–1950* (Belfast: Ulster Historical Foundation).

Hill, M. (1997) "Religion and society: Protestantism in nineteenth century County Down", in L. J. Proudfoot (ed.) *Down: History and Society* (Dublin: Geography Publications), pp. 489–522.

Hirst, C. (2002) *Religion, Politics and Violence in Nineteenth-Century Belfast: The Pound and Sandy Row* (Dublin: Four Courts Press).

Houston, C. J. and Smyth, W. J. (1980) *The Sash Canada Wore: A Historical Geography of the Orange Order in Canada* (Toronto: University of Toronto Press).

Houston, C. J. and Smyth, W. J. (1990) *Irish Emigration and Canadian Settlement: Patterns, Links, and Letters* (Toronto: University of Toronto Press).

Houston, S. E. and Laskin, S. L. (1993) "Responses to poverty, to 1891", in R. L. Gentilcore and G. Matthews (eds) *Historical Atlas of Canada Volume II: The Land Transformed* (Toronto: University of Toronto Press) Plate 56.

*Irish Canadian*, 21 March 1889.

Jenkins, W. (2001) "Geographical and social mobility among the Irish in Toronto, Ontario, and Buffalo, New York, 1880–1910" (Unpublished PhD thesis, University of Toronto).

Jenkins, W. (2002/2003) "Patrolmen and peelers: immigration, urban culture and the 'Irish Police' in Canada and the United States", *Canadian Journal of Irish Studies*, 28/29: 10–29.

Jenkins, W. (2003) "Between the lodge and the meeting-house: mapping Irish Protestant identities and social worlds in late Victorian Toronto", *Social and Cultural Geography*, 4: 75–98.

Jenkins, W. (2005) "Deconstructing Diasporas: networks and identities among the Irish in Buffalo and Toronto, 1870–1910", *Immigrants and Minorities*, 23: 359–98.

Jenkins, W. (2007) "Views from "the Hub of the Empire": Loyal Orange lodges in early twentieth-century Toronto", in D. A. Wilson (ed.) *The Orange Order in Canada* (Dublin: Four Courts Press), pp. 128–45.

Kealey, G. S. (1980) *Toronto Workers Respond to Industrial Capitalism 1867–1892* (Toronto: University of Toronto Press).

Kenny, K. (2000) *The American Irish* (Harlow: Longman).

Lewis, F. (1843) *The Toronto Directory and Street Guide for 1843–4* (Toronto: H. & W. Rowsell).

McAree, J. V. (1953) *Cabbagetown Store* (Toronto: Ryerson Press).

McGowan, M. G. (1999) *The Waning of the Green: Catholics, the Irish, and Identity in Toronto 1887–1922* (Montreal and Kingston: McGill-Queens University Press).

Miller, K. A. (1985) *Emigrants and Exiles: Ireland and the Irish Exodus to North America* (Oxford and New York: Oxford University Press).

Mulvany, C. P. and Adam, G. M. (1885) *History of Toronto and County of York*, 2 volumes (Toronto: C. B. Robinson).

Radforth, I. (2007) "Orangemen and the Crown", in D. A. Wilson (ed.) *The Orange Order in Canada* (Dublin: Four Courts Press), pp. 69–88.

Russell, V. L. (1982) *Mayors of Toronto* (Erin, Ontario: Boston Mills Press).

Sager, E. W., Thompson, D. K. and Trottier, M. (2002) *The National Sample of the 1901 Census of Canada User's Guide* (Victoria: University of Victoria Canadian Families Project).

See, S. W. (1993) *Riots in New Brunswick: Orange Nativism and Social Violence in the 1840s* (Toronto: University of Toronto Press).

Senior, H. (1991) *The Last Invasion of Canada: The Fenian Raids 1866–1870* (Toronto: Dundurn Press).

*Sentinel*, 28 February 1878.

*Sentinel*, 27 July 1899.

*Sentinel*, 1 May 1913.

*Sentinel*, 11 January 1917.

*Sentinel*, 26 April 1917.

Shirlow, P. and Murtagh, B. (2006) *Belfast: Segregation, Violence and the City* (London: Pluto).

Spence, F. S. (1896) *The Facts of the Case: A Summary of the Most Important Evidence and Argument Presented in the Royal Commission on the Liquor Traffic* (Toronto: Newton and Treloar).

Stamp, R. M. (1982) *The Schools of Ontario 1876–1976* (Toronto: University of Toronto Press).

*Toronto Mail*, 20 March 1876.

*Toronto Mail*, 12 March 1888.

*Toronto Mail*, 18 March 1889.

*Toronto World*, 8 December 1890.

Watts, R. L. (1987) "The American constitution in comparative perspective: a comparison of federalism in the United States and Canada", *Journal of American History*, 74: 769–91.

Wilson, C. A. (1994) *A New Lease on Life: Landlords, Tenants and Immigrants in Ireland and Canada* (Montreal and Kingston: McGill-Queen's University Press).

Winder, G. (2000) "Trouble in the North End: the geography of social violence in Saint John", 1840–60, *Acadiensis*, 29: 27–57.

# 15

# "What satire would be more eloquent than reality?" Reporting the northern unionists in the French press, 1919–22

## Ian McKeane

### Introduction

This chapter outlines the degree of reporting in the French press of the social nature and the political ideas of Ulster Protestantism between 1920 and 1923. It also highlights the scarcity of references to Ulster by French writers and the consequent difficulty of describing the political situation there at the time of partition.

### French reportage on Ireland

For the French, Ireland as a concept (to say nothing of Ulster), required a good deal of mental effort and perceptions were distorted since the French usually looked across the Channel and were distracted by England which was, in every sense, in the way. The historian, Louis Paul-Dubois writing in 1921 identified this difficulty:

> It is not easy since if, as Lady Clanricard, Canning's daughter, said, England is the lofty wall which hides the sun from Ireland, this high wall also hides Ireland from our continental gaze.[1]

Thus, for the French, Ireland was only a "geographical expression", to misappropriate Metternich's famous phrase. Few French people had been there and still fewer had written about it—apart from a flurry of interest in the person and activities of Daniel O'Connell earlier in the nineteenth century. Yet, by the early 1920s, this state of affairs had changed and even in the French popular press, Ireland as a separate entity formed part of that mental construction of the outside world which readers took for granted. That there was an essential difference between *l'Irlande* and *l'Angleterre* was understood by 1920 and it is also clear that this understanding was a result of the press coverage of the 1916 Easter Rising and certain events during the Anglo-Irish war.

Before this period, direct reports from Ireland to France were usually linked to military excursions and they were not often complimentary. Reports from Ulster are very rare indeed. One such rarity is a letter to King James II from his Marshal-General, Monsieur de Rozen, commander of the siege of Derry in 1689, who expresses his despair at the prevailing weather conditions. He bemoans

> the impossibility of having to live in the trenches which are flooded either by the river because of the tides or by the continuous rain which will ruin and lose the troops that Your Majesty has before this place.[2]

Ulster does not really feature in French perceptions until the early twentieth century. Even Alexis de Tocqueville, possibly the best known nineteenth-century French commentator on Ireland, never set foot in the province of Ulster on his tour of Ireland in 1835. It was the Ulster crisis of 1910–14 which brought the province into the French press. The Ulster crisis was reported as an essentially parliamentary matter with the action centred on Westminster. This reflects the French perception of Ireland being diffused through the prism of London. It was the situation in Ireland after the end of the First World War that led to the French being confronted with Ulster unionism.

Newspapers are still a relatively unusual source for historians and this is perhaps because study of the press demands a critical approach which crosses the boundary between historical and literary studies. On the historical side there is the doubt expressed that material written in the press cannot be considered a reputable source, given the varied reasons for its writing. Newspapers existed for a variety of reasons and did not always attempt to provide a detached record of events. The personal ambition of owners or editors, their political agendas, creative expression, entertainment and diversion are all elements of newspapers, particularly in the period of this study. In historiography, journalism, particularly in the daily press, is often banished to the realms of popular culture and, therefore, becomes doubly suspect to the traditional academic historian. Yet, James Mill writing in the *Westminster Review* of 1824 noted:

> It is indeed a subject of wonder that periodical publications should have existed so long . . . without having become subject to a regular and systematic course of criticism. (Pykett, 1990: 3)

Pykett goes on to suggest that even in our own time there is a reluctance by historical researchers working on the Victorian period to avail themselves of the resource represented by newspapers and periodicals. Newspapers open a particular window onto the times in which they are published. At the very least, they provide an entry to the actual discourse that was taking place in the popular public sphere as events occurred, something which is difficult to ascertain otherwise.

In probing the French awareness or otherwise of the Irish independence struggle it is essential to look at the reporting of events in Ireland in their press and periodicals. Serious writers on political matters used periodicals such as the *Revue des Deux Mondes* and weeklies like *L'Illustration* and *le Monde Illustré* to transmit their thoughts on developments in Ireland. Not only do these publications give a notion of the discourse on Ireland taking place in France, such as it was, they also provide an insight into the popular perception of relationship between France and the United Kingdom and reveal the effectiveness of the propaganda of the Irish independence movement. We should not forget that this movement drew a deal of its intellectual justification from French revolutionary ideals of the previous century and that many of its leaders looked to the great republics of the United States and France as sources of moral and political support. Many of them were well versed in French literature and a few, like Dáil Minister of Propaganda, Desmond FitzGerald, were fluent in French.

A close reading of the French press is rewarding showing how reporters with less political baggage than their British counterparts moved to recognition of the separate national identity of Ireland. This is a key issue in the coverage of Irish events as French readers realised that a new country had joined the European nations. One of the first actions of the Dáil on 21 January 1919 was to address the "free nations of the world" in Irish, French and English inviting "every free nation to support the Irish Republic by recognising Ireland's national status."(McArdle, 1937: 254) Despite this grand gesture, a year was to elapse before the French began to perceive that Ireland's self-proclaimed independent status was not going to be surrendered. The French press generally took the view that the death of the Lord Mayor of Cork, Terence MacSwiney, played a key role in this defence of the notion of independence. This becomes clear in the reports of his hunger strike and death. That his sacrifice should have had such an effect in France highlights the difference between the views of British and French journalists. Thus, they perceived Irish separation in some form as almost a fait accompli and the only question which remained was how this is was to be achieved and what the exact configuration would be.

This chapter shows how they wrestled with the problem of suggesting a formula for Irish political identity which might encompass the whole island and include the Protestant North-East. It shows also that they ultimately failed, like everyone else, to come up with a solution. By late 1922 Northern Ireland began to drop out of sight, eclipsed by the mystery of the civil war in the South. It was not to reappear until 1969 when, once again, French reporters were on the streets of Irish cities.

## French views on the North and the nation

Terence MacSwiney's hunger strike and death in the autumn of 1920 brought a unique group of young and talented French journalists to Ireland. They were the generation of Albert Londres (1884–1932), the reporter credited with inventing French investigative journalism (Redfern, 2004). For the French, it is clear that there was an element of travelogue in all *grands reportages*, which our modern visual media have made somewhat redundant (Redfern, 2004: 195). Londres' work reflects this. He lived the report. He was on the spot and talked with those who mattered at the time. He sought his interviews, he bribed, he badgered and he cajoled, and his persistence got his reports. Word pictures of newsworthy and sometimes alarming people were skilfully drawn and sent back to Paris with impressions of the exotic places visited as background and atmosphere. While Londres himself never reported from Ireland, his new techniques were used by these reporters who provided a short but brilliant series of reports from Ireland, which was not to be equalled until the work of Mary Holland and David McKittrick in the British press of the 1960s and 1970s.

Reporters in the Albert Londres mould who visited Ireland included Henri Béraud, the war correspondent, Ludovic Naudeau, Joseph Kessel, a young Argentinian-born Russian immigrant fresh from military service in the Far East with some experience of journalism on the quirky *Journal des Débats*, and finally, Simone Téry, daughter of the crusty Gustave Téry, editor of *l'Oeuvre*, who had a reputation for settling differences with opponents on the duelling field. These last three visited or wrote specifically about the North of Ireland.

Kessel's friend, the anglophobe Henri Béraud (1885–1958), was also Londres' drinking partner and came from the same area of the city of Lyons. Perhaps because of poor English, his Irish reports were atmospheric if too reliant on imagination. Béraud later wrote that a reporter could take holidays in the calm knowledge that his work was neither that of a historian nor that of a prophet (Béraud, 1928: 221).[3] In other words, he deserved the accusation that journalists never let facts get in the way of a good story.

Ludovic Naudeau (1872–1949) had established his reputation by reporting the Russo-Japanese war of 1905 and in 1921 was writing for the middle-class weekly, *L'Illustration*. He attempted to explain the Irish situation in four articles of unequal length illustrated with a variety of images. In an article dealing with Ulster in the spring of 1921 he set out the essential differences between Ulster and the rest of Ireland. In a section headed "Orange fears", he attempted to explain the Ulster Protestant dilemma and how it was viewed in Dublin. Naudeau told his readers that the Orangemen

> see popery as a Machiavellian organisation, a permanent conspiracy. The Roman church only has one aim, so they believe, that of its own greatness for which it will sacrifice everything . . . This power of darkness, disposing of immense funds, knows, by all sorts of trickery, how to avoid the constraints of civil law . . . [Furthermore, the Unionists fear that ] . . . the influence of the Catholic clergy would bring the electors of Ireland under their direct control. From that point forward, there is not the slightest doubt that, little by little and with all sorts of underground manoeuvres, these politicians in cassocks would begin to undermine the concessions and protections of Protestant citizens.[4]

The language is extreme but Naudeau claimed he was reflecting the sources for this argument. The report continues

> Against these assertions the Catholics range facts. The population in the South has very frequently chosen Protestant leaders (Robert Emmet, Lord Edward Fitzgerald, Wolfe Tone, Grattan, Parnell and many others). The Orangemen on the other hand have never deigned to follow or elected a single Catholic. Also in the area of the public services statistics show that in the Catholic provinces many Protestants have posts in public service, whilst in the Protestant counties of Ulster, a Catholic stands no chance of such a position.[5]

Here he seems to be on slightly firmer ground in that Irish rebellions since 1798 do appear to have a high coefficient of Protestant leadership.

Naudeau gives his readers a glimpse of the sort of material that was appearing in pamphlets on either side of the North–South divide. For the Orangemen, the North is the Promised Land, where all is wonderful while, according to many in the South so much is wrong up there. High illegitimacy, illiteracy, poor school provision in Belfast and higher criminality are the allegations of the South. Finally, more emigrate from Ulster than the other provinces—the ultimate insult! So this success of industrial Belfast is only an illusion. This formidable capitalist enterprise covers great misery and disappointments. This is Catholic Ireland's accusation of the North. The Northerners reply by citing horrific figures on pauperism in the South:

> We are businessmen here, declare the Ulster captains of industry, and we are far too busy to concern ourselves with politics. Our business is global and we ask for no modification on our part to the situation which has made

us citizens of the Empire. We are and wish to remain British subjects. It would be impossible for us to submit our future destinies to the whims of a majority of narrow [minded] sectarians and dreamers. Our specialities are business, large enterprises, the organisation of labour, while those of the South, are politics and constant useless controversy.[6]

In these articles there is no evidence of actual interviews with Northern Protestants. Naudeau is recounting the results of his research since there are echoes of the work of Yann Goblet and Louis-Dubois—the major sources of information for serious French readers. While attempting to be impartial, he nevertheless leant towards the republican view despite presenting the main strands of the Ulster unionist argument against Home Rule.

The French view of Irish national identity in the early 1920s was based on limited knowledge of Ireland itself and was, therefore, ill-defined. However, it *was* clear to the French that the Irish were fighting a sort of war of independence and that the unifying element in this struggle was a desire among a majority of the population to be no longer subjects of King George V. Yet they realised that, at the same time, there was a size-able minority who wished to preserve the Union with Great Britain, which had served them well for over a century and for which they had fought loyally in the recent world war. This situation was further complicated by the fact that most of this minority was grouped in six northern counties. Add to this that the two communities could be identified in broad terms as Catholic and Protestant respectively and the French reporters had enough labels to help their readers understand what they were being told. What they could not explain were the varying shades of opinion such as: the Irish who were in receipt of British army payments or pensions, ex-British soldiers who were now fighting in the IRA, members of the British establishment who were now leading members of Sinn Fein and Protestant intellectuals who were Gaelic language enthusiasts. The subtle confusion of the Irish social situation was beyond description and the opposing labels were used to outline a picture of Ireland that was, therefore, in the sharp if crude relief of an early woodcut. Yet a new group of social geographers were beginning to understand the tangled links with Britain. Professor Albert Demangeon stated in his contribution to the *Géographie Universelle* in 1925:

Ireland lives off Great Britain; she sells her animals, butter, beer; gets from her capital, coal, cloth, flour, fertiliser and machines. There is a powerful economic link between the two islands and Ireland cannot live apart . . . Certain almost feudal ties which link Ireland with Great Britain have placed her in a kind of situation of colonial exploitation. With Dominion status these ties will fall away. But others draw their strength from the very nature of things, from the geographical proximity of the two countries and from their economic structure. These ties will endure even with changes in the economic circumstances of Great Britain and Ireland.[7]

All this was difficult for the French, since the link between nationality and geography had become an important element in the French notion of nationality. It had been crucial in the definition of France itself since the time of Louis XIV. If France was the land stretching from the Pyrenees to the Rhine and the Alps then all within must be French. A constant denial of diversity in language and religion has been the mark of French national development until our own day. The Huguenots, the Bretons, the Basques, the Catalans and the Alsatian Germans have all endured pressure ranging from outright persecution to bureaucratic indifference at various times since 1648. The result has been the development of the notion of cultural unity within the *hexagone*: a shared socio-cultural experience geographically delimited. This notion has survived for many decades as a model for French national self-definition and the difficulty of reconciling it with the more flexible demands of a multicultural French identity are a very recent phenomenon. All this leads towards an appreciation of the French perception of Irish identity and to their view that Irish nationality must be bound by the natural limits of the island of Ireland. As Professor Albert Demangeon pointed out:

> Many *reasonable* people thought and still think that the Free State should embrace the whole island, one unique and indivisible.[8] (my italics)

It is clear that anyone who did not subscribe to this view would be, therefore, "unreasonable". There is also here a faint echo of that eighteenth-century official definition of the first French republic as *unique et indivisible*. Clearly, unionists would have a problem with reporters from this intellectual atmosphere and there might well have been a propensity for French writers to find the republican/nationalist position more to their taste even without Sinn Fein's effective public relations.

### Interviewing participants

Joseph Kessel (1898–1979) who was later to make his name as a novelist and eventually be elected to the académie Française, published eighteen reports from Ireland in *La Liberté* between 9 September and 26 October 1920. The first contained an interview with Mary MacSwiney in the Sinn Fein London office and, while not very profound, is very atmospheric. Kessel is struck by the force of the Sinn Fein argument. He was also impressed by the inner strength of Mary MacSwiney whom he met in the little smoke-filled office near Charing Cross, which he later described as "the London refuge of the Irish soul"[9] (Kessel, 1968: 42). He described Mary MacSwiney as

> a small, diffident woman, wearing a sad grey mackintosh. Her face also seemed grey and sad, prematurely worn. She spoke quietly, but in a voice in which one could sense power and unswerving belief. The typewriters stopped. All conversation stopped.[10]

He was the first French journalist to interview formally any individuals involved in the Irish crisis. One of these was General Macready, British Commander-in-Chief in Ireland. After a brief biographical note, the interview was presented as a long conversation in direct speech. The general set the tone by stating that he would not discuss politics nor would he give any details of the number or disposition of troops in Ireland but went on to discuss the problem of maintaining order. Troops were there to support the police who were inadequate for the task. Sinn Fein had, in effect, declared war but the government could not and would not reply in like manner. They had to limit themselves to preventing trouble. If there were to be a general revolt then the army would be ready. Peace might come if they were allowed to clean out the terrorists, most of whose names they already knew. If they could do this then Ireland would be peaceful again. Kessel concluded that, while he found the general personally courteous and even charming, his simplistic view of a complex problem was rather disturbing. (Kessel, 1920).

Kessel also visited Belfast and described the tension in the city. He experiences a moment of panic when he hears what he thinks are gun-shots near Royal Avenue but it is apparently a false alarm. The military arrive anyway, armed to the teeth, an event that Kessel describes as an ". . . anachronistic image of war which, in Ireland, pursues and obsesses everyone".[11] This is the only report from Belfast which suggested that foreign journalists were persuaded that the essence of the Irish crisis lay in the nationalist struggle and in Dublin, where Sinn Fein's public relations machine was at its most helpful. Belfast was just too complicated, too dark and too dangerous.

It is clear that the Ulster Unionists lacked a press officer of the calibre of Sinn Fein's Desmond FitzGerald. However, one French journalist made a real attempt to penetrate their thinking. This was Simone Téry (1897–1967) a young left-wing journalist with good English. As a woman, Téry was unique among a fairly tough bunch of male investigative journalists working from Paris. She was also unique in that, in addition to interviewing all the usual suspects in and around post-truce Dublin, she sought out and interviewed in September 1921 leading Ulster Unionists including the Lord Mayor of Belfast, Sir William Coates, and the Northern Ireland Minister of Finance, Horace Pollock. These interviews, which were published as a book in 1923, give us an unusually varied resource (Téry, 1923: 11–12). In Belfast, the truce of mid-1921 has had little effect. Sad and foggy Dublin seems a paradise of light and gaiety beside sinister, dark and menacing Belfast (Téry, 1923: 107). Quizzing her driver about the troubles in the city, Téry asks who is responsible:

> "Ah! Well . . ." and my driver turned a suspicious eye on me. "Some say that it is one lot and others say that it is another. It's difficult to know."
> Listening to the driver one realises that here a careless word can cost dear.[12]

After discovering that in Belfast the popular identification of the opposing groups is Protestant or Catholic, rather than unionists, Orangemen, Sinn-Feiners or republicans, Téry attempts to interview the Lord Mayor, Sir William Coates. This is not a great success and is worth quoting almost in full:

> "Am I speaking to the Lord Mayor [. . .]?"
> "What do you want from me?" The Lord-Mayor is not very welcoming.[. . .]
> "I am here to find out about the situation in Ireland. Could you give me some information?"
> "No."
> "How is it that Belfast, the only city which recognises British authority, is also the only one where the truce is not respected?"
> "It is not up to me to explain that to you."
> "What, according to you, is the origin of these disturbances and what is being done to stamp them out?"
> "I have nothing to say to you."
> "Don't you want to say anything to me?"
> "Not a word."[13]

Little further progress is made when Téry interviews Mr Pollock, Minister of Finance in Northern Ireland. Pollock is more polite than the Lord Mayor but, in the end, not much more forthcoming. He suggests that Ireland is a rich country and that the tumbledown houses in the villages are the fault of the republicans and that the barefoot children just prefer not to wear shoes. The Minister insists that the people just put all their money in the bank rather than spend it on children's shoes. He also insists that business is booming, denies that the streets are full of the unemployed and commerce is grinding to a halt. Téry is appalled and comments:

> If it is enough to deny evil to remove it, Pollock is the man and never has a minister so cheerfully presided over the ruin of his country.[14]

On asking the minister to put forward the unionist position Téry is told that it is difficult to explain. She responds by pointing out that the position seems easy enough to understand. This is ignored and Pollock adds that the unionists have no time for the opinions of foreigners. He is shocked that Téry has met the murderer De Valera and that she cannot see that the southerners are just spoilt children (Téry, 1923: 119).

## Conclusion

The view of the Ulster Unionists, developed in the Paris Press in the early twentieth century, reveals that to the French they were almost beyond explanation. They seemed to have a profound distrust of journalists and to have no sense of the value of presenting their case to outsiders. It would seem that they numbered few if any journalists among their key personalities. This is the opposite of Sinn Fein who had many journalists among their leaders and recognised the value of public relations to their cause. Their view of the value of the press recalls that of Honoré de Balzac expressed in politically incorrect terms back in 1843:

> The press, like a woman, is admirable and sublime when it tells an untruth . . . it deploys the greatest effort in this struggle and the public, like a stupid husband, always falls for it.[15]

There was a revealing moment at the end of the interview with Minister Pollock. He asked to review Téry's notes since, he said, journalists often embroider the truth. Simone Téry agreed to this and then made the comment: "Quelle satire serait plus éloquente que la réalité?" (Téry, 1923: 120–1).

## Notes

1 Ce n'est pas facile, car si, comme disait Lady Clanricard, fille de Canning, l'Angleterre est le mur trop haut qui cache à l'Irlande son soleil, ce haut mur cache aussi l'Irlande à nos regards continentaux (Paul-Dubois, 1921: 366).

2 . . .l'impossibilité qu'il y a de pouvoir habiter dans les tranchées qui sont inondées tant par la rivière, à cause de la marée, que par les pluys continuelles qui vont entierment ruiner et perdre les troupes que Votre Majesté a devant cette place . . . (Tate, 1959: 151).

3 Le reporteur a pris ses vacances avec sérénité, en homme qui ne confond point son ouvrage avec la tâche de l'historien et moins encore du prophète (Béraud, 1928: 221).

4 A leurs yeux, le papisme est une organisation machiavélique, une conspiration de tous les instants. . . . Cette puissance occulte, disposant de capitaux immenses, sait, par toutes sortes d'artifices, éluder les prescriptions de la loi

civile. L'influence des religieux en friande, disent les Ulstériens, mettra le corps électoral sons leur contrôle. Dès lors, il n'y a pas le moindre doute que, peu à peu, et par toutes sortes de manoeuvres souterraines, ces politiciens en soutane ne commencent à détruire les garanties des protestants (Naudeau,1921).

5  A toutes ces assertions, les catholiques opposent des faits. Très fréquemment, les populations du Sud n'ont pas craint de reconnaître pour chefs (les protestants comme Robert Emmet, Lord Edward Fitzgerald, Wolfe 'T'one, Grattan, Parnell et beaucoup d'autres). Les orangistes, au contraire, n'ont jamais daigné, en aucun cas, élire un seul catholique. De même, en ce qui concerne la distribution des emplois publics, la statistique prouve que les provinces catholiques font une place très large aux protestants, tandis que, dans les comtés protestants de l'Ulster, c'est bien en vain qu'un catholique prétendrait à une situation administrative, quelle qu'elle puisse être (Naudeau, 1921).

6  Nous sommes ici des hommes d'affaires, déclarent les capitaines de l'industrie ulstérienne, et nous sommes beaucoup trop occupés pour nous consacrer à la politique. Nos transactions sont mondiales et nous ne demandions, quant à nous, aucune modification de la situation qui nous était faite en tant que citoyens de l'Empire. Nous sommes et nous voulons rester des sujets britanniques. Il nous serait impossible de soumettre nos destinées futures aux caprices d'une majorité d'étroits sectaires et de visionnaires. Les affaires, les grandes entreprises, le labeur méthodique sont notre spécialité, tandis que celle du Sud, c'est la politique, la controverse interminable et vaine (Naudeau, 1921).

7  L'Irlande vit de la Grande-Bretagne; c'est à elle qu'elle vend ses bestiaux, son beurre, sa bière; c'est d'elle qu'elle reçoit ses capitaux, son charbon, ses étoffes, ses farines, ses engrais, ses machines: il y a entre les deux îles un lien économique puissant, et il ne peut être pour l'Irlande de vivre à part [. . .] Certains liens de vassalité qui unissent l'Irlande à la Grande-Bretagne l'ont placée dans la situation d'une sorte de colonie d'exploitation; du fait du statut de Dominion, ces liens tomberont. Mais il en est d'autres qui tiennent leur force de la nature meme des choses, de la proximité géographique des deux pays et de leur structure économique; ceux-là dureront, et dans la mesure même où changeront les milieux économiques de la Grande-Bretagne et de l'Irlande (P. Vidal de la Blanche and L. Gallois, 1927: 115).

8  Beaucoup de gens raisonnables pensaient, et pensent encore, que l'État libre devait embrasser l'île tout entière, une et indivisible (ibid., 87).

9  Le refuge de l'âme irlandaise à Londres (Kessel, 1968: 42).

10  . . . une femme, petite, effacée, habillée d'un imperméable gris et terne. Le visage, également gris et terne, semblait usé prématurément. Elle parla d'une voix timide, mais où l'on sentait une énergie, une foi inflexibles. Les machines à écrire s'étaient arrêtées. Les conversations avaient cessé (Kessel, 1920a).

11  . . . vision anachronique de guerre qui, en Irlande, poursuit et obsède tout le monde (Kessel, 1920c).

12  -Ah! Voilà . . . et mon cocher me regarde d'un œil soupçonneux. Y en a qui disent que c'est les uns, y en a qui disent que c'est les autres. C'est difficile de savoir . . . À entendre le cocher, on se rend compte qu'ici une parole étourdie peut coûter cher (Téry, 1923: 108).

13  —Est-ce au lord-maire que j'ai l'honneur de . . .?—Qu'est-ce que vous me voulez? Il n'est pas très aimable, le lord-maire . . .—Je viens m'informer des choses d'Irlande. Pourriez-vous me donner quelques renseignements?—Non.—Comment se fait-il que Belfast, la seule grande ville qui reconnaisse l'autorité britannique, soit aussi la seule où la trêve ne soit pas respectée?—Ce n'est pas à moi à vous l'expliquer.—Quelle est, d'après vous, l'origine des émeutes, et que fait-on pour les enrayer?—Je n'ai rien à vous dire.—Vous ne voulez rien me dire?—Pas un mot (ibid., 113).

14  S'il suffit de nier le mal pour le supprimer, M. Pollock est l'homme qu'il faut, et jamais on ne vit ministre plus allègrement présider à la ruine de son pays (ibid., 119).

15  La presse, comme une femme, est admirable et sublime quand elle avance un mensonge, [. . .] elle deploie les plus grandes qualités dans cette lutte où le public, aussi bête qu'un mari, succombe toujours. (Balzac, 1943 [1843]: 193).

## References

de Balzac, H. (1943) *Monographie de la presse parisienne* (Paris: Gallimard).

Béraud, H. (1928) *Rendez-vous européens* (Paris: Plon).

Kessel, J. (1968) *Témoin parmi les hommes I: Le Temps de l'espérance* (Paris: Plon).

Kessel, J. (1920) *La Liberté*, Paris (9 September), (21 September 1920, (6 October 1920).

McArdle, D. (1937) *The Irish Republic* (London: Gollancz).

Naudeau, L. "Six semaines en Irlande" in *L'Illustration*, 26 February 1921, 5 March 1921, 19 March 1921, 2 April 1921.

Paul-Dubois, L. (1921) "Le drame Irlandais: les origines 1914–1918", in *Revue des Deux Mondes*, 15 September.

Pykett, L. (1990) "Reading the periodical press: text and context", in L. Brake, A. Jones and L. Madden (eds) *Investigating Victorian Journalism*, (Basingstoke: Macmillan), pp. 3–18.

Redfern, W. (2004) *Writing on the Move: Albert Londres and Investigative Journalism* (Bern: Peter Lang).

Tate, L. (1959) "Franco-Irish correspondence; December 1688–August 1691", *Analecta Hibernica*, 21: 24–50.

Téry, S. (1923) *En Irlande: de la guerre d'indépendance à la guerre civile 1914–1923* (Paris: Flammarion).

Vidal de la Blanche, P. and Gallois, L. (eds) (1927) *Géographie Universelle Vol I : Les Iles Britanniques par Albert Demangeon* (Paris: Armand Colin).

# Part VI

# Identity and culture

# 16

# Identity and victimhood among Northern Ireland border Protestants[1]

*Hastings Donnan*

## Introduction

This chapter looks at Protestant perceptions of "victimhood" along the border with the Irish Republic, focusing on the views of those who self-identify as the "victims" or "survivors" of thirty years of violent conflict, and examining how they represent their status as victims to themselves and to the wider public. It is argued that two styles of Protestant victimhood are apparent, which, though they draw on the same experiences of violence, present these in different ways. The chapter suggests that such differences are no simple reflection of party political positions, but must be seen in context of local social and cultural dynamics.

Following the Good Friday Agreement of 1998, those who suffered during the Troubles have increasingly become a focus of public and scholarly debate (Dawson, 2003; Smyth, 2006). Until then, the "victims of violence" were usually largely lost from view, having appeared briefly in the media only to be promptly dislodged by the latest violent incident (though, see McCreary, 1976), and it was the late 1990s before the first comprehensive study of the "human cost" of the Troubles appeared (Fay et al., 1999).

Much of the recent debate has focused around the definition of "victim", which quickly became politicised as different victims' groups vied for recognition and legitimacy. Not only was there the question of how to identify a victim in a formal sense—recognising proportionately the dead, the injured, the bereaved—but there was also the question of whether some victims were "more deserving" than others, based on what some believed was the nature of their involvement in the violence. Protagonists have much riding on their competing claims, since acceptance of their victim status provides some justification for any violence in which they might have been engaged, while denial of this status casts doubt on the moral legitimacy of their struggle. As Smyth (2006) notes, republicans claim to be victims of British imperialism and a sectarian

state, while loyalists claim to be victims of the IRA. The neutral definition of victim adopted by the Victims Commissioner in 1997, a definition which includes those bereaved or injured by both state and
paramilitary violence, consequently grates against the understandings of
*both* sides. As a result, the politics and morality of victimhood have
remained key features of the victims' debate.

Discussions of victimhood thus fell into well-worn lines, in an oppositional politics that replicates old divides, and making it difficult for
Catholics and Protestants to join a group predominantly associated with
one religion or the other. However, this emphasis on the dichotomised
nature of victims' politics between loyalist and republican has arguably
masked the differences within each side. Focusing here on the Protestant
example, this chapter shows that while a distinctively "Protestant" case
for victimhood has emerged—for the reasons sketched above—it is a case
that obscures some marked differences of style and approach. The contrasts between "Protestant" and "Catholic" victims may be much discussed, but not what different Protestant victims' groups say and about
whether, how and why this varies.[2]

The chapter compares two Protestant victims' groups based in South
Armagh, and draws on fifty semi-structured recorded interviews carried
out in 2004–5 and on field research conducted there in 2000 and 2002.
Researcher participation in a range of formal and informal gatherings
facilitated interaction with respondents "in the round" and not only as
"victims", and established relationships not exclusively based on inter-
viewer and interviewee, or on a single meeting. As Smyth (2006) notes,
many victims' groups were first formed along the border, where the distinctive nature of the conflict provides the basis for the claim of a
uniquely Protestant experience of violence as outlined below.

## Border Protestant victimhood and the experience of violence

Protestant victimhood is mainly distinguished by emphasising that those
who suffered during the Troubles were the innocent bystanders of a conflict imposed upon them by republican paramilitaries. "Innocence" here
is understood as a lack of direct involvement in the conflict, and denotes
the suffering of "ordinary people going about their daily business".

The status of Protestants who became actively involved in the conflict is more complicated, although some of them too were seen as
victims of a conflict not of their own making. Members of the Royal
Ulster Constabulary (RUC) and Ulster Defence Regiment (UDR) were
described as "defending their country" and as "protecting ordinary men
and women from terrorist attack". Some former officers interviewed saw

their primary role as the defence of "our community" (which in their understanding included Catholics), and only secondarily as the protection of the state, so that it was the tangible and overlapping bonds of kinship, friendship and neighbourhood embedded in a particular locality that they claimed to have motivated their actions rather than an abstract ideological commitment and loyalty to a sovereign power. Such a view underscores the innocence of their actions, both in their eyes and in the eyes of their local community, and is a subtlety often obscured in debates about the relative blamelessness or reprehensibility of "pro-state security" versus "anti-state terror".

At the same time, however, others who were involved in the conflict muddy Protestant understandings of victimhood around the edges. Perceptions of loyalist paramilitaries as "victims" is ambivalent and some victims' groups have excluded them. Similarly, members of the police and UDR convicted or suspected of collusion with loyalist paramilitaries are thought to have "brought the violence on themselves" and are less readily classed as "innocent victims". Nevertheless, the Protestant case for victimhood is constructed within the broad perception that Protestants suffered mainly "in the service of the state". Moreover, it is underscored by the distinctive nature of the conflict along the border.

As Fay et al. (1999: 172, 175) have pointed out, South Armagh is a "prime example of . . . the rural war against the security forces" who made up almost 60 per cent of all fatal incidents there. Catholic deaths were disproportionately low in this part of the border where, in contrast to all other areas of Northern Ireland, Protestant fatalities were in the majority, many of them local members of the RUC and UDR (Fay et al., 1999: 173). What such statistics conceal, however, as South Armagh Protestants repeatedly point out, is the manner of these killings, many of which took place when the victim was off duty or at home—"soft targets" with no chance of retaliation or defence—who were subjected to a ruthless violence as border Protestants see it, and which they elaborate in relation to a number of recurrent themes.

The intimidation of Protestant farmers was frequently mentioned as part of border life. Their accounts tell of a landscape of threat and menace, where tractors, farm gates and hay bales were checked for bombs or booby traps. It was a hostile landscape where only hypervigilance might avert the death that could lie behind every hedgerow. Many claimed that the IRA's aim was "to drive us out" and that young Protestant farmers were systematically intimidated from their land, in what some suggested was a campaign of "ethnic cleansing". The children of one border school I visited were asked to raise their hands if someone in their family had been shot or threatened by the IRA. About a quarter of them did so, which the teacher indicated to me was an underestimate, since some were too young to remember.

Many respondents pointed out that their problems were ignored by the government and by Protestants elsewhere in Northern Ireland, and they felt forgotten, marginalised and poorly represented. Some suggested that they themselves were partly to blame for this, because they were anxious that speaking out would identify them as targets and because they valued the ability to "turn the other cheek" and "suffer in silence". Emotions were kept firmly in check: "You just had to get on with life", was how many put it.

There is remarkable agreement among those to whom I talked that this constellation of dominant themes—intimidation, ethnic cleansing, marginalisation, and a silencing of "our story"—typifies their experience. Alongside their claim to the underlying morality of their position, these themes define their identity as victims distinct from border Catholics who tell of a very different set of oppressions, fears and injustices. While individuals may combine these themes in different ways, their inclusion in some form in almost every account gives the narratives a formulaic feel. As Dawson (2004) argues, the cultural memory of "ethnic cleansing" provides border Protestants with "the collective story of their . . . experience of the Troubles", one that resonates with their memory of a history of threat, betrayal and siege (Donnan, 2005). At the same time, however, to see this collective memory as a banner under which diverse experiences and understandings are readily subsumed may overestimate its ability to incorporate this diversity, and privilege a political analysis of victims' issues over one that emphasises their social and cultural variation.

### Telling the past

This section considers the presentational styles of two victims' groups in South Armagh, focusing on how they tell the "story" of the violence sketched in general terms above. Although they remember this violence in similar ways, they narrate it very differently and locate their memories within contrasting contexts, one stressing the political significance of past events, the other its social and emotional effects.

Both groups are based in the predominantly Protestant border town of Markethill (Donnan, 1999). Even though the rate of Protestant casualties here was high as previously noted, it is immediately striking that a settlement of this size (*c.*1,300 inhabitants) has two such groups when other larger towns have none. Families Acting for Innocent Relatives (FAIR) and South Armagh Victims Encouraging Recognition/North

Armagh Victims Encouraging Recognition (SAVER/NAVER) both own their own premises located at opposite ends of the town and both have a small, full-time staff overseen by an elected management committee. Each has 30 or 40 active members and a larger circle of occasional participants, some of whom participate in the public activities of both groups. The membership of both groups is predominantly Protestant, though they claim to have "a few" Catholic members. Membership is made up of small farmers, builders, agricultural contractors, livestock dealers, small shopkeepers, shop assistants, factory workers and housewives. All members share the fact that they have been injured or have had a relative injured or killed in the Troubles. Each group has its own website and both are in the process of building a memorial garden. Both groups recognise that there is now a need to "tell our story", which both understand in terms of the "innocence" of Protestant victims that was outlined earlier, and which both maintain was "hidden" for too long. Both groups participate in the commemorations of South Armagh's worst atrocities and both lay wreaths on Remembrance Sunday. Both have received grants to develop a range of services for their members, such as counselling.

Their history reflects their different approaches to victims' issues. FAIR was founded following a series of informal meetings in 1996. By 2000, differences of approach had split the group, resulting in the resignation of nine of the ten committee members and the formation of SAVER/NAVER under the leadership of a former Greenfinch (female UDR), who explained her departure as follows: "I couldn't see in the environment and in the line that they were going down that I was going to be of any value to the people." Disagreement centred largely on how victims' issues should be addressed and redressed, and the extent to which they should be politicised. As outlined below, such differences are evident from the groups' websites, which contain a number of striking contrasts.

Party political leanings impact on such differences, though they cannot fully explain them. Support for hardline and more moderate political positions is evenly balanced in Newry and Armagh, and in 2005 the DUP and UUP polled 18 and 14 per cent respectively. FAIR maintains close contact with the DUP, and the MPs Dodds and Donaldson are regular figures at its public events including its memorial services in a Free Presbyterian church. In contrast, SAVER/NAVER inclines towards the UUP, and Trimble (former First Minister and MP), Empey and Kennedy regularly attend its functions, including the annual memorial service held alternately in the local Presbyterian and Church of Ireland churches. To this extent, the two groups reflect familiar political configurations in

Northern Ireland and this inevitably manifests in their approach. Todd (1987) has drawn attention to two traditions in Protestant political culture, one emphasising the inextricable connection between religion and politics and associated with the DUP and Orange Order, and the other characterised by a more softly spoken liberal stance that stresses its Unionist connection to Great Britain. However, these are distinctions which the victims' groups cross cut. Any straightforward dichotomy that associates each group with one political party or another is also complicated by other factors. FAIR's relationship to the DUP has often been tense, and has resulted in refusals to cooperate.[3] Moreover, former DUP Northern Ireland Assembly member Paul Berry has been involved with both groups even before he left the party, assisting with grant applications, acting as an advocate at Stormont, and singing at their public events. While some in SAVER/NAVER complain that "the DUP wants to make political capital out of victims' issues", they accept that "that fella Paul Berry has been good", suggesting the existence of a personalised politics that transcends party affiliations. Neither group mentions political party involvement on their website, and membership of both groups includes active supporters of both parties.

Although the structure of the FAIR and SAVER/NAVER homepages is similar, their content and style are very different. For example, while FAIR emphasises graphic accounts of violent incidents and alleged republican links to Gaddafi and Colombia, the SAVER/NAVER site stresses the therapies and training available to members. Unlike the FAIR site, SAVER/NAVER has no commentary on current and past events in South Armagh, and no accounts of personal suffering.

The interpretation of thirty years of violence and the political meanings of these experiences for border Protestants that are stressed by FAIR are intended to reveal a previously unknown "truth" about South Armagh to as wide an audience as possible, and have no equivalent on the SAVER/NAVER site, which stresses instead the psychological and emotional needs of its members. The two sites, therefore, reflect contrasting but equally valid understandings of how best to serve the needs of victims, one stressing the need for political action, the other emphasising the need for familial and emotional support. One of these—the political—can be easily understood outside the group, while the other—the familial—is less likely to be fully shared beyond the immediate victim circle. In this sense, one appeals to a face-to-face community rooted in kin and place, the other to an imagined community of ethno-political belonging.

These different approaches are particularly apparent in how the suffering experienced by members is presented by the two groups. That the groups have different representational styles does not mean, however, that the content of their narrative accounts is arbitrary or invented. It cannot be stressed enough that their accounts recall genuine feelings of hurt, anxiety and threat and stand as expressions of real anguish, grievance and pain. But this is presented in different ways. Although the SAVER/NAVER site includes no accounts of violence, the group recently published such accounts in a book entitled, *A Legacy of Tears* (Patterson, 2006). The decision to publish personal testimony in book form rather than on a website reflects crucial differences in style. "Telling one's story" is recognised by both groups to have potential therapeutic value, though both recognise the trauma that many re-live in the process. Speaking out has been painful for those who have recounted their experiences. Moreover, it has gone against the cultural grain of a rural Presbyterianism that puts a high value on stoic, silent suffering (Donnan and Simpson, 2007). Such concerns impacted upon members of both groups and provided the wider cultural context in which they began publicly to recount their experiences.

There were other concerns too about ownership of the "stories" that were told and about how they might be appropriated for political or other ends once in the public arena. For SAVER/NAVER, book form seemed to allow more control than a website: once published, the text was more "fixed", less easy to alter and to juxtapose with other text or images that might give it a different interpretive load. Many in SAVER/NAVER believed it could "speak for itself" and was more likely to remain "true" to the narrator's experience. Nor was the book as readily available as a web-based account, which some felt was a good thing, believing such easy accessibility could diminish their grief by presenting it as a kind of voyeuristic "entertainment" for casual surfers. Instead, it was felt, a book spoke with a softer, more personal and private voice, and would be read only by those who actively sought it out, and for whom the experiences it described were likely to resonate, since a mainly local, Northern Ireland readership was anticipated. One woman, a member of SAVER/NAVER whose UDR husband had been shot dead by the IRA, and whose experience is included in *A Legacy of Tears*, explained that she had first been approached by FAIR to tell her story: "Sure they wanted me to tell my story in the what do you call it . . . internet . . . and my big son says, 'You'll do no such thing!' "

These principles informed the writing of the book itself. Someone with local connections was approached, a university educated Baptist minister whose father had served along the border with the RUC. He explained to me how he maximised the contributors' "own words" and limited his own interventions to contextualising information. Typescripts of his recorded conversations with the thirteen contributors were returned to them until they were satisfied that their views were "truly represented". In contrast to the FAIR website, which states that the "Contents of the site can be attributed to William Frazer", the emphasis here is on "people's own stories".

Although they agree on the broad narrative themes of the violence they experienced, as outlined earlier, the narrative particulars of the FAIR and SAVER/NAVER accounts differ in language, interpretation, images and tone. While *Legacy* does not shrink from strongly worded comment—its back cover blurb refers to "the republican 'killing fields' of South and North Armagh"—its accounts primarily stress the social networks in which the victims were embedded and the damage that was done to these and to the "communities" to which the victims belonged. The emotional, psychological and social costs, while inescapably present in the accounts given by both groups, are not here subordinated to other interpretations, such as those that communicate a political claim or speculate on the motives and characteristics of the perpetrators. The following examples are typical of the style in the two publications.

From FAIR's website:

On 1st September 1975, one of the worst atrocities was carried out at Tullyvallen Orange Hall one mile from the Irish border where five men were cowardly cut down while carrying out an act of worship . . . The killers entered the hall and began to fire indiscriminately cutting down all that stood in front of them. There was utter chaos as men dived for cover to try and save themselves from psychopathic killers. Fortunately one member in the hall who was an off-duty member of the security forces had his gun and when he fired a shot the cowards then fled still firing through the windows leaving a trail of devastation behind. (FAIR, 2005)

From *A Legacy of Tears*:

Joe Wilson worked at Lester's shop in Armagh and served as a part time soldier in the UDR . . . He also ran the small family farm . . . on 11 September 1975 . . . they fired four or five shots at him from close range hitting him in the chest but he was not seriously injured. Mr Wilson was able to go to his work at the supermarket the next day . . . The family were then advised to move . . . but Mr Wilson refused to move because, "he loved the country and he loved his children, those times we were living on nothing, but he died without any debt" . . . [Following his murder in 1976] . . . hundreds of mourners attended the funeral . . . The minister . . . commented that: "Joe Wilson did not content himself to live life in an ordinary fashion, but gave his time, indeed his life for our community" . . . the resolve and courage of this family . . . stands in marked contrast to the evil and cowardice of the perpetrators of this murder. (Patterson, 2006: 41–7)

While these two accounts share a number of framing themes that are replicated in many other accounts—such as the sense of "ordinary" individuals going about their daily business defenceless against "cowardly" attack—they differ in crucial respects. Both are narrated by a third party, but only the second incorporates directly the voice of those involved, by quoting the dead man's wife and the clergyman at his funeral. By contrast, the first account avoids description of the particularity of individual experience and emotion and is entirely in the narrator's voice. This tendency is reflected throughout the two publications. Particularly striking are the contrasting images and language that describe these tragic events and terms such as "indiscriminate", "atrocity", "cut down" and "psychopathic killers" in the first account contrast with "fired four or five shots" and "this murder" in the second. A selection of the words used repeatedly throughout the publications conveys the cumulative impact of this different language use. Thus, where words such as "ethnic cleansing", "atrocity", "slaughter", "bloodthirsty", "ruthless", "merciless", "savage", "senseless", "psychopathic" and "crazed" appear regularly in one, such words do not feature in the other. In one case there is the sense of excessive force with the killers "cutting down all that stood" before them, and accounts of killings are juxtaposed with images of bodies by the roadside; in the other, the photographs are mainly portraits of the individuals killed and of where they lived. In short, interpretation, opinion and emotion are more subdued and understated in one case than the other.

However, it is not just the language used that constructs the difference between these two styles of accounting, but the contrast in who it is that is described: in one case the killers constitute the main focus whereas in the other it is the man who was murdered. At risk of overstatement, one publication tends to emphasise the nature of the violence while the other emphasises its impact. Where one talks of genocide, extinction and ethnic cleansing, the other emphasises the victim's personality and involvement in family and community. Thus Joe Wilson is described as a hardworking family man who turned up for work the day after he was shot. Like many of those whose experiences are described in *Legacy*, he had worked for the "whole community", which together mourned his loss. And where one emphasises the violence of "bloodthirsty" perpetrators, the other stresses the lives left "in tatters" as a result. Families were "devastated" and "shattered", with lives they had to "battle" to rebuild, an emphasis on life after violence that is largely absent in the other case. This dissimilar focus arguably orients the reader in different ways—in one case towards "the other" as a generalised and diffused threat and in the second case towards the "self"—at the same time as it variously constructs South Armagh as a place of continuing conflict or somewhere that "the community" is in need of repair.

These differences between how these two Markethill Protestant victims' groups represent the violence of the past and its impact upon them suggest that while there is a "shared" collective memory of the violence that South Armagh Protestants experienced—one characterised by a sense of marginality, betrayal and siege—it is a storyline of such generality that it offers only a rough guide to what many of these border Protestants say and think. More than this, however, it is a narrative largely for external consumption and not always how they narrate "their story" to themselves. Such collective storylines might seem to bring people together, and in a broad sense they indeed do just that. But such narratives are situational, and depend on who is talking and to whom, which is to say that in the case considered here we should not overestimate its powers of cohesion or essentialise all border Protestants in its terms. Nor should we overestimate its coherence, and so remain blind to its many constituent and sometimes divergent strands.

## Conclusion

This chapter has suggested that our understanding of what is widely referred to as the "politics of victimhood" must be complemented by a grasp of the local social relations and dynamics in which a particular victims' group is embedded, and especially by what we might call the *"culture* of victimhood"*, which is not only shaped by but shapes Protestant politics at local level and potentially beyond. The culture, content and practice of victims' groups can clearly vary widely, even between groups that draw on a similar constituency for membership and support, and which may perceive and represent the needs and interests of victims in very different ways. The availability of funding and the new opportunities for leadership at local level that victims' issues have created have facilitated the institutionalisation of differences of opinion and style that might otherwise have remained dormant. How past violence is remembered and presented has redrawn the boundaries for those who might have seen themselves as members of the same "community".

Contemporary representations of past political violence along the border such as those in the victims' groups' publications are thus clearly bound up with local power relations and the competition for funding and influence, as much between different Protestant victims' groups as between these groups and their Catholic counterparts. They are also tied up with different unionist political orientations, and with the varied local forms of Protestantism. However, they reflect none of these in any simple way, cross-cutting all of them in terms of membership and cultural style. In whatever ways it is harnessed in social and political life (or framed analytically), personal grief has a way of bubbling up to subvert all the categories in which we might seek to contain it. The power of personal grief lies in its ability to express itself in its own terms.

This chapter has attempted to understand the suffering that border Protestants have endured and the different ways in which they have sought to make sense of it. While many themes are shared, no single form incorporates or communicates the individual grief, so that approaches which aggregate "Protestant suffering" within a single narrative plot risk masking the very real human needs of those involved. The narrative possibilities available to Protestants can sometimes seem heavily constrained by a rigidly formulaic and minimally changing set of rituals and symbols drawn from a limited stock of historic milestones to which every new event must be accommodated, and which provides an interpretive framework in perpetuity for all that follows. As a result, there can seem little room for creative innovation or new forms of emotional expression. So too the specificities of accounts of violence and victimhood along the border are sometimes drawn into this collective storyline, as commentators have often pointed out (Dawson, 2004; Donnan, 2005). Indeed, it is this seeming fixity of the Protestant narrative which gives its themes of stoicism and resilience in the face of threat much of their resonance and power. Yet, at the same time, the weight of this collective recall does not always stifle the individual voices that are gathered to it, which can be worked and represented in different and even divergent ways as shown above. Whatever the discursive frames into which the narratives and memories of violence outlined here might be inserted, these accounts are not infinitely manipulable "through narration or social pressure" (Sorabji, 2006: 4). Even when working within a "cultural script", individuals remain "active managers" of their own memories, with their autobiographical truths performed in different ways. Since the Good Friday Agreement, South Armagh Protestants have increasingly had to grapple with what it means to be a border Protestant, reconciling their community narrative with a broader cultural narrative, something to which they take a varied approach as this chapter demonstrates.

## Notes

1 I am very grateful to Fiona Magowan and Mervyn Busteed for their comments on this chapter and to Kirk Simpson for help with the interviews. A particular debt is owed to everyone in FAIR and SAVER/NAVER. Research

in 2004–5 was funded through the Higher Education Authority North-South Strand 1 Programme.
2   It is potentially contentious to talk of Protestant and Catholic victims' groups, since inclusivity is often a criterion of funding.
3   *Ulster Gazette* 20 June 2002, p. 18 and 8 February 2007, p. 18.

## References

Dawson, G. (2003) "Mobilising memories: Protestant and Unionist victims' groups and the politics of victimhood in the Irish peace process", in P. Gready (ed.) *Political Transition: Politics and Cultures* (London: Pluto), pp. 127–47.

Dawson, G. (2004) "Ulster-British identity and the cultural memory of 'ethnic cleansing' on the Northern Ireland border", in H. Brocklehurst and R. Phillips (eds) *History, Nationhood and the Question of Britain* (Basingstoke: Palgrave Macmillan), pp. 356–73.

Donnan, H. (1999) "Shopping and sectarianism at the Irish border", in M. Rösler and T. Wendl (eds) *Frontiers and Borderlands: Anthropological Perspectives.* (Frankfurt: Peter Lang), pp. 101–16.

Donnan, H. (2005) "Material identities: Fixing ethnicity in the Irish borderlands", *Identities: Global Studies in Culture and Power*, 12.1: 69–105.

Donnan, H. and K. Simpson (2007) "Silence and violence among Northern Ireland border Protestants", *Ethnos*, 72.1: 5–28.

Families Acting for Innocent Relatives (FAIR) (2005) *Tullyvallen Massacre* www.victims.org.uk/tullyvallen.html.

Fay, M., Morrissey, M. and Smyth, M. (1999) *Northern Ireland's Troubles: The Human Costs* (London: Pluto).

McCreary, A. (1976) *Survivors* (Belfast: Century Books).

Patterson, D. (2006) *A Legacy of Tears* (Markethill: Saver/Naver).

Smyth, M. (2006) "Lost lives: Victims and the construction of 'victimhood' in Northern Ireland", in M. Cox, A. Guelke and F. Stephen (eds) *A Farewell to Arms? Beyond the Good Friday Agreement* (Manchester: Manchester University Press), pp. 6–23.

Sorabji, C. (2006) "Managing memories in post-war Sarajevo: Individuals, bad memories, and new wars", *Journal of Royal Anthropological Institute* 12: 1–18.

Todd, J. (1987) "Two traditions in Unionist political culture", *Irish Political Studies*, 2: 1–26.

# 17

# Scenting the paper rose: the Ulster-Scots quest for music as identity

## Fintan Vallely

### Introduction

The island of Ireland is a mixed bag of identities which by origins includes Irishness, Lowland-Scotsness, Scottish-Highland Gaelicness and Englishness. All have contributed to what was established as "traditional" music and song on the island—an artistic and recreational set of practices that have survived into modern time. The use of the term "traditional" for this indigenous music avoids the implication, assumption or ascription of any ownership, and permits acknowledgement of contribution from all social classes and political base-communities. The music as played has a central "standard" style, which is defined by island-wide competition and professionalism, but it also falls into a number of highly distinctive, persistent *regional* voices—one of which is Ulster song style. These "voices" are the equivalent of accents in language, signifiers applied to a basic core of melodies and forms rather than representing different music.

This chapter addresses the adoption of music by the Ulster-Scots movement. It argues that it is a tremendously positive statement to put a community back in touch with valuable aspects of its cultural past; but expresses concern that if this is done in a blinkered or separatist manner, which merely reinforces sectarian values. It is necessary first to digress into a brief summary of the background to traditional music in Ulster, borrowing from the forthcoming *Tuned Out—Protestant Perceptions of Traditional Music.*[1]

### What is traditional music?

Traditional music is played widely in Ireland, Northern Ireland, Britain, Irish diaspora areas abroad, and among many non-Irish in scattered regions internationally, particularly in Europe. As described by the players and aficionados, the music is taken to mean the jigs, reels, hornpipes, etc., dance and style of songs, which were the entertainment of "common" (rural) people prior to the industrialisation and urbanisation of society. It also predates music recording and the development of mass forms of entertainment. More modern music is seen as having already influenced, and continuing to influence, traditional music's ongoing composition and practice. Some writers and academics will refer to "the tradition", a term which indicates the historical continuity of traditional music—its evolution, accumulation and development of repertoire, the process of its being passed on, and the styles of its implementation. Of necessity, the concept of "traditional" is arbitrarily bounded. For instance, the traditional *political* music and song of the North of Ireland are avoided, primarily with regard to the conventions of traditional musicians, but practically because they merit separate description and analysis. Not included in the genre definition "traditional", therefore, is the derivative political music that involves the traditional (Protestant) Orange and (Catholic) Nationalist bands,[2] the distinct Lambeg drum music tradition[3] and the bodies of Orange and Republican song,[4] except in the odd case where items from both are also considered as part of the general traditional repertoire.[5]

Most significant about traditional music is the fact of its revival. Like all older cultural practices, by the 1960s it had become largely redundant for social life, particularly for dancing, usurped by showbands and modern popular music. Older Catholic or Protestant musicians who loved the music they played were faced with a world in which their art had all the appearances of becoming redundant. Some did have an interest in passing it on to the next generation, and managed to do so. But in order to interest youth in music there must be a reason—an occasion for its use, a stage—somewhere to show off, and a feeling of being loved and "thought well of" for playing it. Protestant young people in the 1950s could see their parents and neighbours dancing mostly to cover-pop bands, country and western, country and old-time rather than Céilí or Céilí and old-time. In homes where traditional music or song had once been an actual part of cultural experience, for the children, the music came to have little function other than the pleasing of musical parents and older people, or else the isolated pleasing of one's self. That was not enough incentive to get anything more than a handful of young Protestants to carry on playing or singing. In contrast, by the 1960s the Catholic community had the psychological comfort of the well-attested, nineteenth-century association between indigenous music and Irish identity. They had been in touch with the music ideologically too (no matter how superficially) for all the years after the formation of the two Irish states, and many had learned it courtesy of the opportunity of political complementarity. Most of the action of the 1960s revival was located in the south, towards which Catholics generally were well disposed. There was a full-blown political struggle in progress in Northern Ireland in which there was kudos for Catholics for playing the music, ready platforms and heady, enthusiastic listeners ready to clap players on the back for what was perceived as "great work". Among Catholics, this constituted a significant boost to a music that had been on the wane—an incentive to play, even to learn to play from scratch.

This picture shows a music form which simply moved on in the years of the revival, regardless of religion or collective origins, and with no particular affiliation, for it was played then (as now) by a fair number of Protestants also. Taking this as the background of practice, attention is now turned to the significance of Ulster-Scots interest in the music.

### Style, participation and identity

The overall mixed pedigree of traditional music has been dictated by its task of once having had a "popular" function as well as being artistically driven. By now, arguably, this renders the music as simply *itself*, a tonal *mestizo* of related compatible components. But, collectively, the music is instantly—internationally, like accent—identifiable by core character as being "Irish" and it has, paradoxically in the electronic, global age, been successfully re-established. Borrowed Scottishness is quite obvious in the traditional music repertoire; so too is an acculturated Scottish performance style in particular areas. But most of this dates to post-seventeenth-century time: the Scottish inclusions in dance music coming from the late eighteenth and early nineteenth centuries, the Scottish stylistic accent (found in Donegal) from post famine, seasonal migration to Glasgow and Scottish lowland cities.

Today traditional music has a majority "catholic" participation, this at least partly because of the widely held attitude among Northern Ireland Protestants that—on account of its being regarded as "Irish", and being indulged in by Northern Irish Catholics and by the Irish south of the border—the music does not represent *them*. This was a useful identity marker as long as Northern Ireland's Protestant population felt that they did not need such artistic associations, and their social confidence could be satisfied by being held in high regard by the central government. But with the advent of the Good Friday Agreement things changed, for its strategy involved *identities* and the facilitation of funding for indigenous cultural practices. Following the Agreement, the need for defence of the realm as a core ingredient of unionist politics realistically disappeared, and with it the raison d'etre for Protestant loyalty to Westminster *as a culture*.

## The Ulster-Scots and music

Catholics continued the practice of what they had always subscribed to—standard western-world media culture, popular sport, literature and music, but also including so-ascribed "Gaelic" cultural values. It was, therefore, just assumed that *their* distinctive, representative culture included the classic symbols of all-island Irishness—Gaelic games, Irish language and traditional music. Among Protestants it was less clear. Manifestations of defensive and assertive loyalty are the core elements presently claimed as Protestant culture in this vacuum. In addition to assumed loyalty to the monarch and the British state, recourse was additionally explored by Protestants, however, in linguistics, paralleling what was seen as a package that had worked successfully for Catholics. This uses the foci of Ulster Protestant identity and Ulster-Scots identity. The first embraces all Protestants; the second represents, perhaps, half of Ulster Protestants. Through these tendencies, Protestants have sought ways in which to develop culture and identity via existing music practices. Hence, many strong Ulster Unionists fall to viewing the symbolic, *agitational*, marching-band music as *their* unique, ethnic expression. The Ulster-Scots package additionally proffers the prospect of a more explicitly artistic or "sit-down" culture. Speech- and language-based, this has been gradually expanded in pursuit of identifying, corralling and tapping for Protestant identity cohesion, extant Ulster speech patterns. By the turn of the new century it had moved its interest to music, including the recreational, Irish traditional music repertoire. This can be interpreted in either of two ways, as: Protestants *reclaiming* or affirming what is "rightfully" theirs, or, alternatively, as a desire to "partition" Protestantism *within* traditional music.

As for the first of these Ulster-Scots positions—reclamation—there is no questioning that creation of the body of traditional music has involved people of Protestant faiths (see, for instance, Morton, 1970). And despite several generations having dumped it, it seems appropriate and positive that it should now begin to be appreciated again by them.

The second option, partitioning Protestantism within existing traditional music, which is already happening to a slight degree, seems inappropriate. Not all Northern Irish Protestants are of Scots ancestry. There are English and others there too, all of whom played parts in the music corpus. Moreover, not all people who speak in what is regarded as an Ulster-Scots dialect or language are of Scots ancestry (accent is a matter of locale), and not all who speak the dialect are Protestant. That is, even though there may be a linguistic thread, it does not follow that there is an ethnic group.

Reclamation of cultural use of the music, however, does seem a valid idea. For Protestants, whether of Scots, English or Huguenot origins, traditional music en bloc as it stands *could* be engaged in with unchallengeable historical or cultural validity. The alternative—"partitioning", or the notion of claiming certain tunes, players and forms—as is at present the Ulster-Scots tendency, is implicitly divisive of what is in fact a stable, mixed-religion cultural field, and seems little more valid than screening for religion-specific DNA. More importantly, partitioning of music ignores both the extremely fluid, osmotic nature of folk music development, and the consciousness of traditional music players, aficionados and scholars themselves. Many of the latter are Protestant, and most not politically involved; their engagement is primarily aesthetic, and, when obliged to define the music, regard it in fact as is a signifier of broad-spectrum, *island* Irishness, rather than *flag* Irishness. For the Ulster-Scots however, the "mix" of the music that is available to them in Northern Ireland is problematic, because it is known by repute as "Irish" traditional, and for them "Irish" is a dirty word. The pound of flesh is required without the pound of blood, so the elements of the collective "traditional" music of Ireland—are now being picked over for appropriate, acceptable, Scots-imagined "authenticity".

### Blinkering out "Irishness"

The Ulster-Scots project seeks to replace the ethereal loyal British identity and its one-time political substance with a secular alternative. Going by its media—in particular *The Ulster Scot* newssheet, which is financed by government agency, and given free with the *Newsletter*—its overriding concern is identification with the colonial past and unionist ideology. For many of those who are genuinely interested in Ulster-Scots identity, however, it must be said that the politics may not be the dominant issue. Their desire is to acknowledge and develop cultural characteristics and roots, and, to this end, the movement is assembling a solid, comprehensive cultural package, which might give multi-dimensional meaning to life in a weak economy that is crazily swung by a modern world where tourism, virtual entertainment and escapist hedonism are bewildering realities. Ulster émigré communities in Canada and east-coast America are courted by Ulster-Scots, indicating an overwhelming interest in *that which has been*, those *who have been gone for centuries*, the famous long-dead US presidents whose mettle is claimed for Ulster genes, the entertainers whose talent needs to be seen as conceived by ancestors on the "oul sod".

While the contacts established east-coast USA *are* real, and of tremendous nostalgia value, nevertheless, they seem a shaky foundation on which to build identity. Acknowledging this, real-time models are explored as a more solid base for social cohesion. Therefore, comparable role models are sought in Irish-Gaelic identity in Ireland and its diaspora, as well as in Scots and Scots-Gaelic lobbies in Scotland. To strengthen the Ulster-Scots argument, a distinctive music is sought, not only agitational music, but that which is seen to be of real substance, a "sit-down" music art form. The quest for this draws heavily on Scottishness and shuts out Irishness. Scottish music is not a new dimension of Ulster or Irish ethnic make-up, for as recently as the 1950s Scottish reels, flings and quicksteps were the popular dance music all over the island from Antrim to Kerry, and historically have been hitherto uncontested as a significant part of the traditional music repertoire. Ulster-Scots "Scottishness" does not, however, draw on the clear, chronological historical context which also involved Gaelic language, early Christianity, Gaelic colonisation of Scotland and Scottish origins myths. Instead, it focuses on Lowland Scotland because that is the region from which the majority of seventeenth century Scottish migrants were seen to come. Music, for Ulster-Scots, therefore, comes to be presented as tartan iconology—the sound of bagpipes, marching bands, and Scottish dancing. But these are all a highly-evolved, nineteenth-century Victorian Scottish legacy.

What of the political music practices that are also feted as genuine Ulster-Scots? These are much more credible, even if they do represent significant built-in security too, for they also include (as Ulster-Scots tradition and uniqueness) the general Protestant or loyal flute band, the fife and the Lambeg drum. These are a considerable political safety net. For since they are supremely emblematic in Ulster-British unionist identity, agitational and politically-loyal practices are thus validated as the backbone to the desired aesthetic and cultural identities. By definition, this excludes Catholics.

## Questionable pedigrees

Notwithstanding this argument, however, what is of interest to musicologists, is the desire to develop, or redevelop, a Protestant "traditional" recreational music culture—one rooted in the imagined traditional culture of the neighbouring land mass: Scotland.[6] This in itself is surely no bad thing, but the kind of cultural hybridity that is so encouraged by Ulster-Scots ideologues makes claims that have questionable validity in relation to bodies that they may have had nothing in particular to do with, which are outside their control, and which have been around in Ulster for many generations.

The apparent Ulster-Scots insistence on an "identifying"—but clearly "different"—music seems to draw attention to the fact that such music has not been acknowledged as having been there in the past. Indeed, as the years after 1921 have advanced, Northern Ireland Protestants have been progressively dumping, then distancing themselves from, the body of recreational music and song which is traditional to the island of Ireland, daubing and dubbing it "Fenian", rendering the actual body of music and song all the more irretrievable or untouchable.[7] This process accelerated after 1966 and the re-emerged "Troubles".

Contrary to the popular illusion, Irish traditional music's milieu does not correspond to either Catholic society in Northern Ireland today, or to the population of the south of Ireland. Both are, of course, generally well disposed toward the music, and accept its representativeness, but it is seldom the dominant entertainment of any one local community in anything other than origins. Today, in Ireland, it has a floating community—an "acetate" community,[8] which, while it certainly does not generally see itself as "Catholic", does, mostly, consider itself (Protestants included) as "Irish", "Irish traditional" or "traditional" (most often the latter) and is conscious of the music's Scottish and English borrowings. Undoubtedly, some of its participants are strongly nationalist, and may be outspokenly so, but this is not typical, for it is mostly a middle liberal ground and, indeed, it has a share too of unionist participants. For players and aficionados, however, it typically involves no political identification—it is the art form that is paramount, not the associations that the people involved with it may privately have.

### Inventing traditions

In defence of the Ulster-Scots importation strategy it has been said that Irish and Scottish Gaelic cultures themselves have been "invented" anyway. But whatever is the case for Ireland in this regard also applies to Scotland, and indeed to England, and to Englishness itself. So how true is the idea of "invention"? Firstly, neither Scottish nor Irish cultural practices in their home grounds were arbitrarily conjured up out of thin air. Both drew on tangible and auditory contemporary expressions and material historical, intellectual, academic and music traditions. All of this was well established and visible, part of a continuity that involved archaeology and collecting. Language and song may have been weakening as a result of industrialisation and urbanisation, but in the nineteenth century all countries sought to revitalise and place value on appropriate traditions, a movement, indeed, in which an eighteenth-century one-time Ulster Protestant cleric at Dromore, County Down, Bishop Percy, was prominent. As for Irish music, this is even more real—having had popular function, far from imagined or invented. At the time that the Irish music revival as such began in the 1950s, the music still was well practised, and had always been present– a music utilised all over the island as the soundscape of seasonal and leisure recreation. This music eventually became widely known as simply "traditional" not just out of respect for the contemporary classical music of Irish composers, and the Irish pop music, but occasionally in deference to the fact that some of its Northern Protestant players might have felt insecure or threatened by use of the appellation "Irish".

Ulster-Scots music as such is not a genesis in that it does not arise from an assortment of extant objects and practices. It has come out of the political crucible of late-twentieth-century Ireland, a collation of history and pragmatism assembled in *l'esprit de l'escalier* fashion to mark and clear space for one section of Ulster Protestants. While it may have Scottish antecedents, this identified music does not, however, have Scots continuity in the way it is now presented. Rather, it appears as a defensive strategy to bolster the political. Nor is the Ulster-Scots music project about a new instrumental music, which might have arisen organically from agitational political assertiveness, renaissance, fusion or marginalisation. Instead, it is the opposite—a political movement desiring and devising a recreational music by borrowing, selection and rejection. This has been done before, of course, notably at the birth of the state of Israel. The idea of having a new crop of young people begin to play *some* variety of traditional music that is actually relevant to their community is, to musicians and musicologists, exciting, and deserving of unquestioning support. What weakens the exercise, however, is the notion of directing such a potential as music enthusiasm (and its necessary artistic expressivity) into the imprisonment of a nineteenth-century political straitjacket rather than permitting it to experience the free association and challenge which would raise necessary artistic questions.

There is, of course, a subtext here that is beyond the scope of musicologists. One section of the Protestant population is relocating the implementation of identity from the customary loyal political groupings to recreational music practices that are not directly political. Necessarily, this will involve crisis, for it is something never considered before. In the interim, it cannot avoid becoming a "balaclava in one hand, bagpipes in the other" strategy—perhaps a logical enough transition method.

But there is an alternative to viewing traditional music as political ideology. It is that children be taught music of their localities without any political baggage: all of this music is undisputedly (and undisputed by anyone) *Ulster* music and song. This includes such as the existing artistic practice in areas of both Down and Antrim of Scottish country dance, and also, in the same area, the common involvement of Protestant children in pursuit of virtuosity through so called "Irish" or "step" dancing. Ulster singing is also a distinctive, still practised artefact, which complements a body of contemporary expertise in instrumental music.

## Conclusion

The Ulster-Scots introduction of modern Scottish music to represent their identity mimics the logic of the nineteenth-century Gaelic League's assembly of "Irishness" from then-contemporary cultural hallmarks. As a role model, this is problematic, not least for the fact that what became ultimately identified as "traditional" music was more an associated consequence of that programme. The music's revival on the island was not contemporaneous with political independence, and did not meaningfully begin until the 1950s; it was largely a feature of modernity, a fashionable, post-war reassertion of "people's" identity, of which many Ulster Protestants were a founding part. A programme for redressing the absence of traditional recreational music from Protestant children's consciousness would, therefore, seem better undertaken as a right of place, a celebration of a music which their forebears contributed to shaping. Most of the ingredients necessary to undertake such reappraisal have been already assembled (by Protestants, of Scots, Irish and English ancestry), and are available for consultation. There is, of course, much additional traditional music-related research to be done (in Protestant communities), and, in particular, a great need for building indigenous music awareness. It is vital that the connection with Scotland *should* be acknowledged, but in all its forms, and presented for what it is: a component of local, indigenous or traditional music in Ulster, not a substitute for it. It is of key importance that the reorientation of Protestants toward traditional music should also involve, or be in consultation with, those Protestant performers, music lovers and scholars who have spent their lives involved in that music and who understand it. It also seems better that reintroduction or reorientation be done in a positive fashion, which is respectful of art, rather than as political trophy collection or banner waving allied to dubious irredentism.

## Notes

This material is a refocus on information presented at University of Ulster, Belfast (2002), New York University (2003) and the Society for Musicology in Ireland, Limerick (2003). Additional material on this subject appears in the proceedings of the "Come West Along the Road Conference", held at New York University, 2003.

1  See Fintan Vallely, *Tuned Out: Protestant Perceptions of Traditional Irish Music* (Cork University Press, 2008).
2  Most of the bands are Protestant, making a band culture very much part of Protestant life (see Vallely, 2004, 2008).
3  Lambeg drumming is dealt with in great social detail by Hastings (2003).
4  This has been addressed in various media by, among others, John Moulden (2006), Georges Zimmerman (1967, 2002) and Hugh Shields (1993). May McCann has analysed Republican song practices (1985) whilst Katy Radford (2002) has explored the broader associations of loyalist band players.
5  Orange and Republican songs use both old airs (which may also be used for non-political songs) and more modern pop tunes.
6  Dr Brian Lambkin (Ulster Centre for Emigration Studies, at Omagh, Co. Tyrone), for instance, sees this as similar to the "assembly" of Irishness by the nineteenth-century Gaelic League (personal communication).
7  Robin Morton's *Folksongs Sung in Ulster* (a book urgently deserving republication) documents a period as recent as the 1950s–1960s when traditional song and singing were still part of Protestant life in, for instance, County Armagh and within the Orange Order.
8  "Acetate" here is derived from the notion of marking the locations of traditional music practices and events on a sheet of clear acetate laid upon a map of Ireland, Europe or the world. When the acetate is lifted off, voilá!—the acetate community.

## References

Hastings, G. (2003) *With Fife and Drum* (Belfast: Blackstaff).
McCann, M. (1985) "The past in the present: a study of some aspects of the politics of music in Belfast" (Unpublished PhD thesis, Queen's University Belfast, 1985).
Morton, R. (1970) *Folksongs Sung in Ulster* (Cork: Mercier).
Moulden, J. (2006) "The printed ballad in Ireland 1760–1920" (Unpublished PhD thesis, National University of Ireland, Galway, 2006).
Radford, K. (2002) "Loyal sounds—music as marker of identity in Protestant west Belfast" (Unpublished PhD thesis, Queen's University Belfast).
Shields, H. (1993) *Narrative Singing in Ireland* (Dublin: Irish Academic Press).
Vallely, F. (1993) "Protestant perceptions of traditional music" (Unpublished MA dissertation, Queen's University, Belfast).
Vallely, F. (2004) "Flute routes to 21st century Ireland" (unpublished PhD thesis, University College Dublin).
Vallely, F. (2008) *Tuned Out: Protestant Perceptions of Traditional Music* (Dublin: Cork: Cork University Press).
Zimmerman, G. D. (1967) *Songs of Irish Rebellion* (Dublin: Figgis).
Zimmerman, G. D. (2002) Songs of Irish Rebellion—Political Street Ballads and Rebel Songs 1780–1900 (Dublin: Four Courts Press).

# 18

# The evolution of Ulster Protestant identity in the twentieth century: nations and patriotism

*Thomas Hennessey*

## Introduction

Discussions of national identity in Ireland, particularly within the Ulster Protestant community, have generated much debate. The most perceptive analysis of national identity in Northern Ireland, to date, has been by Michael Gallagher (1995). He also provides a convenient summary of the existing theories. They are: *no nation*—there are no nations on the island of Ireland; *one nation*—there is just one, Irish, nation in Ireland; *a nation and part of another nation*—there is an Irish nation and part of the British nation; *a nation and a bit*—there is an Irish nation and an Ulster Protestant community; *two nations*—there is an Irish nation and an Ulster nation; and *three nations/two nations and part of another nation*—there is an Irish nation, an Ulster nation and part of the British nation (Gallagher, 1995: 718). Gallagher considers the last model—for convenience the "three nations" theory—as that which best fits reality (Gallagher, 1995: 735). This chapter seeks to test these models through a combination of historical (primary source material), quantitative and qualitative evidence (derived from a series of interviews conducted during the Northern Ireland peace process). Here the concept of "affect" may provide an insight into how individuals experience their national identity—and remember that, for Ulster Protestants, this is an identity they see as being under severe pressure; hence it should be of no surprise if the emotions involved are amplified. Affect is a "passion or emotion". The term "affect" is translated from the Latin *affectus*—the physiological shift accompanying a judgement (Brenan, 2004: 3). Affect may be unformed and unstructured but nevertheless highly organised and effectively analysable, a term which denotes a more or less organised experience, with empowering or disempowering consequences (Massumi, 2002: 35). Affect is often used to describe bodily reactions, but it is also a useful concept for understanding the emotional impact of identity in social group capacity—the experience engendered. By understanding the subjective experience of Ulster Protestant national/patriot identities one might become aware that their experience is more commonplace than one might have initially thought.

## Ulster Unionism and national identity in the early twentieth century

In 1911, an "Ulster Imperialist" wrote:

> from the viewpoint of one who consciously adopts all the four varieties of local patriotisms. I am Parochial (literally, being a vestryman as well as a treasurer of our local parish!); I am Provincial, being directly interested in the development of commerce and agriculture in Ulster; I am National, in that I am an Irishman and proud of it, anxious to help Ireland as far as lies within my power . . . I am Imperial, glad of my small share in the proudest boast the world has ever heard—"Civis Britannicus sum"—mark the phrase: it is "Britannicus" not "Anglicanus".[1]

No example better illustrates the ability of Ulster—and indeed Irish—Protestants to inhabit a psychological world of multiple identities. Unionists—of the Ulster and Southern variety—utilised the term "nation" to describe their imagined political community but rejected the concept of "nationalism" as used by home rulers. As one unionist explained "A Nationalist, as the term is used, is a man who holds that the Irish are, or ought to be, a nation distinct from the inhabitants of the adjacent island. The Unionist who thinks that the inhabitants of the two [British] islands should be regarded as forming a single nation is, I think the true Nationalist".[2] Edward Carson pointed out that it was no answer to say to unionists: "You are all Irishmen, go and live together" with nationalists; it was absurd, he said, because "We consider that we are satisfied that we are one nationality with Great Britain, and we are satisfied to be."[3] Carson saw his Irishness in unity with "the great English nation and the great Scottish nation, and the great nation of Great Britain, of whom we claim to be a part".[4] Unionists feared home rule would "repudiate the bond of a common nationality with Great Britain, and would be supported in that repudiation by the majority of the Irish people."[5] William Moore, the MP for North Armagh, rejected the Irish nationalist claim of home rule on the grounds that the ideals of the Ulster Protestant were the "ideals of the whole British nation . . . we have been abused . . . as West Britons. We are West Britons . . . we regard the term Briton as the emblem of liberty . . . we are connected with Britain by ties of blood. . . religion and history."[6]

Conscious expressions of membership of a British national entity did not mean the rejection of a positive identification with Ireland, but it was an Irishness bound up with a sense of Britishness. The Lord Primate of the Church of Ireland, Dr Crozier, denied the right of home rulers to monopolise Irish patriotism:

> Ireland is as dear to us members of the Church of Ireland [as it] is to the so-called Nationalists . . . The real fact is that we share in common a great world-wide dominion, and we are justly proud in the position we occupy in directing the destinies of millions of our fellow-subjects . . . This is the heritage into which we have been born—freemen of the greatest empire on which the sun has ever shone and with a great price we have helped to win this freedom . . . Wherever the flag of Great Britain and Ireland waves, there Irishmen have won honour and fame for their native land.[7]

Crozier's British-Irish identity expresses an Irish identity within a British imperial patriotism—here the emphasis is different to that of Carson, but in no way contradictory, just a variety of Britishness. The key point here was that Protestants did not have to choose between their sense of Britishness or Irishness, but for some this was about change with the advent of the First World War.

The impact of both world wars had, for some within the unionist political elite at least, a seismic impact on their identity. During the First World War, Ireland was the only part of the realm to be excluded from conscription. Captain Hugh O'Neill MP felt humiliated: "I do not know how any Irishman, who is fond of his country, as I am, will ever again be able to hold high his head in the company of a Frenchman, a Russian, or an Italian, or any of our other Allies, or for that matter, before an Englishman, or a Scotsman, or a Welshman."[8] In 1916, Carson was daily receiving letters from Englishmen calling him a coward and accusing him of preventing Irishmen from being included in the same dangers as they were.[9] Carson felt that "in my heart . . . when the hour of victory comes . . . we who are Irishmen will feel ashamed to remember that we expected others to make sacrifices from which we provided our own exclusion".[10]

Significantly, James Craig warned:

> It has always been a pride to a man, no matter what part of the country he came from, to say he was an Irishman . . . But if Ireland . . . refuse[s] to come forward and take . . . [its] fair share . . . then I say for my part if this victory is gained it will be no pleasure to me to call myself an Irishmen, and in future it will either have to be a Britisher or an Ulsterman".[11]

Hugh de Fellenburg Montgomery concluded that: "If the choice is forced upon them . . . of saying which Union they attach more importance to, they will be bound to say that strong as the ties are which attach them to the rest of Ireland, the ties which attach them to Great Britain are stronger, and if one set of ties has to be severed they would regretfully decide that it must be the Irish ties . . ."[12] Sir James Stronge wrote that "For myself . . . I still believe that the people of the British Isles form one nation. But, if they should ever become two nations, I prefer to remain a Briton even at the cost of ceasing to be an Irishman . . ."[13] He warned that "there is serious risk that . . . such Irish feeling as remains among us may disappear. Many events in recent years have tended to weaken our connection with the rest if Ireland, and if it becomes clear that the majority of Southern Unionists desires our absorption into an Irish 'Nation' our conversion into 'West Britons' will be complete."[14] For one man this was exactly the effect the war had on him: the future Northern Ireland premier, Basil Brooke was, after the 1916 rebellion, never happy to be called an "Irishman".[15]

For Brooke, the Second World War only completed the process that the First World War had begun. With the advent of the Second World War, the partitioned Irelands grew further apart psychologically. Lord Craigavon summed up the attitude of many Ulster Protestants when he described Eire's wartime neutrality as "nauseating". Craigavon believed that the war left only two choices: "We have either to fight for Britain in every way we can or we are against her along that horrible, dirty path of neutrality."[16] By the end of the war, Basil Brooke, Northern Ireland's Prime Minister, from 1943, could reflect on the psychological impact of the conflict upon Protestant Ulster:

> We have gone through five to six years of war. We have taken our part—it may not have been in the aggregate a great part; but it was the greatest part we could play—in the maintenance of the freedom of the world, and so far as we could assist we helped the freedom of Eire, which, had it not been for the victory of the Allies, would have suffered the same fate as Holland and Denmark . . . I have heard it said in a boasting manner that Eire men went forward to the war. Of course they did, but they were our men; they were our people who thought as we did . . .What these gentlemen [Nationalists] emphasise is the physical boundary, the physical border, whereas it is the ideological border that really counts. In Eire you have a Government which calls itself Republican, says it has not a King . . . There has been throughout history an anti-British feeling in Southern Ireland . . . Here there is a pro-British feeling . . . that is the boundary of the mind which exists between us and the South . . . strategically Northern Ireland played an immensely important part in the last war. The bridgehead, the Rock of Gibraltar, as it was called, was the mainstay in the Battle of the Atlantic. Is it not better for England and the Empire to make sure of that rock rather than the shifting sands of disloyalty and hostility? I am convinced that our

different outlooks and our different loyalties cannot go on together. Our ideals and feelings are so different that I can see bloodshed and riot if that were to happen.[17]

The final parting of the ways came with the formal declaration of Southern Ireland as a republic in 1948 and the severance of all ties with the Crown. Brooke felt that the formal declaration of a republic meant: "We are two separate communities." He observed that, "Our outlook is different; our politics are different; our religion is different." Eire and Ulster's traditions and loyalties were growing further and further apart. Turning to what he considered the "crucial question", he noted "that is our allegiance to the Crown; that is our sentimental side. The sentimental side of the [Nationalist] Opposition is an Irish Republic, but we differ entirely. Here we look upon the Crown as a symbol of freedom; in the Free State the Crown is said to be a symbol of aggression."[18]

### The Troubles: Northern Ireland since 1968

The psychological changes that had been occurring among some of the unionist political elite in Northern Ireland appear to have spread to wider elements of the Ulster Protestant population as a direct result of the thirty-year crisis, which engulfed the province in the late 1960s. In 1968, for example, it was found that there were three national labels of importance in Northern Ireland: British, Irish and Ulster. Ten years later these had collapsed into British and Irish. Protestants had become more inclined to see themselves as British, and less identified with Irishness, while Catholics overwhelmingly identified with Irish. In 1968, less than two-fifths of the Protestants surveyed described themselves as British; a fifth saw themselves as Irish; and a third saw themselves as having an Ulster identity (see Table 18.1). After a decade of the Troubles only 8 per cent chose to describe themselves as Irish, while two-thirds identified themselves as British and 20 per cent chose the Ulster identity. Subsequent surveys showed a decreasing proportion of Protestants describing themselves as Irish and an increasing proportion seeing themselves as British. The attractiveness of the Ulster identity to Protestants declined strongly between 1968 and 1989 and the availability of the Northern Irish label seemed to provide a viable alternative for those who felt a strong identification with their locality. Significantly, Protestants who identified themselves as Northern Irish differed from Protestants in general. The former were more likely to be younger and female, to come from a non-manual background, to have a degree or A levels and to support the Alliance Party. They were less likely than other Protestants

Table 18.1  Choice of national identity for Protestants 1968–94 (%)

|        | British | Irish | Ulster | N. Irish | Other |
|--------|---------|-------|--------|----------|-------|
| 1968   | 39      | 20    | 32     | –        | 9     |
| 1978   | 67      | 8     | 20     | –        | 5     |
| 1989   | 68      | 3     | 10     | 16       | 3     |
| 1991   | 66      | 2     | 15     | 14       | 3     |
| 1993   | 70      | 2     | 16     | 11       | 3     |
| 1994   | 71      | 3     | 11     | 15       | –     |

Source: Trew, in Social Attitudes in Northern Ireland. The Fifth Report 1995–1996, p. 56.

to consider themselves Unionists and/or more likely to believe that the United Kingdom should unite with Europe, though they did not differ from other Protestants in their view that Northern Ireland should remain part of the United Kingdom (Trew 1996: 1).

The holding of an "Ulster" identity was not usually connected with a desire for an independent Ulster state or the expression of an Ulster nationalism. The British-Irish identity was being challenged from some quarters by an Ulster-British identity. The strike led by the Ulster Workers' Council (UWC) in 1974 was seen by some—such as the Secretary of State for Northern Ireland, Merlyn Rees—as the manifestation of an Ulster nationalism at the expense of loyalty to Britain. But this growth of Ulsterness was more likely to be at the expense of Irishness rather than Britishness. In 1975, The *UWC Journal* complained that when a Northern Irish citizen was quizzed about his or her nationality they were promptly reminded by anti-partitionists that "he is really Irish, because he lives or was born in Ireland". Many loyalists, proud of their British allegiance, reluctantly admitted to being Irish: "geography has made us Irish, but in nationality we are British as this is the political mode of government in Ulster". A reaction against Irishness did not necessarily mean a move towards an Ulster identity at the expense of Britishness, and "that as British Irish, and like other areas of the UK such as the West Country or Yorkshire, we do have a unique regional identity of our own, and have had for centuries . . . But the time has now arrived many feel, when the name 'Ireland' in any context is a liability because of IRA activities, or by association with a southern government." The name "Ulster" was "more appropriate and representative". It conveyed "more aptly" the cultures and traditions of the North Irish people: "just as there are British Scotsmen we are British Irishmen . . . or more correctly—British Ulstermen!"[19] A growth in an Ulster identity did not mean the abandonment of a British identity. Even those, such as the former Stormont cabinet minister William Craig, who warned that Ulster would rather "go it alone" than be absorbed into an Irish Republic,[20] emphasised that "We will not be one bit less British for that", for the allegiance of the "Ulster people" was to the Queen not to the British Parliament, and "like our fathers and grandfathers, we will hold this country in trust for the Queen".[21] Only "if there is no alternative" would there be the "establishment of an independent British Ulster".[22]

While the overwhelming majority of unionists now defined themselves as primarily British and the growth of an Ulster identity was apparent, many were still content to retain a positive sense of Irishness: the problem was that it seemed that the essence of Irishness had become monopolised by nationalists who defined it as separate from a British identity. At the 1992 inter-party talks, the UUP explained to Nationalists what lay at the heart of a positive sense of British-Irishness:

> there is no contradiction in being Irish and British—just as there is no contradiction in being Scottish and British, Welsh and British or English and British. . .Many of us are proud to be Irish, and will always hold ourselves so to be. But we are equally proud to be British and will always feel similarly committed to that sense of identity."[23]

This is borne out in interview data.[24] In terms of his British-Irish identity, Jeffrey Donaldson, then of the UUP but later of the Democratic Unionists, stated that: "I would see myself first of all as belonging to the British nation." And he perceived his British nationalism in a positive way:

> I see the British nation as being a very diverse nation . . . [W]ithin that nation you've got the Scots, the Welsh, the English and the Irish, some people prefer to say the Ulster people, but . . . if you look at the symbols of the British state, look at the Union Flag, it includes the cross of St Patrick . . . I do not believe there is a contradiction between having a regional identity in that sense . . . I believe that it is possible to be Irish and British, or Ulster and British . . . I believe that I can be part of the British nation and still have my own regional identity. (Hennessey and Wilson, 1997: 63)

The link with a Protestant Crown might be a key component of Britishness for many—but it is not necessarily a non-negotiable link. George Patton, of the Orange Order considered himself "a loyalist and a monarchist", but "if push came to shove and the situation arose, I can see where we could live without a monarchy . . . [T]he monarchy is a big thing, there is no doubt about that and it would hurt, it would hurt but I think we would survive that . . . [W]e are all very proud of the monarchy and we are very loyal to Queen and Country, but at the end of the day the presence or absence of a monarchy will not decide our sense of Britishness" (Hennessey and Wilson, 1997: 55–6). Similarly, Ian Paisley Jnr (DUP) described his unionism as more than evangelical Protestantism: his identity was "very eclectic" and including "things which I choose which are British and things which are Irish and things which I choose which are unique to Northern Ireland". But as far as his "Britishness" went, he perceived it in terms of the "British way of life": "I don't look to see what is happening in the Irish exchequer. I am interested in what is happening in the British budget . . . interested in English football teams, in television, such as British soap operas, all those things" (Hennessey and Wilson, 1995: 55).

Bob McCartney (formally the leader of the United Kingdom Unionist Party) defined the identity of any individual as "composed first of all of how he sees himself in terms of the territory where he lives, and I see the territory where I live as part of the United Kingdom of Great Britain and Northern Ireland, so I am a British citizen by definition of territory". McCartney saw himself as British because:

> my whole cultural heritage is British. I was educated on the basis . . . as any other citizen on the mainland would be. I was taught British constitutional history which I identify with. Now as a schoolboy my, if you like, military heroes were people like Nelson, Wellington . . . and so forth . . . So my background in terms of my allegiances and my experiences and my knowledge was very, very much British. But even culturally in terms of . . . literature: I mean I believed that while Shakespeare belonged to the world, he was primarily part of my culture, he was my nation's first before he was given to the world just as Tolstoy is a Russian . . . So my whole development, both culturally, historically and socially, gives me a very, very positive identification as being British. (Hennessey and Wilson, 1995: 56–7)

Alongside the emotional pull of cultural Britishness was a far greater psychological attachment to a British state patriotism than to a cultural sense of Irishness: "I don't see myself as Irish in that sense at all. Indeed, when one talks about what makes you Irish, certainly historically you were not Irish in a classical sense unless you are both Gaelic and Catholic." For him, Irishness was a territorial or geographical identity, similar to a Yorkshireman's regional identity, while his Britishness was bound up with the sense of belonging to a British "national" community: "If . . . simply the geographical accident of your birth is to determine the nature of your political identity then one can say if you are born in Ireland you are Irish—whether it be northern Irish or southern Irish is neither here nor there. But if you apply the litmus paper of which state has real and actual sovereignty over the area in which you live, then you are very clearly British" (Hennessey and Wilson, 1995: 63).

The Church of Ireland Primate, Archbishop Eames, was unusual among interviewees in that he went so far as to place a greater emphasis upon his Irishness than Britishness, while still describing himself as British-Irish: "I see myself as Irish, I see myself as living in that part of Ireland which for historical reasons is still part of the United Kingdom . . . [I]n purely religious terms I am Catholic and reformed. In purely political terms I live in a part of the United Kingdom but in cultural terms I see myself very much as being identified with a part of the island of Ireland." Lord Eames thus saw himself as being a citizen of the UK, with the allegiance which that involved, but also as being part of the island of Ireland. For him, Britishness is a positive identification in a political sense with being part of the UK: "I see a greater affinity with Scotland and Wales obviously in that sense than I would with England, but I also feel that you have got to separate the purely political aspiration of that from the cultural" (Hennessey and Wilson, 1995: 63). But, for someone like George Patton, an event like the signing of the Anglo-Irish Agreement,

> was a defining point and a turning point in who we are because at that stage I personally, and a lot of people that I would know and associate with, would have stopped using the term Irish altogether. I would no longer consider myself even to be Northern Irish: I'm an Ulsterman and I am British . . . We can never turn the clock back, but back in the 1960s it probably would have been easier to eventually convince my community that our future was in a 32–county Ireland. In the foreseeable future that is not going to happen because of the emotional aspects of the terrorist campaign . . . [I]t is a sense of we cannot betray what has happened to a lot of our people.

## Conclusion

Understanding Protestant identity in Northern Ireland seems less a case of Ulster Protestants being confused about their identity and more a case of confused academics. Partly this would seem to be because of the restrictive nature of the purely quantitative methodology employed by some researchers. There are also limitations with primary sources and qualitative research employed here. However, an integrated approach integrating all three offers the prospect of creating a richer interpretation of Ulster Protestant identity. There are a number of points to be made in conclusion. The first is that all of the identities one can observe can evoke a similar and powerful emotional response. The second is that applying too tight a categorisation to these identities will result in a failure to grasp the ability of individuals to exist within a multitude of identities and perceive no contradiction in this. Individuals within communities are themselves aware of belonging to different entities, and much of social life is involved with negotiation through, and the consequences of, "plural membership". Belonging is the "almost inexpressibly complex experience of culture".[25] Attempts to provide fundamental distinctions between patriotism and actively mobilised nationhood fail to acknowledge that the former is almost indistinguishable from the latter.[26]

Individuals construct their own personal national identity from whichever communal myths, symbols or experiences trigger the most significant affect or emotional state within them. In this chapter the schema of the Protestant perception of Ulster/Northern Ireland during the First and Second World Wars has been analysed in the first section. This provides, quite literally, "snapshots" of changes that may be occurring at a deeper level. Ulster Protestant perceptions of how one's own community behaved during those conflicts—sacrifice, loyalty, honour—produced a positive experience; how the "Other"—Irish nationalism—behaved during these seismic events produced a corresponding negative reaction. But the historical affect display—the historical set of actions used to indicate an emotional response within an imagined community—may vary according to what an individual selects, in emotional terms, as important to them: for example the role Ulster/Northern Ireland played as a part of the British imagined community's war effort as a whole; or Ulster/Northern Ireland's role in both conflicts when contrasted with Nationalist/independent Ireland. Neither need be mutually exclusive to the other but may acquire a different psychological relevance in different social episodes. National identification develops as a result of a sense of communal self-esteem by a comparison with other national identities. This can be observed at an elite Unionist level in 1914–18 and 1939–45 in regard to Irishness—with a rebalancing towards Britishness and gradual shift towards Ulsterness at the expense of one's Irish identity. For the first time, some Ulster Protestants felt that they had to choose between their British and Irish identities. The former won. This process was accelerated with the onset of the Troubles.

This evolutionary change need not be irreversible, but it is apparent. An Irish identity of some significance remains, but it has changed. In the early part of the twentieth century, those Unionists who thought deeply about their identity felt comfortable with a dual British-Irish identity. It was perfectly possible to think in terms of multi-layered identities—the nature of the Britannic imperial state encouraged this. Consequently, one could possess an Irish national consciousness/geographical patriotism and British imperial/state patriotism, or an Irish national consciousness and a British nationalism—the emotional affect of these loyalties would have been similar; but note the fundamental difference between *ness* and *ism* in the latter. Unionists could express their identity in terms of an Irish national consciousness/patriotism but still want to be ruled by their fellow members of the British nation. In that sense they were British nationalists. Loyalist rebellion was not a contradiction: it was perfectly logical in the sense that transient governments did not have the right to expel a psychologically coherent community from the state/nation against its will. Expulsion—as unionists believed it to be—would not stop Protestants feeling British. Home rule for the whole of the island of Ireland was thwarted but, for some Unionists, the impact of the First and the Second World Wars made them choose. And they chose their British identity as more important than their Irish identity.

Similarly, the impact of the generation-long IRA campaign from the early 1970s had a wider affect in the Ulster Protestant community. Clearly there has been a shift among Ulster Protestants from an Irish identity—which remains relevant for many—towards an Ulster or Northern Irish one; a British identity has been significantly strengthened. Quantitative surveys allow one to classify, broadly, the expressions of identity but primary source material and qualitative research suggest that Ulster Protestant identities are more complex than at first sight. An individual might possess a British and an Ulster identity: the emphasis, in terms of primary regional/national patriotism/identity will vary according to the individual. Similarly, this will apply to an Irish-British or British-Irish identity; or indeed a British-Northern Irish identity, and its inverse. From this one can argue that there are not, in fact, one, two, three, or no nations within the Ulster Protestant community, but clusters of regional and national identities. But there is a linking identity for all of these Ulster Protestant territorial identities. In terms of Ulster Protestant identity the common denominator revealed by quantitative, qualitative and primary source material is Britishness. Britishness may mean different things to different people, but it is clear that British national identity/state patriotism has been strengthened throughout the twentieth century. It is both a common identity for Ulster Protestants and a primary identity for the majority of them. Ironically, it has been the armed struggle of the Republicans to free Ireland from the British presence that would appear to have done most to cement the Ulster Protestant identity as the British presence in Ireland.

What then of Gallagher's three nations thesis? This chapter suggests that the model is broadly correct—but some modifications can be made. At least three national identities can be identified in Ireland; but in Northern Ireland, among Ulster Protestants, it is doubtful that three nations exist—in the sense that an Irish national consciousness may have declined so much as to be insignificant. This conclusion, however, may be taking things too far and there may be a residual Irish national consciousness (though not nationalism). Therefore, one might say that, among Ulster Protestants there are three national consciousnesses—Irish, Ulster and British—alongside an Irish territorial patriotism, an Ulster/Northern Irish regional patriotism and a British state patriotism. The common denominator, in its various forms, is the emotive power of Britishness.

## Notes

1 *Irish Review*, March 1911.
2 *Irish Times*, "Observer" letter, 25 October 1912.
3 *House of Commons debates*, XLII Col 1615, 10 October 1912.
4 *Irish Times*, 2 October 1912.
5 *News Letter*, 30 April 1912.
6 *House of Commons debates*, XXXIX Cols 1090–1901, 13 December 1912.
7 Belfast News Letter, 17 April 1912.
8 *House of Commons debates*, LXXVII Cols 1500–1, 5 January 1916.
9 Ibid. LXXXII Cols 491–2, 9 May 1916.
10 Ibid. LXXVII Cols 1483–4, 11 January 1916.
11 Ibid. LXXVIII Col 49, 17 January 1916.
12 Public Record Office of Northern Ireland De Fellenburg Montgomery Papers. D627/436/25A&B: de Fellenburg Montgomery to Mary ffolliott, 23 August 1918.
13 Ibid D627/436/30 Stronge to de Fellenburg Montgomery, 26 August 1918.
14 Church of Ireland Gazette, 11 May 1917.
15 *Irish News*, 1 August 1969.
16 *Northern Ireland House of Commons debates*, Vol XXII Col 2491; 29 October 1940.
17 Ibid. XXX Cols 1965–71, 8 October 1946.
18 Ibid. XXXII Cols 3364–8, 30 November 1948.
19 *Ulster Workers Council Journal* 1.1 (1975).
20 *News Letter*, 8 November 1971.
21 *Guardian*, 4 April 1972.
22 *Loyalist News*, 3.5 (1972), 19 February.
23 Multi-Party Talks Papers: Strand Two: Ulster Unionist Party Submission, 7 July 1992.
24 Interviews were carried out during 1995–96 while I was a Research Assistant working for the think-tank Democratic Dialogue. All interviews were recorded and individuals named. A series of focus groups were also held; the individuals participating in these did so on the basis of anonymity.
25 Cohen, A. B. (ed.) (1982) *Belongingness: Identity and Social Organisation in British Rural Cultures* (Manchester: Manchester University Press), p. 16.
26 Canovan, M. (1996) *Nationhood and Political Theory* (Cheltenham: Edward Elgar), p. 16.

# References

Brenan, T. (2004) *The Transmission of Affect* (London: Cornell University Press).

Canovan, M. (1996) *Nationhood and Political Theory* (Cheltenham: Edward Elgar).

Church of Ireland Gazette

Cohen, A. B. (ed.) (1982) *Belongingness: Identity and Social Organisation in British Rural Cultures* (Manchester: Manchester University Press, 1982).

De Fellenburg Montgomery Papers (Public Record Office of Northern Ireland)

Gallagher, M. (1995) "How many nations are there in Ireland?" *Ethnic and Racial Studies*, 18: 1–20.

Hennessey, T. and Wilson, R. (1997) *With All Due Respect. Pluralism and Parity of Esteem*, Democratic Dialogue Report No.7 (Belfast: Democratic Dialogue).

*Irish News*

Irish Review

*Irish Times*

*Loyalist News*

Massumi, B. (2002) *The Autonomy of Affect. Parables for the Virtual* (London: Duke University Press).

*News Letter*.

Ulster Unionist Party (1998) *Multi-Party Talks Papers, Strand Two* (Belfast: UUP).

Trew, K. (1996) "National identity", in R. Breen, P. Devine and L. Dowds (eds) Social Attitudes in Northern Ireland. *The Fifth Report 1995–1996* (Belfast: Appletree).

Ulster Workers Council Journal

# Part VII
# The Orange tradition

# 19

# Pride before a fall?[1] Orangeism in Liverpool since 1945

*Peter Day*

## Introduction

The Irish Protestant diaspora in England remains under-researched, particularly those pockets of Orange culture imported from Ireland and infused with local characteristics. The Orange Order in Liverpool remains one of the few centres of Orangeism outside Northern Ireland. Although the movement in England was initially centred mainly in Manchester, Orange lodges developed rapidly in Liverpool by the mid-1800s, largely as a consequence of Protestant emigration from Ireland during the famine. As a movement of considerable size and some influence in the early twentieth century, the Order on Merseyside has been in decline for some years. This chapter analyses the reasons for that decline, the change in public attitudes to the disruption caused by Orange parades and attempts by the Order to maintain its influence.

The Orange Order in Liverpool has not been good at recording its own history. As Donald MacRaild notes:[2]

> The Liverpool lodge system has left (or can trace) artefacts and records that are directly inversely proportionate to its former size. My student, Dan Jackson learnt that they "might be able to find the records of Star of Halewood" lodge. They used to have nearly 200 lodges, so that's not a very good hit rate on preservation![3]

The role of the Order in Liverpool from the early nineteenth century up to the outbreak of the Second World War has been well covered in Frank Neal's *Sectarian Violence* (Neal, 1988) and in P. J. Waller's *Democracy and Sectarianism* (Waller, 1981). For the period after the Second World War the only secondary sources are a few pages in Waller's book, an unpublished M.Sc. thesis "Religion and Politics in Liverpool since 1900" (Roberts, 1965) and an unpublished paper by Professor Maurice Goldring. This work is, therefore, based largely on newspaper coverage; studies of Reports of Proceedings of Grand Lodges; conversations with lodge members and a questionnaire survey of members of lodges.[4]

## Orangeism in Liverpool prior to the Second World War

The studies by Neal and Waller show that, in the later nineteenth and early twentieth centuries, politics in Liverpool was driven by an association of working-class and Conservative interests forged in the protection of the Protestant heritage. In 1835, the Anglican preacher Hugh McNeile founded the Protestant Association to link middle-class Anglicans with the Orange Order and with the Tories. Liverpool Tories also maintained links with the Protestant working class through the Orange Lodges and the Operative Protestant Association, founded in 1838. It has been said that "no potential Tory councillor could hope to achieve public office unless he was established, in McNeile's eyes, as a "sound Protestant".[5]

The Tory Party in Liverpool at the end of the nineteenth century was dominated by the Working Men's Conservative Association (WMCA). Founded in 1868, with twelve branches by 1872 and 7,000 members by the end of the century, the WMCA was exclusively Protestant. Meetings would begin with the chairman asking those present who had associated with Catholics to confess their crime, and speeches would start with the words "by my protestant faith and conservative principles". In reality, the WMCA was also dominated by the Orange Order who were also affiliated to the Liverpool Constitutional Association and sent delegates to sit on its governing body.

In 1888 Pastor George Wise arrived in Liverpool. Wise had been lecturing for the Christian Evidence Guild in the East End of London and had undertaken a lecture tour in America where he encountered American evangelicism. From 1901 Wise became increasingly anti-Catholic and launched a Protestant crusade marked by huge open-air rallies in Islington Square. His speeches were so vitriolic in his denunciation of Catholicism that they invariably led to violence and Wise was imprisoned on two occasions. In 1903 Wise founded the Protestant Party and three candidates, including Wise, were elected in the municipal elections.

The Labour Party found it difficult to make inroads into the Conservative-Protestant stranglehold of council and parliamentary seats in Liverpool. In 1907 a by-election was held for the parliamentary seat of Liverpool Kirkdale and the Labour Party, encouraged by recent successes in Jarrow and Colne Valley, designated the contest as the "biggest fight in Labour's history".[6] Despite the organisation of almost one hundred open-air meetings and visits by nearly twenty Labour MPs, the Conservative candidate, Charles McArthur, a staunch Protestant, polled 20 per cent more than Labour. Conservative leaflets had played on the "atheist" nature of "socialist" policies and the *Protestant Standard* printed claims that socialism would generate "absolute infidelity" and "the grossest immoralities". More practically, the WMCA had mobilised 500 canvassers in support of the Protestant Tory candidate. After this defeat, Ramsay MacDonald concluded that Labour would never progress in Liverpool until Orangeism was broken.[7]

While it would be untrue to say that sectarianism disappeared from Liverpool during the depression, its importance in elections was much diminished in the face of other, overwhelming problems. Nonetheless, in 1934 there were three Protestant Party councillors in the Council, all representing St Domingo in the heart of the Orange area of the city. The war continued to undermine the strength of sectarian feelings in the City and in 1942 Liverpool gained its first Catholic Lord Mayor. The war also served to disguise Liverpool's long-term decline—prosperity had been based on its role as a port and there was little in the way of a manufacturing base. Despite being granted Development Area status in 1949 this decline accelerated and by 1970 the Docks and Harbour Board faced insolvency. Unemployment in Liverpool had long been higher than the national average, in the 1970s it grew to three times that average.

### The years since the Second World War

The years since the Second World War have been characterised by a decline in the numbers participating in Orange Order activities. Perhaps the most obvious example is in respect of the gathering on the Order's most important event, the celebration, held annually on 12 July, of the Protestant King William's victory over the Catholic King James in 1690. Newspaper reports of the annual Boyne parade held at Southport generally contain estimates of the numbers attending. Estimates in the *Liverpool Echo* and *Southport Visitor* do not always agree, which may reflect attendance by lodges from other parts of the United Kingdom and overseas, some of whom travel directly to Southport and do not take part in the Liverpool parades which converge on St George's Plateau for onward travel to Southport on a fleet of buses. Attendances are also likely to be affected by the day of the week on which the march is held and by the weather, but by averaging the reported numbers (Figure 19.1) it can be shown that while the numbers are highly variable and that that there was a ten-year lull from the early 1960s to the early 1970s, there was a dramatic decline in the early 1980s. The higher numbers in 1985 and 1986 probably reflect a renewed outburst of sectarianism. The Pope made a high profile visit to Liverpool in 1982 and, in the same year, Ian Paisley's Free Presbyterian Church formed an association with the Protestant Reformers Church in Everton. In 1985 the Orange Order's

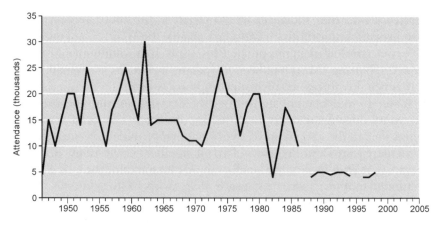

**Figure 19.1** Liverpool 12 July parade attendance, 1946–2000

**Figure 19.2** Parading in Liverpool on 12 July

Provincial Lodge suffered an arson attack. By 1987 attendances had fallen to their lowest level since the war and have never recovered.

The Liverpool 12 July parade has many similar features to Orange parades in Northern Ireland and Scotland. It follows the standard pattern of a lodge walking with its banner accompanied by a band. A distinctive

Merseyside feature, however, is that each lodge also has two junior members dressed as William and Mary (Figure 19.2). It has not been possible to determine when this practice began, even the oldest member interviewed reporting that it had been happening as long as she remembered.

It is not possible to confirm this impression of declining numbers by reference to membership statistics as the Order does not release them[8]. Access to lodge details was, nonetheless, obtained. The number of male lodges was fairly static from 1919 to 1946 and female lodges and, more particularly, junior lodges increased in number. Since 1946, however, there has been a large drop in the number of male lodges and a major reduction in the number of junior lodges—the future of the Order, reflected in lower parading numbers.[9] There is also a suspicion from conversations and through observation at parades that some lodges stutter along with close to the minimum number of members, and that minimum is only five members.

## Assessing the reasons for the decline

As part of the research a questionnaire was distributed to members of the Order in Liverpool. Sixty per cent said that the decline was principally due to the breaking up of the communities by slum clearance and rebuilding, which began in the late 1950s. Some went on to claim that this was a deliberate policy, a policy they describe as "ethnic cleansing", by the council under the influence of Bessie Braddock and her husband John (known as Jack). The Braddocks had been founder members of the Communist Party, and active in the Liverpool branch: Bessie as treasurer and Jack as leader. They left the Communist Party in 1924 and joined Labour, Jack becoming a Labour councillor in 1929. Bessie followed in 1930 and in 1945 was elected MP for the Liverpool Exchange constituency, continuing to sit as a councillor. Jack became leader of the Labour group and, from 1955 when Labour finally took control of the Council, was council leader.

The Braddocks were clearly concerned by the low standard of housing in Liverpool. On being elected as MP, Bessie used her 1945 maiden speech in the Commons to refer to the Liverpool slums as "bug-ridden, lice-ridden, rat-ridden, lousy hell-holes". No evidence has been uncovered, though, to show that she was anti-Orange any more than that she may have been "anti" any religiously-based group. Braddock was a self-declared atheist and her constituency had a large number of Catholic voters, but on election she declared she "would not watch their Catholic interests at the expense of working class interest as a whole" (Roberts, 1965).

The Orange Order, however, was determinedly anti-Braddock. In 1958 *The Times*[10] reported that hundreds of Orange members turned out for a ceremony in Netherfield Road at which Hugh Gaitskell was to officially open two blocks of flats named after Jack and Bessie Braddock. Netherfield Road lies at the heart of the area dominated by the Orange Order in the sectarian geography of the city, and the booing, singing and shouting from the Orangemen and women, accompanied by the waving of Union Jacks, completely drowned out speeches by Gaitskell and the Braddocks. Gaitskell was visiting Liverpool as part of a tour of "unemployment black spots" in the North-west.

Liverpool's Interim Planning Policy identified that 60 per cent of the city's 205,000 dwellings dated from before 1920 and, in 1961, 79,000 were unfit owing to inadequate space standards internally and externally, and a lack of bathrooms and indoor lavatories (Bor, 1965). This, the report noted, was particularly the case in Everton and Toxteth, which formed the hard core of the city's slum clearance problem. Seventy-five per cent of the unfit houses were in the inner residential area that surrounds the city centre, and which includes Everton.

The only suggestions in the planning statements that the city wished to undermine the geographical strength of the Orange Order, or any other sectarian group, came in the following statements:

> concentrations of residents of one particular social class or religious denomination likewise have important local effects . . .
>
> The redevelopment of practically the whole area by the Corporation over the next twenty years, while presenting enormous opportunities, has certain inherent dangers . . .
>
> It will involve a complete upheaval in the structure of the population and great care will have to be taken to secure that a balanced population structure is achieved in new development . . .

The effect of the rebuilding programme on Everton is apparent in Figures 19.3 and 19.4. Figure 19.3 shows that part of Liverpool including Everton as it was in the 1950s. The line running North–South along Scotland Road marks the boundary of the area then considered "Catholic", predominant in the housing lying immediately behind the docks. The area surrounded by the dashed line encloses the "Orange and Protestant" stronghold. The serried rows of back-to-back terraced housing, which cover most of that area, can be easily identified. Plotted onto this are a number of dots, which indicate the locations where Orange Lodges met and show the residences of lodge officials. The picture is not complete as some of the addresses given in the Orange Order Annual Reports could not be identified.

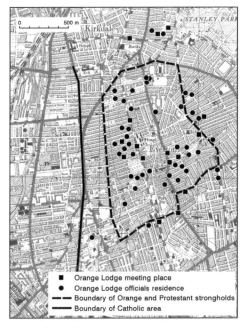

**Figure 19.3** The Everton area of Liverpool in the 1950s.

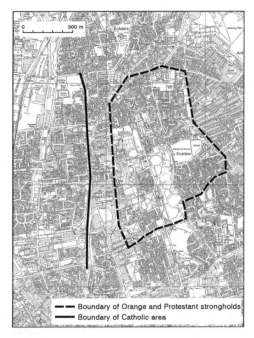

**Figure 19.4** The Everton area of Liverpool in the early 1980s.

Figure 19.4 shows the same area as it is now, following the slum clearance programme of the 1960s and 1970s. As can be seen, all the terraces have gone and been replaced by some low-density housing and by a greater open park area. By contrast, while the terraces behind the docks have gone they have been replaced by low-density housing throughout and by some tower blocks.

These illustrations clearly show that an area which was regarded as a stronghold for the Orange Order, and which returned Protestant Party councillors, was extensively depopulated as part of the slum clearance programme and, unlike the area near the docks where residents came back to the new houses, the residents here were scattered to new estates on the fringes of the city such as Kirkby and Speke, where a small number of new lodges were formed.

This was a problem that some had seen coming. In the early 1960s Pastor Mason of the Protestant Reformers' Church wrote a letter in which he called for action, "to stop the systematic breakdown of the two main Protestant areas of Netherfield and St Domingo, by the obviously planned migration of residents to areas outside the city" (Roberts, 1965).

Other reasons given for the decline in membership were the lack of interest among young people—cited by 27 per cent, and that parades had been suppressed by the authorities, cited by 8 per cent. Others said that reduction in family size was a factor and the questionnaire responses did show that, among members aged over 60, the number of siblings in the family was six, and that 64 per cent of family members had been members of the Order. Curiously, no one mentioned the declining population of Liverpool between 1961 and 2001, a fall of 40 per cent from 745,000 to 442,000. Evidence from the questionnaire responses goes some way to support the view that young people no longer feel any desire to join the Order, as only 6 per cent of responses came from people aged under 25 and nearly half were from respondents aged over 60. Despite repeated visits to the District Lodge, little evidence was seen of the organisation of activities that might appeal to young people such as football or discos.[11]

Members of the Orange Order clearly express, through church attendance and religious belief, a much higher degree of faith than the general population. In this context the answers given in the questionnaires concerning the motivation for membership are revealing. An overwhelming majority, 78 per cent, said that the most important reason for their membership was support for their Protestant religion and a minority, of 13 per cent, gave their primary reason as loyalty to Queen and Country.

The survey also looked into frequency of attendance at church and showed that:

- 44 per cent attended weekly;
- 31 per cent attended less than one per week but more than one per month;
- 11 per cent attended once a month;
- 14 per cent attended less than one per month.

Clearly, in the face of declining religious belief among young people, a membership which expresses its values in this way will not be attractive to those young people. Nonetheless, the figures emphasises the continuing centrality of Protestantism in a cultural-religious organisation.

### The parades issue

Until the 1970s, press reporting in Southport of the annual 12 July Boyne parade was generally favourable. After all, the Order brought considerable numbers of visitors to a place that exists as a resort town. There were complaints from the public as early as 1949 and, for a time in the 1960s, some catering establishments took the opportunity to close for the day of the Orange parade saying they could not cope with the rush, and for fear of "hooligans" who stayed behind in the town when the marchers had left and created disturbances. Nonetheless, in 1967 the *Southport Visitor* said "Orange Day" was a bonanza for local traders and that was, for a time, the prevailing mood.

The tone of reporting changed in 1970. With the parade about to take place on a Saturday for the second consecutive year, the Chamber of Trade made representations to the Council objecting to the holding of parades on Saturdays. Local publicans and landlords were reported as fearing trouble and disturbances and one local businessman said, "One is always worried about possible trouble and Orangemen seem to bring trouble in their wake."

In 1973 a further attempt was made to ban visits to Southport by Orangemen, following reports that several public houses had been damaged during an outbreak of hooliganism on "The Twelfth". The Southport Licensed Victuallers' Association called for a report on how the troubles started, who the troublemakers were, and whether they were Orangemen or just hangers-on. An editorial in the *Southport Visitor* asked if the trade brought to the town was too high a price to pay, particularly given the situation in Northern Ireland. Criticisms were made about the levels of drunkenness, and the numbers of children waiting for their parents outside pubs. In 1974 the *Liverpool Echo* reported that the Chamber of Trade believed there was no financial benefit to the town and that as the parade the following year (1975) would again take place on a Saturday a concerted effort would be made to have it stopped. Richard Roberts, Grand Master of the Liverpool lodges, said, "This organisation will not be blackmailed or threatened by anybody." and claimed it was the democratic right of people to conduct their marches where they wished.

In 1979 and 1980 the *Southport Visitor* ran editorials questioning whether or not the parade should be allowed. By the late 1990s the *Liverpool Daily Post* was carrying readers' letters every year as 12 July drew near, calling for the parade to be banned—though it has to be said the issue did not arouse quite as much passion as Liverpool's new, purple, wheelie-bins.

An unfortunate double-booking in 2003 meant that Southport's Pier Festival had to be cancelled because the date had already been booked by the Orange Order. Sefton Council's cabinet member for the environment said, "I am sympathetic to the view that they should not march in Southport any more" and Southport's Liberal Democrat MP, John Pugh, joined the criticism saying, "I think there should be a big question mark about it continuing. It is a fact that people stay out of the town on 12 July to avoid the march, and it is noticeable. I am sure the town loses business as a result".[12]

In 2004 the *Liverpool Echo* report on "The Twelfth" said, "For those who take part, it is their day of days, July 12, when thousands of men, women and children come together to celebrate their Protestant identity. But for many others, it is an outdated show of supremacy, which creates nothing but religious division, disharmony and sometimes disorder." Ron Bather, the Grand Master, replied:

> It's a show of loyalty to the crown and to the Protestant religion. We're celebrating the Battle of the Boyne, not because it's something that happened 314 years ago. It is because we're celebrating our heritage. How long ago the battle happened doesn't matter—it's about the heritage that has been passed down to us that we're upholding it. We don't look upon it as sectarian; that went out of the window years ago. It's a carnival day and the Liverpool parade is very different to the ones that take place in Northern Ireland and Scotland.

### The Orange Order and politics

Waller (1981) says that "Orange lodges in Liverpool were neglecting political work" in the late 1950s and early 1960s. A strict reading of the situation would be that the organisations they used as an entrée into the political life of Liverpool had significantly declined in importance and the influence of the Order had no other outlet. The WMCA was moribund, the Protestant Party and Protestant Association no longer held sway over the local Conservatives who, in any event, were now under intense pressure from Labour. The Order's lack of political organisation was a reflection of a changed reality.

The 1945 General Election produced an excellent result in Liverpool for Labour, as it did elsewhere, and they won eight of the eleven Liverpool seats. Attempts were made by some to have Reverend Longbottom, leader of the Protestant Party and Grand Master of Grand Orange Lodge of England, adopted as the official Conservative and Protestant candidate for Kirkdale, but the influence of the WMCA and the Orange Order was no longer very important. He stood as an Independent Protestant, but his vote was halved from the 25 per cent he had won in 1931.

Nevertheless, the Protestant Party, aided by an electoral pact with the Conservatives who did not stand against them, had six councillors between 1946 and 1951 and Longbottom was elected by the Council to serve as Lord Mayor of Liverpool in 1951, having already served a number of years as an Alderman. Longbottom had become Grand Master in 1946, but was replaced in 1956. Waller (1981) claims this was because he had become too extreme and anti-Catholic. He does seem to have become embittered towards the Order and in 1961 was expelled after the Order brought the following charges:

- Public reflections upon the Imperial Grand Master
- An attack upon an Officer of the Loyal Orange Institution of England, namely the Grand Chaplain
- Slighting references about the "Orange Vision", the official publication of the Institution.
- An incitement to Orangemen to disobey lawful authority within the Institution
- Reflections upon the leadership of the Institution generally.[13]

Religion and sectarianism continued to decline in importance as an electoral issue. Strongly sectarian politics was confined to only half a dozen wards and was perhaps as much to do with anti-socialist feeling as with true religious emotion. Over the next fifteen years, with a decline in the number of Orange members and in the size of congregations at evangelical Protestant churches, sectarianism further declined in electoral matters. The working class of Netherfield and St Domingo voted Labour in increasing numbers and by 1964 there were only two Protestant Party councillors. In 1952, there was even an Orangeman who stood for, and won, Netherfield as a Labour candidate.

The WMCA had become a pointless organisation. By 1964 there were only two functioning branches and in 1971 the Liverpool Conservative Party agent wrote that their rules "were not in line with present day thinking". The leader of the Conservatives, Alderman H. Macdonald Stewart, said that sectarian bitterness was a spent force and affirmed that his party made no sectarian appeal whatsoever. The electoral pact in Netherfield and St Domingo continued, however, and the Conservatives never opposed a Protestant Party candidate. Although sectarianism had ceased to be a major factor in Liverpool politics, it was noted as late as 1965 that, "To understand Liverpool politics, even today, one must be well versed in the attitude of Orangemen and Catholics . . . Not more than one Catholic in ten votes Conservative. A majority of Protestants do" (Goldring, 1984).

Unable to continue a campaign against Catholicism through democratic politics, the Order took, to some extent, to "guerrilla" action. In 1959 they wrote to the Director of Education complaining that children in Liverpool schools had been forced to observe two minutes silence on the death of the late Pope. Later the same year, *Orange Vision*, the official publication of the Loyal Orange Institution of England, carried an article critical of plans for the Queen Mother to meet the Pope and, on a lighter note, criticised those Liverpool Orange bands which had joined the parade of Billy Smart's Circus from Lime Street to Sefton Park—not for the levity or lack of dignity involved, but because the parade took place on the Sabbath.

The potential election of a Catholic to the presidency of the United States, visits by the Archbishop of Canterbury and the Prime Minister to the Pope, and the Treaty of Rome, all served as grist to the mill of the Order's continuing anti-Catholic campaign. In the Treaty of Rome they saw, "grave danger to the spiritual welfare of our peoples . . . the death knell of that political and religious freedom so dearly purchased for us by our martyred sires".

The growth of the ecumenical movement caused problems for the Orange Order, which found it increasingly difficult to find churches prepared to host its religious services. This problem came to a head in Liverpool in 1979. On several occasions Liverpool Provincial Grand Orange Lodge applied to Liverpool Cathedral for permission to hold an Orange Service. The requests were all refused because of the unavailability of dates. In an attempt to force the issue, the Grand Lodge requested facilities to hold a divine service of worship in the cathedral on any Sunday, in the month of October, during the next five years. The *Orange News of England* in April 1979 reported that the Grand Lodge received the following reply from the Very Reverend Edward Patey, Dean of Liverpool:

I think we ought to be quite honest with each other and say that we at the Cathedral and you of the Orange Order take such different views about ecumenism that were you to hold a service here it would puzzle many of our friends, not only in the Roman Catholic Church, but also among Free Churchmen and our fellow Anglicans. The Cathedral is not a public hall to "let out" to organisations. Everything that happens here is seen as part and parcel of our ministry and mission. The Church of England does not observe Reformation Day and, I think, rightly so because of the perpetuation of a backward-looking view of history which has certainly been overtaken by such events as the formation of the World Council of Churches, the Anglican/Roman Catholic Commission, and the new atmosphere created by the second Vatican Council. We here value our close links with the Metropolitan Cathedral. Unless I am much mistaken these are things which your members deplore, preferring to maintain the divisions of the past.

We do not deny you the right to hold your views and I know that some Anglicans share them. But I think it would be less than honest to blur the issues by having a Reformation Day service in the Cathedral. We therefore feel that we are unable to grant your request.

The Order petitioned the Queen to have this decision overturned. The claim is made[14] that a sympathetic member of the Privy Council, James Molyneaux, the leader of the Ulster Unionist Party, told the Order that the Queen intervened on their behalf. This may be an erroneous claim from the Orange Order, as Molyneaux did not become a Privy Councillor until 1982.

Following an Orange Order "invasion" of the cathedral where Orangemen attended in numbers and donned their regalia during the service, an injunction was taken out by the cathedral authorities to prevent a repetition of such behaviour. However, the Dean had a change of heart and a "Reconciliation" service was held in the cathedral in June 1982 attended by thousands of Orangemen following an invitation from the Dean and Chapter. There is now an annual service to which the Orange Order are invited, to celebrate St George's Day, and the Order claim they have recently been asked, by the cathedral, to increase their presence to two visits annually. Nonetheless, the cathedral does not have a Reformation service.

Pope John Paul II's visit to England in 1982, the first visit of a Pope to this country since 1531, prompted nationwide agitation by ultra-Protestant organisations. The British Council of Protestant Christian Churches called on all Christians to "pray earnestly that the Lord would keep the Pope out of this land", and carried out a campaign of resistance to "alert the nation to the danger of the hour". Protestants were particularly angered by plans for the Pope to visit both Canterbury Cathedral and the Anglican Cathedral in Liverpool for "celebrations of faith". For his part in organising this, Dr Robert Runcie, a native of Liverpool and then Archbishop of Canterbury, was howled down by "anti-papists" in Liverpool.

The Orange Order claims they were not responsible for this and that exhaustive meetings and consultations were held in deciding that no public opposition would be mounted. One member of the Order described those involved in the protest as "concerned citizens", but it is difficult to believe that, while the Order may not have been officially involved, those making the protest were not associated with the Order. They argue that no Orange insignia was in evidence, but removing the collarette does not stop an Orangeman being an Orangeman. In their publication, *The Anchor*, the Liverpool District of the Orange Order said:

> When the man who assumes the title belonging only to God desecrated this land in May, the Orange Order in Liverpool decided, democratically, that there would be no Orange Protest or Parades. This decision was upheld and Orange people avoided and ignored the imposter's visit. There was no trouble.

Members of the Order are prepared to admit that there were Orangemen in the protest, but also point out that in 1982 Ian Paisley's Free Presbyterian Church of Ulster became associated with the Protestant Reformers' Church, which has a base in Liverpool and it is difficult not to agree that members of that congregation may well have made up a good number of those protesting. The Reverend Gordon McCracken, former Deputy Grand Master of the Orange Order in Scotland, claims that the decline in Orange membership in the 1980s can be directly attributed to a perception among some that the Order was powerless to prevent the Papal visit.

Lingering sectarian tensions on Merseyside had one, perhaps final, outing in the mid-1990s, when the improving political climate in Northern Ireland led to the city's (dwindling) Irish community deciding to hold a St Patrick's Day Parade in 1996. The physical protest against the parade outside the city's now defunct Irish Centre was sufficiently strong for organisers to call off the parade. An assortment of loyalists blocked the parade and although the Orange Order was not formally part of any protest, some of its members were present. The flare-up prompted agitated local debate, but this soon melted and the following year's parade met only token opposition. A 2001, Irish republican hunger-strike commemoration march through Liverpool was met with isolated verbal opposition, but nothing more serious. Two members of the Independent Orange Order in Liverpool, a smaller, more militant grouping, were convicted in 2006 of terrorist offences associated with their membership of the loyalist paramilitary group, the UVF, but the Northern Ireland issue did not appear to have impacted hugely upon the city.

## Conclusion

The Orange Order's current position in Liverpool is that, while they have lost the political influence they once enjoyed, and while the number of lodges has fallen and the numbers supporting the annual Boyne parade is now less than 25 per cent of the 20,000 reported as recently as 1980, the parade does still take place and still manages to attract about 5,000 walkers and supporters. Sectarianism is not demonstrated through violent conflict in the way many people "remember", though memory is an unreliable indicator—memory has it that football in Liverpool split along sectarian lines with Everton playing "in the blue of Mary's colour",[15] but Everton had their origins in St Domingo and an early patron was John Houlding, known as "King John", a staunch Orangeman.[16] The views expressed about Catholicism by members of the Order today would not have been considered unexceptional in 1950s Liverpool, or in other towns and cities in England. That 1950s world was both more religious[17] and more conscious of the Protestant nature of the state, under-lined by the monarch's coronation promise to defend that Protestant religion.

So the question remains: is it simply that the world has moved, and the members of the Orange Order have not? Is the decline of the Order due to structural changes, to slum clearance and the changing nature of employment on Merseyside, or does it reflect a fundamental cultural change with the rise of secularism and the post-1950s decline in church attendance? The leaders of the Order believe the former and suggest there are many who share their views but who are unwilling to turn out to demonstrate their beliefs—the phenomenon Grace Davie calls, "Believing without Belonging" (Davie, 1994). Further research is working toward untangling that paradox.

## Notes

1  This title was inspired by a feature on Scotland in *National Geographic Magazine* of July 1984. The article included a photograph of an Orange Walk in Glasgow and described the march as "A Pride of Protestants".
2  E-mail to the author, 29 May 2004.
3  There have recently been suggestions from senior officials within GOLE (Grand Orange Lodge England) that substantial records do exist; permission to study them is awaited.

288 *The Orange tradition*

4  Several conversations were held with Lodge officials at Liverpool Provincial Orange Hall, Everton Road, Liverpool and a questionnaire was circulated to Lodge members. Fifty-one completed questionnaires were returned for analysis.

5  See *Saoirse* (Irish Freedom) "Orangeism and the Irish in Liverpool" on their website at: http://homepage.tinet.ie/~eirenua/mar99/saoirse4.htm (accessed 22 January 2007).

6  *The Times*, 27 September 1907.

7  P. J. Waller, *Democracy and Sectarianism*, 233–5.

8  Some intriguing clues to the level of membership are available. In 1960, writing in *Orange Vision*, the Grand Treasurer reported on the progress of fund-raising through their Gideon campaign. The figures given would suggest there were 2,930 adult members in Liverpool province at that time.

9  Writing in *Orange Vision* (the official publication of the Grand Orange Lodge of England) in 1959 the Grand Treasurer said, "The future of our Order is with our young people and it is quite possible that our future Grand Lodge officers are today members of our juvenile lodges."

10  *The Times*, 23 September, 1958, p. 5.

11  In 1978 an international tournament was held for youth football teams representing the Order in Northern Ireland, Scotland and England. There was some difficulty making up an English team then—and England came third in the tournament.

12  *Southport Visitor*, 18 July 2003.

13  Taken from *Orange Vision*, issue 10, undated.

14  Conversation between the author and Lodge officials.

15  Quoted in e-mail to the author from Dr Rogan Taylor, Director, Football Industries Group, University of Liverpool, 12 May 2006.

16  See www.liverweb.org.uk/lfcs1.htm (accessed 27 January 2007).

17  Throughout the 1940s and 1950s the *Liverpool Echo* carried a weekly column "Pulpit and Pew" listing significant Church comings and goings.

## References

Bor, W. G. (1965) *Liverpool Interim Planning Policy Statement* (Liverpool: Liverpool City Council).

Davie, S. (1994) *Religion in Britain since 1945: Believing Without Belonging* (Oxford: Blackwell).

Goldring, M. (1984) "Working class Conservatism in Liverpool: the Orange Order" (Working Class conservatism conference, University of Paris).

Neal, F. (1988) *Sectarian Violence: The Liverpool Experience, 1819–1914. An Aspect of Anglo-Irish History* (Manchester: Manchester University Press).

Roberts, D. A. (1965) Religion and politics in Liverpool since 1900 (Unpublished M.Sc. thesis, University of London).

Waller, P. J. (1981) *Democracy and Sectarianism: A Political and Social History of Liverpool 1868–1939* (Liverpool: Liverpool University Press).

# 20

# The contemporary Orange Order in Northern Ireland

*Jonathan Tonge and James W. McAuley*

## Introduction

The history of Orangeism in Ireland dates back to the late eighteenth century. Today, as the largest organisation in civil society in Northern Ireland, the Protestant Orange Order remains a significant vehicle for cultural and religious expressions of British Protestant identity. Since the demise of UUP majority rule in the early 1970s, however, the Order has been bereft of direct political influence and has struggled to maintain its relevance amid paramilitary violence, secularism and ostracism.

The Orange Order's difficulties have been reflected in declining membership. Although put as high as 80,000–100,000 as late as 1999 (Elliott and Flackes, 1999: 380) a more realistic current figure appears to be nearer to 40,000, spread across 126 district lodges and 1,400 private lodges. There are also smaller organisations, the Apprentice Boys of Derry, the Royal Black Institution and the Independent Orange Order which are regarded as part of the Orange "family".

Previously an integral part of a coalition of religious and political unionism with the UUP, the Orange Order divorced its "political wing" in 2005, cognisant of the shift of political allegiance of many of its members to the more hardline DUP. As the 1998 Good Friday Agreement (GFA) divided unionists, the Orange Order rejected the deal on both "moral" and political grounds and contributed to the realignment of Unionist anti-Agreement political forces. This chapter surveys the attitudes and profile of current Orange Order members, examining their contribution to the unionist political realignment suggested above, and analysing the Order's ongoing struggle for relevance.[1]

## The changing Orange Order

The Orange Order in Northern Ireland is a large and complex organisation with Protestant unionism at its core. The key internal characteristics of the Orange Order are ritual and fraternity. Religious tradition and ritual are evident in most aspects of Orange activity. Meetings in Orange halls include prayers and Bible readings. Regalia is worn by members, with specific insignia varying according to the individual lodge and status of the individual. Membership of a lodge involves joining a social, cultural, religious and political network, these four aspects being impossible to disentangle, with members almost evenly divided over whether the Order's primary role is religious or cultural. Overwhelmingly, new members join because they are asked to do so by family or friends, almost nine in ten joiners being recruited in this manner. Private and district lodges exist at the bottom of the Orange pyramid structure. Localism is important, but their activities are overseen and coordinated by county lodges and, at the apex of the structure, the Grand Lodge of Ireland in Belfast (perhaps ironically, despite partition, Grand Lodge has an all-Ireland remit). Although in decline numerically, the Orange Order in Northern Ireland remains by far the most important centre of Orangeism in the United Kingdom, although Orange lodges are still active across the west of Scotland and on Merseyside.

The Orange Order has declined in political influence in recent decades, while its social base has altered. Instrumental in forming the Ulster Unionist Council (UUC) in 1905, the Order helped bind disparate Unionist elements into a loose but effective governing coalition, with the UUP operating more as a movement than a party, until the demise of devolved government in 1972. The Orange Order and the UUP operated as an integrated movement, not immune from internal squabbles, but intent on securing the Union and infusing the Northern Ireland polity with a distinct sense of Protestant Britishness. This was reflected in the famous polemic from the first Northern Ireland Prime Minister, James Craig, that he was "an Orangeman first and a politician and a Member of this Parliament [of Northern Ireland] second", whilst basking in the construction of a "Protestant parliament and a Protestant state".[2] The Twelfth of July, the climax of the Orange Order's celebrations of the Protestant King William over the Catholic King James in 1690, was declared a public holiday by the Unionist leadership in 1926.

The UUP and Orange Order operated in substantially reduced circumstances following the imposition of direct rule from Westminster amid the violent conflict of the early 1970s. With direct rule the norm for the remainder of the Troubles, apart from the brief ill-fated Sunningdale power-sharing experiment of 1974, the Orange Order faced difficult times. It attempted to maintain influence within a political party that was stripped of power by the British government and faced challenges from the DUP and loyalist paramilitary ultras. Unionist tactics on how best to defend the Union differed at times during the Troubles and intra-unionist rivalry climaxed after the UUP backed power sharing with Sinn Fein in the GFA.

Orangemen remained solid in their British identity, 69 per cent of those surveyed identifying as such, with "Northern Irish" or "Ulster" providing a further 25 per cent of preferred identities. However, the Order was undergoing social transformation. During the 1950s, three-quarters of its central committee possessed a title, but four decades later, the figure was less than one-quarter (Kaufmann, 2007: 254). The Order became more proletarian with, by 2004, 50 per cent of its members describing themselves as working-class and only 16 per cent self-identifying as middle-class. Thirteen per cent of Orange Order members have university degrees, although 23 per cent possess no formal qualifications. Membership has declined from the 1960s onwards, particularly in Belfast. Contrary to popular wisdom, however, the Order's membership is not composed largely of the elderly, as 62 per cent of members are aged below 55.

According to internal critics, the Orange Order has lost influence and members because of failures of leadership (Kennaway, 2006). The apex of the organisation, Grand Lodge, is largely insulated from censure from below, cases having to be referred upwards through private, district and county lodges, an elaborate system that discourages prolonged internal dissent. When grass-roots members diverged from "official" policy, Grand Lodge appeared reluctant to act against those dissidents and rebels within the movement, whose actions, for religious figures such as Kennaway, appeared less to do with God-fearing Protestantism than with base antagonistic sectarianism.

From the mid-1980s onwards, increasing numbers within the Order became involved in disturbances and street confrontations around parades, often without sanction from a leadership which officially remained implacably opposed to violence. Irrespective of its internal discipline, the Order was always seen by critics as sectarian (Farrell, 1980; McGarry and O'Leary, 1995). Its rules prohibit marriage to a Roman Catholic or participation in Roman Catholic church services, while the children of Orangemen must be brought up as Protestants. Within the UUP, the Orange Order opposed the admittance of Roman Catholics and was seen as instrumental in turning the 1921–72 Unionist state into a sectarian laager.

Despite the perceptions of the Orange Order as sectarian, the organisation claims to be opposed to the doctrines of the Roman Catholic church, rather than hostile to Roman Catholic individuals. For many Unionists, Orangeism was associated with moderation and respectability, based upon faith and Crown and offering loyalty to party and political institutions. At the Order's core, observance of the Protestant religion remains. A large majority of members (68 per cent) claim to attend church weekly and 91 per cent of members attend at least monthly. Given this religious commitment, it was unsurprising that the loyalist paramilitary violence, which erupted partly as a response to republican violence during the post-1970 conflict, was unequivocally condemned. The Order offered constitutional responses to the violence and encouraged its members to join the security forces rather than loyalist paramilitaries.

The imposition of direct rule and fair employment legislation, allied to a diminished local economy, greatly reduced the Order's scope for patronage to its members. Increased population mobility, the impact of mass university education and the demise of deferential "grandee unionism" all contributed to a reduced status for Orangeism, which came to be viewed with some disdain by sections of the Protestant middle class, a contempt that grew amid the violence associated with protests over parades. The Order has struggled to maintain relevance among some working-class militants who, whilst sympathetic to its parading traditions, had less interest in its religious associations, preferring to confine their "Orangeism" to support for "Kick the Pope" bands outside the direct control of the Grand Lodge.[3] In rural areas, however, the Order continued to play an important role in the community, offering social networks and reinforcement of cultural and religious beliefs (Dudley Edwards, 1999). The Dudley Edwards perspective sees the Order's role as a fusion of "Bible" and "tea and sandwiches", with the Orange Order offering continuity of values amid growing secularisation and political disengagement. The Orange hall present in all Protestant villages continues to serve as a primary meeting point. The Kennaway analysis, in contrast, sees a retreat from the religious orientation of the Order, matched by movement towards greater political militancy.

As perceptions of the Orange Order as an outdated sectarian organisation have mounted, it has struggled for recognition as an important contributor to civil society. It was ignored by the Opsahl Commission in 1992–93 (Opsahl and Pollak, 1993), despite the plethora of soundings taken by that body in its analysis of ways forward for Northern Ireland. The supposedly inclusive GFA established a Civic Forum designed to allow societal organisations consultative input to legislation. Despite the Order's status as the largest organisation within civil society, it was not offered participation. Meanwhile, the Order has attempted to improve its often negative image via better public relations and by attempting to re-brand its Twelfth of July parades as community festivals. Grand Lodge has explored how to increase participation in its activities in an era of declining social capital by, for example, inviting the American political scientist, Robert Puttnam, to address the organisation in 2005.

### Cultural defence? The parades issue

The supposed cultural retreat of Orange Protestantism preceded the GFA. During the mid-1950s, restrictions had been placed upon some contentious Orange parades, which had led to grass-roots accusations of betrayal by "their" Unionist political representatives and the Orange leadership (Kaufmann, 2007). However, this was a rare interruption to the normal deference towards such leaders. During the mid-1980s, in Portadown controversies over parading were reignited with a vengeance, which eventually led to serious reverses for the Order. Amid strong protests from nationalist residents, the Portadown district lodge insisted on exercising its right to take its "traditional" route which included the Garvaghy Road on the way back from Drumcree parish church. With the threat of widespread disorder evident, the police eventually allowed each march to proceed until 1998, when the route was finally blocked to the Orange Order. Widespread rioting followed as Orangemen and other loyalists mobilised across Northern Ireland. These confrontations were repeated, on a much lesser scale, for the remainder of the decade, as the prohibition on the Drumcree parade remained.

For moderates within the Order, the insistence upon unfettered rights to march was provocative, took little account of changing demography and reflected an unhealthy new militancy within an organisation that had lost much of its religious grounding. Militants within the Order believed that any impositions upon the Order's rights, amid confrontations orchestrated by "Sinn Fein/IRA residents' groups", were an unacceptable dilution of Protestant rights. The Spirit of Drumcree group, formed during this period, represented the strongest expression of uncompromising Orangeism.

Within the Orange Order, there is considerable hostility to the Parades Commission, the body established in 1998 to adjudicate on the routes of contentious marches. Eighty-seven per cent of members believe the Commission should be abolished, a similar percentage to that which believes the Order should have the right to march through nationalist areas. Nonetheless, there is a pragmatic wing—31 per cent of the membership—which believes that the Orange leadership should negotiate with the Commission. The refusal for many years to recognise the Commission meant that the Order fared badly in determinations on parades. This situation might have eased (albeit slightly) if direct discussions with residents' groups and the Commission had been held, although for many within the Order, "freedom to walk the Queen's highway" was not a privilege to be negotiated. In this respect, the Order appeared at odds with mainstream Protestant opinion, 61 per cent of "ordinary" Protestants (and 96 per cent of Catholics) believing that the religious mix of an area ought to be considered by parade organisers prior to a decision to march.[4]

For the Orange Order, the parades issue remains unresolved. Although few (less than thirty annually) of the Order's 3,000 annual parades are contentious, the restrictions upon the controversial parades has added to the sense of an organisation under siege. Parading remains at the heart of Orange activity and the number of parades and length of the "marching season" have increased since the mid-1980s (Bryan, 2000). Restrictions on routes imposed by the Parades Commission are legally binding. They apply to different types of parades: church, commemorative or celebratory. The Order has its own rules on parading and band conduct. Indeed Grand Lodge's regulations for marching bands are strict and designed to be non-provocative. Introduced after trouble at parades during the mid-1980s, notably in the "Orange citadel" of Portadown, the list of regulations includes requirements that only hymns are played at church parades; bans upon alcohol; dress codes and stipulations regarding flags and banners (Bryan, 2000: 125).

## The Orange Order and the Northern Ireland conflict

The beleaguered status of the Orange Order has been heightened by the changed nature of violence during the peace process. Throughout the conflict, Orangemen, particularly in border areas, felt victims of ethnic cleansing. This perception was not diminished by the actuality that the majority of Protestants killed or injured were targeted because of security force, rather than Orange Order membership. As the peace process gathered pace and the IRA's "war" subsided, low-level sectarian violence increased. While much of this was undertaken by loyalists, there were attacks upon 229 Orange halls, more than one-quarter of the 800 across Northern Ireland, between 1994 and 2002 (Jarman, 2004). Although such attacks were condemned by Sinn Fein, they served merely to reinforce loyalist scepticism over the "non-sectarian" claims of Irish republicans. The Orange Order lost 296 members through violence during the conflict. Table 20.1 indicates both the number of deaths of "ordinary" Orange Order members and those working for the security forces.

Over half (53 per cent) of Orange Order members killed during the conflict were serving members of the security forces. This figure rises to

Table 20.1  Deaths of Orange Order members through republican violence in
the Northern Ireland conflict, according to security force membership

| County Lodge | RUC | UDR | Prison officer | Civilian |
|---|---|---|---|---|
| Antrim | 3 | 1 | 1 | 11 |
| Armagh | 15 | 18 | 1 | 32 |
| Down | 8 | 8 | 0 | 15 |
| Fermanagh | 12 | 13 | 0 | 6 |
| Derry City | 1 | 3 | 0 | 2 |
| Co Derry | 4 | 3 | 0 | 4 |
| Tyrone | 14 | 37 | 0 | 22 |
| Belfast | 5 | 7 | 3 | 47 |
| Total | 62 | 90 | 5 | 139 |

*Source*: constructed from *News Letter*, "Orange victims" tribute", 7 April
2006.

69 per cent if former members of the security forces (a further 47
victims) are added to the tally. Of the 300 RUC officers killed during the
conflict, 21 per cent were members of the Orange Order. From the
Order's perspective, Orangemen had offered selfless service in defence of
their country. From a nationalist perspective, the sizeable number of
Orangemen within policing ranks offered further evidence of the sectarian, partisan nature of the security forces, with Orange effectively
policing Green.

As substantial reforms of policing loomed during the peace process,
however, Orangemen appeared less welcome within the force. The final
Chief Constable of the RUC, Ronnie Flanagan, indicated that he would
prefer members of his force not to belong to the Orange Order.[5] The
Patten Report on policing, which led to the replacement of the RUC by
the Police Service of Northern Ireland (PSNI) recommended that all
police officers should "be obliged to register their interests and associations", which would require an indication of Orange Order membership,
but declined to insist on an outright ban on PSNI officers belonging to
the Order.[6]

No longer desired by the security forces they had served, the isolation
of the Orange Order appeared complete. Indeed, the organisation came
to be viewed as an unwanted harbinger of sectarianism and, in some
instances, violence. The Order was blamed by the Chief Constable of
Northern Ireland, Hugh Orde, for instigating some of the worst rioting
seen in Belfast for decades in September 2004. While much of the violence appeared to be orchestrated by loyalist paramilitaries, the catalyst was the restrictions placed upon an Orange parade in Belfast. The
constitutionalism and non-violent approach, which had characterised

the Order's activities, appeared in jeopardy. By 2004, 20 per cent of Orangemen declined to agree with the proposition that "loyalist violence was never justifiable".

### The severing of the contentious alliance: farewell to the UUP

The 1998 GFA was seen by many members as a further dilution of Protestant-British culture. As Walker (2004: 263) puts it, "to Orangemen, the 'equality agenda' of the Agreement was code for attacks on Protestant culture". Moreover, the Agreement contained conflict resolution measures, such as the early release of paramilitary prisoners and the establishment of an independent commission to examine policing, which were seen by many within the Order as morally unacceptable. For the Orange brethren, there had been no "war", merely terrorism. Moreover, very few Orangemen (5 per cent) thought that the IRA's campaign was over. Grand Lodge resolved that "failing clarification of certain vital issues, it cannot recommend it [the Good Friday Agreement] to the people of Ulster", but declined to issue a direct "Vote No" edict to members for the May 1998 referendum on the deal (Kaufmann and Patterson, 2007). Nonetheless, the brethren were hardly unaware of the feelings of the Orange leadership. An editorial, headlined "No", in the organisation's newspaper, the *Orange Standard*, warned of the "disaster course on which our Province is embarked upon", and described the GFA as a "green-tinged document which has been carefully compiled to placate the pan-Irish nationalist front of which Sinn Fein/IRA is an integral component".[7]

Opposition to the GFA put the Orange Order in direct opposition to a major plank of UUP policy. Previous decades had seen episodic tensions between Order and party, but this was the first serious rupture and one that was to lead to severance of a contentious relationship. The Order's antipathy to the UUP leadership's position was exacerbated by the feeling that a pro-GFA position was increasingly at odds with the views of most Protestants, a perception for which there was growing electoral and opinion poll evidence. Hostility was further heightened by antipathy towards the UUP leader, David Trimble. In 1995, Trimble's election as party leader had been hailed as a "masterly performance for Unionism", as the Order looked forward to the maintenance of the cordial relations with the UUP evident under Trimble's predecessor, James Molyneaux.[8] Trimble, an Orangeman, had been prominent in supporting the right of the Order to march down the Garvaghy Road, once famously linking arms with Ian Paisley upon conclusion of the parade in a rare moment of undiluted unionist unity. Subsequently, however, Trimble had distanced himself from the parades issue, despite growing restrictions upon lodges.

For disaffected Orange Order members, Trimble's support for the GFA placed him within the "Lundy" tradition of unionist "sell-outs". They were unimpressed by his vision of a civic, pluralist unionism, believing it naive amid continuing republican pressure for concessions for the rival community. The presence of Sinn Fein in government, with one of the party's ministers a self-declared former IRA member, was anathema to many of the brethren.

The support of the Orange Order for the GFA was courted by Tony Blair who, for the only time during his premiership, invited its leaders to 10 Downing Street to outline the deal's advantages. Blair found the Orange delegation unreceptive to the moral compromises of the package and only one-third of Orange Order members supported the GFA in the 1998 referendum on the deal. After its implementation, Orange opposition hardened, with Grand Lodge seeking to unite cross-party opponents of the deal with a "solemn pledge" of "lawful opposition" to the deal (Kaufmann and Patterson, 2007). By 2004, only 12 per cent of Orangemen indicated that they would support the GFA in a further referendum. Overall Protestant support for the GFA fell from 57 per cent to 33 per cent between 1998 and 2002 (Irwin, 2002). Trimble's personal popularity rating among members of the Order, averaging 3.5 out of ten, was closer to that of Gerry Adams (0.2) than that of Ian Paisley (7.3)!

Discord over the GFA proved the catalyst for the fracturing of the historic UUP-Orange Order alliance. As the Agreement was implemented and the UUP entered power sharing with republicans, the Orange Order still provided 122 delegates to the 858-member UUC, which remained responsible for the broad direction of UUP policy. Moreover, half of the UUP members were also members of the Orange Order (Tonge and Evans, 2001). Although Grand Lodge influence upon UUP policy had diminished markedly, the "Orange vote" within the party remained significant. The chaotic structure of the UUP had facilitated Orange dissent in the past against the reformist leaderships of Terence O'Neill, James Chichester-Clark and Brian Faulkner and provided a similar protest forum in respect of the GFA. Special meetings of the UUC could be called if a mere sixty delegates so demanded, and opponents of the GFA regularly used this device in attempting to steer the UUP from its pro-Agreement stance (Tonge, 2005).

In 2000, Reverend Martin Smyth, Grand Master of the Orange Order for the previous twenty-five years, challenged Trimble in a UUP leadership contest. In courting the Orange vote, Smyth made clear how he had "first been an Orangeman, then a politician".[9] Among Orange Order members, Smyth outpolled Trimble (51 per cent to 49 per cent) with the leader saved only by the votes of non-Order members (Tonge and Evans,

2001), who contributed substantially to Trimble's unconvincing 57 per cent to 43 per cent victory. Controlling other variables, Orange Order membership was an important factor in support for Smyth (more likely) and opposition to the GFA (again, more likely). Age (younger UUP members were more hostile to the GFA) was more significant, but clearly the Orange membership continued to shape political preferences. Kaufmann and Patterson (2006, 2007) indicate how Orange UUC delegates tended to hold more middle-class occupations compared to grassroots Orange members, a factor which worked in Trimble's favour. Had UUC Orange delegates been more typical of ordinary Orange Order members, the pro-GFA UUP leadership might have found itself in deeper trouble. Among these Orange delegates to the UUC, those who were most active within the Order as office-bearers were most likely to be hostile to Trimble and the GFA. Urban-based Orange delegates were also overwhelmingly more likely to be hostile to the GFA, compared to their rural counterparts.

Although Trimble had spoken of reviewing the relationship between party and Order, he was careful not to attack the Orange section of the UUP directly, couching any possible move within a need for general party restructuring. Few believed that severance of the historic link would lead to a rapid influx of Catholics into the party, but the presence of the Orange Order was seen by critics as a sectarian anachronism. Those supporting retention of the link tended to be anti-Agreement Orangemen within the party, who wanted to shift the UUP leadership from support for the GFA as basic constitutional security for the Union towards a stouter defence of Orange interests. In the event, the Orange Order jumped first. In March 2005, Grand Lodge voted by 82 votes to 16 to sever its links with the UUC.

That severance came from the Orange Order rather than the UUP was something of a surprise, given that the Order was divided on the issue. Forty per cent of lodge masters had indicated a preference for disaffiliation as early as 1994 (Kaufmann and Patterson, 2007). Ten years later, ordinary members were also split, 37 per cent backed severance compared to 49 per cent supporting retention of the Orange-UUP link. The UUP leadership preferred to retain the association, partly because of the local benefits in terms of support bases and the facility of Orange halls for party meetings. Trimble's idea was to bring Orange delegates directly under the control of party associations, a move rejected by Grand Lodge for fear of losing control over their delegates. With the Assembly having collapsed, the DUP having overtaken the UUP in the 2003 election to a suspended institution and defections of prominent Orangemen to Paisley's party, the benefits of association with a split party in freefall were far from apparent to Grand Lodge. Continued linkage to the UUP might have worsened the unfashionable image of the Orange Order.

## The Orange Order and the DUP

The Order's link with the UUP was not replaced by any formal association with the DUP. Nonetheless, rapprochement with Ian Paisley's party was apparent. Previously, the DUP had represented a form of rebel unionism associated with political militancy and, institutionally, the Independent Orange Order, founded in 1903, or the Free Presbyterian Church, established by Paisley in the 1950s (Kaufmann and Patterson, 2007). These institutions and their politics were regarded with suspicion within "traditional unionism", represented by the established order of the UUP and the Orange Order, which identified with the Church of Ireland or Presbyterian Church. Such was the antipathy to more militant Protestant-Unionists that Free Presbyterian ministers were barred from acting as lodge chaplains from 1951 until 1998. Paisleyism was regarded as an uncharitable, perverted form of extreme Protestantism, based upon political polemic and religious bigotry, and still struggled for credibility among sections of the Orange Order until the realignment associated with the GFA.

Grand Lodge was following its membership, however, in detaching itself from the UUP. In the 2001 Westminster election, the DUP enjoyed a narrow lead (of 4 per cent) over the UUP among Orangemen, but by 2004, 66 per cent of Orange Order members surveyed by the authors indicated they would vote DUP "in an election tomorrow", with only 30 per cent backing the UUP. These figures were replicated among the broader Unionist constituency at the 2005 Westminster and local elections. Support for the DUP was increasing across all social categories within the Orange Order. By 2004, two-thirds of manual workers declared support for the UUP's rival, with 58 per cent of middle-class members also indicating backing for the DUP. Support for the DUP was not income-dependent, nor was it confined to the Orange grass roots. Among Northern Ireland Assembly unionist representatives there was a higher percentage, post-2003, of DUP Orange Order members than among the UUP.

Nonetheless, remnants of the old UUP-Orange Order ties were still evident. Even by the mid-2000s, less than half (49 per cent) of Orangemen aged 55 or over declared support for the DUP, having received their political socialisation in an era of close UUP-Orange affiliations and UUP dominance. Moreover, membership of the "moderate" Church of Ireland was also significant as an indicator of UUP support

(McAuley and Tonge, 2007). The DUP's links with the Free Presbyterian Church remained unappealing to some, although the party tended towards a pragmatic separation of church and politics on some issues, such as Sunday leisure activity, where a rigid religiosity was electorally unappealing.

Orange Order members had become rational consumers within a reshaped unionist electoral marketplace. No longer bound by the loyalties of previous generations to a broad unionist alliance, Orangemen defected to the party they felt was the stouter defender of their interests. Whilst the UUP recognised the risks involved in the GFA, the party leadership believed that constitutional guarantees for the Union provided sufficient security for Protestants in Northern Ireland to continue to be "Simply British", to cite the UUP's 2005 election slogan. For the DUP and the Orange Order, basic constitutional guarantees were insufficient amid a perceived hollowing-out of the Britishness of the state. The new allegiance of Orange Order members may, of course, be tested as the DUP presides over a revised Agreement, albeit one with substantial further movement from republicans, in government with Sinn Fein, but there is little evidence thus far of any UUP revival within the Order.

## Conclusion

The Orange Order in Northern Ireland has attempted to maintain a distinctive sense of Protestant-British Unionism not found elsewhere in the United Kingdom. Enduring political marginalisation since the early 1970s, the Order has struggled for relevance in a polity where key decisions have not been made locally for decades and where religious identification and observance, although still very strong compared to elsewhere in western Europe, is in decline. That the DUP neither courted, nor coveted, the electoral support of the Orange Order is indicative of the limited importance of the organisation.

Nonetheless, the durability of Orangeism should not be underestimated. It represents a fusion of cultural, religious and political aspiration that chimes with that section of the unionist population underwhelmed by the peace and political processes in Northern Ireland. In disaffiliating from the UUP, the Orange leadership recognised the changed tastes of its members, and the modern-day Order acts as an outsider pressure group competing for influence, rather than as insider organisation with a special political relationship.

With the armed conflict in Northern Ireland over, there is likely to be a new focus on sectarianism, which will bring renewed scrutiny of the role of the Orange Order. Traditional songs associated with its bands on parade have already been labelled as "sectarian" and discouraged or pro-hibited in, for example, sporting arenas. The Order's central symbols of faith and Crown face struggles for relevance amid secularisation and dis-interest in the monarchy. Continual rebranding of the Order's traditions seems likely, most notably the "folk festival" approach towards the Twelfth, but minor controversies over parades seem likely amid chang-ing demography. The challenge for the Orange Order will lie in adhering to its strong religious and political traditions whilst making them more appealing or benign to those from alternative backgrounds.

## Notes

1 The authors acknowledge with thanks the assistance of Dr David Hume and Drew Nelson at the Grand Orange Lodge of Ireland, Belfast, for facilitating the membership surveys. The main study was funded by the Economic and Social Research Council from 2006–8. (R000-23-1614)
2 Parliamentary Debates, Northern Ireland House of Commons, XVI, 1091–5, 24 April 1934.
3 The term "Kick the Pope band" is sometimes used to describe those militant loyalist marching bands who are not affiliated to the Grand Lodge of Ireland and are thus not bound by its rules. Such bands are seen as more overtly sec-tarian than lodges affiliated to Grand Lodge.
4 Independent Review of Parades and Marches, *Public Attitudes to Parades and Marches: Northern Ireland Survey* (Belfast: HMSO, 1997).
5 House of Commons Northern Ireland Affairs Committee, 18 March 1998.
6 Independent Commission on Policing, 1999: pp. 89 and 119.
7 *Orange Standard*, May 1998, p. 1.
8 *Orange Standard*, October 1995, p. 10.
9 *Belfast Telegraph*, 27 March 2000.

## References

Bryan, D. (2000) *Orange Parades* (London: Pluto).
Dudley Edwards, R. (1999) *The Faithful Tribe: An Intimate Portrait of the Loyal Institutions* (London: HarperCollins).
Elliott, S. and Flackes, W. (1999) *Northern Ireland: A Political Directory 1968–1999*, (Belfast: Blackstaff).
Farrell, M. (1980) *Northern Ireland: the Orange State* (London: Pluto).
Independent Commission on Policing (1999) *A New Beginning: Policing in Northern Ireland* (The Patten Report) (Belfast: HMSO).
Irwin, C. (2002) *The People's Peace Process* (Basingstoke: Palgrave).
Jarman, N. (2004) "From war to peace? Changing patterns of violence in Northern Ireland 1990–2003", *Terrorism and Political Violence*, 16.3: 420–38.
Kaufmann, E. (2007) *The Orange Order: A Contemporary Northern Irish History*, (Oxford: Oxford University Press).

Kaufmann, E. and Patterson, H. (2006) "The dynamics of intra-party support for the Good Friday Agreement", *Political Studies*, 54: 509–32.

Kaufmann, E. and Patterson, H. (2007) *Unionism and Orangeism in Northern Ireland Since 1945* (Manchester: Manchester University Press).

Kennaway, B. (2006) *The Orange Order: A Tradition Betrayed* (London: Methuen).

McAuley, J. and Tonge, J. (2007) ' "For God and for the Crown": Contemporary political and social attitudes among Orange Order members in Northern Ireland', *Political Psychology*, 28.1: 33–52.

McGarry, J. and O'Leary, B. (1995) *Explaining Northern Ireland* (Oxford: Blackwell).

Opsahl Commission and Pollak, A. (eds) (1993) *A Citizens' Inquiry: The Opsahl Report on Northern Ireland* (Dublin: Lilliput Press).

Tonge, J. (2005) *The New Northern Irish Politics?* (London: Palgrave).

Tonge, J. and Evans, J. (2001) "Faultlines in Unionism: division and dissent within the Ulster Unionist Council", *Irish Political Studies*, 16: 111–32.

Walker, G. (2004) *A History of the Ulster Unionist Party* (Manchester: Manchester University Press).

# Part VIII

# The Protestant working class: political and paramilitary representation

# 21

# Duck or rabbit? The value systems of loyalist paramilitaries

*Lyndsey Harris*

## Introduction

A common assumption, expressed particularly in the media, is that loyalists, unlike republicans, are incapable of strategic thinking. Essentially, by assuming a lack of strategic thinking we are drawn into a discussion on what we mean by rationality. In other words, did loyalists simply apply violence irrationally and in an ad hoc way in the hope of achieving something? The question then arises, what did they try to achieve? The assumption that loyalists are incapable of strategic thinking is countered by an examination of the perceptions and belief system held by the UDA and UVF.

It is necessary to stress that the strategic tradition within academic analysis assumes that behaviour is rational. The question is, what sort of rationality? What does it mean to act rationally? Everyday understanding of "rational strategy" equates to the implementation of a preconceived and premeditated plan that is systematically followed through. The end is identified and the means are selected according to their efficiency in obtaining that end. The assumption that can be found in much of the prevailing literature on the Northern Ireland conflict is that Republicans had such an end and the means were rationally proportionate. Loyalists are often portrayed as having no such end and so their means were incommensurate and hence irrational (McDowell, 2001; Anderson, 2002; Lister and Jordan, 2003). This understanding of loyalists has been confirmed in the popular mind since September 2005 by events such as loyalist rioting throughout areas of Belfast and Antrim following the prohibition of an Orange Order parade on the Whiterock Road; rioting due to the early release of the Republican, Sean Kelly, who was involved in the Shankill Road bombing in the early 1990s; and also disillusionment amongst the loyalist community about the social and economic deprivation in their areas.

## What do we mean by "strategic tradition"?

By complementing the work conducted by M. L. R. Smith (1997) on the strategic tradition of the Republican movement, it is believed that a similar method of enquiry can be employed to examine loyalist paramilitaries and this will add to our understanding of the, so far inadequately documented, military dimension of the "Troubles".[1] Smith states that an analysis of a strategic tradition should examine, "schematically the evolution of number of ideological themes . . . which have a bearing upon the employment of the movement's use of armed force"(Smith, 1997: 6). Therefore, if we are attempting to expose the strategic tradition of loyalist paramilitary groups we need to address:

1. the identification of loyalist political objectives;
2. their perceived history;
3. their relationship with the British government/Irish government/ Republican "movement";
4. the identification of any images that encapsulates and enforces their ideology, and from which they draw strength;
5. the establishment of their primary means of violence.

In addition to these factors it must be remembered that loyalist military objectives will be dependent on their clear identification of the enemy, and what their adversary's preference structure entails. Furthermore, an examination of the strengths and weaknesses of loyalist analysis of the points raised above is required.[2] However, the purpose of this chapter is to reveal loyalist value systems and how they believe they are perceived by the "other" actors involved in Northern Irish politics by drawing upon empirical research conducted across Northern Ireland in 2005.

## What is loyalism?

Throughout the conflict a major concern of loyalists was that of media misrepresentation, aiding republicans in a propaganda war against them. Indeed, this was the view articulated by loyalists in the April 1998 issue of *Combat*,[3] which included a discussion of the "Arrogance of the USA and its pro-republican lobby" and claimed that the Americans were misinformed and making "blind and rash judgements against anything Loyalist or Unionist". Historically, the negative coverage loyalist paramilitaries attracted from the media was deemed an attempt to weaken the loyalist position and create further opposition to their aims. In a UDA statement published in June 1973, loyalists expressed their distaste at the negative media coverage and discussed the language used to describe them:

> Mountains of words have been written about us in the past four years and our role in the affair is cast by the press in a certain way and all comments about us are based upon these assumptions: That we are narrow minded. That we are fanatical. That we are similar to the IRA. That we hate all Catholics. That we are repressive, "right wing" Fascists. That we cannot be reasoned with. (Dillon and Lehane, 1973: 280–3)

Loyalists complain that the Protestant side of the conflict has not been accurately reported to the rest of the world. Consequently, sometimes they see themselves as being "wrongfully cast into the role of villains" (Galliher and DeGregory, 1985: 133). This antagonistic relationship with the media has been a constant feature and the UDA and UVF have often issued statements, similar to that above.

Responses to the question, "How do you think Loyalists are portrayed by the media?" demonstrate that this perception is still maintained. For example, the majority of respondents surveyed referred to the media portraying loyalists as criminals or focusing upon a criminal element within the UVF and UDA and not placing the same emphasis on criminality within republicanism:

> I think that they are portrayed and given a harder ride by the media. I think that the media seem to place more emphasis on alleged criminality within Loyalism. Although, I will accept that there is criminality in the ranks and there has been, but the media seem to be more focused on that than on criminality in Republican ranks. (A, UVF, County Down, 2005)

Respondents also stated that the media was partial when examining paramilitary organisations in Northern Ireland and their aspirations; loyalist political or community initiatives are not as favourably examined as Republicans.

> Again, everything in society today is about republicans—the media would see that the Loyalists don't have a case simply because they believe themselves to be a reactionary force and defence groups; if you attack us we will retaliate. They [media] have never seen them as forward thinkers, as a result of that there is certainly less [positive] media attention on the Loyalist side than there is on the republicans. (Tommy Kirkham, Ulster Political Research Group, Newtownabbey, 2005)

Another cause for complaint is revealed in the following excerpt where all Loyalist paramilitary organisations such as the UVF, UDA, Red Hand Commando (RHC) and Loyalist Volunteer Force (LVF) are portrayed by the media as a collective group and therefore feed into a stereotype:

[The portrayal by the media is][h]orrendous usually. The red tops on a Sunday are particularly vicious and they have created more trouble than anything else; they are just looking for a sensational headline or stereotype and they have added to the difficulties of the violence I would have to say. The odd few papers takes [*sic*] an odd look but journalism has changed from twenty years ago and there are not many in depth studies; now papers demand three hundred words on a certain topic so there is not a big lot of explanation and usually when it comes to Unionist or Loyalists politics there is a lot of explanations of ifs and buts and whys and modern day journalism doesn't allow for that so it hasn't got a strict explanation or one answer. In my own situation if I am asked a question I have got three different paramilitary organisations I work with: if you answer one that would fit one group but it may not fit the other two groups so you have to try and get an answer and explain that and that can be very hard to do in a short space of time. (Mervyn Gibson, Chair of Loyalist Commission, 2005)

By not grasping the thinking behind loyalist actions it is often possible to portray them in ways described above, especially concentrating on the sectarian nature of their operations. Loyalists claim that the press has deviously misled the public in their coverage of loyalist military campaigns. Indeed, they are often not recognised as military campaigns at all, but as actions of "gangster hoodlums". An obvious criminal element does exist and this was not denied by those surveyed within loyalist paramilitary circles. However, the relationship between British public perceptions of loyalist paramilitaries and the media portrayal of them is something that respondents were asked to consider. It was apparent that respondents felt the media exploited and fed into public opinion of the UDA and UVF. Responses obtained from the interview question, "How do you think Loyalists are perceived by the general British public?" support this assertion, "[As] [t]hugs, hooligans, terrorists, just a bad lot and receive a bad press. They don't understand us. I have been on holidays and they think Orangemen are terrorists . . . They have no interest in us and we get a bad negative press" (N, UVF, County Down, 2005).

The common perception that the general British public has of loyalist paramilitaries is said to include a picture of organisations that are steeped in sectarianism and hooliganism: as Respondent M (UVF, County Down, 2005) summarises, "Thugs, drug dealers, extortionists and very intransigent and always saying no." The late Billy McCaughey, once a prominent PUP member and ex-UVF, described how these perceptions are fed and formed by the media:

I would doubt whether they [British public] even know what Loyalism represents. I would suspect that if they have a perception it is one of the sort of cardboard cut out larger than life, with tattooed skinheaded characters like football hooligans, totally controlled by sectarianism, probably unemployed all their lives and most definitely uneducated. If they have any understanding I would suspect that that is the perception that would be there; formed obviously by the tabloid press rather than any direct contact or any serious attempt to find out where loyalists came from and what it is about and how it came to exist. (Billy McCaughy, UVF, Co. Antrim, 2005)

As demonstrated in the previous quotation, there is also a general concern by those interviewed that loyalists are mainly seen as "an anonymous group of people . . ." and that over the years of the Troubles, "they [the British public] know more about the Republican community than they do about Loyalism as a branch of Unionism . . ." and, most significantly, fail to ". . . understand Loyalism as a political philosophy" (Respondent F, UDA, Londonderry, 2005).

However, it is important to note that the negativity surrounding loyalism is not merely due to media portrayals. Many scholars of the Northern Ireland conflict are hostile towards loyalist paramilitaries due to the seeming sectarian randomness of their victims and criminal activities (Cairns, 2000; Silke, 1999, 2000; Bruce, 1992a). The majority of loyalist victims did not belong to any republican paramilitary organisation and the notion of deterrence of the other community often seemed a thin veneer for sectarian tendencies.

## Modification of the rationalist view

Wittegenstein's use of Jastrow's image that alternates between a duck and a rabbit is employed by Minogue to illustrate how perceptions might switch from one thing to another and, importantly, it is an example of a "potentially conflicting judgement about the world." Minogue states that:

> sometimes perceptual equivalences may arise because we oscillate between two senses of rationality. Attempting to understand the actions of a terrorist organisation such as the IRA, we enter into their belief system to find a duck, but without drawing from this belief system into our own notion of what is rational, we find ourselves confronting a rabbit. (Minogue, 1996: 129)

Whilst Minogue applies this statement to the IRA, the same assertion can be made about loyalist paramilitary organisations. We need to attempt to examine their value systems in order to make any judgement or understanding of the use of the military instrument to achieve their set goals, and so dispel the idea that loyalist paramilitary action is always irrational. The following section reveals how loyalists believe they should be portrayed; how they perceive themselves; and who, or what, loyalists are loyal to. The importance of this method of enquiry is not to dispel the portrayals of loyalists revealed in the previous section but to add to our understanding of how loyalists create their own value system. Hence, it is not important whether loyalists see themselves as a "duck" or a "rabbit" but why they perceive themselves in this way.

Fundamentally, loyalist paramilitaries stress their history and identity. They often counteract the "propaganda war" against them by stating that the press have never documented their history in a true light; and that their actions are understandable the strength of their claim and the legitimacy of their organisations are examined:

> I think that we get a very negative press in the media. I mean, I am not gen-erally happy with the media attitude to Loyalism from a political point of view we as representatives of Loyalism tend not to get 1) the space to put our message across and 2) we don't get any respect from media people in relation to statements that we make unless its something negative. If it is a negative issue within Loyalism we are the first people that the media contact; if it is positive we are the last. (O, UVF, Co. Tyrone, 2005)

In establishing that loyalists, on the whole, do not believe that they are accurately portrayed by the media and perceived by the British public, all participants were asked how they would like to be perceived. The late David Ervine, then leader of the PUP, suggested that, "Loyalism would love to be loved" and "be venerated and it would love to be greatly appreciated in a wider sense than it already is . . ." This is certainly a theme that existed throughout all of the interviews conducted and it can be related to loyalist value systems. It is important to note here that there were distinctions between how members of the UDA and UVF would like to be perceived, and this translates into an establishment of varying value systems. In relation to the question, "How would Loyalists like to be per-ceived?" a characteristic response from UVF associated members was that they believed they were defending the Northern Irish state to ensure that it remained British.

One UVF member from Ballymena provided an interesting assessment of what it means to be a loyalist, which reveals that in his mind although loyalists share with all Unionists common support for the maintenance of the Union between Northern Ireland and Great Britain, Loyalism is a separate term used to describe those who would be willing to ensure the maintenance of the Union by using violent means:

> Well, we should be seen basically for what we are. Loyalism means, or has come to mean, somebody who has taken up arms in defence of the Protestant and Unionist cause, taking up arms illegally. Now, defining that

as Loyalism as opposed to Unionism: people tend to look that if you are a Unionist you would tend to be Protestant and support the Union but you wouldn't consider stepping outside the law. Whereas the term Loyalism has generally come to mean someone who has joined one of the main paramilitaries and has stepped outside the law to fight Republicanism. (A, UVF, Armagh, 2005)

The commitment to being prepared to "step outside the law" is a key role that many of the respondents identified and the belief that they were the "defenders of Ulster" when the security forces of the state seemed, in their eyes, to be incapable of countering the Republican paramilitary threat to Northern Ireland:

Loyalists like to be perceived, and again, they would believe that they *are* the defenders and the only ones who stood between the lines in the sense of defending the protestant people from republicanism over the last thirty years. They would believe that they have done society a favour. If they weren't there, then the British forces wouldn't have coped with republicanism. So, they would look at it like that; they wouldn't see themselves as being criminals and murderers in any sense. They would say that they came up to the mark to defend Ulster when Ulster needed to be defended. (P, UVF, East Belfast, 2005)

In comparison, most UDA respondents, although believing that they were defending the Northern Irish state, placed greater emphasis on defence of their local communities against Republican attacks. Respondent A8 suggested, "the UDA would want to be seen as defenders of the community, okay, especially, this brigade: The North-West, North Antrim, and Londonderry Brigade. We are the defenders of the community; we look after our people . . ." (Londonderry, 2002). The belief that the UDA is defending their communities is reinforced throughout its publication, *Warrior*.

There is a very strong belief among its members that the UDA should be perceived as defenders of their community and that they would never have existed if it were not for Republican violence:

[Loyalists should be perceived] [a]s genuine Loyalists; what they were when they originated from the vigilante groups—when everyone just did what they did: when they stood around the fires at night on the street corners looking after areas and then they formed themselves into a paramilitary organisation but they were all there for the right reasons. When it was formed obviously people had been in the British Army and that is where the structure was formed from. That was when leaders just came to the fore and they did whatever they had to do with great pride within their communities to form themselves into a paramilitary organisation that everybody was proud of: the community, the people, their families, even the

security forces were begrudgingly accepting that there were a well organ-ised outfit. (UDA "Brigadier", North Belfast, 2005)

Essentially, both of the main loyalist paramilitary groups, the UVF and UDA, wished to be perceived as "defenders" and draw upon the conven-tional wisdom that they are "pro-state terrorists"(Bruce, 1992a, 1992b). Some respondents conveyed a sense of dismay in being branded as crim-inals often using the infamous saying, "our only crime was loyalty". The question then becomes inevitable—loyal to whom or to what?

## To whom, or what, are loyalists loyal?

The previous section drew upon empirical data regarding how loyalists would like to be perceived. However, in order to examine why they wish to be conveyed as "defenders"—albeit with slight variations in the defin-ition of defence between UDA and UVF understandings—a deeper analy-sis into what it is they believe they are defending is required. Ultimately, this leads us to ask to what, or to whom, are loyalists loyal? Why is the maintenance of the Union between Great Britain and Northern Ireland important? Are there any other factors which influence the belief systems of the UDA and UVF?

The empirical data discussed supports the analysis provided by Aughey and McIlheney (1981, 1983) that loyalists see themselves as "arbiters of Ulster's destiny" or, as stated in *Warrior*, a belief that "Ulster's future lies in our hands" (*Warrior*, 13: 3). Aughey and McIlheney's examination of loyalism revealed two aspects of loyalty, which were also supported by empirical data collected for this study. First, is the concept of Britishness, which concentrates on being distinct from Irishness. This is something that respondent M conveyed forcefully:

> I don't identify myself as Irish in anyway; I just can't. I don't connect with anything Irish . . . I don't think I would like to be ruled by a state that was heavily influenced by the church. I definitely wouldn't want my children, if they were growing up, educated by a school that was heavily influenced or controlled by the church. It is not so much about I want a British way of life it is more of that I don't want an Irish one. I know that we are dictated by our government too but I think it is the better of the two evils. (M, UVF, Co. Down, 2005)

All respondents from the UVF referred to a wish to uphold their British identity and "British way of life". Respondent G stated, "From my per-spective my Britishness is paramount and that is why I got involved in Loyalism. As far as I am concerned my number one priority is to remain British" (G, UVF, Londonderry, 2005). Respondent O, gave his understanding of what it was about the British way of life that loyalists wished to defend, "Loyalists are basically loyal to the Crown; to the British way of life; I think that is the concept of our Britishness—the freedom to be who we are and what we are and say what we want, when we want. Being loyal—we are loyal to the Crown" (O, UVF, Tyrone, 2005).

Respondents also indicated a desire to maintain loyalty to Unionist and Protestant culture and their heritage. This, again, supports the second of Aughey and McIlheney's categories in understanding the nature of loyalty espoused by loyalist paramilitaries who discuss the "deep political allegiance to the symbols of the union and the rest of the United Kingdom."(1983: 2). This is articulated in depth by one UVF respondent, A, who describes it as follows:

> I think that it could be said that we are simply loyal to what our forefathers were loyal to: "For God and Ulster"; our religion; and our country. Now whether the Northern Ireland state survives, as we know it, only time will tell, but that is our basic strength and definition of our loyalty. Inside those two main components are a whole lot of other things that make up our Protestant culture, our heritage, and our way of life; whether that is our Loyal Orders, marching cultures, flute bands, supporting Rangers, Lambeg drumming, our Ulster Scots connection, or our basic sense of identity of being Ulstermen but being within the broader British Isle context within the Union. All of those things come together to make up what we are loyal to. (A, UVF, Co. Antrim)

Within the cultural realm differences can be identified between the value systems of the UDA and UVF. First and foremost, the UVF stress the need to defend the Crown and point to this being a part of their heritage from the early 1900s, and the creation of Carson's Ulster Volunteer Force to defend against the Home Rule Bill. This also goes further, and many UVF respondents stress the sacrifice made by the 36th Ulster Division who fought gallantly in the Battle of the Somme during The First World War. These memories are often used to demonstrate their "loyalty" to the British Crown and have remained a constant feature. Throughout the *Combat* journals there are reminders of the sacrifice made during the First World War and these are especially emphasised in July, among commemorations of the Battle of the Boyne.

Loyalty to the Crown and, intrinsically linked with this, the maintenance of the Union, is a significant part of the UVF's value system and was identified by all of the UVF-related interviewees. Respondent N stated that he was loyal to the "maintenance of the Union" and "loyal to the British State—not a particular government because governments change—and a British way of life" (N. Co. Down, 2005). Respondent P typified answers to what, or who, the UVF are loyal to:

Loyalists, I think, in the sense of the true word of Loyalism are loyal to the Crown; The British Empire; we are the British presence in Ireland and that is where their loyalty is. It is not loyalty to any such governments but it is the ethos of being British and the British Crown in its entirety. So, when people talk about being disloyal to governments or something like that, it is not about being loyal to governments, it's the ethos of being British. (P, Co. Antrim, 2005)

Drawing upon the cultural heritage, Billy Mitchell stated that:

Basically, the traditionalists within the UVF and Red Hand [Commandos] would say that they are loyal to the principles of the Ulster Covenant and probably some of the key elements of the covenant would be the material well-being of Ulster; that is something that the criminal element can't say they are loyal to. The principled element of Loyalism say: we are loyal to the principles of the covenant; the material well being of Ulster; civil-religious freedom; equal citizenship within the United Kingdom; and the right to resist unjust political impositions. So, it is the key principles of the covenant. Probably the key one in that would be equal citizenship within the United Kingdom. (Billy Mitchell, ex-UVF and PUP, North Belfast, 2005)

The UVF's Billy McCaughey described how loyalty to the Crown is ultimately loyalty to the Northern Irish state, distinctive from the Irish state and characterised by Britishness:

Well, historically I suppose Loyalism would have been loyal to the British Crown. I personally am not a monarchist—I am not really on a crusade to abolish the monarchy, I am not really interested in whether Charles marries Camilla or not—to me the Crown on its own is the Head of State. Until there is a republic in the UK I have no difficulty accepting the Queen as the Head of State, although it wouldn't be my first choice; it would be republican—not in the Irish sense but in the American sense. (Billy McCaughey, UVF, Co. Antrim, 2005)

By identifying oneself as a citizen of the United Kingdom, the *Principles of Loyalism* (PUP, 2002) document highlights that this concept ultimately leads to a "reciprocal loyalty". One loyalist is quoted by the document as describing loyalty:

As a unionist I choose to be a citizen of the United Kingdom and while I am not a monarchist by conviction, I accept that the political state in which I choose to hold citizenship is a constitutional monarchy. Therefore as a loyal citizen of that state I am happy to pledge loyalty to the *Queen in Parliament* and, unlike some unionists, my loyalty is not conditional upon the Sovereign's adherence to any particular religion. It is conditional only upon the Sovereign remaining subject to the will of a Parliament that is freely elected by the citizens of the United Kingdom and that endorses and supports my right to equal citizenship under the Crown. (PUP, 2002: 28)

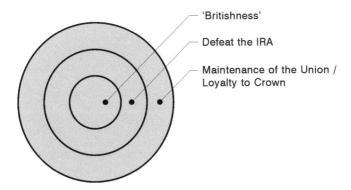

**Figure 21.1** The value system of the Ulster Volunteer Force

This identification of being British by maintaining the Union between Great Britain and Northern Ireland and drawing upon cultural symbols and heritage indicates that the UVF's value system can be identified as being informed by notions of Britishness, which translated into a paramilitary mindset requiring the defeat of the IRA to maintain their ultimate value of loyalty to the Crown and preserving Northern Ireland as a part of the UK. This was observed by a member of the UDA who stated:

> [T]hose who did belong to the UDA firstly seen [*sic*] that loyalty to its own people, i.e. the communities within Northern Ireland, the working class people—as defenders of those communities who were besieged by republican aggression. The Ulster Volunteer Force, on the other hand, see themselves firstly being loyal to the Crown and secondly to the Union and thirdly to the people. There is a difference in the analysis of the two organisations. (F, UDA, Londonderry, 2005)

UVF value systems can be represented as in Figure 21.1. Todd's (1987) analysis of Ulster loyalism, which is said to include a primary imagined community based on northern Protestants with a secondary identification to Great Britain does not seem to apply in its entirety to the UVF. It can, however, be said to apply more consistently to the value system of the UDA.

The UDA also claims a long-standing history of loyalty to the Crown, but ultimately their rationale is the protection of their countrymen. They maintain that their origins lie in the Ulster Defence Union (UDU), established in 1893. The UDU, they assert, was "established to defend the Protestant inhabitants"; consequently, they continue by stating that 'the contemporary UDA is merely continuing the great historical tradition of Republican "defenderism"' (*Warrior*, 22: 5). It is entirely justified to question these links as simply historical ones. What appears to be certain is that the UDA hopes to gain some credibility by explaining their origins

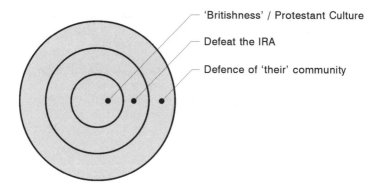

**Figure 21.2** The value system of the Ulster Defence Association

and, consequently, indicates that their role as loyal protector of their community's interest is a constant one that will continue whatever the situation. Therefore, an argument is put forward to the media that while they seem to portray the IRA as part of a long-standing Irish rebel tradition, stemming from the Irish Republican Brotherhood, loyalists are portrayed as a new sectarian response to circumstances.

Respondent T, a UDA member from Co. Down stated very clearly his belief that the UDA need to be loyal to and work for, their communities. This was echoed by respondent X, a UDA brigadier, who identified his community as the "Protestant community":

> My motto of the UDA would be defenders of the faith and the Protestant community that would be my motto. So, I keep going back to the community issue and Sammy [Duddy] and I, we were there to defend the communities. It is a different type of thing now with attacks going on; it is interfaces. Sammy said about the geography and about nationalists and republicans moving into these arterial routes, that is where the parades issues come in . . . That is our culture, the Orange Order. My motto would be that we are still defenders of the faith and the Protestant community. (X, UDA, Belfast, 2005)

This identification of the Protestant community does not necessarily correspond with wishing to uphold any doctrinal religious commitments but from the empirical evidence gathered it appears to support Cairn's (2000) and Shirlow and McGovern's (1997) analysis in that it aids the creation of the "collective self" in comparison with the "other". Essentially, Protestantism has been used as a way to differentiate between two communities, which also strengthens Bruce's (2001) description as Protestantism being used as a "badge of identity". Therefore, in relation to the above extract from Respondent X's interview, the belief that culture is being eroded or lost due to "the other" actor's action would correlate with Todd's (1987: 3) description of an Ulster loyalism that is characterised by evangelical Protestantism and that the core assumption is that the only alternative to Ulster loyalist dominance is Ulster loyalist defeat and humiliation.

The Ulster Defence Association's value system can, therefore, be said to contain notions of Britishness, which includes the desire to maintain cultural practices and the need to defeat the IRA to ensure the defence of "their" communities (see Figure 21.2).

## Conclusion

The problem is not whether the commentator or student of Northern Irish politics thinks that the belief structure of loyalist paramilitaries is viable but that we must understand the values of loyalist paramilitary organisations to begin any analysis of their behaviour. With the value systems of the UDA and UVF clearly identified and illustrated in Figures 21.1 and 22.2 it is believed that this will aid future examinations of loyalist paramilitaries and will establish what impact this has on loyalist understanding of the strategic environment. In other words, what matters is how loyalists respond to events, other actors and their own communities in the Northern Irish political arena.

## Notes

1   For further information on the absence of work examining the military dimension of the Northern Ireland conflict see Smith (1995, 1999).
2   For further information on the strategic approach see Harris (2006), Smith (1991, 1997), Neumann (2003)
3   *Combat* is a journal created and edited by members of the UVF and is sold in Loyalist areas as a way to fund raise and provide information to the Loyalist community about the actions and intent of the UVF. *Warrior* is the equivalent publication produced by the UDA.

## References

Anderson, C. (2002) *The Billy Boy: The Life and Death of LVF Leader Billy Wright* (Edinburgh: Mainstream Publishing).
Aughey, A. and McIlheney, C. (1981) "UDA: Paramilitaries and politics", *Conflict Quarterly* (Fall), 32–45.
Aughey, A and McIlheney, C. (1983) "Law before violence? The Protestant paramilitaries in Ulster Politics", ECPR Workshop on violence and conflict management in divided societies, Freiburg, March.

Bruce, S. (1992a) *The Red Hand: Protestant Paramilitaries in Northern Ireland* (Oxford: Oxford University Press).

Bruce, S. (1992b) "The problem of pro-state terrorism: Loyalist paramilitaries in Northern Ireland", *Terrorism and Political Violence*, 4.1: 67–88.

Bruce, S. (2001) "Terrorists and politics: the case of Northern Ireland's loyalist para-militaries", *Terrorism and Political Violence*, 13: 27–48.

Cairns, D. (2000) "The object of sectarianism: the material reality of sectarianism in Ulster Loyalism", *Journal of Royal Anthropological Institute*, 6: 85–104.

Dillon, M. and Lehane, D. (1973) *Political Murder in Northern Ireland* (Middlesex: Penguin).

Galliher, J. F. and DeGregory, J. (1985) *Violence in Northern Ireland: Understanding Protestant Perspectives* (Dublin: Gill & Macmillan).

Harris, L. (2006) "Introducing the strategic approach: an examination of Loyalist paramilitaries in Northern Ireland", *British Journal of Politics and International Relations*, 8.4: 553–49.

Lister, D. and Jordan, H. (2003) *Mad Dog: The Rise and Fall of Johnny Adair and "C" Company* (Edinburgh: Mainstream Publishing).

McDowell, J. (2001) *Godfathers: Inside Northern Ireland's Drug Racket* (Dublin: Gill & Macmillan).

Minogue, K. (1996) "Machiavelli and the duck/rabbit problem of political perception", *Government and Opposition*, 31.2: 216–26.

Neumann, P. (2003) *Britain's Long War: British Strategy in the Northern Ireland Conflict, 1969–1998* (New York: Palgrave Macmillan).

Shirlow, P. and McGovern, M. (eds) (1997) *Who Are The People? Unionism, Protestantism and Loyalism in Northern Ireland* (London: Pluto Press).

Progressive Unionist Party (2002) *Principles of Loyalism*. An internal discussion paper (Belfast: PUP).

Silke, A. (1999) "Ragged justice: Loyalist vigilantism in Northern Ireland", *Terrorism and Political Violence*, 11.3: 1–31.

Silke, A. (2000) "Drink, drugs, and rock "n" roll: financing Loyalist terrorism in Northern Ireland—part two", *Studies in Conflict and Terrorism*, 23: 107–27.

Smith, M. L. R. (1999) "The intellectual internment of a conflict: the forgotten war in Northern Ireland", *International Affairs*, 74.1: 77–97.

Smith, M. L. R. (1997) *Fighting for Ireland? The Military Strategy of the Irish Republican Movement* (London: Routledge).

Smith, M. L. R. (1995) "Holding fire: strategic theory and the missing military dimension in the academic study of Northern Ireland", in A. O'Day (ed.) *Terrorism's Laboratory: The Case of Northern Ireland* (Aldershot: Dartmouth).

Smith, M. L. R. (1991) "The role of the military instrument in Irish Republican strategic thinking: an evolutionary analysis" (PhD dissertation, University of London).

Todd, J. (1987) "Two traditions in Ulster political culture", *Irish Political Studies*, 2: 1–26.

*Warrior* Ulster Defence Association.

# 22

# A weapon in the struggle? Loyalist paramilitarism and the politics of auto/biography in contemporary Northern Ireland

*Stephen Hopkins*

## Introduction

Writing about individuals and their experience of the Troubles has been well-represented in recent published works about the conflict in Northern Ireland, whether in autobiography, biography or political memoir. This chapter is predicated on the belief that Northern Ireland's perceived movement towards a "post-conflict" environment has given fresh impetus to the long-established tradition of political auto/biography associated with the historical development of Anglo-Irish relations. Many protagonists or ex-protagonists of the "Troubles" now feel the time is ripe to tell their stories to a wider public, to explain their motivations and to try to shape the debate over the rights and wrongs of the conflict.

This chapter analyses several authors and subjects, some of whom have used this type of publication to engage in self-critical reappraisal of previous commitments and actions, but more generally writing in this genre and at this juncture has involved a large measure of self-justification. The auto/biographical design may well, in this event, represent a proxy weapon in an ongoing ideological struggle. In interpreting political auto/biography in the Northern Irish context, therefore, we need to be mindful of what Roy Foster (2002: 3) has described as "the deliberate gap in the narrative: the momentous elision, the leap in the story". Auto/biographical writing may have a significant role to play in contemporary political discourse in Northern Ireland, by providing an opportunity for individual narratives to be told in their entirety, retaining their integrity, unlike for instance legal process: "law does not permit a single witness to tell their own coherent narrative; it chops their stories into digestible parts" (Hegarty, 2002: 100). This writing may also provide a symbolic, collective and communal element to this process of narrative construction, particularly when the authors or subjects are viewed as emblematic individuals. However, as these examples of loyalist and Protestant auto/biography demonstrate, the lacunae that often characterise these stories make this process complex and uncertain, especially where there is still no public consensus about the essential causes of conflict.

### Loyalist paramilitarism and auto/biography: a new phenomenon?

There has been a long tradition of Irish republican and nationalist writing that has conflated individual protagonists' lives with the "story" of the nation. This personalisation of Irish republican history can be traced back at least as far as the nineteenth century, and this approach remains popular in the contemporary period (e.g., Adams, 1982, 1990, 1996, 2003; Morrison, 1999, 2002; MacStiofain, 1975).

By contrast, within loyalist paramilitarism it is difficult to discern a similar tradition, at least until recently, even if republican efforts to "re-write the script" and control the narrative of the peace process have proved irksome (Gillespie, 2006: 139). With only a few exceptions, loyalists have seemed inarticulate and slow to react to this transparent republican strategy to control the narrative "telling" of the conflict. Within Ulster unionism, the prevailing tradition of auto/biographical writing has been the ministerial memoir, firmly based upon the parliamentary arena, and mirroring the Cabinet reminiscences of Westminster politicians; in this sub-genre, Brian Faulkner's *Memoirs of a Statesman* (1977) is a classic. There is also a range of autobiographical works from within the wider Protestant working-class community, although these are not always explicitly political in outlook (e.g., Harbinson, 1960; Boyd, 1985, 1990). Also, there is a fine tradition of autobiographically-inspired writing for the theatre, specifically documenting the Belfast Protestant working-class experience (e.g., Thompson, 1997; Mitchell, 1998, 2001; Reid, 1984).

With regard to loyalism and specifically self-writing from within the paramilitary milieu, until recently there was a paucity of material available. There have been several fictional attempts to imagine the world of the UDA and the UVF—some more successful than others; the neglected *Silver's City* (1981) by Maurice Leitch is a persuasive portrayal of an ageing loyalist leader. There are several possible explanations for this: sociologically, it could be argued that working-class Protestant culture in Northern Ireland and the social groups that formed the bedrock of loyalist paramilitary personnel did not set great store by literary forms of cultural presentation. In what is now considered something of a clichéd view, but one that, nevertheless, may contain some truth, working-class Protestant educational values placed greater emphasis upon craft, technical and scientific training than upon the arts and humanities. For loyalists, auto/biographical literary production was simply less likely to be considered as a vehicle for self-expression, or political articulation. There has also been considerable debate concerning the alleged "defeatism" and "fatalism" within Northern Ireland's Protestant population and we can speculate that this may have inhibited the production of life-writing (Finlay, 2001; Aughey, 2001).

Second, both unionists and loyalists felt no requirement to construct a personalised narrative of their history, in which the political experiences of emblematic individuals could stand as symbols of their community's forbearance and suffering. After all, unionists were in control of the machinery of the state through much of the twentieth century and thus had little need to develop a mythologised version of their historical fortitude. Many working-class loyalists, despite their precarious social circumstances, could also buy into this "official" history of Northern Ireland's elite. On a broader canvas, it was also the case that loyalists strongly identified with the British imperial grand narrative. Interestingly, in a study of the British military and its literary output, it has been argued that recent autobiographical works about soldiering and war identify "militarism and imperialism as central concerns of British national identity" (Newsinger, 1997: 39). There has been a significant growth in this type of memoir in the period since the Falklands conflict, and some of it has dealt specifically with the British Army's experience in Northern Ireland (e.g., Curtis, 2003; Rennie, 1996; Lewis, 1999). Arguably, we can also place the recent spate of memoirs by former police officers of the RUC in a similar sub-genre, and publishers clearly believe there is a similar market for this kind of narrative (Hermon, 1997; Barker, 2004; Latham, 2001; Brown, 2005). We can agree with Newsinger (1997: 39) that these "military memoirs are a literary form that has received little critical attention, at least in part, one suspects, because the experiences recounted are so uncongenial to most students of literary and cultural studies".

Third, as republican "dissident" Anthony McIntyre (2003) has pointed out, "in the world of publishing, loyalism is not the marketable commodity that has earned Republicanism considerable capital in terms of public interest". In terms of "popular" literature and journalism, some recent works have begun to rectify this gap: Jim Cusack and Henry McDonald have completed general histories of both the UVF (1997) and the UDA (2004) and Peter Taylor's *Loyalists*

(1999) undertook a general survey. Geoffrey Beattie's *Protestant Boy* (2004), detailing the author's relationship with his family and his past in Ligoniel in North Belfast, inevitably explores aspects of the loyalist paramilitary experience in one of the crucibles of the conflict. Other works, including the same author's *We are the People: Journeys through the Heart of Protestant Ulster* (1992), and Susan McKay's *Northern Protestants: An Unsettled People* (2000), also include significant sections devoted to loyalist politics. Among academics, the apparent aversion to the study of loyalism has been partially addressed since the 1990s in the work of Steve Bruce (1992, 1994), Peter Shirlow and Mark McGovern (1997), Colin Crawford (1999, 2003), Jim McAuley (1994; 2005), Ian Wood (2006) and others. Nonetheless, both in terms of academic and popular writing, "the republican/ loyalist imbalance shows few signs of being incrementally adjusted, loyalism [is] permanently locked in the catch up spot" (McIntyre, 2003). Bearing in mind these potential explanations for the relative dearth of interest in loyalist paramilitarism, at least until recently, we turn now to an examination of contemporary writing about loyalist paramilitary actors and their political world.

### A line in the sand? Authorial motivation and loyalist paramilitary auto/biography

At one level, it is not too surprising that there has been a growth in auto/biographical writing among (and about) loyalists in Northern Ireland. After all, memoir as a genre (and political auto/biography as a sub-genre) has been a publishing phenomenon in the latter part of the twentieth and the early years of the twenty-first centuries. Equally, there are specific causes for this increased output: as Northern Ireland moved tentatively towards a transitional, "post-conflict" phase, some of the key protagonists of the thirty-five year "Troubles" began to contemplate telling their "stories" to a wider public, explaining their interpretation of the conflict, its genesis and its outcome (if, indeed, the conflict could be said to be definitively over).

Indeed, the "truth" about which of the antagonistic groups had been primarily responsible for the outbreak and continuation of violent conflict and even what had been at stake, was pushed to one side in the understandable desire to end the violence. Since 2001, five key individuals in the contemporary history of loyalism have either published autobiographical accounts or been the subject of biographies (whether "authorised" or not): Roy Garland wrote *Gusty Spence* about one of the veteran members of the reformed UVF (2001); Henry Sinnerton wrote the biography of another political representative of this strand of loyalism, organised in the PUP, *David Ervine: Uncharted Waters* (2002); Michael Stone, the notorious Milltown cemetery loyalist terrorist, published a ghost-written autobiography (2003); David Lister and Hugh Jordan (2003) produced a collective biography of the UDA's Lower Shankill organisation and its leader through the 1990s, Johnny Adair; and Chris Anderson (2004) wrote a biography (or perhaps necrography) of the leader of the Loyalist Volunteer Force (LVF), a splinter group from the UVF, Billy Wright (2002). In addition, Adair has published his own autobiographical account (2007).

Two distinct trends could be observed in these works: on one hand, there may be a sincere effort on behalf of protagonists to draw a "line in the sand", to move away from sterile ideological antagonism and inflexibility towards a self-critical reappraisal of previous commitments and shibboleths. On the other, the idea of a "line in the sand" may, of course, be used in a more traditional loyalist sense also, summed up in the classic slogans of "No Surrender!", "What we have we hold!", and "Not an Inch!" (Longley, 1997: 110). There is probably clearer evidence of this trend in the autobiographies under consideration here. Fionola Meredith, in an insightful interview with Richard English, author of a recent major study of the IRA based largely on interviews with republican activists, makes a telling point with regard to the utility of these auto/biographical projects:

> Why then should we accept the "authenticity" of their self-reflexive accounts as holding any more significance, insight or weight than a more "objective" analysis? The experiential narrative offered by "someone who's been through it" can be as duplicitous and untrustworthy as it is vivid. The truth-claim based on experience is often furthest from veracity.

Meredith goes on to conclude that "the most fundamental impulse in the stories of those who have committed politically-motivated violent atrocities will nearly always be self-justification. That's the difficulty with narrative accounts—their need for legitimacy means that the truths they offer are partial, loaded and incomplete" (Meredith, 2003).

It may well be the case that loyalists are keen to contest the republican version of the rights and wrongs of the Northern Ireland conflict, but there may also be more prosaic (and less edifying) reasons for this spate of publications. As has been pointed out, "the political memoir has become an expected rite of passage for political celebrity, and also a highly profitable one" (Gamble, 2002: 142). This element of celebrity (or notoriety), allied with a widespread unease about the financial gains that erstwhile paramilitaries might make from writing sensationalist accounts of their exploits, has been the subject of lively debate in Northern Ireland. This trend towards the conflation of celebrity, violent crime and sensationalism is now well established in mainstream British popular culture, as evidenced by the glamourisation of gangsterism in recent films such as *Lock, Stock and Two Smoking Barrels* (1998) and the growth in the "true crime" genre.

In the context of Northern Ireland, it was probably inevitable, though nonetheless a matter of regret for many, that (ex-)paramilitaries would also haul themselves onto the bandwagon. A victims' group, Relatives for Justice, sought legal advice to try and prevent Michael Stone from reaping profit from the publication of *None Shall Divide Us*, but the Northern Ireland Office issued a statement indicating that the Proceeds of Crime Act "does not cover the writing of a memoir, however profitable".[1] In 2006, it was reported that Johnny Adair had been signed up to publish his autobiography by John Blake, for a reputed advance of nearly £100,000. Adair argued that, "when I look at my bookshelf, there are at least four books about me written by journalists. If they can make money writing about my life then why can't I do the same?" He betrayed some confusion regarding the motivation for his venture, however, stating that he wanted to "tell it as it is, warts and all . . . I don't intend to hold anything back, and I want to expose these so-called loyalists [the UDA leadership that expelled Adair in 2002] for the gangsters, bullyboys and informers that they are"; in the same interview, he also admitted he would be taking legal advice to make sure "I don't talk myself into any trouble when I look back at my past".[2]

Home Secretary John Reid announced in October 2006 that he would be seeking to introduce new legislation to prevent (ex-)criminals from indulging in this kind of profiteering. Expressing sentiments that are undoubtedly widely shared in Northern Ireland, Gail Walker excoriated Adair and others who had gone into print with their "250 pages of bold-type whitewash PR, with murder and mayhem thrown in to titillate the bloodlust of the reader". She was disturbed by the fact that publishers liked "to flog them as if they are contributing to the scientific knowledge of Ulster's war", but she was even more disconcerted at the "large market for these "kill and tells" here".[3]

Of course, emotions continue to run high in an atmosphere where ideological differences over past deeds are never far from the surface of political discourse. However, the tendency to dismiss these narratives, even though they may well be untrustworthy and contemptuous of victims' sensitivities, is mistaken on at least two counts. First, the act of self-writing often tempts authors on to the paths of "vindication, exculpation and the byways of personal interest", whether intentionally or subconsciously (Egerton, 1994: 344). Whether being deliberately self-serving or manipulating the historical narrative for contemporary ideological purposes, "the memoirist is almost invariably self-betrayed into the hands of the later historian" (ibid: 347).

Second, professional political scientists or historians, accustomed to the rigorous demands of a disciplined historiography, have displayed an understandable tendency to downplay the significance of political memoir, but there is often a paucity of reliable documentary evidence with which to work. In these circumstances, reliance upon the historian's usual injunction to collect, collate and evaluate documentary material will not yield a complete picture. Indeed, it is in the nature of the Northern Ireland conflict, where a good deal of "political" activity (particularly, but not exclusively, the use of violence for political ends) has been necessarily clandestine and conspiratorial, that much of what is now accepted by historians as "conventional wisdom" has been gleaned from memoir and personal testimony, and the related field of oral history. For example, in possibly the most rigorous academic study of the UDA, Wood (2006: 150) explicitly praises the biography of Adair by Lister and Jordan as "compelling and meticulously detailed." So while these accounts must be treated with due caution, not least because they are often mutually contradictory and sometimes internally inconsistent, they ought to be recognised for their potential as a valuable resource for researchers.

### A confusion of voices: author and subject in loyalist auto/biography

Alongside the question of the motivation behind some of the recent crop of loyalist auto/biographical publications, it is also important to consider the confused authorship of some of these works. In some cases, like the biography of Billy Wright, there is little room for doubt about the nature of the enterprise: after all, the subject of the biography could not cooperate in this project, having been killed inside the Maze by republican inmates in December 1997. In their introduction, the authors of *Mad Dog* "are at pains to stress that this is not an autobiography of Johnny Adair" (Lister and Jordan, 2003), which is a rather strange statement, given that Adair's name is not featured anywhere as an author of the book. Adair himself was certainly interested in the project, but this is definitely not an authorised account of his life: "During a lengthy interview inside Maghaberry Prison and a series of telephone conversations, Johnny Adair blew hot and cold. When the mood took him, he spoke freely and we acknowledge that contribution" (ibid.).

However, it is clear that the authors do wish to make it known that they have received at least some cooperation from their subject. They lay bare Adair's instrumental approach to telling his life story: "In May 2003, during the first of many telephone conversations from the jail, he said he wanted to write his autobiography and offered to do this with the authors" (ibid: 18). Informed that this was not the plan of the biographers, Adair then asked for some share of the profits, if he were to cooperate further: " 'What's in it for me? What am I going to get out of this?' he demanded . . . The minute Adair realised there was no money in it for him, his interest died" (ibid: 18). At various points in the story, Lister and Jordan question the veracity of his version of his life, as presented to them by Adair. Another author who interviewed Adair on several occasions underlined the fact that he "can be highly selective about what he wants to remember" (Wood, 2006: 171).

Michael Stone's autobiography is presented *as if* Stone himself had written it; his name alone appears on the cover and title page. However, in the introduction, journalist Karen McManus claims some sort of authorial status: "to my critics, of whom I expect there will be plenty, I would say just one thing: I do not intend this book to be a glorification of the life of Michael Stone. I do not intend this book to glamorise his life as a paramilitary" (Stone, 2003: xi). It is not unusual for autobiographies to be "ghosted" by sympathetic journalists, of course, though such works tend to have celebrities or sportspersons as their subject, or individuals not otherwise known for their literary dexterity. It is also usual for this relationship between "author" and ghost-writer to be made plain to the reader. As Malachi O'Doherty shrewdly recognised, "this is not a psychological portrait of a killer, but it is the raw material from which such a book might be written. Everywhere there are stories which an astute reader will understand better than the writer and his assistant have done."[4]

In his biography of Gusty Spence, Roy Garland is both personally and politically close to his subject, and much of the material in the book consists of edited transcripts of the men's "conversations", a word he uses advisedly, arguing that " 'interview' seems much too formal a description of our many discussions" (Garland, 2001: ix). The copious use of this first-person testimony and the relative lack of interpretative text from Garland, means that the reader is constantly encouraged to read this book as if Spence himself were the author. Garland's obvious admiration for his subject does not prevent him from stating that "in writing this book it has not been my intention to glamourise or lionise Gusty Spence, nor would he want this" (ibid: 311) and it is certainly no hagiography. A key interviewee for Garland was leading PUP figure, David Ervine, the subject of Henry Sinnerton's biography, which adopts a similar approach, and is also based upon the active collaboration of the subject.

However, it could be that greater critical distance between biographer and subject would ultimately have left less room for ambiguity concerning who was really directing and narrating the project. In the case of both Stone and Spence, the authentic "voice" of the subject has clearly been mediated or filtered by a journalist/biographer. What is more difficult to discern is the precise nature of the relationship between mediator and subject. Who is really in control of the structure and content of the narrative? Who speaks through whom? Paradoxically, it does seem as though Spence and Ervine might enjoy a greater degree of influence over the narrative structure of their "biographies" than Stone does over his own "autobiography".

### An enclosed world? Localism and loyalist auto/biography

A key criterion when judging the historical utility of these autobiographies is the authors' willingness or capacity to place their individual experiences within a broader political framework. However much controversy they have generated, and however disputed their accounts of life within the loyalist paramilitary milieu, they do differ significantly in their attitude to this wider context. Ultimately, some of these memoirs are of limited interest to the contemporary political historian in that they are primarily concerned with the minutiae of paramilitary activities and personalities, engagements with the "enemy", and so forth. This may well be the result of a deliberate authorial or publishing decision to highlight these aspects, often with an eye on sales and the sensationalist appetites of populist audiences, or it may be that these "foot-soldiers" have a relative lack of concern, knowledge or even understanding of the broader framework within which their particular dramas were played out. These works are useful, nonetheless, in pointing up the diverse experiences of the 'different "worlds"' that exist in Northern Ireland in relation to the "Troubles" (Smyth and Fay, 2000: 133).

For instance, some of the works studied here show how defiantly parochial the experience and interests of many loyalist paramilitaries are: Johnny Adair was relatively unconcerned with the wider political context within which he directed the activities of the UDA's Lower Shankill C Company. He often seems to have been exasperated with the internal political compromises required in a relatively loose organisational structure such as the one utilised by the UDA and, in discussions with "brigadiers" from other areas in the province, Adair showed little patience or desire to contemplate pressures that were not central to the experience of the Shankill loyalist community. Indeed, he seemed uninterested and even bored by political or intellectual discussion, and rarely intervened in meetings, such as the one held with Secretary of State, Mo Mowlam in the Maze in January 1998 (Lister and Jordan, 2003; Wood, 2006; Stone, 2003). He was streetwise enough to understand that after the renewal of the IRA ceasefire in 1997, resuming the simplistic, but powerful, militaristic campaign of the early 1990s was not a realistic option for loyalists; but, building a genuine non-violent political career was not something that appealed to Adair in the new dispensation.

Unlike some of those who had served lengthy jail terms for UVF activities, and who had fallen under the influence of Gusty Spence (for example, David Ervine, Martin Snodden and Billy Hutchinson of the PUP), Adair's spurious claim to be keen on constructing such a political route, based around his close relationship with John White (Wood, 2006), was proved groundless by the subsequent ignominious collapse of the C Company "empire". He simply did not have the skills or aptitude for such a transformation. Within the UDA, whilst Adair was a charismatic leader of his immediate "team", he was never wholly trusted outside his confined, claustrophobic geographical area and he could not articulate a mobilising political vision along the lines of some other leading figures from the organisation's recent past, such as John McMichael or Ray Smallwoods. Other than "fighting fire with fire" and "taking the war" to the republican movement and the community from which it drew its support and sympathy, Adair's political strategy was almost entirely undeveloped. In some ways, as a microcosm of the brutalisation visited by the "Troubles" upon the Shankill, and the political-cultural vacuum at the centre of loyalist West Belfast by the 1990s, Adair and C Company could be said to authentically "represent" or symbolise the impoverished political culture of this area.

Yet, for other loyalists, sometimes of a different political generation, similar objective social circumstances could certainly produce highly divergent political trajectories; this is most obvious in the highly localistic sectarian patchwork of Belfast (Shirlow and Murtagh, 2006). The position of loyalist paramilitaries in South or East Belfast, where David Ervine and Michael Stone became active, was rather different from that of loyalists in the West or North of the city and different again from the Portadown experience of Billy Wright (Anderson, 2004). Crudely, loyalists were in the overwhelming majority in East Belfast, and their position was relatively secure, whereas in West and North Belfast the perception that hostile, enemy forces were just around the corner (on occasion, literally) produced a highly unstable and fearful mentality, both the fabled "siege mentality", but also, as Longley has argued, a "self-besieging" posture.

The socio-economic deprivation endured in working-class loyalist districts of the city in the earlier years of the twentieth century is vividly recalled in the testimony of Gusty Spence. For Johnny Adair and Michael Stone social conditions were somewhat less deprived by the 1960s, but the labourist ideological impulses (exemplified in the mid-century evolution of the Northern Ireland Labour Party) of the earlier generation were in steep decline by the mid-1970s. Ervine and others in the PUP would try to reinvigorate this tradition as progressive loyalism in the 1990s (Edwards and Bloomer, 2004) but with little obvious electoral success and to the scorn of loyalists like Adair. The latter's early ideological influences had come from a very different source: the neo-fascism and violent rhetoric of the late-1970s skinhead movement.

The most astonishing example of the same circumstances coinciding with very different political beliefs comes from Spence who, together with his brother, Ned/Eddie, was raised in the hard conditions of the Hammer district of the Lower Shankill during the 1930s. Ned broke with Orangeism, became a socialist and trade unionist, then a member of the Communist Party and, in the late 1960s, joined the Northern Ireland Civil Rights Association. Meanwhile, Gusty served in the British Army in Cyprus and on his return to Belfast joined the reborn UVF and was convicted of the 1966 murder of a Catholic barman, Peter Ward. He served almost nineteen years for the crime, before his release in 1984. Spence wrote privately to his brother:

> As you know I have very much changed—not because of what prison has done to me, but because of what I have done for myself. If I had to serve a lifetime in dungeons like these, I wanted to know for what reason, and I searched for the truth . . . I feel deeply embarrassed when I think of my former "truths" which when investigated did not stand up to scrutiny or fact. (Garland, 2001: 244–5)

The localism of Spence's experience was extreme and it is clear that his remarkable approach to his long years in prison and the autodidactic education he gained there helped him to transcend his enclosed world and draw broader lessons for his own ideological beliefs, the future of the UVF and loyalist politics generally.

Other loyalist prisoners made much less of their prison experiences. Michael Stone, who was convicted for the Milltown cemetery attack on republican mourners in 1988 and other offences, served twelve years before being released in 2000 under the terms of the Belfast Agreement. There are a number of tensions, if not downright contradictions, in Stone's account of his motivation for publishing his autobiography. In the foreword he offers an apology to the families of those he killed, but immediately nullifies this by stating: "I regret that I had to kill [. . .] I committed crimes as an Ulsterman and a British citizen and that was regrettable but unavoidable" (Stone, 2003: xiv). The sincerity of his expression of regret is further undermined by the decision (either Stone's or the publisher's) to include in the book the celebratory "Ballad of Michael Stone", which refers to those killed at Milltown as "rebel scum". His autobiographical tone is that of a veteran, though Stone was only 50 at the time of publication. But what is most instructive about Stone's reflection on his prison experiences is how little he appears to have connected with the political developments that were taking place during the 1990s.

The emphasis upon self-discipline and self-improvement in the prison regime set up by Gusty Spence for UVF inmates in the 1970s and 1980s, stands in stark contrast to the picture painted by Lister and Jordan, Anderson and Michael Stone for a later period. Dillon (2003) has argued that the solitariness of loyalist paramilitary prisoners' experience could lead some individuals to embrace religion and adopt born-again fundamentalist Christian tenets, and Billy Wright arguably provided one example of this phenomenon. For Adair, his periods behind bars from 1995 until 1999 (and subsequently) seems to have provided the opportunity to plot and embark on personalised rivalries and vendettas (not least with his erstwhile "hero", Stone). This dispute is not political in origin or content, but is better understood as emanating from internecine power struggles, petty jealousies and a competitive urge to be viewed as the most "notorious" of the loyalist icons.

### Conclusion

Ultimately, this survey of recent loyalist auto/biography tends to confirm an emerging academic consensus with regard to some core distinctions to be drawn between the trajectory of many leading figures in the UVF/PUP, on the one hand, and those within the UDA/Ulster Democratic Party tradition, on the other. Whether auto/biographical works are characterised by a politically conscious and, at least partial, self-criticism (as in the cases of Spence and Ervine), or whether they are apparently motivated primarily by commercial and parochial interests (as in the cases of Stone and Adair), all of them can shed light upon the multiple loyalist narratives of the Northern Ireland conflict, even where it is the "gaps" in the stories that appear most telling. Of course, researchers (especially from outside Northern Ireland itself) may be expected to take a more detached attitude towards these works than those who have lived day to day with some of the consequences of paramilitary violence, particularly the direct victims/survivors of some of the protagonists considered here. Still, this chapter has argued that political auto/biography by prominent or (in)famous actors in the "Troubles" can provide a symbolic and collective aspect to a necessary process of addressing, if not "coming to terms", with the past in Northern Ireland. However complex or even contradictory some of the results, a fuller, more rounded understanding of what motivated these actors is only one necessary condition for edging towards a public consensus, concerning the rights and wrongs inflicted and suffered by all parties to the civil strife. It will almost certainly be impossible to find agreement about the essential character of the Northern Ireland conflict, its causes and even its outcome. For all their many problematic elements, these auto/biographical works can be used to contribute to this very necessary debate about the past.

## Notes

1  *Sunday Life*, 8 June 2003; *Belfast Telegraph*, 29 August 2003; *An Phoblacht/Republican News*, 29 May 2003.
2  *Observer*, 21 May 2006.
3  *Belfast Telegraph*, 31 October 2006.
4  *Belfast Telegraph*, 11 June 2003.

## References

Adair, J. (with McKendry, G.) (2007) *Mad Dog* (London: John Blake).
Adams, G. (1982), *Falls Memories* (Dingle: Brandon).
Adams, G. (1990) *Cage Eleven* (Dingle: Brandon).
Adams, G. (1996) *Before the Dawn: An Autobiography* (Dingle: Brandon).
Adams, G. (2003) *Hope and History: Making Peace in Ireland* (Dingle: Brandon/Mount Eagle).
Anderson, C. (2004) *The Billy Boy: The Life and Death of LVF Leader Billy Wright* (Edinburgh: Mainstream).
Aughey, A. (2001) "Learning from 'The Leopard'", in R. Wilford (ed.) *Aspects of the Belfast Agreement* (Oxford: Oxford University Press).
Barker, A. (2004) *Shadows: Inside Northern Ireland's Special Branch* (Edinburgh: Mainstream).
Beattie, G. (1992) *We Are The People: Journeys Through the Heart of Protestant Ulster* (London: Heinemann).
Beattie, G. (2004) *Protestant Boy* (London: Granta).
Boyd, J. (1985) *Out of My Class* (Belfast: Blackstaff).
Boyd, J. (1990) *The Middle of My Journey* (Belfast: Blackstaff).
Brown, J. (2005) *Into the Dark: 30 Years in the RUC* (Dublin: Gill & Macmillan).
Bruce, S. (1992) *The Red Hand: Protestant Paramilitaries in Northern Ireland* (Oxford: Oxford University Press).

Bruce, S. (1994) *The Edge of the Union: The Ulster Loyalist Political Vision* (Oxford: Oxford University Press).

Crawford, C. (1999) *Defenders or Criminals? Loyalist Prisoners and Criminalisation* (Belfast: Blackstaff).

Crawford, C. (2003) *Inside the UDA: Volunteers and Violence* (London: Pluto).

Curtis, N. (2003) *Faith and Duty: The True Story of a Soldier's War in Northern Ireland* (London: Andre Deutsch).

Cusack, J. and McDonald, H. (1997) *UVF* (Dublin: Poolbeg Press).

Dillon, M. (2003)*The Trigger Men* (Edinburgh: Mainstream).

Edwards, A. and Bloomer, S. (2004) *A Watching Brief? The Political Strategy of Progressive Loyalism since 1994* Conflict Transformation Papers, 8 (Belfast: LINC Resource Centre).

Egerton, G. (ed.) (1994) *Political Memoir: Essays on the Politics of Memory* (London: Frank Cass).

Faulkner, B. (1978) *Memoirs of a Statesman* (London: Weidenfeld & Nicolson).

Finlay, A. (2001) "Defeatism and Northern Protestant 'identity'", *Global Review of Ethnopolitics*, 1.2: 3–20.

Foster, R. (2002) *The Irish Story: Telling Tales and Making it Up in Ireland* (London: Penguin).

Gamble, A. (2002) "Political memoirs", *British Journal of Politics and International Relations*, 4.1: 141–51.

Garland, R. (2001) *Gusty Spence* (Belfast: Blackstaff Press).

Gillespie, G. (2006) "Noises off: loyalists after the Agreement", in M. Cox, A. Guelke, and F. Stephen (eds) *A Farewell to Arms? Beyond the Good Friday Agreement* (Manchester: Manchester University Press).

Harbinson, R. (1987[1960]) *No Surrender: An Ulster Childhood* (Belfast: Blackstaff Press).

Hegarty, A. (2002) "Truth, justice and reconciliation? The problem with truth processes", *Global Review of Ethnopolitics*, 2.1: 97–103.

Hermon, J. (1997) *Holding the Line: An Autobiography* (Dublin: Gill & Macmillan).

Latham, R. (2001) *Deadly Beat: Inside the Royal Ulster Constabulary* (Edinburgh: Mainstream).

Leitch, M. (1981) *Silver's City* (London: Secker & Warburg).

Lewis, R. (1999) *Fishers of Men* (London: Hodder & Stoughton).

Lister, D. and Jordan, H. (2003) *Mad Dog: The Rise and Fall of Johnny Adair and 'C' Company* (Edinburgh: Mainstream).

Longley, E. (1997) "What do Protestants want?" *Irish Review*, 20: 104–20.

MacStiofáin, S. (1975) *Revolutionary in Ireland* (Edinburgh: Gordon Cremonesi).

McAuley, J. (1994) *The Politics of Identity: Protestant Working-Class Politics and Culture in Belfast* (Aldershot: Avebury).

McAuley, J. (2005) "Whither new Loyalism? Changing loyalist Politics after the Belfast Agreement", *Irish Political Studies*, 20.3: 323–40.

McDonald, H. and Cusack, J. (2004) *UDA: Inside the Heart of Loyalist Terror* (Dublin: Penguin Ireland).

McIntyre, A. (2003) "Uncharted waters", *The Other View*, Autumn.

McKay, S. (2000) *Northern Protestants: An Unsettled People* (Belfast: Blackstaff).

Meredith, F. (2003) "Rounded, intelligent, articulate, human and murderous", *Fortnight*, 412.

Mitchell, G. (1998) *Tearing the Loom* and *In a Little World of Our Own* (London: Nick Hern).

Mitchell, G. (2001) *As the Beast Sleeps* (London: Nick Hern).

Morrison, D. (1999) *Then the Walls Came Down: A Prison Journal* (Cork and Dublin: Mercier).

Morrison, D. (2002) *All the Dead Voices* (Cork and Dublin: Mercier).

Newsinger, J. (1997) *Dangerous Men: The SAS and Popular Culture* (London: Pluto Press).

O'Doherty, M. (2003) "Book review: Michael Stone—Wee Mikey looking for a pat on the head", *Belfast Telegraph* (11 June).

Reid, G. (1984) *Billy: Three Plays for Television* (London: Faber & Faber).

Rennie, J. (1996) *The Operators* (London: Century).

Shirlow, P. and McGovern, M. (eds) (1997) *Who are "The People"? Unionism, Protestantism and Loyalism in Northern Ireland* (London: Pluto).

Shirlow, P. and Murtagh, B. (2006) *Belfast: Segregation, Violence and the City* (London: Pluto).

Sinnerton, H. (2002) *David Ervine: Uncharted Waters* (Dingle: Brandon).

Smyth, M. and Fay, M.-T. (2000) *Personal Accounts from Northern Ireland's Troubles: Public Conflict, Private Loss* (London: Pluto).

Stone, M. (2003) *None Shall Divide Us* (London: John Blake).

Taylor, P. (1999) *Loyalists* (London: Bloomsbury).

Thompson, S. (1997) *Three Plays: Over the Bridge, The Evangelist, Cemented with Love* (Belfast: Lagan).

Wood, I. (2006) *Crimes of Loyalty: A History of the UDA* (Edinburgh: Edinburgh University Press).

# 23

# Containment and the politics of loyalist-based conflict transformation

*Brian Graham*

## Introduction

The particular focus of this chapter is on loyalist politically motivated former prisoners and the factors constraining their capacity to contribute to conflict transformation in Northern Ireland. I examine the ways in which they are involved in peace building and societal transition and evaluate the impediments placed upon their activities, not least of which stem from the effects of residual criminalisation. While the issue remains on the table as a result of the 2006 St Andrews Agreement, as yet, neither British nor Irish governments have been prepared to remove all the barriers to full citizenship that face politically motivated former prisoners. It has been found useful in assessing these issues to compare and contrast loyalists with their republican counterparts.

## Conflict transformation

In general terms, conflict transformation refers to methods that alter the nature of the conflict from violence to some other means (Lederach, 1997). There is a vital distinction, however, between loyalists and republicans regarding the nature and meaning of conflict. The essential key to its ideological mindset is to understand that physical-force republicanism was—and remains by other means—engaged in resistance against the British state rather than loyalists. That state is held to have been responsible for the oppression and torture of republicans while, simultaneously, trying to deny that it was an active participant in the war. For loyalism, the conflict was much more straightforwardly a "civil war", being caused by republicans seeking to "bomb" northern Protestants into a united Ireland.

The concept of containment emanates from the idea of isolating a political opponent from either a support base or wider civic society (usually achieved by demonisation or stereotyping). Containment is thus concerned with isolating and marginalising opponents by controlling political, media, cultural and even military environments. It is usually presented in terms of controlling those who aim to subvert democracy, the anticipated result being that as opponents become more contained, any additional subversive acts that they undertake will create additional isolation and further hinder their political and ideological effectiveness beyond a faithful rump of supporters. Sinn Fein effectively challenged British strategies of containment by entering constitutional politics, a tactic which allowed that organisation to set aside the ideological framework of militant republicanism shaped by their claim to be the true heirs of the "martyrs" of 1916. Loyalism, however, remains contained from within, not so much by the activities of the state as by the negative and marginalising attitudes of the so-called "middle unionism" of the DUP and UUP.

Within this framework of containment, the specific objectives of this chapter are threefold: first, to discuss the general contribution of loyalist politically motivated former prisoners to processes of conflict transformation, but also to examine the constraints on those activities. It then moves to a discussion as to how these activities are constructed both within loyalist communities and between then and their republican counterparts. Finally, the chapter compares and contrasts the contribution of loyalist and republican former prisoners to conflict transformation, demonstrating that the relative exposure of the former to containment strategies within unionism renders them singularly less effective. The chapter draws upon evidence from a much larger research project conducted with former prisoner groups in north and west Belfast during 2004–05, which was the first sustained attempt to investigate the impact of imprisonment and the role of politically motivated former prisoners—loyalist and republican—in the process of conflict transformation in Northern Ireland (McEvoy and Shirlow, 2008). All quotations included in this present chapter—unless otherwise referenced—derive from interviews, workshops and focus groups conducted as part of this larger research project.

## Former prisoners and conflict transformation

The fate of former prisoners and combatants in the process of transition from conflict has been widely recognised as central to attempts at peacemaking (McEvoy, 2001). The traditional focus of much of this kind of work has been to break up armed groups as quickly as possible and remove their weapons in order to better protect and provide security. More recently, however, the gaze of the international community on this issue has shifted somewhat. As the then Secretary-General of the United Nations, Kofi Annan, argued in 2004 during a speech at the University of Ulster's Magee campus in Derry/Londonderry, peace cannot be secured without "providing the fighters with an alternative, peaceful means of earning their living. Nowadays we no longer contemplate demobilisation and disarmament—the two "D's"—without adding an "R", which stands for reintegration into the civilian economy" (Annan, 2004).

While reintegration can be about securing individual rights and entitlements, former prisoners in Northern Ireland are making a much broader impact upon the peace process. Indeed, although the point does not apply to many members of the present-day *Ard Chomhairle*, former prisoners remain highly influential in the Sinn Fein leadership. But this present discussion goes beyond "high" politics. It is contended that many former combatants and prisoners have provided leadership, or have that capacity, in preventing the resumption of organised political and communal violence, a role that may involve physical engagement on the streets. Despite the rhetoric of a "shared future" being promoted by the British and Irish governments, the conflict in Northern Ireland remains inherently territorial, and the "ground" a key political resource.

Identities remain constructed around territoriality which essentially replicates nationalist ideologies at the local scale. This territoriality reflects the continuing importance of place to social networks and mental and emotional bindings, while control of space is still regarded as being crucial to identity, power and politics (Graham and Nash, 2006). It also remains a key factor in the contested nature of Northern Ireland's society, "a symbol of political domination and political practice" (Shirlow, 2001: 69). The effects of territoriality are experienced most acutely at interfaces being transmitted primarily through "chill factors" (fears regarding entering a community dominated by the ethno-sectarian "other"). Territorial separation is both symbolic and practised through the minutiae of daily routine, travel patterns and social networks that evolve around ethno-sectarian allegiance. Nowhere are these issues more profoundly apparent than in north and west Belfast (Shirlow and Murtagh, 2006).

At this stage, it is important to enter two caveats. First, it is not suggested that all former prisoners are necessarily "leaders" in such local communities. Although it is difficult to quantify, many loyalist and possibly some republican former prisoners simply returned to their previous forms of employment, accepting prison as the price to pay for their involvement in the conflict. For republicans, however, former prisoner groups and their activities can be seen as constituting another mode of resistance which offsets the negative impacts of criminalisation. Second, it is also important to stress that I am not postulating some form of naive eulogising of all of those who once took up arms. As in any post-conflict society, some former prisoners may become involved in individual acts of political or sectarian violence or individual criminality. At an organisational level, it is certainly possible to argue cogently that at least one of the paramilitary organisations whose members benefited from early release provisions under the 1998 Belfast Agreement (the UDA) has largely morphed into a criminal gang involved in drug dealing, racketeering and prostitution (McDonald and Cusack, 2004). In addition, UVF members have been involved in drug dealing and "ordinary" criminality (McDonald and Cusack, 2000). The UDA has had little involvement in conflict transformation. Thus it was claimed that "People from a UVF/RHC [Red Hand Commando] background seem to want to engage, but for whatever reason, people from a UDA background don't".

While the IRA has not been credibly linked to drug dealing or distribution, its long tradition of robberies, smuggling and related criminality to fund the republican "cause" allegedly survived beyond the ceasefires of "military" operations in the mid-1990s (Neuman, 2002). It is also obvious that members of the respective organisations have been involved in punishment attacks. Within such a societal framework, involvement in peacemaking work is not without its personal risks, particularly for former loyalist prisoners. As one argued: "You could be shot dead—it's as simple as that". "The biggest risk", however, "is going too far ahead of your constituency. And yet if we are CT practitioners then we have to go ahead of our constituency."

The effectiveness of former prisoners in conflict transformation is constrained by the impediments under which they work. Both loyalist and republican former prisoners are stigmatised by the system of criminalisation invoked by the British government during the Troubles. For loyalists, however, that stigma also helps define their position within their own communities. Unlike republicanism, loyalism since partition has had no culture or history of political prisoners, of going outside the law. Instead, loyalists wore uniforms: "We just put on a B Specials uniform or police uniform and you could shoot as many people as you wanted." For republicans, conversely, the status of former prisoner is a "badge of honour", denoting activists imprisoned by the British state for their part in the war against that state but also now continuing the "struggle" by other means. As a generalisation, therefore, republican former prisoners have a higher status in their own communities than that accorded to their counterparts in loyalist areas: "The community is with you in republican areas: the community is against you in loyalist areas." Republican former prisoners are "everywhere" as community activists, reflecting the point that, unlike loyalists, their stigmatisation is only without the community rather than both without and within: "If you throw a stone in any direction, say in the New Lodge—there's former prisoners involved in whatever, residents' groups, training, welfare." For republicans, criminalisation was part of the apparatus used by the British state to depoliticise the "war" whereas they insist on the British government as being a principal party to the conflict. The scale of engagement is, however, much more local for loyalists; criminalisation is a mode of suffering, something that has been—and still has to be—endured for the greater good of unionism.

What can former prisoners contribute to the process of conflict transformation? Loyalists and republicans have a shared concern with the deprivation of working-class areas in north and west Belfast and beyond and the need for community regeneration and programmes such as restorative justice. They have an understanding of each other, which builds upon their common structural position; the shared experience of prison and also more recently acquired mutual skills in preparing applications for funding and dealing with the agendas of funding agencies. Moreover, it has been shown that relatives of former prisoners have significantly more entrenched attitudes to the "other" than the former prisoners themselves who, in being more open to their former opponents, can also bring analytical, reflective and organisational skills to conflict transformation and thus, based on experience, possess an expertise and ability to engage across community boundaries (McEvoy and Shirlow, 2008). For republicans, former prisoner status also brings credibility to conflict transformation, although that is much less likely to be the case in loyalist areas. A shared openness and expertise in the skills that can deliver conflict transformation and agreement on its desirability should not obscure, however, the vital point that irreconcilable ideological differences still separate loyalist and republican politically motivated former prisoners.

### Working within and without communities

As already suggested, the capacity of loyalist former prisoners to contribute to conflict transformation work within their own communities is seriously compromised by the stigmatisation resulting from criminalisation: "What recognition we do get is begrudgingly given . . . because there are people involved in criminality, all ex-prisoners are then tarred with the same brush. It's hard to break out of that." The "middle" or "political unionism", to which loyalist former prisoners often refer, is doubly alienated. Loyalist former prisoners are working on behalf of:

a community within a community . . . an underclass [marginalised] by middle unionists, the media . . . middle unionism doesn't like [conflict transformation] because they don't want a working class movement . . . The other thing is social engineering which is destroying our communities. North Belfast has lost 50–60,000 people . . . The peace process has meant absolutely nothing to them [inner-city working class] . . . Educational disadvantage within working class Protestant communities is abysmal. Those who are trying to take a lead are ex-POWs and there are very few of us.

Middle unionism also categorises loyalist former prisoners as criminals whose presence stigmatises and criminalises entire communities. To some extent, this ignores the fragmentation of loyalism and regards former prisoners through the "hard man" or gangster perspective of the UDA (which in colouring republicans' attitudes to loyalist former prisoners allows the former to portray themselves as being somehow more principled and ideologically consistent). This is not to deny, however, that such criminalisation exists:

What we're seeing is the criminalisation of whole communities within loyalist areas . . . by the selective handling and protection of key individuals involved in criminality. Drugs have been put into our community . . . [creating] a criminal culture [organised] by the lowest element in loyalist communities, that means the whole community is stigmatised by the media, politicians and in some cases by nationalists. It's come to the stage now that many ex-POWs are afraid to build an extension, buy a new car or own their own house because they'll be stigmatised as drug dealers, criminals or gangsters.

The issue of stigmatisation emerges as the key factor in constraining the effectiveness of loyalist former prisoners in working within their own communities. At best, they receive only grudging recognition from the communities and even from their families: as one loyalist observed:

I would say that there is a greater understanding from republican politicians that what there would be among unionists in terms of the role that former prisoners can play . . . one of the ironies is that among the Catholic/ nationalist community, I would find a better understanding of my position in life . . . there is not the same prejudice.

Loyalist former prisoners express no sense of continuing the war by other means: the constitutional war is over and the key issues are now those of their own communities and, in particular, their criminalisation by the drugs, which are destroying those communities. Unlike their republican counterparts, loyalist former prisoners are working within their communities, not specifically as former prisoners or in former prisoner groups, but in community organisations that also include former prisoners. Republican former prisoner community organisations are different, being aligned to the macro-politics of Sinn Fein. Even the presence of a former prisoner may be sufficient to stigmatise the group or community centre: "Take the centre I work in. It is a church based centre employing both Protestants and Catholics. As far as the DUP is concerned—this is a UVF centre." Such constraints are crucial to the effectiveness of loyalist former prisoners in conflict transformation. Nevertheless, they still bring valuable experience and, perhaps, a form of personal status: "Because of the background that ex-prisoners have they have been able to argue successfully for moderation in terms of dealing with conflict . . . The whole thing is about moral and transformative leadership . . . Moving away from militarism using dialogue and discussion as a way forward."

As emphasised here, there are very marked contrasts between the status of republican and loyalist former prisoners within their respective communities. In the first instance, republicanism has a long historical experience of imprisonment from earlier campaigns during the 1940s, 1950s and 1960s. Also, a number of republican former prisoners were already involved in community work before they went to prison and returned to this on release, whereas loyalists went back to their trades and other forms of employment. There are higher expectations of republican former prisoners than their loyalist counterparts, whom the former regard as dupes of the state—or more charitably, victims of a "false consciousness"—who have assumed criminality upon themselves. Thus unlike republicans, they are alienated *within* their own communities. This lack of stigmatisation within extends to the democratic election by the republican macro-community of the former prisoner and combatant leadership of Sinn Fein as their representatives. Former prisoner groups are thus seen as being legitimate and part of the wider ideological and leadership structure of militant republicanism. As Mike Ritchie, Director of Coiste na n-Iarchimí (Coiste) (the umbrella organisation for republican former prisoner groups throughout Ireland) explains: "I've often described ex-prisoners as middle managers in the Peace Process."

The very different ways in which loyalist and republican former prisoners are regarded within their own communities is replicated in their dealings outside—or without—those communities. This means, inevitably, that the effects of exclusions and impediments vary between the two groups, as do the constraints on their activities and the extent of containment with respect to conflict transformation. The idea of working "without" refers both to the relationships of these groups with each other and also to the state and its agencies. It is readily apparent that "within" and "without" are interconnected domains in that the capacity to work within relates to that without and vice versa. If mutual prison experiences, originally built on simple, everyday exchanges, paved the way for dialogue between loyalist and republican combatants, the shared experience of criminalisation has had negative impacts on the abilities of both sets of former prisoners to work with each other because part of its purpose was to separate the two blocs: as one loyalist graphically describes:

> We were the cannon fodder who were marched up to the top of the hill and like eejits [Belfast colloquial for idiot] we went over it . . . You had a whole community backing you and supporting you . . . a lot of those men from the Catholic church, even the most moderate of politicians . . . the crimi-nalisation process succeeded because middle (mainstream) unionism backed it . . . everyone in civic society were (sic) opposed to us—we were the criminals in this.

Nevertheless, it is clear that this legacy of criminalisation and the strate-gies applied to achieve it have diminished the capacity of former prison-ers to work without. Despite the small physical distances involved, there is often a sense of parallel worlds. Face-to-face contact notwithstanding, fundamental misunderstandings remain between republican and loyalist former prisoners, as do stereotypical depictions of the other. Differences remain irreconcilable and loyalists and republicans continue to see the world from dissimilar perspectives and mindsets that can be paralysing for dialogue.

There is one further problem for loyalist former prisoners in circum-venting these barriers and impediments to conflict transformation. That is the major gap between unionist macro-politics and the "real" work on the ground which helps explain the low-level expectations of attainment with respect to conflict transformation. For the Loyalist Ex-Prisoners Interpretive Centre (EPIC—the principal loyalist former prisoner organ-isation), the biggest problem is the DUP and that legacy of criminalisa-tion, which prevents it being perceived as a legitimate expression of loyalism. Given all the impediments, however, and despite the DUP's conversion to power-sharing presaged by the 2006 St Andrews Agreement, loyalist former prisoners (as demonstrated by EPIC's activi-ties in conflict transformation work) are well in advance of conventional politicians in working with republicanism. This includes practical issues such as interface projects, but also mutual attempts to understand oppos-ing mindsets through studies of political theory and the multiple inter-pretations of shared histories. Loyalist former prisoners are likely to be more committed to conflict transformation than conventional politi-cians, have skills—no matter how imperfect—in dialogue with the other, and also experience of attempting to control militarism and paramilitarism in their own communities. The problem, however, is how far to go.

Working without is difficult, face-to-face and grinding work, which depends on individuals and the personal contacts that former prisoners can establish between each other. It involves risk, and betrayal of trust is a constant hazard. There may be a sense of lip service to the idea of interconnectedness but also one of passive dismissal along the lines of: "we really don't know these people" (who are literally one mile away in physical terms, if sometimes almost invisible in psychological distance). Republican former prisoner groups are working at the local level too but are connected much more effectively to macro-politics than are their loyalist counterparts. Their community work is part of a greater whole and they derive additional legitimacy from that. Nevertheless, the thrust of their activities is within, not without. It is through their interconnections with the state and funding agencies rather than in conflict transformation work with loyalists that they function most effectively without.

### The comparative effectiveness of loyalist former prisoners in conflict transformation

It has been established that politically motivated former prisoners have experience in conflict transformation work and often so in the "hard places" on the actual ground. Their activities are motivated by various factors, some personal, some ideological but the effectiveness of their capacity to deliver on conflict transformation is still compromised by residual criminalisation and stigmatisation. Although former prisoners are involved in "high politics", most notably in Sinn Fein, this chapter is more concerned with the lived experiences of everyday lives than the political renegotiation of Northern Ireland's future: as one loyalist former prisoner remarks: "[people] don't want conflict; they don't want to be throwing stones at each other; they want their children to have a good education. It's day-to-day basics they want. People want to move on." At this scale, it must be accepted that people's expectations may be very low-key, but this is where the peace process has to be "sold".

Despite the official "shared future" and accompanying "neutral space" rhetoric, post-conflict society in Northern Ireland is, arguably, still predominately conceived on the ground in terms, not of a radical departure from segregation but of: "interconnected separation"; "benign apartheid"; "separate but equal"; containing conflict by working together to live apart; or even "malign apartheid". For many therefore, "good relations" means agreement on living apart. Little (2004: 196) describes

Northern Ireland as an example of what he calls "conflictual consensus", a society that embodies a basic level of agreement, but in which the "political" remains a sphere of conflict and disagreement spatially apparent on the ground through territoriality. "Conflictual consensus" does, however, involve an acceptance of the legitimacy of opponents and an understanding as to how their perspectives embrace a different way of thinking to one's own. Even agreement on living apart, the de facto reality of life in Northern Ireland, represents a huge incremental advance on the violence of the period prior to the paramilitary ceasefires in 1994.

It is argued here, that as part of this unavoidable contestation, former prisoner groups have a role to play although there are significant variations in their respective capacities to deliver on these expectations. Certainly, both republicans and loyalists have a shared agenda for reintegration of former prisoners and a state commitment to remove the barriers of residual criminalisation. Even given this, the comparative failure to mobilise wider support from within unionism—and also internationally—appears as a fault line with regard to many of the differences experienced between the loyalist and republican former prisoner communities. Evidently, there are clear discursive and ideological differences between loyalists and republicans and these divisions are manifest in terms of the alternative roles undertaken by each with regard to the "prison experience". However, there is also an evident place for republicans to locate themselves within geographically bounded communities that offer distinct cultural and political support. Conversely, for loyalists, the failure to garner such significant political or community support confines them to being one group within a more heterogeneous political community.

The division between loyalist and republican former prisoners is more than that of ideological intent. The variable unpacking of the prison experience as a form of resistance and the uneven capacity to draw upon community support indicate that the former prisoner groups do not possess the same levels of political effectiveness: in essence, "republicans have been successful in changing their military clout into political clout which loyalists haven't been able to do and are never likely to be able to do so". Former prisoners can bring "analytical, reflective, and organisational skills and experience" to conflict transformation but only republicans gain credibility within their own communities from their status. Indeed, the involvement of republican former prisoners can *add* to the credibility of community organisations.

In sum, in terms both of working within and without in this imperfect peace that constitutes Northern Ireland's present, and will shape its future and the ways in which that might be negotiated if not shared,

republican former prisoners have the advantage over their loyalist counterparts in that:

- They are empowered by the close relationship between former prisoner groups and macro-politics through Sinn Fein.
- The stigmatisation of former prisoners within loyalist communities
contrasts to the central role which their republican counterparts have
in community politics.
- The experience of criminalisation reflects on relationships both within
and without for loyalists but largely only without for republicans.
- Republican former prisoners acquire legitimacy and confidence from
their integration into republican communities.
- Both groups of former prisoners are involved in conflict transformation in the sense of promoting social, cultural and economic change
within their respective communities.
- Loyalists see themselves as being more committed to pushing conflict
transformation towards relationships with the other community
although, in part, this may reflect their less secure position within their
own community.

## Conclusions

We return here to the ideas on containment that frame this chapter. The
constraints experienced by loyalist politically motivated former prisoners in contributing to conflict transformation processes reflect both their
marginalisation at the macro-scale by the apparatus of state residual
criminalisation but also at the meso- and micro-scales within their own
communities where they have been demonised and contained by "middle
unionism". Republican former prisoners, on the other hand, while
sharing in the constraint of residual criminalisation—which particularly
impacts on their effectiveness without their own communities—have
benefited hugely from Sinn Fein's macro-policy political shift into constitutional politics which has, successfully, served to countermand their
previous ideological containment. Within this overall framework of relative constraints, politically motivated former prisoners do constitute a
source for conflict transformation, especially in translating the ambiguities and elisions of high politics into effective working agreements on the
ground, which, moreover, extend across the urban interfaces where the
conflict was at its most bitter. Dialogue is still impeded by suspicion and
lack of understanding of the other's position and by stereotypical representations of the other. Republicans, for example, often see loyalists as
gangsters, "hardmen", engaged in insular territorial violence that con-

trasts markedly with their own non-parochial ideology. Even though prisoner groups have been prepared to promote change by working within the state since the inception of the peace process, the goal of both working within and without is best summed up as an "interconnected separation". It does seem to be the case that former prisoners have a shared expertise that is helping attain this modest but still important form of transition from conflict to conflict transformation. It may be at a local scale but their work on the ground has to be legitimated by macro-politics because the interface is a mindset as well as a physical entity. It may often be modest work but, none the less, valuable for that: as one loyalist argues

> The real interface is the one between people. That's where the work is needed. We shouldn't fall into the trap of feeling that everybody wants to do what we are doing. People ask what peace means to you and what they are saying to me is "a brick doesn't come through my window", or "I got a good night's sleep", or "I don't have to worry about my child going out over the door". Everyone's peace is different. They might support us but we don't need the masses behind us. Social profit can be that we have a few new faces and we have the support of the community in what we do. They don't have to be involved to gain the benefits of the work. Everyone has their own expectations of what they want to see in terms of peace.

Politically motivated former prisoners can thus contribute to the incremental, flawed, fragile and deeply contested process of transition and conflict transformation. Their activities—and especially those of loyalists—have been constrained by processes of containment. As one remarks:

> Criminalisation as a policy was set out to define some people as criminals for a political purpose . . . the repercussions are still going on. Middle unionism see themselves as legitimate, the RUC see themselves as legitimate, the British army see themselves as legitimate, everybody else isn't and that's not the way it is and that's not the way it should be.

Northern Ireland remains an arena of conflict, not only between identities, but between the formal and procedural processes of consociational democracy and the persistence of the interconnection of ethnicity, territoriality and political process. While the Belfast and St Andrews' Agreements reflect the consociational concern with the scale of the state (Tonge, 2005) it is the failure to formulate ways of addressing the continued potency of these forces at the sub-state scale that, at present, undermines strategies for a "shared future", which cannot be achieved through the endlessly repeated but deliberately ambiguous rhetoric of both British and Irish governments. The politically motivated former prisoners—both individuals and groups—discussed here are one resource in renegotiating a future society. It may not be a society that emulates the aspirations of the governments but the capacity to help sponsor ideas of coexistence within and without the working-class areas that sustained, but also suffered grievously from the "war", marks a significant progression in the everyday lives of those communities and their ultimate economic and social regeneration.

## References

Annan, K. (2004) "Learning the lessons of peace building", The Tip O' Neill Lecture, Magee Campus, University of Ulster, 18 October.

Graham, B. and Nash, C. (2006) "A shared future: territoriality, pluralism and public policy in Northern Ireland", *Political Geography*, 25: 253–78.

Lederach, J. P. (1997) *Building Peace: Sustainable Reconciliation in Divided Societies* (Washington, DC: United States Institute of Peace Press).

Little, A. (2004) *Democracy and Northern Ireland. Beyond the Liberal Paradigm?* (Basingstoke: Palgrave Macmillan).

McDonald, H. and Cusack, J. (2000) *UVF* (Dublin: Poolbeg).

McDonald, H. and Cusack, J. (2004) *The UDA* (Dublin: Penguin Ireland).

McEvoy, K. (2001) *Paramilitary Imprisonment in Northern Ireland: Resistance, Management and Release* (Oxford: Oxford University Press).

McEvoy, K. and Shirlow, P. (2008) *Beyond the Wire: Former Prisoners and Conflict Transformation in Northern Ireland* (London: Pluto Press).

Neumann, P. (2002) "The imperfect peace: explaining paramilitary violence in Northern Ireland", *Low Intensity Conflict & Law Enforcement*, 11: 116–38.

Shirlow, P. (2001) "Fear and ethnic division", *Peace Review*, 13: 67–74.

Shirlow, P. and Murtagh, B. (2006) *Belfast: Segregation, Violence and the City* (London: Pluto Press).

Tonge, J. (2005) *The New Northern Irish Politics?* (Basingstoke: Palgrave Macmillan).

# 24

# The Northern Ireland Labour Party and Protestant working-class identity

*Aaron Edwards*[1]

## Introduction

The Northern Ireland Labour Party (NILP) is an under-studied and poorly understood phenomenon in Irish political studies. Its significance lies in the fact that it was the only bi-confessional democratic socialist party to hold opposition status in the Northern Ireland Parliament during the 1921–72 era of devolution. Moreover, the NILP's legacy is a remarkable illustration of how a rich tradition of class-based politics could mobilise cross-sectarian electoral support on a practical level despite the existence of deep-seated ethnic, religious and national divisions. It was in its roles as a political opponent of Ulster unionism and Irish nationalism that the NILP is perhaps best remembered. For most of the post-war period Northern Ireland Labour challenged the basis of the province's confessional party system and "sought, with only partial success, to redefine the fault-lines of Irish politics" (Coakley, 2002: 140). Although the NILP pooled its members and supporters from across the religious divide, working-class Protestants constituted the largest proportion of its party activists. However, with the possible exception of Henry Patterson (1980, 2005), Graham Walker (1985, 2005), Terry Cradden (1993; 1996) and Bew et al. (2002), surprisingly few commentators have sought to illuminate the dynamics underpinning this labourist tradition in the political culture of the Ulster Protestant community.

## Northern Ireland labour and the Protestant working class

In an early scholarly review of Northern Ireland's political landscape, Richard Rose found that of the twenty-nine party labels then active in the region, only three stood out "as specially visible to the mass of the electorate"—the Unionists, the Nationalists and the Northern Ireland Labour parties [*sic*]" (Rose, 1971: 222). Observing the NILP at close quarters he concluded that it was "truly a working class party, and not a place of refuge for middle-class people seeking an alternative to parties divided along sectarian lines. More than three-quarters of its support comes from manual workers, a figure similar to that of the British Labour Party" (Rose, 1971: 283). Beyond Rose's early assessment few commentators have attempted to audit the salient features of the NILP's ideology and discourse, the social groups which constituted its membership and support base, or, indeed, the reasons for its successes and failures in the post-war period. This chapter fills out the picture of the NILP's political successes vis-à-vis the Protestant working class, arguably its core constituency, and the social grouping with which it is commonly identified by academic commentators (see McAllister and Nelson, 1979; Walker, 2005; Edwards, 2007).

According to one early historian of the NILP, the party's *raison d'être* from 1949 onwards, when the party eventually ended its ambivalence on the constitutional question and declared openly in favour of partition, was part of a much wider "consensus-forming strategy"[2] (Graham, 1972: 2). Graham argued that ultimately it was a means to an end for the NILP in its quest to make its democratic socialist politics electorally viable in the confessional socio-political environment of Northern Ireland. Moreover, it was a strategy framed within realistic parameters. Briefly, it had a dual aim: to breach the Ulster Unionist Party's (UUP's) electoral bulkhead in the medium term and thereby challenge unionism's broader political, social and cultural "hegemony" over the province in the longer term. The actual tactical manoeuvres deployed by the party to attain these objectives ranged from a radical turn in policy making to the instigation of a renewed propaganda drive to win over ambivalent working-class support. By freeing itself from its previous "constitutional ambivalence", argue McAllister and Nelson, "the NILP was able to make a direct appeal to the Protestant working class" (McAllister and Nelson, 1979: 294). Furthermore, by confounding accusations that it was "sitting on the fence" on the partition issue, the NILP of the 1950s could concentrate its efforts on developing more vigorously the pluralist, non-sectarian and democratic socialist dimensions of its political ideology.

By summer 1957, mass redundancies, twinned with industrial unrest, left 10 per cent of the province's workforce unemployed. Unionist government hesitancy over socio-economic issues, such as Family Allowance and the "Rent Bill" legislation, also led to increased enthusiasm for NILP policies (Walker, 2004: 124–7). The NILP's assistance to the Belfast working class in their "hour of need" was to be greatly rewarded at the polls in March 1958 when the party saw four of its high-profile candidates elected to the Stormont Parliament. Within these four Belfast constituencies Labour polled a clear majority in Pottinger, but won on only slender majorities in Oldpark, Woodvale and Victoria. Overall the party polled 16 per cent of the total vote, a significant increase on the 1953 figure of 12 per cent (Elliott, 1973: 116). In 1962 the four MPs confidently doubled their majorities in all Belfast constituencies, attributable mainly to the rapid mushrooming of the party's membership, the diligent grass-roots activism of its new MPs and much favourable media coverage of its political programme.

As the leading centrist party in the region during the 1950s and 1960s, the NILP advocated an integrationist community agenda, rather than a radical class-based reordering of Northern Irish society. This was reflected in official party discourse, which played up the progressive legislation introduced by Clement Attlee's post-war British Labour government. NILP election literature from 1945 onwards frequently claimed that "The future development, the future prosperity, of Northern Ireland depends on her inclusion as an integral part in the greater plan for the United Kingdom as a whole" (NILP, 1964b). The prominent Belfast solicitor (and senior NILP strategist) Charles Brett had been chiefly responsible for drafting these policy documents at a time when the welfare state was seen to be delivering for the British working class. The challenge, as far as Brett was concerned, was to make welfarism work for a region of the United Kingdom that had serious disparities in the inner workings of its locally devolved administration (Brett, 1970).

### The NILP's democratic socialism

Above all, the NILP projected itself as a democratic socialist party. True to its ideological commitment to a British style of Labourism, the NILP faithfully reproduced Clause 4 of the British Labour Party (BLP) constitution in its entirety and fashioned its political programme from a parliamentary socialist and mainly working-class perspective (NILP, 1964a). Usually its members behaved as socialists first and foremost and were prepared to put aside their ethno-religious differences to forge a cross-sectarian partnership. David Bleakley, who served as a Stormont MP for Belfast Victoria between 1958 and 1965, has remarked that for those involved in Ulster's Labour tradition, "Collective action between Protestants and Catholics was high on our list of priorities and we were encouraged to rebuke sectarianism in any shape or form" (Bleakley, 1995). For Bleakley, like so many others in the party, the NILP was "a Keir Hardie party"[3] with a strong social conscience and moral fibre. This kind of socialism, as Bernard Crick points out, is "both an empirical theory and a moral doctrine" and is part of a strong ethical impulse in the broader British Labour movement, which places "more stress on personal exemplifications of socialist values than on public ownership or class legislation" (Crick, 1987: 79). In the Northern Ireland context the NILP's unique brand of democratic socialism was forged in a working-class culture, which placed a premium on ethical labour values. As Bleakley recalled in interview:

> There were a lot of Christian socialists in the party . . . I don't want to emphasise that but it was not unusual for a person in the Labour Party to be very very active [religiously]. Take Billy Boyd, he was a Methodist lay preacher. Vivian Simpson had been a [Methodist] missionary in Africa and Tom Boyd [a Presbyterian] was a very very highly respected man and respectable man . . . And so we had a lot in common holding us together and I think anybody who was in the Labour Party tended to put the service ethic high on [their list of priorities].[4]

Despite the admirable personal qualities this religious conviction imbued in some NILP activists it is, nevertheless, often paraded as a debilitating aspect of the party's development in the 1960s, especially at times of intra-party conflict (McGarry and O'Leary, 1995: 156; White, 2007).

For those members who found the Christian socialist strand running throughout the NILP unappealing there was still great scope to hold more closely to material conceptions of society. This "agnostic" strand could be found permeating the party's membership just as evidently as the Methodist one, suiting many of those who had been disenchanted with the binding sanctions imposed on everyday life by organised religion. This strand included almost as many Catholics as Protestants, as the NILP claimed by 1965 that its religious balance reflected that of Northern Ireland society more widely (*Irish News*, 1965; Graham, 1972: 286). For agnostics from a Protestant background, Catholics were welcomed on comradely terms. As Jim McDonald recalled, "I mean you had people like Paddy Devlin and all who were in the Labour Party. All good socialists. It didn't matter whether they were Catholic, Protestant or whatever; they were working class people".[5] NILP activists like McDonald were typical of many working-class Protestants who found a political home for their strong socialist beliefs in the NILP at a time when the party was offering a "radical alternative" option to the ethnic politics of Ulster unionism and Irish nationalism.

Although something of a minority trend within Protestant working-class political culture, one further ideological strand worth mentioning here is liberalism. Those of a liberal disposition, like Charles Brett, were representative of a huge chunk of middle-class people who had joined the NILP in the 1950s and 1960s, a recognisable proportion who were agnostic or atheist in comparison to the devout Christian social-ism espoused by David Bleakley, Vivian Simpson and Billy Boyd. Disproportionately pooled from the professional classes, liberals promoted a view of society wherein rational individuals could enjoy unbridled freedom from religious dogmatism and any accompanying dis-crimination. Most liberals within the NILP were discouraged from taking a more active role in public life by the ugly scars of religious bigotry and fundamentalism displayed by militant Paisleyites. With the outbreak of violence in 1969 it became much more difficult for those of an affluent disposition to stomach the *realpolitik* of street-level activism in ways that did not affect Christian and agnostic members.

## Tensions between Labourism and loyalism

By the mid-1960s, the Protestant working class was becoming increas-ingly more susceptible to the Reverend Ian Paisley's rhetoric, in which he warned of the dangers of ecumenicalism and liberalism. Billy Boyd and David Bleakley undoubtedly saw support for extreme loyalism as an erosion of their political powerbases (Graham, 1972: 124–35). Consequently, they sometimes behaved in ways inimical to the NILP's non-sectarian ethos. Perhaps the most public illustration of this was in the intra-party conflict arising from the so-called "Sunday swings" issue. The extent to which some commentators have wheeled out the "swings" incident as proof of the NILP's inherent Protestant sabbatarianism (and therefore, by implication, a rejection of its integrationist community agenda) is unhelpful and has effectively tainted the party with a hue that it does not altogether deserve (see Rumpf and Hepburn, 1977: 206). The incident arose when some of the NILP's councillors in the Woodvale area refused to endorse a corporation motion to open children's playgrounds on Sundays. As the local MP, Billy Boyd supported the right of his local constituents to decide on whether to retain Sunday opening. The former NILP chairman Erskine Holmes explained:

> Billy [Boyd] was faced with this challenge from fundamental Protestants on the effect on little Protestant communities where they had play centres. The misuse of these playgrounds if they were opened on Sundays, not by chil-dren but hooligans [was apparent]. Therefore I think that Billy Boyd advo-cated a form of local option; that if the people wanted these open then they could vote to have them open, but he never was a supporter of keeping the swings locked up on a Sunday, but he was represented as if he was. Historians of the movement with a nationalist bias will always represent that as some fundamental division within the party.[6]

A detailed analysis of the episode undertaken elsewhere (Edwards, 2006) reveals how it was more about a gulf between central NILP policy and what local people actually wanted than a question of "pandering" to the whims of evangelical Protestants. Nevertheless, as the leading Falls Road NILP activist Paddy Devlin asserted, it was a "risky strategy because such tactics . . . compromised the NILP vote in other constituencies where the Catholic vote was important" (Devlin, 1993: 79). Indeed, if anything, the episode unveiled a differential in the centralised-localised dynamic of party policy, and its effect on discipline and morale, rather than the confessional convictions of its membership.

Conversely, there were other instances when Billy Boyd chose to jeopardise the loyalty of his constituency base to push forward controversial legislation in the Northern Ireland House of Commons. Probably the most exemplary piece of Private Member legislation proposed by the local Parliamentary Labour Party was the Racial Discrimination Bill (1964), which went forward to a second reading only to be thrown out by the unionist government.[7] The request for legislation to curb discrimination on the basis of race, creed and religion (as well as the incitement to hatred) was to form an essential ingredient in the BLP-linked Campaign for Democracy in Ulster's call for a return to "British rights for Northern Ireland citizens" the following year in, 1965.[8] It was unfortunate that Boyd chose to dither on the "swings" issue several months later. Notwithstanding its internal difficulties, the 1960s proved to be, above all, a decade of great promise for the NILP with "unprecedented breakthroughs" taking place beyond Belfast in places like Lisburn and Newtownabbey (Devlin, 1993: 80).

Walker has indicated that the sort of socialist culture propagated by Labour in these working-class districts "often co-existed with sectarianism and with an unshakeable suspiciousness about the intentions of the Nationalist minority, and was thus vulnerable to Paisleyite populism" (Walker, 2004: 159). His analysis echoes a central theme explored in the fictionalised work of the renowned Ulster playwright (and NILP activist) Sam Thompson. In his critically acclaimed 1960 play, *Over the Bridge*, Thompson intuitively encapsulates how sectarianism could often have a debilitating effect on workplace solidarity. The play's arch-bigot, Archie Kerr, is one of those who believe wholeheartedly in the visceral outpourings of religious fundamentalists when they warn of the dangers of accommodating Catholics. His ill-tempered rants about an impending "showdown" in which not only "Popeheads . . . [are] the enemies of Ulster", but also "mealy mouthed Prods . . . who aid and abet them" are indicative of working-class intolerance (Thompson, 1970: 45). In a very poignant climax the lead character, Protestant trade unionist Davy

Mitchell, faces down a marauding mob of loyalists baying for "Fenian" blood, but is brutally beaten to death for sticking to his non-sectarian principles. The play's cruel twist in many ways personifies what Stephen Howe has recently termed the "stifling environment" of Protestant working-class life in which "the pressures to conformity were intense: anyone inclined to question the shared truths of the community was labelled a Communist or a Fenian" (Howe, 2005). Howe's argument, however, somewhat exaggerates the strength of religious fundamentalism and overt sectarian bigotry and neglects discussion on how ethnic loyalism ultimately triumphed over non-sectarian labourism.

From 1965 the spectre of militant loyalism began to rear its head in West Belfast, first under the *nom de plume* Ulster Protestant Action and later in the form of the much deadlier Ulster Volunteer Force. The threat that these loyalist organisations posed to the NILP's position was considered so great that party secretary Sam Napier quickly produced a detailed report of possible political implications.[9] Up to this point the NILP proved capable of appealing electorally to individual loyalists and Orange Order members who harboured socialist political outlooks. As one *Round Table* correspondent observed, following the NILP's encroachment in staunchly Protestant working-class districts:

> The Orange Order did not counsel its members that they should vote for the Unionist Party. The presence among them of independents and supporters of the Labour Party would have made any such declaration on the part of Grand Masters invidious and prejudicial to solidarity. (*Round Table*, 1958: 277)

Rather than serving as an ideological adhesive binding the workers to the ruling class, Orangeism, as Patterson rightly points out, "could at various times be disruptive of Protestant unity when it conflicted with ruling class strategies which appeared to compromise with the traditional enemy" (Patterson, 1980: 144).

Undoubtedly, the months running up to the November 1965 Northern Ireland general election were a difficult period for the NILP, owing primarily to the internal friction now persisting among the party's front ranks. Graham attributes the party's difficulties to O'Neill's reorganisation of the Ulster Unionist Labour Association. This organisation sought to win the "hearts and minds" of Protestant workers, especially those now residing in new housing estates across the greater Belfast area, like Rathcoole in North Belfast, and Highfield in the west of the city. Over ten thousand new homes were circulated with a personal message from the premier appealing for industrial workers to join him on his onward journey to the new Ulster. In many of his campaign speeches O'Neill attempted to discredit Labour's democratic socialist programme by depicting it as vulgar and suspect.[10] Although flawed on many levels, O'Neill's modernisation ideology was an ambitious piece of political theatrics and "could function quite simply to defend sectarian activity by defining nationalist and NILP concern as 'reactionary' or 'living in the past'" (Bew et al., 2002: 130–1).

Thus, the political conflict, which had been bubbling to the surface between labourism and loyalism, particularly in urban working-class districts, was to have profoundly damaging consequences for the NILP. The closing months of 1965 confirmed that the electoral investment placed in Labour by the Protestant working class was conditional upon an absence of anti-partitionist feeling and the presence of high rates of unemployment: in flagging up one while dealing energetically with the other O'Neill could effectively administer a *coup de grâce* to the NILP. In Woodvale and Victoria unionist candidates backed by powerful interest-groups beat sitting MPs Boyd and Bleakley. Only Tom Boyd and Vivian Simpson (who held strong cross-sectarian support-bases) held onto their seats. Napier blamed the low morale occasioned by the emerging split among party elites for making it "less attractive than usual to the Labour voters".[11] O'Neill had outmanoeuvred the NILP on this occasion but his success in reversing the party's political fortunes would have profound long-lasting effects for his premiership as it effectively removed the one vehicle which could have channelled civil rights agitation into the parliamentary arena and not—as it later transpired—on to the streets.

By the 1960s the NILP was arguing for the advantages of devolution to be seized, while heavily criticising legislative discrepancies (NILP, 1964b). The party's years in parliamentary opposition allowed it to highlight disparities in taxation, social services and what it termed "citizens" rights", that is matters relating to discrimination in employment, housing and the electoral franchise (Brett, 1970). This period witnessed a distillation in NILP policies and presented a party that was more self-confident than ever before. Calls were also made for the acceleration of house building and the distribution of new stock on a fair and non-discriminatory basis by way of a rigorously imposed standardised points system (NILP, 1965). By 1967 the newly formed Falls Labour Party had agreed motions supporting the emerging civil rights movement (Edwards, 2006: 242–5). Although individual NILP branches, including Ballynafeigh, Woodvale and Shankill, supported civil rights, the party as a whole did not endorse the use of civil disobedience to highlight these grievances. Instead the NILP chose to place its trust in parliamentary democracy at a time when the Unionist Party sought—largely successfully—to fix a Catholic image onto the public's perception of the civil rights movement (Purdie, 1988: 33–41). In many ways, the NILP had to fight off unionist propaganda on two fronts: while avoiding the Catholic label it also had to resist being portrayed as Communist in orientation. Jim McDonald remarked how, as an NILP member in the staunchly Protestant working-class Shankill Road, there were "people out there who think that when you tell them that you are a socialist they think that you are a Communist. You know you had that sort of baggage [as a member of the NILP]".[12]

To younger members in the 1960s the NILP offered a vehicle from which to challenge the governing Unionist Party. The drift of many university students into the Young Socialists[13] certainly stiffened the resolve of those who rejected the baggage attached to their ethnic backgrounds in favour of the NILP's non-sectarian style of politics.[14] At a time when the Nationalist Party had opted out of the political system it is true to say that many Catholics felt disenfranchised and wanted something more politically satisfying. "As the official opposition", remarked Erskine Holmes, the NILP "tried to make Northern Ireland Parliament function as a normal Parliament; before they were the opposition it didn't function as a proper Parliament".[15]

## Conclusion

In the 1960s the NILP won between 16 and 26 per cent of the total vote in Northern Ireland Parliamentary elections and, according to O'Leary and McGarry (1996: 162) "posed a straightforward threat to the UUP's electoral hegemony, especially in the Belfast urban area". During the post-war period, the party demonstrated its political foresight by formulating full-bodied policies on academic selection at age 11, the death penalty, electoral discrimination and the continued exclusion of the Catholic-maintained Mater Hospital from the NHS system (Edwards, 2007: 26). Above all, the party's electoral successes demonstrated how non-sectarian democratic socialist values could be fostered and articulated in a cohesive manner from within the most progressive sections of the Protestant working-class community.

Nevertheless, with the advent of O'Neillism in the mid-1960s, economic factors, including the dissipation in the high tide of unemployment (previously the centrepiece in the NILP's critique of the Unionist government and the bridging used to reach across the ethno-religious divide in Belfast), almost certainly alleviated pressure on the Stormont Government.[16] O'Neill was shrewd enough to package his economic strategy as a positive way out of the morass. Paradoxically, however, his superficial reform plan—while it masked underlying structural deficiencies in the state—only served to exacerbate a potentially explosive situation. O'Neill's impressive lobbying for new regional industrial initiatives, such as his encouragement of inward investment by multinational companies, may have reasonably improved the lot of broad sections of semi-skilled and manual labourers, but it did not lead to the emergence of "capitalism with a human face". In 1969, under increasing pressure from his own party and civil rights protesters, O'Neill resigned as Prime Minister. Ironically, by counter-attacking the NILP's position in Belfast, O'Neill had left the door open to further challenges by extra-parliamentary forces.

By 1970, the NILP's political fortunes had peaked at an impressive 98,194 votes in that year's British general election, after which it entered a period of protracted electoral decline. Despite its decline, the party remained at the forefront of attempts to broker a truce between warring paramilitary factions at the height of the "troubles" in 1972 (Edwards, 2006: 325–31). Few commentators have acknowledged how the NILP attempted to get among its long-established support bases and exert a calming influence once armed conflict became centralised in the Ardoyne, Shankill, Woodvale and Falls districts after 1969–70. As sectarian animosity worsened, many committed Methodists in the NILP—including Vivian Simpson (Stormont MP for Belfast Oldpark, 1958–72) and the former shipyard worker turned Methodist preacher the Reverend John Stewart—emerged to exercise responsible leadership in inter-communal conflict zones. They were joined by the prominent agnostic socialists Paddy Devlin (Stormont MP for Belfast Falls, 1969–72), Brendan Mackin (Falls Labour Party chairman, 1969–70) and Harry Donaghy (Councillor for Belfast Falls, 1967–73) in a desperate bid to diffuse tensions. Unfortunately, for the NILP common socio-economic grievances were beginning to fade into the background as the security situation worsened.

The facilitation of a "bottom-up" peace initiative was greatly hampered by a lack of resources and by the fact that after 1973 the British government favoured a "top-down" arbitration approach in which Ulster Unionists and the SDLP were pressured into embracing a power-sharing or consociational settlement. At a time when the newly formed Alliance Party was challenging the NILP for the cross-community vote, competition between these two centrist parties became inevitable. The NILP's political fortunes took a further downswing at the Constitutional Convention election in 1975 when its overall vote dipped to an all-time low of 1.4 per cent. Despite David Bleakley's re-election at this critical juncture it became increasingly obvious that the electorate had consigned his party's integrative community agenda to atrophy. Arguably, the prospects for a centrist working-class party gaining political momentum from within the Protestant working class have remained bleak ever since.

## Notes

1 I would like to thank Professor Graham Walker for supervising the doctoral research on which this chapter is based and to those former NILP members who made themselves available for interview. I also wish to acknowledge the Northern Ireland Department for Employment and Learning for funding my PhD research between 2003 and 2006.
2 The NILP's "strategy" was apparently couched in a realist philosophy. It rested on the presumption that the party ought to contest Protestant working-class areas first and, then, once a foothold was established, repeat the same process with working-class Catholics until cross-community consensus for its non-sectarian democratic socialist programme was secured.
3 Interview with David Bleakley, 21 March 2006.
4 Interview with David Bleakley, 21 March 2006.
5 Interview with Jim McDonald, 5 May 2005.
6 Interview with Erskine Holmes, 21 September 2005.
7 See, for example, Billy Boyd's sophisticated critique of discrimination in his tabling of the NILP's Racial Discrimination Bill (1964) in the Northern Ireland House of Commons Debates (*Hansard*) Vol. 57, Col. 1238–1242, 1244, 1374, 3 March 1964.
8 PRONI, D/3026, *CDU Papers*, CDU Constitution.
9 PRONI, D/3702/C/1/12, *Sam Napier Papers*, Report on UPA.
10 PRONI, PM/5/9/6, speech made by Terence O'Neill at Carrickfergus, 22 November 1965.
11 PRONI, D/3233/5/5, Secretary's Report to the Executive Committee on the General Election, March 1966.
12 Interview with Jim McDonald, 5 May 2005.
13 The "Young Socialists" was a ginger grouping inside the NILP.
14 Interview with Sydney McDowell, 24 August 2005.
15 Interview with Erskine Holmes, 21 September 2005.
16 The unemployment rate stood at 36,400 (7.4%) in June 1963; by June 1965 it had fallen to 29,200 (5.8%). Interestingly there were only 17,000 new jobs created in the same two-year period. See the *Ulster Year Book 1969* (Belfast: HMSO, 1969), pp. 254–55.

## References

Bew, P., Gibbon, P. and Patterson, H. (2002) *Northern Ireland 1921–2001: Political Forces and Social Classes* (London: Serif).
Bleakley, D. (1980) *Sadie Patterson: Irish Peacemaker* (Belfast: Blackstaff).
Bleakley, D. (1995) "Home truths for a man of peace", *Belfast Telegraph*, 17 April.

Brett, C. (1970) "The lessons of devolution in Northern Ireland", *Political Quarterly*, 41. 3: 261–80.

Brett, C. (1978) *Long Shadows Cast Before: Nine Lives in Ulster, 1625–1977* (Edinburgh: John Bartholomew).

Coakley, J. (2002) "Conclusion: new strains of unionism and nationalism", in J. Coakley (ed.) *Changing Shades of Orange and Green: Redefining the Union and the Nation in Contemporary Ireland* (Dublin: UCD), pp. 132–54.

Cradden, T. (1993) *Trade Unionism, Socialism and Partition: The Labour Movement in Northern Ireland, 1939–1953* (Belfast: December Publications).

Cradden, T. (1996) "Labour in Britain and the Northern Ireland Labour Party, 1900–1970", in P. Catterall and S. McDougal (eds) *The Northern Ireland Question in British Politics* (Basingstoke: Macmillan), pp. 71–87.

Crick, B. (1987) *Socialism* (Milton Keynes: Open University Press).

Devlin, P. (1993) *Straight Left: An Autobiography* (Belfast: Blackstaff).

Edwards, A. (2006) "Labour politics and sectarianism: interpreting the political fortunes of the Northern Ireland Labour Party, 1945–1975" (unpublished PhD thesis, Queen's University Belfast).

Edwards, A. (2007) "Democratic socialism and sectarianism: the Northern Ireland Labour Party and Progressive Unionist Party compared", *Politics*, 27.1: 24–31.

Elliott, S. (1973) *Northern Ireland Parliamentary Election Results, 1921–1972* (Chichester: Political Reference Publications).

Farrell, M. (1976) *Northern Ireland: The Orange State* (London: Pluto Press).

Graham, J. (1972) *The Consensus-Forming Strategy of the Northern Ireland Labour Party, 1949–1968* (unpublished MSc thesis, Queen's University Belfast).

Howe, S. (2005) "Mad dogs and Ulstermen: the crisis of loyalism: Part one", *Open Democracy*, 28 September. Archived at www.opendemocracy.net/globalization-protest/loyalism_2876.jsp (accessed 15 October 2005).

McAllister, I. and Nelson, S. (1979) "Modern developments in the Northern Ireland party system", *Parliamentary Affairs*, 32.3: 279–316.

McAughtry, S. (1981) "A question of politics", *Irish Times*, 13 May.

McGarry, J. and O'Leary, B. (1995) *Explaining Northern Ireland: Broken Images* (Oxford: Blackwell).

Mulholland, M. (2000) *Northern Ireland at the Crossroads: Ulster Unionism in the O'Neill Years, 1960–9* (Basingstoke: Macmillan).

NILP (1964a) *Constitution: Revised 1964* (Belfast: NILP).

NILP (1964b) *Signposts to the New Ulster* (Belfast: NILP).

NILP (1965) *Manifesto for the Northern Ireland General Election* (Belfast: NILP).

O'Leary, B. and McGarry, J. (1996) *The Politics of Antagonism: Understanding Northern Ireland* Second Edition (London: Athlone).

Patterson, H. (1980) *Class Conflict and Sectarianism: The Protestant Working Class and the Belfast Labour Movement 1868–1920* (Belfast: Blackstaff).

Patterson, H. (2005) "William Walker", in F. Lane and D. Ó Drisceoil (eds) *Politics and the Irish Working Class, 1830–1945* (Basingstoke: Palgrave), pp. 154–71.

Purdie, B. (1988) "Was the civil rights movement a republican/communist conspiracy?", *Irish Political Studies*, 3: 33–41.

Rose, R. (1971) *Governing Without Consensus: An Irish Perspective* (London: Faber & Faber).

Rumpf, E. and Hepburn, A. (1977) *Nationalism and Socialism in Twentieth Century Ireland* (Liverpool: Liverpool University Press)

Rutan, G. and Gerard, F. (1967) "The Labor Party in Ulster: opposition by cartel", *Review of Politics*, 29.4: 526–35.

Thompson, S. (1970) *Over the Bridge* (Dublin: Gill & Macmillan).

*Ulster Year Book 1969* (Belfast: HMSO, 1969).

Walker, G. (1985) *The Politics of Frustration: Harry Midgley and the Failure of Labour in Northern Ireland* (Manchester: Manchester University Press).

Walker, G. (2004) *A History of the Ulster Unionist Party: Protest, Pragmatism and Pessimism* (Manchester: Manchester University Press).

Walker, G. (2005) "The Northern Ireland Labour Party, 1924–45", in F. Lane and D. Ó Drisceoil (eds) *Politics and the Irish Working Class, 1830–1945* (Basingstoke: Palgrave), pp. 229–45.

White, B. (2007) "A working class hero is something to be", *Belfast Telegraph*, 16 January.

# 25

# The Protestant working class and the fragmentation of Ulster Unionism

*Graham Walker*

## Introduction

The Protestant working class remains central to attempts to establish a peaceful future for Northern Ireland. However, the problem constituted by this group's increasingly disaffected and alienated condition over the course of what has come to be known as the "peace process" was often forgotten or unacknowledged, at least until the eruption of violence in loyalist areas in the late summer of 2005. This chapter attempts to provide some pertinent observations about the Protestant working class, both in historical and contemporary contexts. It highlights the Protestant working class's difficult relationship to political change in Northern Ireland, and the complexities of its historical relationship to Ulster unionism and the Ulster Unionist Party (UUP). The chapter also examines portrayals by nationalist commentators and other unsympathetic observers, which have profoundly influenced and arguably distorted debates surrounding the Ulster Protestant community and Protestant identities more broadly.

## Unionism and labour

Historically, the UUP placed a premium on the internal containment of dissent and the preservation of its broad-church and cross-class character (Walker, 2004a; Harbinson, 1973). From 1918, the party—"movement" is perhaps a better term—had incorporated Labour representation through the Ulster Unionist Labour Association (UULA) (Morgan, 1991, chapter 10), and this group was closely looked after in a paternalist spirit after the party took over the governance of Northern Ireland in 1921. The UULA has been derided as the stooge of the bosses who ran the Ulster Unionist Council (UUC—the UUP's ruling body) (Goldring, 1991: 119–35), but it should be remembered that its trade union credentials were genuine, and that its success as a pressure group can be measured by the way the government prioritised the issue of remaining "step by step" with the rest of the United Kingdom in respect of welfare benefits and social legislation throughout the inter-war era (Walker, 2004a: 63–6). Northern Ireland's first Minister of Labour and later Prime Minister, John Andrews, presided over the UULA and championed the cause of "step by step" in the cabinet (Scouler, 2004) while William Grant, another UULA stalwart and shipyard worker, was made a government minister by Andrews in 1940 and remained in the cabinet until his death in 1949.

The UULA was certainly a peculiar product of the circumstances of the division in Northern Ireland over national allegiance and its attendant sectarian discords. Nevertheless, allowing for the "tribal" dynamic of the UULA, it is still arguable that it resembled the kind of defensive and narrow form of Labour advocacy also to be found in Britain in the same period. If David Marquand's description of Labour politics and working-class values in his seminal study *The Progressive Dilemma* is taken as a guide, then "Unionist Labour" in Northern Ireland might qualify as a species of a British Labour culture in which the values held were essentially conservative (Marquand, 1991, chapter 5). Neither, it may be added, did the greater success achieved by Labour Party politics in Scotland remove sectarian tensions and divisions there; it contained and managed them at best. Strong religious-based identities coexisted with Labour and socialist ones (Smyth, 2000; Gallagher, 1987; Walker, 1995, chapter 5). In Merseyside, the Labour Party did not properly break through until after the Second World War, so hampered was it by sectarian divisions (Waller, 1981). In Salford and Manchester it had to tailor its appeal to take account of the local power of the Catholic Church and Irish Catholic identity (Fielding, 1993). In sum, the peculiarly entrenched nature of the communal division in Northern Ireland should not preclude notice being taken of similarities and resemblances with other parts of the UK, the phenomenon of Labour identity or Labour culture being a case in point.

The UULA's actual strength and degree of political vigour for a long time mattered less than the powerful symbolism of its existence within the unionist machine. Thus, when Basil Brooke, Prime Minister of Northern Ireland from 1943 to 1963, declared in 1947 that the UULA was "the backbone of Unionism" and that it would not be satisfied if the Northern Ireland government rejected the social benefits gained through the British link, he was sending a message to the wider constituency of Protestant working-class voters, many of whom were suspicious about the government's intentions in respect of the reproduction of the British Labour government's welfare state legislation after 1945 (Bew et al.,

1995: 103–4; Walker, 2004a: 104–6). Significantly, the Northern Ireland government's continuing fidelity to the "step-by-step" policy after 1945 was primarily the result of its fear of alienating this support base. In the face of much middle-class unionist anguish over "socialistic" measures, and amid calls for the province to go advance towards greater autonomy, which pointed to dominion status, the claims of this section of unionism prevailed upon the leadership (Patterson, 2006: 114–18; Walker, 2004a: 106–7). The welfare measures were duplicated in Northern Ireland and an effective working relationship with the Labour government was established. In this period, and beyond, Brooke and most of his colleagues took care not to identify the UUP too closely with the Conservative Party in Britain; indeed, there was unease among many Northern Ireland unionists over the generally slavish pro-Conservative voting behaviour of the Ulster Unionists at Westminster (Walker, 2004a: 106, 119–20).

The UUP, of course, took nationalist opposition for granted and concentrated its electoral strategies on holding in check the Northern Ireland Labour Party (NILP)—which it did comfortably until the late 1950s—and containing the threat posed by varieties of "independent" unionism. Indeed, most UUP anxiety was focused on those who made a populist appeal to working-class voters on the twin grounds of class interest and ultra-loyalism. The best examples of these were the irrepressible Tommy Henderson and John W. Nixon, both of whom held Stormont seats for decades and used their position to castigate successive unionist governments over social and economic questions and for letting down the very people, the poorest Protestants, to whom they believed the government owed its power and pomp (Kelly, 1995: 93–9). The success, albeit localised in west Belfast, of Henderson and Nixon, illustrated to the UUP the dangers of unionist fragmentation, and the wider damage which might be caused and consequently exploited by their opponents. In the 1950s, Henderson and Nixon were replaced as *Independent* threats by mavericks such as Norman Porter, and, by the 1960s, Ian Paisley.

The late 1950s and early 1960s witnessed a crisis in the relationship between the UUP and the Protestant working class, the effects of which are arguably still being felt. It was a period of economic anxiety: the unemployment rate in Northern Ireland was several times that of the British average; there were lay-offs at firms such as Shorts aircraft manufacturers and Harland and Wolff shipbuilders; and the long-term future of the province's traditional heavy industries appeared bleak. Brooke's unionist government, notwithstanding frantic lobbying of the Conservative government in London, could not secure the relief measures and the Ministry of Defence orders required to improve matters. Indeed, the unionists were embarrassed by orders going to rival British shipyards such as the Clyde, and by the Tory government's special measures for the north-east of England. In January 1963, the Ulster Unionist MPs at Westminster obtained an audience with Prime Minister Harold Macmillan and Home Secretary Rab Butler to protest about the unemployment situation, and to explain that they were under "heavy local pressure to show that Northern Ireland's interests were not being overlooked or given lower priority than those of Scotland or of the North-East [of England]" (Walker, 2004a: 144).

By this time it was too late to prevent the destabilising effects of the loss of confidence felt by many Protestant working-class voters in the UUP. In the 1958 election in Northern Ireland the Unionists lost four seats in Belfast to the NILP, two of which, Woodvale and Victoria, were overwhelmingly Protestant working class in complexion. The NILP, which since 1949 had taken a pro-Union constitutional position, began to build a significant base of support and held their seats with an increased vote in the 1962 election (Edwards, 2007). The NILP encouraged Protestant workers to pursue the goals of the working class in Britain, and in this period the Protestant working class became painfully aware of the gap between their position and that of the working class in comparable parts of Britain. The spirit of "step by step" was perceived as having been broken, and there was a feeling of being treated unequally in relation to the rest of the UK. The UUP, having for so long fostered the impression that it had the power to protect working people's interests vis-à-vis London, had to bear the costs of being revealed as lacking such power.

The NILP successes sparked much soul-searching within the UUP, and concern was expressed over the UUP's identification with an increasingly unpopular Tory government in London, and over the demise of the UULA. The latter factor reflected the absence by this time of a "broker" figure with whom Brooke could deal. The death of William Grant in 1949 had removed the personal link between the cabinet and the world of the urban Protestant working class (O'Neill, 1972: 32). Grant had been an invaluable conduit who was never adequately replaced. Harry Midgley, Minister of Education in the 1950s, had impeccable working-class and Labour movement credentials and was also chairman of Linfield Football Club, yet he was never completely trusted on account of his non-unionist past (Walker, 1985). Senators Joseph Cunningham and Robert Armstrong, other crucial working-class influences from the time of the establishment of the northern state, were fading from public life by the late 1950s. Against the background of economic gloom, the UUP suddenly appeared too distant from working-class concerns and, in view of the unionist government's failure to secure help from London, demonstrably unable to deal with the problems. The London Tory government's economic policies, in particular the restriction of credit facilities, were adversely affecting Northern Ireland, yet the province, on account of its devolved status, was expected to tackle its economic problems on its own.

The final years of Brooke's premiership were thus notable for the fracturing of the relationship between the UUP and the Protestant working class, and the way in which the NILP challenge oriented Northern Ireland much more towards the left–right political culture of the rest of the UK. Nevertheless, Northern Ireland's political history also made it likely that cracks in the UUP monolith would provide opportunities not just for the NILP, but also the current of "independent unionism". This tradition found its most dynamic and powerful expression in the Reverend Ian Paisley, who took independent unionism to a new level. He built on the disruptive genius of his mentor John Nixon to recreate the climate of crisis within unionism which only Thomas Sloan and the Independent Orange Order (IOO) had managed to cause in the Edwardian years, one of the factors which led to the formation of the UUC itself (Morgan, 1991, chapter 3). Paisley was quite simply better value in the eyes of some: hard-hitting, colourful, humorous, and without peer in the art of "rumbling up" the UUP at a time when the Protestant working class had become disenchanted with the ruling party. It was also a time when Protestant workers had become oriented, through economic worries, to protest politics and protest voting. It turned out to be Paisley, rather than the NILP, who would benefit most from the UUP's Labour problems as the outside world's attention began to focus on the plight of the Catholic and nationalist community and as the civil rights era commenced: hence the symbolic nature of the victory of Paisleyite docker John McQuade, albeit nominally a UUP candidate, over NILP Stormont MP Billy Boyd in the Woodvale seat at the 1965 election.

McQuade would go on to promote Paisley's brand of populism. The advent of Terence O'Neill's premiership at this juncture, with his campaign of economic modernisation, technocratic rhetoric and lack of class empathy did little to re-kindle the faith of the older craft workers or restore confidence in the "step-by-step" creed. O'Neill, indeed, set out to make Northern Ireland's devolved status more meaningful in the sense of a readiness to diverge from Britain and at least appear more self-reliant (Mulholland, 2000). This only fed uncertainties and misgivings which, when linked to the perception that O'Neill was "soft" on the constitutional position, compounded the UUP's difficulties. The Protestant working class tended to identify liberal unionists like O'Neill—and Brian Maginess before him—with indifference to their class interests, and with insufficient commitment to the Union which was basic to working-class improvement and central to their identity as a people. It is a mistake to assume that hard-line unionists were necessarily "right wing" unionists; most, in fact, prioritised the interests of working-class unionists. Liberal unionists were, by contrast, rarely in tune with the culture of the working class, whose sectarianism prevented the championing of social and economic causes. At the Bannside by-election of 1970 Paisley conquered his relatively liberal UUP opponent with the same blend of uncompromising loyalism and social and economic agitation with which he had almost unseated O'Neill the previous year (Walker, 2004b).

With the onset of the Troubles, from 1969 the Protestant working-class was central to the political flux around unionism's dilemmas. The context of violence ensured the emergence of loyalist paramilitarism with its claims to defend Protestant working-class districts from IRA attack (Wood, 2006). Politically, the NILP was marginalised, notwithstanding the achievement of polling almost 100,000 votes in the 1970 British election, and the British Labour Party did not recognise any obligation to break with the tradition of effectively keeping Northern Ireland out of the British party system; this had become a constitutional "convention" since Northern Ireland received devolution in 1921.

The suspension of Stormont in 1972 and the onset of direct rule from London left this unaltered, although Ian Paisley, for one, reacted by calling for the greater political integration of Northern Ireland into the UK, if only to drop the issue barely a year later. The integration argument was to develop within unionism and find its fullest expression some time later in the aftermath of the Anglo-Irish Agreement of 1985 with the demand for "equal citizenship" and the right of Northern Ireland citizens to vote for, and participate in, the British parties, which competed to govern them (Aughey 1989; Farrington, 2006, chapter 2). By then, Irish Republicanism had in effect "appropriated" socialism and to a degree even labourism, a process decidedly facilitated by the British Labour Party's pro-Irish unity (albeit by consent) position from 1981 until 1994. In the event, the UUP and Paisley's Democratic Unionist Party (DUP) vied for Protestant working-class support over the duration of the Troubles with the latter emerging as the clear winner in the wake of the Belfast Agreement of 1998.

## A privileged class?

The Protestant working-class's ostensible sense of "privilege" over the Catholic working class has been tirelessly discussed by scholars and commentators; it is seldom observed, by contrast, that this group's political behaviour may also have been shaped by a sense of relative deprivation with regard to the British working class, to which it perceived itself as belonging. The thrust of the argument in the previous section constitutes an attempt to shift the focus in this respect. And maybe it is time that more critical scrutiny is applied to the promiscuous use of the term "privileged" in connection with the Protestant working class.

Arguably, the use of such terms is inappropriate and unhelpful. Both scholars and journalists indulge in the practice. Kevin Bean has recently made reference in an essay on Northern Ireland in the post-Second World War era to Protestant "privileges"; the use of the term is casual—almost throwaway—unthinking, and devoid of any attempt to specify or contextualise (Bean, 2005). Similarly, the journalist Fionnuala O'Connor in her book on the peace process, *Breaking the Bonds*, throws the term around like a polemical grenade, with no attempt to define clearly what it means (O'Connor, 2002). Writing in the wake of the 2005 loyalist disturbances, the nationalist journalist Briedge Gadd refers to Protestant workers being knocked off their "top dog podium" and having the "certainties" of traditional employment terminated (Gadd, 2005). The purpose of such writing and language is to apportion blame, to condemn, and to put the Protestant working class in the dock. Language, of course, is a political weapon and this is a classic case.

The historian Marc Mulholland has written of the Unionist government "pampering" the Protestant working class during the 1960s (Mulholland, 2000: 58). It may be wondered if he would use this term to describe the British government's propping-up of the shipbuilding industry on the Clyde in the early 1970s. By what criteria, it could be asked, were the people of the Shankill and Sandy Row and Ballymacarret ever "top dogs"? Would any of these writers use the term "privileged" about those whose only realistic target in life was a job in a similar industrial outfit in Clydeside, Tyneside or Merseyside? The Protestant working class was only "privileged" in the sense of being typical of the British working class of the twentieth century, to which they belonged and wanted to be seen to belong, although nationalists (and even those of a nationalist persuasion in the same trade unions) were inclined to talk of them as aberrant and peculiar.

In a recent television profile of James Ellis, the Belfast actor from a Protestant working-class background, some discussion took place of the trilogy of television dramas written by Graham Reid—popularly known as "The Billy Plays"—which starred Ellis and were broadcast in the early 1980s. The point was made by Kenneth Branagh, another product of Protestant Belfast, that the plays signalled the end of "a kind of working class life" which was eminently familiar to those watching in Britain.[1]

The "Billy" trilogy was perhaps the first time Protestant working-class people had been dramatically represented in a form that they themselves recognised, and as similar to their counterparts across the water. Significantly, there is nothing in Reid's plays which smacks of a privileged caste of workers adopting superior attitudes to Catholics. Following the paramilitary ceasefires of 1994, more Protestant working-class voices would be heard, particularly through the PUP, challenging the facile use of terms like "privileged" to describe their backgrounds and their personal and family histories.

The Protestant working class generally did not enjoy the level of job security that is often suggested. It is only necessary to refer back to the unemployment and the economic troubles of the heavy industries in the 1950s and 1960s, to say nothing of the stricken times of the inter-war years. They had a relative advantage in objective terms over the Catholic working class, again generally speaking. But that is all it was: not privilege. The latter is a word most commonly applied to country squires or well-heeled suburbanites, not industrial workers. Their lot was anything but privileged where working and living conditions were concerned. This is not just to quibble with words. The use of the word "privilege" precludes a proper understanding of the Protestant working class and the politics of that class. It precludes appreciation of its own self-image and view of the world. It is a word that prevents appreciation of the dislocation and demoralisation suffered by the Protestant working class over the past half century of deindustrialisation, an experience they have shared with the working class across the water. These years have witnessed nothing less than the decomposition of the urban British working-class culture to which the Protestant working class is related. The term "privileged" is used by those who wish to parcel up the Protestant working class and dispatch them to the dustbin of history with a label that indicates that they deserve their fate. Such language also cannot help appreciation of how the Protestant working class retained a strong Labourist culture and trade unionism, while being confused by the peculiar structure of trade unionism in Northern Ireland and the indifference of the British Labour Party (Clifford, 1986: 25–6).

To use terms like "advantage" and "disadvantage" instead is not to deal in soft or "cop-out" language. It is simply more appropriate to the task of reaching a balanced perspective. Several factors came together to create employment sectors dominated by Protestants: the apprenticeship system; the different educational priorities in the schools attended by Protestants and Catholics respectively; the location of industries. It is an issue that cannot be reduced merely to naked sectarian exclusiveness. Many years ago an intense debate took place among scholars about the suitability of the term "Labour aristocracy", and the extent to which such a concept was helpful (Hobsbawm, 1984, chapters 12–14). At the very least, there is a need for a similar debate around the extent to which terms like "privileged" help us to understand the experience of the Protestant working class, and the development of identity issues over time in relation to it.

It seems to suit a certain mode of argument on the Irish conflict to distance Northern Ireland from developments in the rest of the UK and to imply that Northern Ireland, under the Unionists, did not share in progressive social developments where they occurred. This is disingenuous. Northern Ireland, in such treatments, is too often set speciously at odds with notions of British homogeneity, which are misleading. To return to Kevin Bean: in his essay on the post-war era he argues in effect that Northern Ireland did not march in step to the "New Jerusalem" of the welfare state. As evidence he cites the case of the Mater Hospital in Belfast, which was not brought into the National Health Service (NHS). Rather a lot rests on this one case. However, what is not acknowledged is that welfare state legislation was implemented and administered differently in different parts of the UK. Exceptions and anomalies existed elsewhere, too. Scotland, indeed, had enjoyed a proto-health service experiment during the war and, in many ways, moulded the NHS to its own needs and conditions (Stewart, 2003). The political climate in Britain was less consensus-oriented than often suggested. Debates about the wisdom of "New Jerusalem" took place throughout the UK. In the development of the welfare state, as in so much else about the UK, there was territorial diversity, unevenness and dispute.

For all the reactionary impulses of the UUP, the Unionist government defended the highly significant innovation of the Housing Trust under pressure from its grass roots and stood by the Education Act of 1947, which had aroused intense opposition in the party over the increased funding to Catholic schools without state representation on the boards of these schools (Walker, 2004a: 112–21). In these ways, and allowing for the diversity that characterised so much of UK public policy, Northern Ireland marched along with the UK in housing and education as well as matters such as family allowances and the NHS, and was shaped by the same post-war context with huge consequences for the working class—both Protestant and Catholic. For all the persistence of sectarian tensions and its continued exclusion from the party system, Northern Ireland was brought more substantially into the UK through the integrative effects of the welfare state; ties became significantly harder to break.

## Conclusion

Finally, some observations might be made on the Protestant working class in a contemporary context. For an insight into this community it would be difficult to better a recent novel, Glen Patterson's *That Which Was*. This work has as its main character a Presbyterian minister and it is set mainly in Protestant working-class east Belfast. This novel highlights the resentment felt by those badly-off Protestants over what they believe is the success with which Catholics have played the victimhood card: "Them ones only have to ask and they get" snipes one of Patterson's female characters, a single mother (Patterson, 2004: 91). The novel testifies to a people who feel left behind and marginalised, uncomprehending of how they could ever have been viewed as winners rather than losers. This feeling has hardened to such a point that the DUP's brand of ethnic "community defence" politics has been able to prevail. There has been a failure to convince Protestants—and especially working-class Protestants—that they have a future and are valued and that their aspirations and desires are respected and understood. As Neil Southern has argued, perhaps it is time to take seriously loyalists" stated desire to be part of a wider British community and not insist on viewing this as code for a tribal wish to dominate Catholics (Southern, 2006).

Patterson captures very well the sullen and cynical outlook in this community, laced as it sometimes is with a stoical humour. In a key episode in the novel—a Remembrance Day church service—Patterson artfully conveys the emotions invested by these people in the occasion. At its root is a deep wish to belong and to have their contribution to the making of the UK, to Britishness, and to British history recognised (MacDonald, 2005, chapter 8). Patterson draws our attention to the still evident "honourableness" of many in this community at the same time as he makes all too clear the savage depths to which other elements in it have sunk—directionless, nihilistic, raging against a political process they perceive to be inexorably moving away from them.

Part of this problem, it might be suggested, is the amorphous and "non-specific" quality of the UK and the very diversity and complexity of British identity, which makes it unique. There is little that is solid to reflect back the strength of Ulster Unionist loyalty and conviction. In other parts of the UK local identities are usually primary, with Britishness an overarching layer, thought to be useful for protection whether in terms of the NHS and welfare state, or in relation to the cause of a stronger voice internationally. Ulster Protestants, however, seek the security and protection of the British link because of the Irish nationalist threat, and this makes them wish for a Britishness that is more coherent, more conscious and proud of itself, more redoubtable. In this they are unlikely to get their wish; even Gordon Brown's recent attempts to foster a prouder British identity seem ambiguous about Northern Ireland's possible role in the enterprise. Nevertheless, a case can be made for the Ulster unionists and loyalists being entitled to assume their place in the multinational, multicultural UK, forming one of the series of partnerships that constitutes that entity.

Over the years, there has been no shortage of spokesmen for the Protestant working class who have been willing to indict mainstream unionism for exploiting their loyalty. From Tommy Henderson to David Ervine—whose death left a significant void—there has always been a critique of unionist political leadership from within the unionist community. This has always encouraged nationalists and republicans, but they have seldom appreciated how the Protestant working-class's unionist identity could remain unswerving at the same time as they develop a critical perspective towards unionist political leaders, and use the language of class conflict to express it. Only those on the left—from Herbert Morrison to the British and Irish Communist organisation in the 1970s—who did not subscribe to a nationalist solution of the Irish Question were in a position to appreciate how class consciousness could co-exist with unionist/loyalist identity.

The Protestant working class need to be given back their history, particularly the Labour political aspects of it, which Ervine was in the habit of claiming had been taken away from them. "There was a great Protestant contribution to the trade union movement", Chris McGimpsey has remarked, "and to left-wing causes generally but it seems to have been lost to some extent".[2] McGimpsey was for years a rare UUP voice for working-class interests and indeed attempted in vain in the mid-1990s to reinvent the Unionist Labour Association for the purpose of getting his party to re-engage with working people. Mark Langhammer, a socialist councillor from a Protestant background in Newtownabbey, reflected after the rioting of 2005 that a generation previously:

> every street in Newtownards Road, Tigers Bay, Sandy Row, the Shankill or Rathcoole would have had a convenor, or shop steward, or health and safety representative as a result of mass participation in the great unionised, manufacturing enterprises of shipbuilding, aircraft, engineering and textiles.

These communities today, he went on to observe, are devoid of such people with capacity for leadership (Langhammer, 2005). There now remains a real sense of pessimism which, however much nationalists and republicans may seek to address it with promises of a new Ireland, is intimately related to unionist and loyalist frustration over being seemingly denied their place in a wider UK scheme. Whatever the future holds in this respect, this community undoubtedly deserves to have its place in British working-class history properly acknowledged.

## Notes

1 BBC Northern Ireland, 19 December 2006.
2 "Who's sorry now? Chris McGimpsey speaks to Ruth Graham", *The Vacuum*, "The Sorry Issue", December 2004.

## References

Aughey, A. (1989) *Under Siege* (Belfast: Blackstaff).
Bean, K. (2005) "Roads not taken", in *Portraits from a 50's Archive*. (Belfast: Belfast Exposed)
Bew, P., Gibbon, P. and Patterson, H. (1995) *Northern Ireland 1921–1994: Political Forces and Social Classes* (London: Serif).
Clifford, B. (1986) *The Unionist Family* (Belfast: Athol).
Edwards, A. (2007) "Democratic socialism and sectarianism: the Northern Ireland Labour Party and the Progressive Unionist Party compared", *Politics*, 27.1: 24–31.
Farrington, C. (2006) *Ulster Unionism and the Peace Process in Northern Ireland* (Basingstoke: Palgrave).
Fielding, S. (1993) *Class and Ethnicity* (Buckingham: Open University Press).
Gadd, B. (2005) "Unionist argument is hard one to sustain", *Irish News*, 11 October.
Gallagher, T. (1987) *Glasgow: The Uneasy Peace* (Manchester: Manchester University Press).
Goldring, M. (1991) *Belfast. From Loyalty to Rebellion* (London: Lawrence & Wishart).
Harbinson, J. F. (1973) *The Ulster Unionist Party 1882–1973* (Belfast: Blackstaff).
Hobsbawm, E. J. (1984) *Worlds of Labour* (London: Weidenfeld & Nicolson).
Kelly, J. (1995) *Bonfires on the Hillside* (Belfast: Fountain).
Langhammer, M. (2005) "Politics of hopelessness", *The Daily Ireland*, 5 October.
MacDonald, H. (2005) *Colours* (Edinburgh: Mainstream).
Marquand, D. (1991) *The Progressive Dilemma* (London: Heinemann).
Morgan, A. (1991) *Labour and Partition* (London: Pluto).
Mulholland, M. (2000) *Northern Ireland at the Crossroads* (Basingstoke: Macmillan).
O'Connor, F. (2002) *Breaking the Bonds* (Edinburgh: Mainstream).
O'Neill, T. (1972) *Autobiography* (London: Hart-Davis).
Patterson, G. (2004) *That Which Was* (London: Penguin).
Patterson, H. (2006) *Ireland Since 1939* (Dublin: Penguin).
Scouler, C. (2004) *John M. Andrews* (Belfast: Killyleagh).
Smyth, J. (2000) *Labour in Glasgow 1896–1936: Socialism, Suffrage, Sectarianism* (East Linton: Tuckwell).

Southern, N. (2006) "Protestant alienation: The Shankill and Beyond". Paper delivered to Conference of the Social and Policy Research Institute, University of Ulster.

Stewart, J. (2003) "The National Health Service in Scotland, 1947–1974: Scottish or British?" *Historical Research*, 76: 193.

Walker, G. (1993) *The Politics of Frustration: Harry Midgley and the Failure of Labour in Northern Ireland* (Manchester: Manchester University Press).

Walker, G. (1995) *Intimate Strangers: Political and Cultural Interaction Between Scotland and Ulster in Modern Times* (Edinburgh: John Donald).

Walker, G. (2004a) *A History of the Ulster Unionist Party: Protest, Pragmatism and Pessimism* (Manchester: Manchester University Press).

Walker, G. (2004b) "The Ulster Unionist Party and the Bannside by-election 1970", *Irish Political Studies*, 19.1: 59–73.

Waller, P. J. (1981) *Democracy and Sectarianism: A Political and Social History of Liverpool 1868–1939* (Liverpool: Liverpool University Press).

Wood, I. S. (2006) *Crimes of Loyalty* (Edinburgh: Edinburgh University Press).

# 26

# Unionist identity and party fortunes since the Good Friday Agreement

## *Neil Southern*

For political parties in divided societies, a process of transition from violence toward a political settlement can be hazardous. While there is considerable hope that something better will be achieved, the process is often overshadowed by uncertainty and mistrust. The period after the signing of an agreement can prove to be just as risky, if not worse. Political courage on the part of a party is no safeguard against the power of unanticipated post-settlement factors to endanger its prospects of future electoral survival. A party may prove significant in helping to bring an end to political violence and display leadership in moving its community in a progressive direction, but electorates that have been bruised by violence are likely to be unforgiving, especially if what is hoped for does not materialise. Rethinking treasured features of an identity is not something that an ethno-national community finds easy. The electoral cost of misjudgement or imprudence on the part of a party can be high. These points are germane to any discussion of the Ulster Unionist Party (UUP) and the Democratic Unionist Party (DUP) since the signing of the Good Friday Agreement (GFA) in 1998.

Let us briefly familiarise ourselves with a few election results. In the Westminster elections of 1997 David Trimble's UUP won 10 parliamentary seats compared to the two won by Ian Paisley's DUP. The UUP won this election whilst in talks about Northern Ireland's future, and despite the fact that the IRA had called off its ceasefire the pervious year.

Following the signing of the GFA, the elections to the new assembly in June of the same year resulted in the UUP having 28 seats to the DUP's 20. The United Kingdom Unionist Party (UKUP), an anti-Agreement party under the leadership of Robert McCartney, had five seats bringing the total number of seats held by unionist parties opposed to the GFA to 25. The UUP, however, could call upon the support of the Progressive Unionist Party and its two seats—a unionist party that had been involved in the GFA negotiations and whose participation, along with the Ulster Democratic Party, benefited the UUP (see Bruce, 2001). The message of the first assembly elections was that "Trimble's majority, given the problems that inevitably lay ahead, was dangerously thin" (Taylor, 1999: 254).

Unionist support for the UUP fell in the 2001 Westminster elections when the party ended up with six MPs to the DUP's five. This downward trend in the UUP's electoral performance was demonstrated in the assembly elections of November 2003, when the DUP took charge with 30 MLAs to the UUP's 27 (buttressed further in early 2004 with three UUP defectors). As Tonge (2005: 60) states: "When the latter [UUP] was defeated in the 2003 assembly election, outpolled by the DUP, it was apparent that a realignment of unionism had occurred." The realignment was acutely felt in the 2005 Westminster elections when the UUP suffered the humiliation of being reduced to a single MP, whilst the DUP—an avowedly anti-Agreement party—enjoyed the unprecedented success of gaining nine MPs. In 2005, UUP leader, David Trimble, resigned and by May 2007 Ian Paisley had become First Minister in the restored Northern Ireland Assembly.

John McGarry (1998) suggests that unionists were not overly enthusiastic about the multi-party talks (Sinn Fein were excluded at their starting point) which began in 1996, nor was it a reflection of unionist goodwill that resulted in the UUP accepting the GFA or, latterly, the DUP working within its fundamental framework. Accordingly, he claims that "as a dependent group within a region of the UK, they [unionists] were particularly susceptible to British government policy, reached in cooperation with the Irish government. It was largely British-Irish policy which produced unionist flexibility" (McGarry, 1998: 855). Yet it would be unfair to think that unionists had refused to become more flexible in their thinking. There were signs of unionist willingness to integrate forms of civic and pluralist discourse within a basic pro-Union outlook (see Walker, 2004; Farrington, 2006). Certainly, significant sections of unionism appeared willing to raise questions about the nature of unionist identity, especially the nature of that identity in a society that required solutions to its conflict-generating political divisions. This internal intellectual exploration helped reduce the amount of friction as the talks in 1996 proceeded to the negotiations leading to the signing of the GFA. It should be acknowledged that a sufficient and unprecedented number of unionists seemed willing to countenance an agreed settlement with nationalism.

At the level of design, the consociational achievements of the GFA have been praised (Horowitz, 2001). However, before investigating post-GFA developments in an attempt to account for the shift in unionist support from the UUP to the DUP, it is necessary to consider briefly two aspects of the GFA. The first relates to the signatories of the Agreement in 1998, while the second concerns what might be described as its structural imperfections or shortcomings. Simply, the fact that the Agreement was not the product of *all* major political movers in Northern Ireland created problems from the moment that it was signed. The self-imposed exclusion of the DUP and UKUP from the negotiations because Sinn Fein had been admitted to the talks, allowed for a crucial rallying point for all varieties of post-Agreement unionist alienation. The second point concerns the GFA's shortcomings, which had one main effect: the trust-building potential of the Agreement was weakened. These shortcomings lay in the failure of the Agreement to deal comprehensively with divisive issues. For unionists, the issues of decommissioning, policing and parading were particularly relevant.

These structural imperfections in the Agreement proved to be invaluable to the DUP (the UKUP suffered internal divisions which resulted in its anti-Agreement assault increasingly being conducted from the margins) not least because they prevented political closure on key issues. True, given the emotionality associated with each of the three issues, to have made it a requirement of the 1998 Agreement that they be negotiated and agreed upon might have precluded an agreement being struck. In the case of policing, for example, the decision to make the matter the concern of a subsequent commission (see Ryder, 2004) may have been a sound calculation for those who wanted to consolidate the peace process politically after four years of paramilitary ceasefires (although broken by the IRA in 1996–97), but it proved to be costly for the UUP. In respect of the decommissioning of illegal weaponry, the GFA merely asked that following the necessary endorsement of the Agreement the parties: "continue to work constructively and in good faith with the Independent Commission, and to use any influence they may have, to achieve the decommissioning of all paramilitary arms within two years". The parties with influence, which did not include the UUP, were not really being tied down to delivering on so crucial an issue for unionists. Similarly, and in disregard of the deep inter-ethnic polarisation that had been caused by the Drumcree dispute in the years immediately preceding the GFA, the Agreement did not confront the issue head-on. This allowed anti-Agreement unionists to argue that the sustained opposition to Orange parades by nationalist communities under the political influence of Sinn Fein, signified Sinn Fein's unwillingness to share space. Ongoing disputes over these issues assisted the DUP, whose strategic approach concentrated on making optimum use of anything that assisted them in portraying the GFA as deleterious to unionists. The DUP also centred their attack on Trimble by repeatedly accusing him of political ineptitude and the UUP of collective sell-out.

With the GFA only supported by a slender majority of unionists in 1998, the cost of political miscalculation could not have been higher. The fact that the Agreement did not pin down Sinn Fein (or the loyalist paramilitaries and their political associates) on the question of IRA decommissioning was a structural flaw. Trimble has been recognised as someone who took enormous risks to share power with the Social Democratic and Labour Party (SDLP) and Sinn Fein (Godson, 2004). A distinction, nonetheless, needs to be drawn between a preparedness to take risks and cognisance of potentially destabilising issues. In defence of the UUP leadership, it could not have predicted with certainty how the decommissioning issue would unfold. However, the wisdom of gambling on such a significant subject was certainly questionable. If the republican movement—unionists' ideological enemy—refused to decommission and the GFA only requested that those parties with influence vis-à-vis paramilitary groups should use it in order to help bring decommissioning about, then this would undermine the UUP position.

Another imponderable for the leadership was that of how the wider unionist community would respond either to delaying tactics by republicans or their refusal to decommission—although the term "no guns, no government" seems to have been the standard unionist expectation. The continued support for the UUP in 2001 reflected the willingness of many unionists to see the GFA work. At this stage, however, the Agreement had not delivered much by way of satisfying unionists. Contrariwise, the accruement to the nationalist community via the concerns which Sinn Fein had successfully negotiated as part of the GFA was considerable: prisoners were being released; demilitarisation was evident; the Patten Commission recommended far-reaching changes to policing, not to mention Sinn Fein ministers having been admitted to government. That loyalist prisoners were released as part of the GFA was relevant only to a small unionist constituency. The sight of loyalist prisoners walking out of prison was not interpreted by most unionists as one of the advantages of the Agreement. Instead, it pointed to the effectiveness of parties associated with paramilitary groups to win a major concession and have it built into the Agreement itself. The consolidation of the GFA was also unaided as a result of other factors, which suggested that Northern Irish society was neither post-conflict nor post-sectarian: ongoing attacks by loyalist paramilitary and republican dissident groups; the Holy Cross dispute; loyalist feuds, and suspected IRA involvement in the training of Fuerzas Armadas Revolucionarias de Colombia (FARC) terrorists in Colombia. These factors highlighted the abnormal nature of Northern Ireland, regardless of the GFA. Eventually, in October 2002, amid suspicions of an IRA spy ring in operation at Stormont, the Secretary of State suspended the assembly.

The dissolution of the UUP's electoral support can be looked at from a number of different angles. At a general level, it is clear that the UUP under the leadership of Trimble failed to grasp the political implications of a rising mood of Protestant alienation, which is more than a one-dimensional phenomenon and although exacerbated in the post-GFA period, predates the Agreement (Southern, 2007a). The UUP's Dermot Nesbitt, who helped negotiate the GFA, made reference to a few issues that he felt had been detrimental to his party:

> Parties succeed when they are seen to have a clear message; when they are seen to act as a team and when they can be trusted—reverse that: we were divided, we had Jeffrey Donaldson saying one thing and Martin Smyth saying another. You had all of the disparate views within unionism. We did not have discipline; we did not have a clear simple and consistent message that people could understand.[1]

When a disgruntled Jeffery Donaldson left Trimble's side before the completion of the GFA, it was evident that following the acceptance of the Agreement in a referendum, any setbacks during its implementation would likely cause serious dissension within the UUP. Not only had pro-Agreement unionists in the UUP to fend off the attacks of the DUP and UKUP, they also had to contend with anti-Agreement forces within their own party. Given that the issue of decommissioning repeatedly hampered the implementation of the Agreement, the anti-Agreement group gathered strength, with the result that deeper fractures began to appear in the party. Failure to deal with the internal dissent, owing to a lack of party discipline (a problem exacerbated by the chaotic structure of the UUP) can be blamed for sending confusing messages to the unionist community and rendered the party seemingly less trustworthy.

In contrast, the DUP, operating according to a tightly organised party system presided over by the charismatic and uncontested authority of Paisley, aimed and fired every shot in unison. Nesbitt pointed out certain advantages enjoyed by the DUP:

> So on one hand you had the DUP banging away "they [UUP] can't be trusted—they've sold you out, they can't be trusted". They [DUP] had a consistent, clear message "forget the UUP we're going to give you a better deal"—a clear simple message, highly disciplined whereas we were highly ill-disciplined and we didn't have a clear message.[2]

When the topic of the UUP's dramatic loss of support was raised with the party's David McNarry, self-critical reflection was also evident. McNarry stated that, because the unionist community was divided over

the GFA, the UUP ought to have slowed down the process of implementation in order to allow the community to keep up with the speed of
change:

> We certainly got ahead of the people. Having brought, you know, a slender
> majority of them to support the Agreement, I think that's when we took too
> much for granted. I also think we weren't able to stand up to the govern-
> ment as we should have and said to the government what our gut reaction
> was, "hang on, Tony, now we've got this far, we've got to slow down" . . .
> the pressure that Trimble was under was immense.[3]

With a slim unionist majority in favour of the Agreement, coupled with
the uncharted nature of the political waters that lay ahead, swift developments at the level of the implementation of the GFA threatened the
maintenance of voter support, especially if the process appeared uneven.
In particular, a speedy approach to the issues that satisfied republicans
and loyalists—like the prisoner release scheme—and other benefits, like
demilitarisation, which Sinn Fein ensured were in the Agreement, was
not balanced by the decommissioning of illegal weaponry.

In a deeply divided society like Northern Ireland, a political settlement
that lacks the total support of one of the ethnic blocs means that the way
in which the pro-Agreement party handles the anti-Agreement electorate
is significant. Political moralising by the pro-Agreement party can drive
a wedge not only between the 'yes" and "no" camps but also between
the pro-Agreement party and the "no" group. McNarry made reference
to such problems and said:

> I think that our mistake looking back was that too many of my own col-
> leagues—I don't think they did it deliberately—began to demonise other
> unionists. They demonised those who hadn't voted for the Agreement and
> they started to put great distance between the "yes" and the "nos" and that
> was very, very damaging particularly when it was such a close call.[4]

The problem with demonising groups who choose to reject the contents
of an agreement is that it becomes all the more difficult politically to persuade and convert them.

However, the apportionment of blame stretched outside the realms of
UUP self-criticism and rested firmly on the shoulders of the British government, along with Sinn Fein and the IRA. Sir Reg Empey pointed out
that the unionist community became increasingly alienated because of a
weak policy in relation to dealing with republican stubbornness: "what
has not happened are the promises that were made particularly by the
prime minister and republicans and so on; the fact that they've failed to
deliver on the ground has alienated people."[5] That Trimble and the UUP
suffered because of the bad faith of other actors is a theme running

through the work of some commentators. For example Michael Kerr (2005: 31) has argued that "Sinn Fein's intransigence over IRA decommissioning and the British and Irish governments' refusal to punish Republicans for reneging on their commitments under the Belfast Agreement irreparably damaged the UUP in the eyes of the Unionist electorate." However, irrespective of which group was responsible for causing unionist disenchantment with the GFA, the DUP stood to gain by it.

Perhaps the most remarkable feature of the period from the signing of the GFA to the restoration of the Assembly in 2007 has been the politics of the DUP. From being vehemently opposed to the Agreement, the party is now in government with Sinn Fein. Further, Ian Paisley and Martin McGuiness (a self-confessed IRA commander) occupy the positions of First and Deputy First Minister, respectively. These facts give rise to an important question: what is the essence of Paisleyism and Democratic Unionism? Indeed, the work of a number of commentators stressed the ideological rigidity and inflexibility of Paisley and the DUP (see Bruce, 1986, 1994: Moloney and Pollak, 1987; Smyth, 1987; Cook, 1996). Yet the pragmatic aspects of Democratic Unionism were also identified and it was argued that the party was capable of working the GFA even in such circumstances where Sinn Fein was the predominant nationalist party (Southern, 2005).

Ideological transformations as a reflection of a transitional society like Northern Ireland are, however, political minefields for parties. The recent resignations which the DUP has suffered (most notably its MEP, Jim Allister) testifies to a degree of dissatisfaction, but not to the degree that demands a policy rethink. In addition to Paisley's ideological flexibility which, of course, is a sine qua non to his political participation in an executive with Sinn Fein, political developments and realities, and even gambles, also had a part to play.

As we have seen, the issues that bedevilled the GFA allowed Paisley persistently to snipe at the UUP, thus undermining the confidence of those unionists who supported Trimble, as well as reinforcing the attitudes of those who opposed him. There were two important vote-winning buttons that required pressing: on the unionist side, Paisley was most effective at pressing the *insecurity* button, while his opponents, Sinn Fein, were adept at pressing the *equality* button within the nationalist community. Having suffered a prolonged and violent terrorist campaign, designed to rupture Northern Ireland's constitutional position within the United Kingdom, unionists demanded decommissioning. If Sinn Fein and the wider republican movement were sincere about their commitment to the ballot box without the armalite, then the retention of weapons was needless. Obviously, Sinn Fein wanted to delay decommissioning because it was a key bargaining chip, but this was lost on the unionist community. It was hardly Paisley's duty to explain the bargaining side of politics, especially when it bred such discontent among the UUP voters whom he desperately wanted to see defect. Hence, the post-GFA debacle over decommissioning enormously benefited Paisley.

While the DUP's (and UKUP's) decision to withdraw from the talks in 1997 in protest at the inclusion of Sinn Fein was no doubt motivated by principle, the party was, nonetheless, gambling. Refusing to participate in a process that had the potential to alter significantly pretty much everything about a society, is not a decision a party takes lightly, given that the costs could be great. Yet Paisley stayed outside the talks, became the voice of anti-Agreement unionism and leader of the largest unionist party, but has ended up pro-Agreement to the extent that he functions within the framework of the GFA. The gamble, then, has paid off, if measured in terms of his leadership of the largest unionist party. Ironically, however, and this is where the gamble has not worked out that well, Paisley has ended up working a political settlement that he refused to help design and which he and his party rejected. Had the party (and the UKUP) have been involved in negotiating the Agreement, then in all likelihood a better deal would have been negotiated on behave of the unionist community. The fact that unionism was bitterly divided weakened the negotiating power of the UUP and the small loyalist parties. Admittedly, the participation of the DUP and UKUP might have precluded a settlement (Kerr, 2005). However, had the DUP have played a part in the GFA they would have done so as the subordinate party within unionism. Thus, if the GFA had have worked the first time round then the DUP might well have remained the junior partner within unionism. Participation in the Agreement would also have established a sense of collective responsibility. In the case of the unionist community's disgruntlement with any aspect of the Agreement, each party would have had to shoulder the responsibility—there would have been no easy option of shifting loyalty to a party outside of the framework. Again, this may well have kept the DUP in the electoral shadow of the UUP.

The suspension of Stormont in 2002 provided the DUP with an advantageous hiatus. The four years since the signing of the GFA, although stormy, nonetheless confirmed that the Agreement was solidly grounded. It was then necessary for the party to address seriously two interconnected problems. The first problem was less difficult and involved the defeat of the UUP, which was well afoot due to the DUP's acidic attacks on the confidence of the UUP electorate. The second problem, however, required more careful thought: how could the party end up working an agreement that it had persistently condemned? The integrity of the DUP was on the line as well as the reputation of Paisley who had argued that he was a qualitatively different sort of unionist leader to that which Trimble had proved to be. The problem became more pressing when the DUP defeated the UUP in the 2003 elections. It was at this point that political reality dictated a strategic shift in policy. Basically, the party began to exhibit traits more in keeping with the shrewdness and cleverness of the Machiavellian fox at the expense of the thunderous—yet strong, yet clumsy—roar of the Machiavellian lion. The foremost concern of the DUP was how to prevent disillusionment being generated within the ranks of their traditional supporters, as well as retain the support of those voters who had shifted their allegiance in protest at the UUP's post-GFA performance. Given the strong anti-Agreement line that the DUP had peddled, the party had the tricky task of carefully softening its approach in a way that it hoped would alter the overall perception of the unionist electorate. Accordingly, in September 2004 Paisley travelled to Dublin in a political capacity, while, more unexpectedly, in October 2006 he met Archbishop Sean Brady and a Roman Catholic delegation in Stormont. These meetings were part of the party's new politics of recognition and were preparatory steps leading to the massive ideological leap—working in an executive with a Sinn Fein deputy first minister. Republicans, of course, had their part to play if they were to attain the goal of high political office: hence the serious move by the IRA on decommissioning in September 2005 and Sinn Fein's support for policing in January 2007. At the same time, there were moments when Paisley spoke in stormier tones. For instance, when giving his speech at an Independent Orange Order parade in July 2006 Paisley stated: "No unionist who is a unionist will go into partnership with IRA/Sinn Fein", and continued: "They are not fit to be in partnership with decent people. They are not fit to be in the government of Northern Ireland and it will be over our dead bodies if they ever get there."[6]

It could be argued, however, that the IRA's acts of decommissioning were unsatisfactory because they lacked the transparency and visual evidence that the DUP had demanded. In fact for purposes of confirming that an act of decommissioning had occurred, it is somewhat ironic that Paisley was left having to depend on the word of two clergymen whose respective denominations he has continually railed against, namely, the Roman Catholic Church, and the Methodist Church, which embraces ecumenism. Additionally, given the DUP's demand for the dismantling of paramilitary structures, it is odd that the party has entered government with Sinn Fein whilst the IRA's Army Council remains in place. In the light of these facts it would seem that Trimble and the UUP have been unfair losers since 1998 not least because the GFA seems to be a dragon that the DUP are unwilling to slay. The absence of a widespread outcry within the unionist community at the DUP's recent approach suggests that the more successful the DUP are in making the GFA work then the greater the likelihood that they will maintain their new position as the predominant unionist party. But it is possible that those voters who deserted the UUP in protest may at a future date return to the party, particularly if it can successfully reinvent itself in terms of hard work at a basic constituency level.

## Conclusion

Two concluding remarks can be made about the DUP's recent political success and its working alongside Sinn Fein ministers in the Stormont executive. First, while the DUP had refused to acknowledge Sinn Fein's democratic mandate because it viewed Sinn Fein to be inappropriately linked to the IRA, this position could not be held indefinitely. Although the DUP's argument was morally persuasive for democrats, the more Sinn Fein moved towards becoming a normal party the less morally objectionable it would become. As a religious fundamentalist, Paisley would have wished for members of Sinn Fein and the republican family to have sought genuine and public forgiveness for the sins that he believed they had been guilty of committing against the unionist community, but the chances of this happening were remote. Hence, democracy has placed Paisley on a conveyor belt that his theological leanings might have preferred him get off. Certainly, for some in the Free Presbyterian Church, like the Reverend Ivan Foster, the DUP is not honouring its principles by sitting in government with Sinn Fein. When asked for his views regarding the DUP and Sinn Fein working in an executive at close quarters, Foster pointed to possible moral problems associated with the political alliance: "Sinn Fein/IRA is pro-abortion, pro-sodomy and pro-Rome. Since the DUP can now do none else but concede something on these issues, the result will be that which will be detrimental to the gospel."[7] Despite such disgruntlement Foster did not feel that the denomination would suffer a split although he admitted that some members may leave in protest and worship elsewhere. However, the Free Presbyterian minister suggested that deception, and not honesty, has played a part in former UUP voters and longstanding DUP voters supporting the DUP: "Basically, because they were deceived! Deceived about Plan B, the power of the Deputy First Minister and on the willingness of the DUP to hold the line!"[8]

There was tension in the Free Presbyterian Church between supporting Paisley as its moderator and supporting his political actions and

Paisley quit as leader of both within one year of the DUP—Sinn Fein deal. These were concerns that Trimble did not have to confront. While the evangelical convictions of the leadership of the DUP help provide ideological cohesion and establish discipline in the party, such religious beliefs do not always dovetail neatly with the requirements of politics. The second remark to be made about the DUP's working of the GFA concerns the content of the Agreement. Unionist "street" mobilisation against the GFA was not considered to be an option, even though Paisley had been involved in many protests of this type throughout the years. Also, mobilisation at a popular level was a cultural response mechanism within unionism, which had a pedigree history. But the fact that the UUP (and the two loyalist parties) had been involved in negotiating the Agreement reduced its sting. More significantly, however, the reason why street-level action was ruled out was that the GFA did not unbearably burden unionists. Unionists were not being asked to abandon their sense of Britishness, which they sentimentally cherish (Southern, 2007b), nor was Northern Ireland's membership of the United Kingdom considered to be changeable by any other means but the consent of the majority. The GFA demanded that unionists revise their identity, but as Herbert Kelman (2004) has pointed out, in relation to a theory of identity change in ethnic conflict zones, this was tolerable because the revision still allowed the *core* of unionist identity to remain intact. True, the consent principle did not provide a never-ending constitutional guarantee, but it established the only mechanism by which such change could be achieved, and unionists of all shades appear to have found this satisfactory. Unionists desired peace. Thus, the protest options available to Paisley and the DUP were quite limited. Traditionally, Paisley was well suited to opposing respective British governments and had done so on numerous occasions, but he did not have the same licence over his own community. Therefore, when the DUP took the political scalp of the UUP it did not seek to pursue the politics of opposition despite being in a strong position within unionism. Instead, the party set about designing a more constructive approach which has led it into a power-sharing executive involving Sinn Fein. In essence, however, the durability of Northern Ireland's peace settlement and the workability of the Assembly is only something that time will tell.

## Notes

1 Interview with Dermot Nesbitt, 16 December 2005.
2 Ibid.
3 Interview with David McNarry, 8 December 2005.

4  Ibid.
5  Interview with author, 28 June 2005[0].
6  Speech by Ian Paisley at Independent Orange Order parade, 12 July 2006.
   http://news.bbc.co.uk/1/hi/northern_ireland/5174000.stm
7  e-mail response to questionnaire, 11 May 2007[0].
8  e-mail response to questionnaire, 11 May 2007.

## References

Bruce, S. (1986) *God Save Ulster! The Religion and Politics of Paisleyism* (Oxford: Oxford University Press).

Bruce, S. (1994) *The Edge of the Union* (Oxford: Oxford University Press).

Bruce, S. "Terrorists and politics: The case of Northern Ireland's loyalist paramilitaries", *Terrorism and Political Violence*, 13.2: 27–48.

Cooke, D. (1996) *Persecuting Zeal: A Portrait of Ian Paisley* (Dingle: Brandon).

Farrington, C. (2006) *Ulster Unionism and the Peace Process in Northern Ireland* (New York: Palgrave Macmillan).

Godson, D. (2004) *Himself Alone: David Trimble and the Ordeal of Unionism* (London: HarperCollins).

Horowitz, D. (2001) "The Northern Ireland Agreement: clear, consociational and risky", in J. McGarry (ed.) *Northern Ireland and the Divided World* (Oxford: Oxford University Press), pp. 89–108.

Kelman, H. (2004) "Reconciliation as identity change: a social-psychological perspective", in Y. Bar-Siman-Tov (ed.) *From Conflict Resolution to Reconciliation* (Oxford: Oxford University Press), pp. 111–24.

Kerr, M. (2005) *Transforming Unionism: David Trimble and the 2005 General Election* (Dublin: Irish Academic Press).

McGarry, J. (1998) "Political settlements in Northern Ireland and South Africa", *Political Studies*, XLVI, 853–70.

Moloney, E. and Pollak, A. (1986) *Paisley* (Dublin: Poolbeg).

Ryder, C. (2004) *The Fateful Split: Catholics and the Royal Ulster Constabulary* (London: Methuen).

Smyth, C. (1987) *Ian Paisley: Voice of Protestant Ulster* (Edinburgh: Scottish Academy Press).

Southern, N. (2005) "Ian Paisley and evangelical Democratic Unionists: an analysis of the role of evangelical Protestantism within the Democratic Unionist Party", *Irish Political Studies*, 20.2: 127–45.

Southern, N. (2007a) "Protestant alienation in Northern Ireland: a political, cultural and geographical exploration", *Journal of Ethnic and Migration Studies*, 33.1: 159–80.

Southern, N. (2007b) "Britishness, 'Ulsterness' and Unionist identity in Northern Ireland", *Nationalism and Ethnic Politics*, 13.1: 71–102.

Taylor, P. (1999) *Loyalists* (London: Bloomsbury).

Tonge, J. (2005) *The New Northern Irish Politics?* (New York: Palgrave Macmillan).

Walker, G. (2004) *A History of the Ulster Unionist Party: Protest, Pragmatism and Pessimism* (Manchester: Manchester University Press).

# Index